WALDO: PIONEER AVIATOR

A personal history of American aviation, 1910 - 1944

by
Waldo Dean Waterman
with Jack Carpenter

To order additional copies, please see page 485.

International Standard Book Number: 0-9600736-0-4
Library of Congress Catalog Card Number: 87-73013

Printed by Capital City Press, Inc., Montpelier, Vermont.

ARSDALEN, BOSCH & Co

GJ (Jack) Carpenter
1710 Ave. Sevilla, Oceanside
CA 92056-6204 (619) 414-1424

To Jane,
and Carol Jack Carpenter

Clover Field - 1926

THE EARLY BIRDS

(Incorporated in the District of Columbia, not for profit)

HOTEL CARLTON
WASHINGTON, D. C.

THE EARLY BIRDS OF AVIATION, Inc.

*An organization of pioneers
in aeronautics who flew solo
before December 17, 1916.*

October 1, 1987

I found the book *WALDO: Pioneer Aviator* one of the most fulfilling stories I have ever read. Waldo fills in so many blanks in the story of aviation. He was there when it happened and tells it from the view point of a pioneer who loved aviation and was willing to bear all the hard luck that was so common in those grim days. Because of the persistence of him and those other devotees, aviation has reached the point where it is today.

Waldo's path and mine did not cross until in 1961 I joined The Early Birds. He was a member of the Board of Governors that had to approve my qualifications for membership. I found him to be very gruff and demanding and bluntly critical of anything he disapproved of. No doubt the *"slings and arrows of outrageous fortune"* had made him a tough man to deal with. But as I got to know him I grew to admire him, and was happy to assist him in any way possible.

Waldo was really the cement that kept The Early Birds of Aviation functioning. He was the one responsible for my becoming secretary of the organization. He was my mentor and friend to the end of his life.

Sincerely yours,

Forrest

Forrest E. Wysong, President
The Early Birds of Aviation, Inc.

This letter and photo of Forrest Wysong, the *senior* Naval aviator, commissioned March 30, 1916, USNR, is superimposed on a sheet of original stationery.

An Association of Oldtime Airmen

PREFACE

This is the true story of Waldo Waterman, pioneer aviator, aircraft manufacturer, engineer, barnstormer, inventor and test pilot. Those that were his idols and contemporaries - Glenn Curtiss, the Wright brothers, Bill Stout, Lincoln Beachey, Billy Mitchell, Carl Spaatz, Tony Fokker, Amelia Earhart and Charles Lindbergh - are gone now, but they and the others that helped break the bonds of man to earth will never leave us, especially when we relive their successes and failures through the memory of Waldo.

When Waldo first flew his hang glider in 1909, the euphoria of man's conquest of the air was but a year old. The Wrights did fly in 1903, but the world didn't comprehend it until 1908. It was Glenn Curtiss who first captivated America when he flew before awed spectators on the Fourth of July, 1908; and it was Curtiss who won the coveted Gordon Bennett Trophy by being the fastest at the world's first air meet at Reims in 1909. In 1910 he was the hero at the first American air meet and the *"first to fly on the Coast"*; this event also marked the beginning of his friendship, with Waldo.

Waldo went on to become an aviation legend. In his eighty-two years he participated in virtually everything in that fabulous era that brought us, from aeroplanes of bamboo, wire and muslin, to the Space Age. He was no casual spectator, but was constantly working at *"improving the breed."* He was a pilot's pilot, and a strong voice for air safety. Decrying the harem-scarem flying of the Twenties, he was convinced that aviation would never come of age until it was a viable force for the good of man. Briefly a barnstormer, Waldo was not a "flying fool"; there were better and bolder pilots, but few who survived him.

Waldo's life is a story for all who have flown - from the aviation buff to the passenger sitting in quietude and comfort, possibly in awe of it all, racing through the skies at nearly the speed of sound - the same skies that Leonardo daVinci once dreamed about. We'll watch as Waldo and the other pioneers push back the horizon and broaden the scope of the daring - opening the heavens to a world unknown when he first flew only seventy-eight years ago.

GJC

CONTENTS

San Diego Bay, from Point Loma, 1893

J.T. McCutch

x

Chapter 1

1894 - 1912

THOSE EARLY YEARS

It was June 16, 1894, when I was brought, kicking and bawling, into this world - in San Diego, a California city of only 17,000 people in a state then of barely a million population. It was a time when wonders were about to unfold. There were few telephones and fewer electric lights. Steam trains connected cities, and there were the new (Sprague) trolley cars in towns. Horses - over 25 million - provided basic transportation, unaware that their final decade was at hand. The 'safety' bicycle was the craze for millions, the automobile but an inventor's curiosity, and balloons were the only flying vehicles. There were no radios, television, or computers, let alone even the remotest thought of satellites or space travel, and Coca Cola had just been put into bottles. Work was hard and lowly paid, and there were no such things as labor-saving appliances. Very few went to college and fewer yet travelled much beyond 20 miles from their birthplace. Medicine was primitive, medical training sparce, and the great killer was tuberculosis. It was truly a time of birth - both for me and the modern age.

1

WALDO: PIONEER AVIATOR

My father, Waldo Sprague Waterman, was a graduate of the University of California at Berkeley. He managed the San Diego, Cuyamaca & Eastern Railroad, a line which had evolved from my grandfather's mining interests. My mother, Hazel Wood Waterman, had met my father at Berkeley. She was an accomplished artist and would achieve local renown as an architectural designer.

Robert Whitney Waterman

My grandfather, Robert Whitney Waterman, came to California across the plains from Illinois as a *forty-niner* (in 1850). Later he would become a merchant, rancher, gold and silver mine owner and railroad builder. His prominence led to his Republican nomination for Lieutenant Governor, and after a successful campaign followed by the death of the Democratic Governor Bartlett, he became the *Governor of California*. He served from September 1887 to January 1891, and though not particularly distinguished as a politician, *"Old Honesty"* was a champion of the University of California and of prison reform.

While he was Governor, Coronado's Hotel del Coronado opened in 1888, at the height of San Diego's first land boom, and he and my grandmother, Jane Gardner Waterman, led the opening ball's Grand March.

J. T. McCutch

Hotel del Coronado - 1893

Though the surroundings have changed much during the past century, this hotel remains gracefully the same, a magnificent reminder of Victorian California.

I was the youngest of three children. My sister, Helen, was four years and my brother, Robert, five years older than I. Until I was eight we lived a comfortable and secure life, but in 1903 father died. From that time on mother's architectural career evolved, and the state of the family's finances was somewhat tenuous.

Once, when I was very young, my mother and several friends were enjoying one of that era's favorite pastimes, having fortunes told by a 'Gypsy Queen,' and she told my fortune:

> *"Mrs. Waterman, your son will someday build ships that will cross the oceans in the air."*

The memory of that strange foretelling must have influenced mother, for in later years she assented and quietly encouraged my burning desire to fly. Remember, at this time man hardly succeeded in controlling the flight of balloons, and knew nothing of *'aeroplanes'*. In 1900, flight was still an age-old dream few thought possible. It was as far-fetched as Jules Verne's flight to the moon, or of man's first steps upon it!

In the years before my father's death I spent most of my spare time after school in the railroad's shops - and as the boss's son I got awfully good treatment from the men there. They taught me about operating machine tools, forging and blacksmithing. I dreamed of being an engineer, like my father, and in 1903 made a drawing of a steam engine, signing it *"Waldo Waterman, Mechanic."* But after father's death I felt a bit strange hanging around there, and began frequenting the machine shop of Clarence and Will Hunt. The Hunts' father had been the physician for grandfather's Stonewall (Jackson) Mine, and had brought both my brother and sister into this world. I have always been very grateful for their taking me in and giving me both needed companionship and training in pattern making, foundry work and automotive mechanics.

Me, at 11 years old

3

Clarence Hunt was the pattern maker and Will ran the shop. They gave me my own lathe and bench, letting me do pretty much as I pleased as long as I didn't damage things too much. As I now look back, they were rare individuals to let a kid loose in their shop. They had ambitions of becoming automobile manufacturers, and while I was around their shop they built several cars on a custom basis for local San Diegans. In 1908 they formed the Great Western Motor Car Co. in National City, but soon it went the way of 95 percent of the over-175 early automobile manufacturers in the United States.

The first money that I ever earned was at the Kessler Machine Shop during a grammar school vacation. I was 12 or 13 years old. By then I'd already received considerable training from both the railroad shops and the Hunt's. I could drive an automobile and do enough around a shop to be a general do-anything handy boy. For this I was working the usual hours; 10 hours a day, six days a week, which came to a 60-hour week for which I was paid $3 - the equivalent of 5 cents per hour.

My first job in the morning was starting the huge single-cylinder distillate engine (distillate was a fuel less volatile than gasoline, more like kerosene). The engine's power was transmitted by belts to the shop's machine tools through two long shafts in the rafters going the full length of the building. These belts were always connected to the engine - there was no declutching mechanism - and therefore when the engine was turned over to start, the entire overhead system turned, too. Of course, the machine tools themselves were not clutched-in except when being used.

To start the engine I first pulled a lever releasing the cylinder's compression - if I didn't do this it was almost impossible to turn over by hand. Then I'd retard the spark so that it wouldn't kick over backwards, and open a petcock, squirting gasoline, which would ignite much easier than distillate, into the combustion chamber. I'd then close the petcock and climb up on the spokes of one of the two big flywheels - about 4-1/2 feet in diameter - and I'd walk the wheel around, rotating the entire system. When the engine reached the reduced compression stroke, just as it went over center, the 'make and break' ignition (which produced a spark by the opening and closing of contact points inside the combustion chamber) would go 'clack'. Then, the spark would hopefully ignite the charge and away she'd go! I've often wondered what would have happened if I'd

4

forgotten to retard the spark (causing it to ignite on the wrong side of center). I would have been shot up through the tin roof like a skyrocket!

(Incidentally, as we go along, I'll try to give somewhat rudimentary descriptions of the various engines and mechanisms that I was involved with - not as a scientific discourse but rather to help explain them. While some readers will feel that this may be boring, others will think that it's insufficient. The middleground stance will hopefully satisfy most. For instance, the 'make and break' ignition system, the same type that the Wright brothers used for their first aircraft engine, was the predecessor of spark plugs.)

There was another young chap working with me at Kessler's, Harry Titus, 15 years old, a couple of years older than myself. Harry was sort of a wild boy, and his father, Kessler's lawyer, had got him the job in order to keep him corralled during vacation. He wasn't as experienced as I, so he was assigned to me as my helper. But there was a bit of an inequity, for he was paid $5 a week while I received only my $3 - one of life's first lessons! When I received my first pay envelope there was $3.50 in coin in it. I'd only worked that first week so I took the envelope back to Mr. Smith and told him that I'd been overpaid by 50 cents. (Wilson Smith kept the books and the payroll, and later became the Franklin automobile dealer in town.) He said *"Well, it's always a pleasure meeting someone like you, and I'll gladly recommend you as an honest man."* Some people that I've tangled with over the years may question that appellation, but all of my life I've tried to live up to what his recommendation was in 1907.

Almost all of us kids had some sort of job with which to earn spending money or help out with the family finances, and much of what I did was related to machines and automobiles. One night I was attending a lecture at the YMCA by Clarence Hunt for a group of automobile owners. There were only 10 or 15 cars in town then; San Diego's first Motor Vehicle License had been issued in 1905. During the meeting I asked several questions which must have indicated that I knew something about the subject. When the lecture was over a local banker, Julius Waggenheim, contacted my mother about my taking care of his car. It was a 6-cylinder Model K Ford, an unsuccessful luxury model preceding the famous 4-cylinder Model T introduced in late 1908. She OK'd his suggestion, as he lived only a couple of blocks from our house. He then advanced me enough money to construct a 20 by 20-foot garage-type building behind the house. When I'd completed it, Mr. Waggenheim had me drive his car from its downtown garage to my house where I began taking care of it, eventually earning enough money to repay the loan and later to build my glider, which we'll soon come to.

*Ford Model K
1906 - 1907*

But I didn't spend all of my time around machine shops and garages. I did most of the things that kids did then, though I never was much for sports. I've never played baseball, only played one semester of football while in grammar school, and went out for track once in high school - all with discouraging results. When it came to the normal fistfights, I invariably came-off second-best, for having no father I had little training in fighting and could care less. But I had one characteristic that I abhorred - I cried very easily. Physically I could take a lot of punishment, but if I were crushed mentally, the tears flowed, thus letting the neighbor kids add insult to injury. But these were the normal pains of growing up, and by the time I reached my mature height of 6 feet and weight of 185 pounds, I found that these problems had disappeared.

There was one thing that I really excelled in, though: kite making. There was very keen competition amongst us kids as to who could build the best and biggest kites. Since we had a real productive backyard clump of bamboo (the best kite frame material), with my other skills I was soon making some outstanding kites. One, a Hargrave box-kite de-

6

sign, had a 10-foot wingspread and looked like the Wrights' 1900 Kitty Hawk glider.

I never was much for exercise, and even before my flying injuries I was a bit stooped, a characteristic that in the Twenties Clyde Forsythe would catch when he caricatured me in *"Joe's Car."* Also, I had big feet - size 12's while a teenager and 13 when I was adult. At least no one ever claimed that Waterman aircraft didn't have enough foot room.

During these years - 1907, '08 and '09 - flying was increasingly the rage and about all we talked about. There were balloonists, parachute jumpers, and one daredevil, Dan Maloney, who, on April 29, 1905, had successfully flown in a balloon-lofted Montgomery *"Aeroplane"* glider in northern California. He was killed on July 18, 1905, while attempting it again, though.

I was engrossed in reading about Chanute and Lilienthal and their great gliding exploits, and somewhat later I'd treasure Victor Lougheed's 1909 treatise, *Vehicles Of The Air.*

The January 24, 1907, *The Youth's Companion* had this interesting and accurate comment:

"Man-Flight. The scientific journals give considerable attention to the recent feat (Oct. 23, 1906) of Santos-Dumont in Paris...where he made a flight of about 80 yards in the presence of a multitude of spectators. This has been called the 'first manned flying machine'.

But the question has been raised whether the first flight of this kind should not be credited to America. More than a year ago, according to their published report, the Wright brothers of Dayton, Ohio, made much longer flights with a motor-driven aeroplane. But their experiments have been conducted in private."

Santos-Dumont, September 13, 1906

(*The Youth's Companion*, actually a *family* magazine, was published by Perry Mason Company, Boston. It was the oldest, most widely-read weekly publication in the United States at this time.)

7

I wasn't aware - for I'd been too young - of what *McClure's Magazine* had published in its June 1897 issue, *"The Flying Machine "* by Professor S.P. Langley (with photographs by A. Graham Bell, Esq.). This article detailed Langley's work with his *"aerodrome"* and its over-3000 foot level flight, and was possibly the first publication of its type.

THE "FLYING–MACHINE."

BY PROFESSOR S. P. LANGLEY.

With illustrations made directly from Professor Langley's machine and approved by him.

McClure's Magazine
June 1897

THE AERODROME IN FLIGHT, MAY 6, 1896. TWO VIEWS FROM INSTANTANEOUS PHOTOGRAPHS TAKEN BY A. GRAHAM BELL, ESQ. SEE PAGE 659.

In the summer of 1908 there was a great stir - a man named Glenn Curtiss had flown a motor-powered aeroplane on the 4th of July in New York State. There wasn't any doubt of it. The photographs and articles proved that *man with power had mastered flight and now could go further*

8

than the winds of chance. Like most, then, I first learned of the Wright brothers in the fall of 1908. Hardly anyone believed that they'd flown as early as 1903, but they surely were also flying in 1908.

The Wright Flyer III of 1905 was the *"first practical aeroplane"* in that pitch, roll and yaw were controllable. However, very few knew of its flights, for they were conducted in semisecrecy. In fact, the Wrights were darned unhappy that Curtiss was getting the lion's share of publicity for something they said they'd invented!

The Youth's Companion, October 1, 1908, with a cover photo of the Wright's Fort Meyer War Department trials, stated:

> *"...while Wilbur Wright was astonishing France...Orville was preparing the machine...that surpassed previous achievements...caused many people to revise their opinions regarding the practicability of flying machines...Mr. Wright carried an Army officer on a nine minute's journey; remained in the air during his second flight for nearly an hour and a quarter, and rose to the greatest height an aeroplane has ever reached... 250-feet. ...the machine travelled more than 39-miles an hour.*
>
> *The Wright machine is one of the simple aeroplane type, a heavier-than-air, motor-driven vehicle, constructed mostly of steel and wood and canvas. It is about 30 by 40 feet over all, and weighs about half a ton."*

The idea of flying was a contagious fever to me, an exhilarating and heady prospect! Through my kite flying experiments I'd become fascinated with flying's potentials and began itching to do something about it. My opportunity came in April of 1909. The new issue of *Popular Mechanics* had an article on "how to build" a Chanute-type glider. (Later I learned that this article had been 'lifted' from an earlier article, *"How To Build A Gliding Machine"* by Carl Bates in the March, 1909 issue of *Fly* magazine!) Like countless others, young and old, I read that issue as if I'd found buried treasure.

I immediately got right to work in my private domain, my garage-shop in the backyard of our house at Hawthorn and Albatross streets. I bought several pieces of long, clear spruce at the lumber yard; nuts,

9

WALDO: PIONEER AVIATOR

OCTOBER 1, 1908   PRICE FIVE CENTS

THE YOUTH'S COMPANION

NEW ENGLAND EDITION

PHOTOGRAPHS COPYRIGHTED, 1908, BY WELDON FAWCETT, WASHINGTON

The Wright Brothers' Aeroplane in a World Record Flight

Orville Wright at Fort Myer, Va.   Scene of the Disastrous Accident of September 17th.

bolts, and piano wire at the hardware store; and unbleached muslin at Marston's department store. I was now a high school freshman, and since the school had an arrangement for teaching shop at Barth's Machine Shop, I was able to use their equipment and table saws for the preliminary cutting and ripping of the glider's spars, ribs and struts. Cutting spars for the glider's wing span of 20 feet was a tricky job - and they were the devil to get home. Finally, though, I had everything ready for assembling the *'gliding machine'*, which I named *"White Swan No. 1"*.

For weeks I worked every minute I could spare, and by early June, just in time for summer vacation, the glider was almost complete. Now I had to figure out where to fly it. Hansel Schnoover, a classmate, lived close by, and his father had a Stoddard-Dayton touring car. It was one of America's finest automobiles, the pace car at the first Indianapolis '500' Race, and, coincidently, the same make of auto then owned by Glenn Curtiss. With the top down it would be ideal for carrying the glider. I talked Hansel into helping me out, and one morning late in June we loaded-up for my first flying attempt.

We drove north on Albatross Street a couple of short blocks to Juniper, a street going east-west with a steep hill. We unloaded the glider, I reread the article's instructions, and I gave it a try. Result: a lot of running and puffing, but no flying. The hill wasn't steep enough; I couldn't get up enough speed to become airborne without sinking too fast. We then went further up to Laurel, a steeper hill. But it still wasn't steep enough; results didn't indicate that I was getting off the ground. We'd now been at it for about two hours, and I was really getting tuckered-out. *What this flying needed was horsepower, not Waldo-power!* The glider was bashed up a bit, and with that excuse we called it quits for the day, returning home for repairs.

Later that afternoon Hansel and I cased the neighborhood looking for a still steeper hill. We thought we found it just a block further north of Laurel, where Albatross and Maple met, dead-ending at a very steep canyon or barranca. There wasn't any road there, but it sure looked steep enough. We decided to axe and machete-out the worst of the brush, and give it a try in the morning.

Shortly after dawn the next day Hansel and I, with the glider again atop the Stoddard-Dayton, drove up Albatross to Maple, where we unloaded and got set to try again. (Today, this location overlooks Lind-

[*March, 1909*] F L Y 5

How to Build a Gliding Machine

By CARL BATES

A gliding machine is a motorless aeroplane or flying machine propelled by gravity, and designed to carry a passenger through the air from a high point to a lower point some distance away.

Flying in a gliding machine is simply coasting down hill on the air, and is the most interesting and exciting sport imaginable.

The style of glider described in this article is known as the "two-surface" or "double-decked aeroplane, and is composed of two arched cloth surfaces placed one above the other.

In building a gliding machine the wood material used should be straight-grained spruce, free from knots.

Now to build the machine, first prepare from spruce planks the following strips of wood:

Four long beams 3/4 inch thick, 1 1/4 inches wide and 20 feet long. (If 20-foot lumber cannot be had take 10-foot strips and splice them together by the method shown in drawing.) (Fig. 5.)

Twelve cross pieces, 3/4 inch thick, 3/4 inch wide and three feet long. Twelve uprights 1/2 inch thick, 1 1/2 inches wide and four feet long.

Forty-one strips for the bent ribs 3-16 inch thick, 1/2 inch wide and four feet long.

Two arm-sticks, 1 inch thick, 2 inches wide and three feet long. Two rudder-sticks 3/4 inch by 3/4 inch and 8 feet long.

Several strips 3/8 inch by 3/4 inch, for building the vertical and horizontal rudders.

The frames for the two main surfaces should be constructed first by bolting the cross-pieces, marked "C" in (Fig. 1) to the long beams "L", and spaced apart as shown in dimensions (Fig. 1.)

All bolts used should be 3/8 inch in diameter, and fitted with washers at each end. These frames should be braced by diagonal wires marked "W". (Fig. 1.) All wiring is done with number sixteen piano wire.

Now the forty-one bent ribs may be nailed to the main frames on the upper side by using fine flat-headed brads 3/4 of an inch long.

These bent ribs are spaced one foot apart and extend one foot beyond the rear edges of the main frames, as shown in (Fig. 1).

These bent ribs are arched by bending. The front end being nailed to the front long beam first, the rear end being sprung down and nailed last. The ribs should have a curve as shown in B.R. (Fig 3). The amount of curvature being the same in all the bent ribs. The frames of the main surfaces are now ready to be covered with cloth.

Cambric or bleached muslin should be used for the covering. The cloth should be tacked to the front edge, stretched tightly over the bent ribs and fastened securely to the rear ends of the ribs. The cloth should also be glued to the ribs for safety. In the centre of the lower plane surface there should be an opening two feet by four feet, for the body of the operator (see Fig. 2).

Place the two main surfaces four feet apart and connect by the twelve uprights, see "U" (Fig. 2) and (Fig. 3). The uprights "U" are fastened by bolting to the cross-pieces "C" as shown in drawing (Fig. 4). The whole structure is made strong and rigid by bracing the diagonal wires both laterally and longitudinally.

The vertical rudder "V.R." (Fig. 3) is to keep the machine headed into the wind, and is not movable. It is made of cloth stretched over a light wooden frame nailed to the rudder-sticks "R.S." (Fig. 3.)

The horizontal rudder "H.R." (Fig. 1) is also made of cloth stretched over a light wooden frame, and is arranged to intersect the vertical rudder at its centre. This rudder is

held in position and strengthened by diagonal wires and guy-wires. The horizontal rudder is also immovable; its function being to prevent the machine from diving, and also to keep it steady in its flight.

The rudders are fastened to the glider by the two rudder-sticks "R.S." (Fig. 3), and these sticks are held rigid by diagonal wires, and also by guy wires leading off to the sides of the main frames as shown in (Fig. 1).

The two arm-sticks marked "A.A." in Fig. 1 should be spaced about thirteen inches apart and bolted onto the long beams in the centre of the opening in the lower plane, where the operator is located. The glider should be examined to see that the frame is not warped or twisted. The surfaces must be true or the machine will be hard to balance when in flight.

Now to make a glide take the glider to the top of a hill, get between the arm-sticks, lift the machine up until the arm-sticks are under the arms, as shown in Fig. 2. Run a few steps against the wind and leap from the ground.

You will find that the machine has a surprising amount of lift, and if the weight of the body is in the right place you will go shooting down the hillside in free flight.

To make a landing, push the weight of the body backwards, this will cause the glider to tip up in front, slacken speed and settle; the operator can then land safely and gently on his feet. Of course, the beginner should learn by taking short jumps, gradually increasing the distance as he gains skill and experience in balancing and landing.

The proper position of the body is slightly ahead of the centre of the planes, but this must be found by experience. The machine should not be used in winds blowing faster than fifteen miles an hour. Glides are always made against the wind, and balancing is done by moving the legs. The higher the starting point the farther one may fly. Great care should be exercised in making landings, otherwise the operator might suffer a sprained ankle or perhaps a broken leg.

Fig. 6 shows line of flight in starting, flying and landing, and the angle of descent.

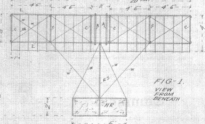
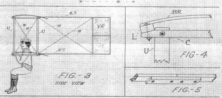

FIG.-2 FRONT VIEW
FIG.-1 VIEW FROM BENEATH
FIG.-3 SIDE VIEW
FIG.-4
FIG.-5
FIG.-6

bergh Field.) There was a slight breeze blowing in from the bay when I lifted the glider and positioned myself. Then, with a short run climaxed by as high a jump as I could make, I propelled the glider off the crest of the hill. There was the slightest of hesitations, and then I found myself airborne. *I was flying!*

It was an eerie, unreal feeling - floating there. All I could hear was a faint whistling of the wind passing over the wings and Hansel's whoops and hollars. Then, the glider settled into the brush about halfway down the slope. Golly-gee-whilikers. That was exciting! I felt like Edward Stratemeyer's Tom Swift or Rover Boy, and the blood was thumping something fierce in my chest. After clambering back to the top of the hill, I tried it again and again. And by the end of the morning I was getting an occasional glide the whole distance, from the top of the hill to the bottom, around 125 feet. I rarely rose higher than a couple of feet above the brush, and every once in a while my feet would catch the branches, often causing the end of the flight and usually some damage to the fragile wing covering. But it was not enough to stop the flying - only fatigue did that.

It was July 1, 1909 - I'd just turned 15 years old, and I had become the first person to fly within San Diego, by then a city of almost 40,000 population.

Now I wanted to try some other things that I'd heard about. The Wrights used a catapult for launching their craft. Their aeroplanes didn't have wheels, only skids, and thus could only be airborne by catapulting. But, Curtiss was using wheels, and I therefore dreamed-up the idea of using both a catapult and wingtip wheels for my glider. I hoped that the wheels would lessen the damage, resulting in fewer bashed-in rib ends, while making it easier to launch and land. Also, I rigged up *"balancing planes,"* hoping that they'd give me more control over the tendency of one wing or the other to drop. (These were small movable wings between the outer ends of the main wings - a Bell-Curtiss innovation adapted from Frenchman Esnault-Pelterie's concept, now called *"ailerons".*) The catapult was little more than a 20-foot 2" x 8" wood rail with a roller at one end. A rope passed from the glider's leading spar, over the roller, and back to our winch, the Stoddard-Dayton.

13

Me on my glider, "White Swan No. 1," in August 1909, on launching rail; Hawthorn street between Albatross and Front streets. (Note wingtip wheels)

With this arrangement I could sit on the glider rather than run underneath it, but we never could get enough momentum to get airborne. And almost every time we tried it we'd damage the glider, something like Langley's problems in 1903.

My next idea was to pull the glider behind the car. It wasn't until late in July that we were able to try this, though, for I had to spend alot of time repairing the glider from the beating that it had already taken. Also, I strengthened its frame so that it could better withstand the jolts and strains of being towed. It was early in the morning when Hansel and I loaded the Stoddard-Dayton and headed up Sixth Avenue, a wide, dirt street along the west side of Balboa Park, and stopped near Maple. There was very little traffic at this time of day or, for that matter, not much anytime. But we were very secretive about what we were doing and wanted as few eyes watching as possible.

We unloaded the glider and got everything all set to go. With a rope running about 50 feet from the glider to the car, we headed south, with me squatting on the glider and Hansel carefully accelerating the car.

14

The wingtip wheels occasionally flicked the dirt as we gained speed, and I was very shortly airborne. But after about three swoops to the left, the glider veered way off and struck a newly planted palm tree beside the road. That ended the flight and smashed up the wing enough to cause us to head for home. We did stop to prop up that tree, stomping some dirt around its base so it wouldn't lean so much. It was still leaning a bit, though, and we worried some about catching it from the Park Department. You can still spot that tree today, a leaning runt in a line of 100-foot-tall palms!

When I got home I was greeted by a very agitated mother; why I did not know. I soon found out when she told me about receiving a phone call at 6:30 A.M. from a very upset Mrs. William Clayton, the socially prominent wife of the manager of the Spreckles Company. Mother had designed their lovely home at Sixth and Laurel - right where we'd picked for our morning's experiments - and therefore knew her well.

"Mrs. Waterman, what is your son doing destroying the park's shubbery with that flying machine of his?"

"But Mrs. Clayton, it couldn't be Waldo. He's still in bed."

"Oh no, he isn't. I know Waldo. You go look and see if he's in bed."

Which my mother did, and found that I was somewhere else.

That put a damper on my flying activities; there were to be no more flights with the glider. Many years later I'd build another glider, though. It now (1974) hangs in the Smithsonian, a true reproduction of the *"Popular Mechanics Glider"*, the tenth most important aircraft in American aviation history.

When things had cooled down I figured that I'd learned about all that I could from gliding. Now it was time to build an aeroplane, a *powered* glider, as soon as I could get an engine. Initially I'd toyed with simply putting a motorcycle engine and a propeller on the glider, but it was so bashed-up after the collision with the palm tree that I discarded that idea. Then, in the fall of 1909 our newspaper, The Union, carried some stories about the upcoming *First American International Aviation Meet at Los Angeles* at Dominguez Field, northwest of Long Beach, January 10-12, 1910. This was to be the first American air meet following the one at

15

Reims, France, the world's first. (At this time, France was the world leader in aviation with its Center of European Aeronautical Experiments, and today the bi-annual *Paris Air Show* is still the world's premier aviation showcase.) This meet was being promoted by actor Dick Ferris with Pacific Electric Railway's Henry Huntington's money, and was really going to be some affair. Many of aviation's heroes would be there: Glenn Curtiss, Louis Paulhan (Europe's top pilot, the *"Napoleon of the Air"*), Charles Hamilton, Charles Willard. My head was swimming.

Curtiss, in his 1912 book, wrote:

"The Pacific Coast, always progressive and quick to seize upon every innovation, no matter where it may be developed, had been clamoring for some time for an aviation meet. The enterprising citizens of Los Angeles got together and put up a large sum of money to bring out from Europe and the eastern part of the United States, a number of representative aviators for an international meet, the first ever given in this country. Louis Paulhan, one of the most celebrated French aviators, was brought over with a biplane and a monoplane, and there were a number of American entries, including Charles F. Willard and myself. Los Angeles furnished the first opportunity for a real contest in this country between the French and American machines, and these contests aroused immense interest throughout the country."

The prize monies at these meets were very impressive by any standard, particularly if one realizes that a dollar in 1910 was worth far more than one today. A pair of boots cost $5 then; today the same pair would cost approximately $75. Paulhan was enticed to Dominguez by a $7,500 appearance fee, and won $14,000 more during the meet. I could never be in that league, but the $5,000 available for California amateurs really interested me. Maybe I could build an aeroplane and win some of it!

I designed a biplane with a 25-foot wingspan, 5-foot chord, Curtiss-type ailerons, Wright-type front elevator and rear rudder, and skids plus wheels. Wheels were the best for takeoffs, but Curtiss had broken many when landing too hard. Therefore, I planned on using wheels for takeoffs, and then retracting them for landings. When I had everything all

16

figured out I found that it was going to take more money than I had, and require a lot more manpower to build than just myself.

At this same time another San Diegan, Charles F. Walsh, was promoting a huge monoplane that he'd designed and built, but never flown. It was displayed in a haybarn downtown, and they were trying to sell stock to finance a company to manufacture it. I was intrigued with it, but I didn't think much of Walsh's design or mechanics. Nonetheless, one day I was looking over his plane when I ran into Kenneth Kendall, a school chum. Kenneth was quite a lawn tennis player, but also very interested in aviation. Therefore, for three reasons I thought that he and I ought to get together: his family was well-off; I needed an extra pair of hands; and he lived close to our house. I showed him my designs and told him about the Dominguez prize monies, and we shook on it, forming the *Waterman-Kendall Aviation Partnership*.

Kenneth and I set to work, devoting every spare minute after school and on weekends towards building the biplane. A couple of times he begged-off to attend a tennis tournament somewhere. This bothered me, but there wasn't much that I could do about it. However, he made up for this failing by being an excellent photographer. He took many photographs during the period of our association which provided far more benefit than the loss of his labors in 1909. (Sadly, most of these were lost in the 1978 San Diego Aerospace Museum arson-fire.)

The plane was finally completed enough to take out of the shop and assemble, minus the engine, for a photograph. The engine, a Speedwell 2-cylinder small auto engine which I'd borrowed, promising its owner 25 percent of our winnings, was still in the shop being tested.

In the early days of aviation two of the toughest problems were finding suitable engines and propellers. We had a devil of a time fashioning our propeller. What we ended with was no thing of beauty, but it looked like it would do the job. However, engines weren't something that you could make very easily. Manly made his fine radial for Langley in 1901; the Wrights had built their own; and the French had Levavasseur's 50-hp steam-cooled V8 *"Antoinette"* engine, which was ideal, having been designed for motor boats originally. Curtiss's involvement in aviation originated from his superb motorcyle engines. His engine powered Baldwin's *"California Arrow"* airship in 1904, and also the *first* American military aircraft. None of these, though, were available to high schoolers building airplanes in their backyard.

17

Levavasseur's Antoinette engine, Gastambide-Mangin aeroplane,
Scientific American, Jan. 18, 1908

Popular Mechanics, March, 1908

Scientific American, January 18, 1908

The more I tested the Speedwell engine, the more convinced I became that it wasn't going to be powerful enough to lift our 500-pound aeroplane. But, I'd heard that Barney Oldfield doped his fuel with ether to get more power. If it was good enough for him, it was good enough for us, and I proceeded to add a good slug of ether to the Speedwell's gasoline. Boy, it sure gave us a lot more power; it blew

18

one of the cylinders right out of the crankcase! There went our hopes for Dominguez.

But we were already officially entered; we'd received our passes and badges designating us as *"Aviators"*, and we were still determined to attend the Aviation Meet.

Shortly after the new year Kenneth and I packed our bags and took the train up to Los Angeles. The Pacific Electric trolley then took us the rest of the way to Dominguez Field, where we arrived just when the meet started, January 10, 1910. Our *"Entrant"* credentials got us into the big infield where there were two huge circus-type tents, one for the French contingent and the

other for Curtiss' American group. As it was the first time we'd ever seen these aeroplanes, we gawked a bit at the French Farmans and Bleriots, and then hurried straight for the Curtiss tent.

As soon as we spotted Curtiss we went up to him and asked if we could work with his group. But this offer must have been what every kid

19

in America wanted to do, for he indicated that there wasn't any need of us. This made us feel a bit dejected - but the feeling didn't last for long because there was too much excitement going on.

The front page of *The Los Angeles Times* for January 10, 1910, carried this headline:

"GLENN CURTISS FLIES OVER AVIATION PARK"..."The first flight of an aeroplane west of the Great Plains was made by Glenn H. Curtiss at Aviation Park yesterday afternoon at 3:30 o'clock... It marked an epoch in the affairs of the West, for a flight had never before been made on the coast and native sons were skeptical of its accomplishment until they actually set eyes on the performance."*

Therefore, what we were witnessing was indeed historic. It may add even more perspective to consider that it was just the year before that I had successfully flown the glider, and at this time Kenneth and I had substancially completed an aeroplane that was virtually 'state-of-the-art'.

It does make one wonder, though, about today's common belief that everyone then was aware that the Wrights had flown in 1903. Here it was 1910 and there were great multitudes of nonbelievers - especially in that one region of the world that would become a center of aviation development!

We kept an eye on what little flying was yet going on. A couple of times we wandered over to the French tent to curiously look over their operation, but we always came back to Curtiss'. After sneaking in and out of his tent several times, and watching the half-dozen or so men assembling his aeroplanes, we thought of another ruse that might get Curtiss interested in us.

It was about midafternoon when we again sidled up to him - with the photographs of our biplane. Curtiss was more approachable this time. He took the photos, looked them over with interest and said:

20

"Aren't you the two boys that were here this morning looking for a job?"

"Yes we are, sir," said I.

"Well, I can't pay you anything, but if you want to work just for the experience, I think I can find something for you to do."

"Oh - we don't expect to get paid. We just want to work for you," we chorused.

With that, Curtiss took us over to Henry Kleckler, his chief mechanic, and he turned us over to a chap assembling a pusher-biplane for Frank Johnson, one of Curtiss' first aeroplane buyers. (Johnson would become the first native Californian to own and fly an aeroplane, on February 12, 1910, a distinction that I almost did him out of.) For the next few days we worked on Johnson's plane, and learned more from all of the conversations and aeroplane flying than we ever would have in months and months on our own. It was a fantastic education.

Curtiss and Johnson

21

Towards the end of the meet Curtiss said:

> *"Aren't you boys from San Diego?"*
> *"Yes sir," we replied,*
> *"Is there any place down there close to the water that would be suitable for a flying field?"*
> *"Yes sir," I said, "there's a place like that called North Island."*

When I was a young boy, my father's railroad had a contract for supplying the granite boulders for building the big jetty that projected seaward from North Island's Zuinga Point. Completed in April 1905, it formed a protected entrance to San Diego Bay. Some of my fondest memories are of accompanying father there when he inspected the work. I'd become very familiar with the terrain and the bays and beaches, so I could answer Curtiss' question in some detail:

> *"Sir, there's a mill pond - a shallow lagoon called Spanish Bight - on the inside of the sand spit connecting North Island - an excellent place for a flying field - to Coronado, and as you go on around the island counterclockwise from the bight, the water gradually gets rougher and rougher until you get to the jetty and ocean breakers."*

That was about all I said. But, I've always thought that it planted the seed that led to his establishing his winter experimental station and flying school at North Island less than a year later. As best I recall, here's how the events transpired. Following the Dominguez Meet, Curtiss visited the Aero Club of San Diego, of which I was a member. Due to the enthusiasm of its D.C. Collier and the Chamber of Commerce, negotiations were worked-out with North Island's owner, John Spreckels and his Coronado Beach Company, to lease the island to the club for three years at $1 per year rent. The club, in turn, made the choicest two sites available to Curtiss and to Harry Harkness, a wealthy New Yorker, who arrived in 1911 with three lovely French Antoinette monoplanes. Thus, due to the temperate climate and unique geography, the Aero Club of San Diego pulled off a coup - bringing America's first aircraft manufacturer to North Island - and I have always felt a part of it.

But, back to Dominguez. It followed by only a few months the great Reims meeting when Eugene Lefebvre, Henri Farman, Hubert Latham, G.B. Cockburn, Bleriot, and Curtiss had first competed in the air - and Glenn Curtiss had won the coveted *International Cup,* the Gordon Bennett Trophy, *"The Blue Ribbon of the Air".*

1909 GAMY lithograph - Curtiss winning Gordon Bennett Trophy

But progress was incredibly rapid in those first few years - and when Paulhan (a circus bareback rider turned aviator) arrived at Dominiguez he was flying with Seguin's new 70-hp Gnome *rotary* engine, mechanically different and far more reliable than all others. Its combustion gases were drawn into the cylinders through the crankcase. This would dilute petroleum lubricating oils, so vegetable *castor oil* was used, producing an unpleasant, pungent odor. In tractor (pulling) use, it splattered the pilot, necessitating the 'dashing' use of scarfs by those intrepid *'knights of the air',* and the fumes caused diarrhea!

A week after Reims, Lefebvre became the first pilot to die. *(Curtiss' Aerial Experiment associate, Thomas Selfridge, was the first American to die in an aeroplane, while a passenger with Orville Wright in 1908.)* There'd be many others going to the same fate. Pilots had little protection in those frail contraptions of the lightest construction possible: spruce, bamboo, muslin and piano wire.

Records fell right and left, rarely lasting more than a few months. Many new records were being set at Dominguez, attested by Cortlandt Field Bishop, president of the Aero Club of America and chairman of

23

the judge's committee. Paulhan won his first $10,000 for an amazing flight to Santa Anita and back, covering 64 miles in just under two hours. Finding one's way in the air for any distance then was very difficult, much as it was for early motorists. Paulhan also gave Mrs. Dick Ferris a ride, and she thus became the *"First American lady passenger to fly in the air."* But, the speed and altitude events caused the most interest. Before thousands of spellbound spectators Curtiss again proved that he was the world's fastest aviator as he raced at over 55-mph. And then it was Paulhan's turn. He struggled higher and higher in his Farman; at his zenith, the ground triagulators determined his altitude was 4,165 feet. When that was blared out, I remember Curtiss exclaiming,*"Oh, that's a wonderful record. It'll be many years before it's broken"*. Within a year, Lincoln Beachey in a Curtiss had flown three times as high!

Attendance was over 50,000 on Sunday, the 16ᵗʰ. The total meet attendance was of over 175,000, quite a crowd gazing skyward acquiring "the aeroplane neck" when Los Angeles' population was less than 75,000.

We were all intrigued and a little skeptical of the Bleriot tractor-monoplanes. These were virtually the same as the one that had conquered the English Channel six months earlier. Their two front wheels and single rear tail wheel caused them to look precarious during their takeoffs, like they were knife-edge-balanced upon the front wheels. But later when we flew these 'tail-dragger' aeroplanes we discovered that they were very stable, and that there wasn't a problem at all.

During the Dominguez meet I became acquainted with Charlie Willard, Curtiss's first pupil, known as the *"Boy Wonder of the Air,"* and the next best aviator after Curtiss. For several years following this meet Willard flew the exhibition circuit as America's first barnstormer. He was also involved in aircraft design and manufacturing, and was project engineer for one of Curtiss' largest flying boats, the Model T Triplane, in the mid-teens. I think that he should have received the Aero Club of America's FAI license No. 4, after the Wrights and Curtiss, but due to the way Alan Hawley ran things, he was awarded No. 10.

The FAI (Federation Aeronautique Internationale) was the international licensing body, recognized until well into the 1920's. In the United States the Aero Club administered its rules and *alphabetically awarded the first five licenses, No. 1 to Curtiss, No. 2 to Army Lt. Frank Lahm, No. 3 to Paulhan and Nos. 4 and 5 to Orville and Wilbur Wright.*

24

Curtiss' Reims Racer

Curtiss & Clifford

Curtiss & Johnson

Charles Willard

Paulhan & Farman

Paulhan's Farman

Our Dominguez photos

25

1910 Dominguez composite: l-r, top, Paulhan, Paulhan, Curtiss; center, Paulhan (Bleriot); lower, left-Willard, right-Hamilton; Beachey in balloon.

26 *Charles Willard - fine detail of the Reims racer in Curtiss tent, Dominguez, 1910*

*My photo of Willard, Hamilton, and Curtiss - Dominguez 1910
(Reims Racer in background)*

The editor of *Scientific American* on April 8, 1911 wrote:

"Sport for Sport's Sake

*The presentation of the Scientific American Aviation Cup to Mr.
Glenn H. Curtiss, as recorded elsewhere in the issue, gave the donors an opportunity to draw attention to the sportsmanlike spirit displayed by the winner in his persistent quest of this trophy. Although
Curtiss is engaged in the manufacture and commercial exploitation
of aeroplanes, and is therefore a professional, he has exemplified the
best traditions of the amateur in his three-year quest of a trophy
which brings no cash to the winner, and whose principal value lies
in the distinction which it confers. The Scientific American has always deplored the fact that there was no competition for this trophy,
and our regret was due, not so much to the consideration that we
were its donors, as to the fact that the lack of interest in the cup
proved that the spirit of commercialism was dominant among the*

27

ranks of the aviators, not one of whom, outside of Curtiss, cares to turn momentarily aside from the hunt for large money prizes and make a effort to win a cup which has the distinction of being the first trophy of any kind offered in America in commection with the new art of aviation."

This may somewhat clarify things when I state that Glenn Curtiss was the man dominating American aviation then: he was *THE* hero to boys like myself. There was even a song heralding his historic 1910 Hudson River flight, *"King Of The Air"*, a march and twostep!

When the Dominguez Air Meeting was over, Kenneth and I packed-up and went home to San Diego. My mind was bursting with all that I'd seen and I was itching to try out some of the things on our aeroplane.

Following the meet, Charles Hamilton came to San Diego and with Curtiss' Reims racer put on an exhibition at Coronado's polo field on January 22 and 23, 1910 - thus becoming the first person to fly an aeroplane in my home town.

The exhibition's promoters offered Charlie Walsh $500 to fly his monoplane for the crowds. He started off properly headed into the wind, but when he reached the end of the field he was only going 10 or 15-mph - far too slow to become airborne. Then he did a foolish but not uncommon thing; he got out, lifted the nose wheel and walked the plane around to the opposite direction. Now, as he gunned the engine he was headed downwind and it looked like he was really racing - but with the tailwind he was actually going slower than before relative to his airspeed. He didn't take off, and was rolling so fast that he couldn't stop. He ran into the low ballstop circling the field and smashed-up his landing gear. It surely wasn't flyable anymore - if it ever had been - but his Cameron air-cooled 4-cylinder automobile engine was undamaged and I immediately approached him, propositioning for its use, and received his hesitant but tentative OK.

Late that January and on into February, Kenneth and I worked on our biplane. While Hamilton had been at the polo field I'd arranged for the use of his tent after he departed, and it was Feb. 12th when we carted the plane over to Coronado, assembling it in front of the tent's framework. The Union newspaper took photographs and wrote an article about our achievement, which appeared on the 13th.

But just when we were about ready to follow Hamilton skyward, Walsh told me that we couldn't use his Cameron afterall. He'd ordered a new Elbridge *"Featherweight"* 3-cylinder engine, and wanted the Cameron available if his monoplane would be repaired and ready to try to fly before its delivery. We were back to using the now-repaired Speedwell engine!

Flying With the Elbridge at Denver

29

February 13 1910 THE SAN DIEGO UNION

HIGH SCHOOL BOYS PUTTING
LAST TOUCHES ON BIPLANE

Kenneth Kendall, in seat, Waldo Waterman, standing, and biplane built on original designs which is nearing completion in tent on Coronado Aviation field.

—Norton & Bennett Staff Photographers.

BIG LEAGUERS USE CARSON AND MYERS

Press Dispatches Tell of Members of San Diego's Star Battery.

By the Associated Press

New York, Feb. 12.—If an early start counts for anything, the New York National League club will have an advantage over all rivals this year. Leaving New York today, the advance guard of the Giants will reach its training quarters at Marlin Springs, Texas, well before any other big league teams begin a similar move.

The advance guard sailing on the Southern Pacific steamship Porteus for New Orleans, includes First Baseman Fred Merkle, Coach Arlie Latham, Pitchers Dailey, Kleber and Scott; Outfielders Zacher and Lush, and others.

Manager McGraw, with Pitcher Christy Mathewson and a bunch of recruits will follow southward as soon as next week's National league meeting at the Waldorf-Astoria is ended, and Catcher Ja·k Myers will meet the others at St. Louis.

Marlin Springs is a town of about 5000 inhabitants, close to the Mexican frontier.

Waldo Waterman and Kenneth Kendall Patent New Principles.

Waldo Waterman, grandson of the former governor of California, and Kenneth Kendall, who attained the semi-finals in men's singles in last week's tennis tournament, both high school boys of this city, have practically completed the construction of a biplane, which involves the original ideas of both. The big machine is housed in a tent on Coronado field, where Hamilton's Curtiss biplane stood two weeks ago, and attracted nearly as much attention last week as the tennis tournament and the polo practice games.

In general lines the partnership machine of the local boys is much like the Curtiss aeroplane, but it embodies several new ideas, original with the two youthful inventors. One of the new features is the arrangement of the three wheels. They are set so they may be folded under the machine, and are controlled by the same lever by which the engine is shut off, when the aviator wishes to descend.

The Waterman-Kendall machine is fitted with both the wheels and with the running skids peculiar to the Wright biplanes. Much trouble has been experienced by Curtiss machines in descending on rough ground, the wheels frequently collapsing and breaking. In the Wright machines this trouble is obviated, the aeroplane leaving the starting carriage, which is mounted on wheels, when sufficient momentum is gained and lighting on the skids when returning to earth. The disadvantage of the Wright method, however, is that the machine and its wheels are often miles apart at the finish of the flight.

This difficulty will be done away with in the local biplane. The motion which shuts off the engine when it is stopped preparatory to the final glide to the earth, will also fold the wheels beneath the body of the aeroplane, and the aviator and machine will glide along smoothly for a few yards on the tough spruce runners. The machine can then be tilted and the wheels replaced in position.

Another new feature, for which the inventors already have obtained a patent, consists in the automatic control of the small lateral balancing planes, between the main planes of the machine. By a special device the machine will be automatically balanced, the small planes warping so as to present a concave or convex surface either up or down. Kendall and Waterman declare that on account of this later patent, which they declare is superior to the Wright principle, their design will not conflict under the law with the patents already issued.

The main planes of the machine are 2½ feet shorter than those of the Curtiss machine, but are wider and give a greater lifting surface. The parabolic curve is also accented to a greater degree, and the vertical and horizontal steering apparatus are both larger. The main planes are 5 by 25 feet, the forward planes 2 by 10 feet and the rear planes 2 by 5. It is estimated that the completed weight, with engine and aviator, will be 450 pounds.

Waterman and Kendall are trying to secure the use of the engine which C. F. Walsh had in his unfortunate monoplane. If they get this it will be installed in their biplane and a flight will be attempted in a few weeks.

San Diego Union - February 13, 1910

We knew that it wouldn't get us airborne, so we decided to try automobile towing for takeoff, hoping that once aloft it would then keep us aloft. Before we installed the Speedwell, we trained by trying several tow-takeoffs behind Wilson Smith's Franklin automobile, but these were terminated in a crackup when Kenneth was piloting. He wasn't injured - but, by golly, he had to immediately participate in a lawn tennis tournament, leaving me to complete the repairs alone. That didn't make me a bit happy.

At this time an ex-locomotive engineer named Sigmund was garaging his Buick in my shop. He became very interested in my aeroplane projects, helping as much as possible with the repairing of the biplane. Since he had two wooden legs he wasn't much help outside of the shop - but he did volunteer to drive his Buick as a tow car. Kenneth was still away when I'd completed the fixup, and I got another chum, Milton Wolf, to help me, and it was back to Coronado, trying again.

I was using an alligator-type release hook holding the tow rope to the biplane, and with this arrangement we made several successful straightaway flights. But the Speedwell, powering a propeller that wasn't as efficient as it might have been, couldn't keep the plane airborne long. I was getting in some abbreviated flights, though, and it was a consuming sensation trying to keep the craft level and flying. However, on the fifth flight the hook release didn't work for some unknown reason, and the tow rope kept pulling me. I found myself in an untenable position, 30-feet above the ground attached to an automobile whose driver was unaware of my predicament. When Sigmund turned the Buick to the right at the predetermined spot, I started pulling the controls, trying to turn right also. But, when I got abreast of the car, my momentum stopped. The plane stalled, went into a sideslip and dove into the ground.

Damn, did it hit hard! The biplane was demolished. Almost everything was broken except the top wing. The way that I'd been positioned, with everything landing on my feet, meant that my legs took a terrible shock with the blow being transmitted right to my tailbone. I was surrounded by the wreckage with jagged, splintered pieces thrusting towards me like daggers, but fortunately none jabbed me seriously. The pain in my back was excruciating. I was sure that something serious was damaged there when, after a couple of seconds, the pain in my ankles became fiercer than in my back.

Sigmund and Milton rushed over to help me. Since Sigmund had had problems like this himself, he took charge, seeing that I was extricated and then laid flat on the ground. They tore loose some broken struts and fashioned a makeshift stretcher, rolling me onto it and then gingerly lifting me up on the rear of the Buick. I was thus ignominiously carried home with Sigmund driving very slowly and carefully up the hill from the ferry landing.

It was a shocked mother that immediately took command, getting me to my room, out of my clothes and into bed. She then called a new, young physician in town, Doctor B.J. O'Neill, and he hurried over by the Electric Rapid Transit trolley. He determined that I'd badly broken my right ankle plus several small bones in my left foot: eight bones in all. After pulling and pressing, he got the bones repositioned as best as possible, and then he applied heavy plaster casts to both feet, admonishing me to stay off of them and in bed. No X-rays were then used; it was simply feel and skill the doctor used in setting broken bones.

When Kenneth had returned from his tennis tournament and found me laid up, he'd seen to it that the hapless Speedwell engine was returned to its owner. We then ended the Waterman-Kendall Aviation Partnership.

For the next couple of months I was confined to home, with my classmates bringing me my studies so that I wouldn't drop behind in school. It wasn't long, though, before I was propped-up in bed designing a new aeroplane. It would be called my "tractor biplane," for I was planning to have the propeller up front, pulling, instead of the more common pusher designs.

After about six weeks Dr. O'Neill decided that the casts could come off, as long as I used crutches and stayed off my feet. I was soon hobbling around on crutches at school, and by the time the semester ended I was fairly mobile again. However, I must have pushed things a bit as my left foot never healed properly. The arch was gone, and it has given me lifelong problems.

Mother now thought that I'd benefit from a vacation: farming at Aunt Abby's Waterman Ranch in Barstow, a section of land homesteaded by my grandfather in the 1870's. It was in the middle of the Mojave Desert - about the hottest, most desolate and inhospitable place that I'd ever seen. Working under the conditions existing in those days was surely no vacation! I stuck it out, though I never did become a desert fan. Years later I'd have much to do with that property.

When I thankfully returned home, ready for my junior year in high school, I immediately started gathering the materials for my next aeroplane. I paid for them, and the doctor's bill, by taking care of Dr. O'Neill's new Stanley Steamer, plus two or three other automobiles.

Charlie Walsh had now received his Elbridge engine and was flying in a Curtiss-copy that he'd built, doing exhibitions at Imperial Beach, just south of Coronado. The Cameron engine was at Trepte's cabinet shop, where Walsh owed a bill, and after a bit of negotiating I got the use of it. It was then full-speed ahead building my tractor aeroplane. Now, for the first time, I had a powerful-enough engine.

During this time Bernard Roehrig had the Baker Machine Works fabricate a beautiful copy of a Paulhan Farman, equipping it with a 6-cylinder, 60-hp engine. I spent quite a bit of time around Baker's watching the Farman's construction, and upon its completion it turned out to be a better aeroplane than its owner was a pilot. Roehrig teamed-up with one of Paulhan's Dominguez teammates, Didier Masson. They first did exhibition flying at Imperial Beach and then, in the fall of 1910, moved up to the Playa del Rey Motordrome, near Venice, southwest of Los Angeles. *This was the first of the very popular steeply-banked, wooden-planked automobile speedways* - and its infield was ideal for exhibition flyers. Roehrig won the *Los Angeles Times' "Harrison Gray Otis"* gold medal for being the first Californian to stay aloft in excess of a minute, and thereafter faded from the scene.

Didier Masson continued exhibition flying. Then he got involved as a mercenary in the Mexican Revolution, earning the dubious distinction of being the first to drop bombs for real in the Americas - in May, 1913, over Guaymas Bay. In 1916 he was one of the heroes of the Lafayette Escadrille.

Walsh continued building aeroplanes and doing exhibition flying. After Dominguez he became associated with Curtiss' designs, and in 1911 he built a plane for Harry Harkness at North Island powered with the pioneering and very innovative Iowa-made Adams-Farwell *horizontal* rotary engine. However, his manufacturing was not too successful, and he went East as a Curtiss exhibition flyer, becoming secretary of the Aero Club of America just prior to his fatal crash in 1912.

33

Another aviation experimenter near San Diego was Don Gordon, a farm boy living near Bostonia. Like I, he had built gliders in 1909, and then took the 7-hp engine from his Curtiss motorcycle and with considerable ingenuity fashioned a successful aeroplane. *(Prior to getting into aviation, Curtiss had become "the fastest man in the world", racing his motorcycle at 136.3 mph in 1907, and he also invented the twist-handle throttle.)* Gordon was, like I, an *"Aviator"* entrant in the first Dominguez meet. In 1915 he astounded everyone with the beautiful monoplane that he built and flew over to North Island. The Army made quite a fuss over it - but nothing ever materialized for Don. We were good friends in those years due to our common interest in flying. Gordon's family, however, discouraged his efforts, and that, coupled with his near-deafness, led him to become a Mt. Palomar forester and almost a recluse. *I'm sure that his life affected mine.*

But back to Glenn Curtiss and his coming to San Diego. The Wrights had sold their first aeroplane to the United States Army (and appeared to have it as their customer). Thus, Curtiss was determined to secure the Navy's business - hopefully by developing *"a new amphibious machine"*, an aeroplane that could operate from the water. In selecting Curtiss, the Navy's Captain Washington Irving Chambers found him always ready to experiment and *as progressive as the Wrights were conservative.*

Curtiss' hometown, Hammondsport, was on Lake Keuka, one of the smaller Finger Lakes located in upstate New York. It was far too cold in the winter to carry on such experiments on a frozen lake, hence the desire for a warmer, water-oriented location.

Between mid-December 1910 and early January 1911, Curtiss, accompanied by his own family, plus his mother and much-younger half-brother, Carl Adams, arrived in San Diego, setting up the *Glenn H. Curtiss Aviation Camp* on North Island. (During this same time Curtiss was a major figure at the second Dominguez Air Meeting.) Also, with him were Navy Lt. Theodore G. (Spuds) Ellyson and Army officers Paul W. Beck, G.E.M. Kelly and John C. Walker, Jr. Ensign Charles Pousland came in February, and Hugh Robinson, C.C. Witmer of Chicago and R.H. *"Lucky Bob"* St. Henry of San Francisco, civilians, arrived in March. Curtiss' head mechanician, Damon Merrill, was there but returned to Hammondsport in February, replaced by John D Cooper.

With many Aero Club members helping, the brush and jackrabbits were cleared away for an airfield about half-a-mile long and three hundred yards wide, and a few temporary buildings were erected for hangars and shops, plus a boat landing. Curtiss returned from the San Francisco Air Meeting at Tanforan Racetrack to open the camp on January 17th, just a day before Eugene Ely, flying from the Army's Selfridge Aviation Field, successfully dared the first landing and takeoff from a ship, the USS Pennsylvania in San Francisco Bay. Ely's life preserver was several inner tubes wrapped around his body, but nerve was his only protection when he brought his Curtiss biplane in to land, to be stopped by the world's first arresting gear. This was a Curtiss innovation of ropes stretched across the deck between 100-pound bags of sand which would snag the grappling hook hanging below his aeroplane, *a system little-changed today!*

Pragmatic, determined and impatient, Curtiss' goal was to prove the practicality of water-borne aircraft. He was ready to try anything to do so. Secondly, he wanted to train his nucleus of military flying students.

At this time there were 26 FAI-licensed American aviators. France had 353, England 57, Germany 46, Italy 32 and Belgium 27.

To introduce his activities to San Diegans (and probably to help out the bank account as well) Curtiss held an exhibition at the Coronado polo field on January 28th and 29th under the auspices of the Aero Club of San Diego. Several thousand spectators watched as he and Ely showed how the fledgling pilots were instructed. The Curtiss method was termed *"grasscutting"* because the student was put in an aeroplane that had its throttle blocked to preclude its taking off, permitting only the repetitious whizzing back and forth across the field. After some time, when the student became accustomed to the plane and its controls, he would be permitted to try flying by releasing the blocked throttle.

Spuds Ellyson, a red-haired, freckle-faced 25-year-old Virginian, was Curtiss' star pupil, and was doing very well showing the crowd how grass-cutting was done. But on the second day of the exhibition the throttle block must have loosened, for he suddenly was airborne. He wasn't yet proficient enough to cope with that situation, and slewed off left, cracking up the plane somewhat by making a wing-first landing. Ellyson wasn't injured, but from then on he was considered to have made his *"first flight"*.

35

John Walker, Spuds Ellyson and Eugene Ely - January 29, 1911
(Ely was killed October 9, 1911)

Curtiss exibition, Coronado Polo Field, January 29, 1911

36

But I'm ahead of my story. I was at the polo field that day not as a spectator, but as one in the group around Curtiss. When I'd learned that he was at North Island I'd raced over there and made it known that I was available. From that time on I was part of the Curtiss camp, never paid, but always an eager helper with my eyes and ears wide open.

Flying lessons and aircraft development were going on at the same time, and in an effort to clarify each, I'll discuss them separately.

As noted, instruction was by the grasscutting method. The engine's throttle was controlled both by foot, like in a car, and by hand. But all of the training was done with only the foot control, with the stop set to conform to the student's progress. The flying was always done when there was almost no wind, either in the early daylight hours or just before dusk, thus permitting the students to go back and forth, learning each way. The first thing to learn was how to steer the plane on the ground. This feat was far harder in practice than it sounded because turning was dependent solely on the air forces upon the rudder, not on a turning wheel on the ground. It was further complicated because the Curtiss pushers had three wheels, one forward and two aft of the center of gravity, making turning more difficult than even with tail-draggers.

Ellyson, Beck, Curtiss, Kelly and Walker - March, 1911

37

Paul Beck was the most advanced of the students, having briefly flown with Curtiss at Dominguez. He soloed only about a month after arriving at North Island. Ellyson and Witmer were also very apt pupils and appeared to be natural flyers, but Kelly and Walker were a different story. Walker simply didn't catch on, and Curtiss soon recommended that he be dropped. I don't know if Curtiss repeated that recommendation for Kelly, but I sure thought that he ought to have.

Walker, Robinson and Kelly - March 1911

GH (Curtiss) was always on-hand when grasscutting was going on, and usually after each run he'd offer some comment, counseling the student. Many of these I overheard and stored away for future reference. One day Kelly was roaring towards the hangar from the west end of the runway as fast as the throttle setting permitted, when, for some reason or other, he froze with his foot hard-down on the throttle. The training plane, affectionately called *"Lizzie"*, was charging right at us gathered at the corner of the hangar when Curtiss yelled for everyone to *"get out of the way!"*. He dashed in front of the onrushing craft, grasping the lead-

38

ing edge of the lower wingtip and swinging his body under, acting as a drag. Lizzie pivoted, barely missing the hangar, and shaking Curtiss up while raising a cloud of dust. This jolted Kelly into moving his foot, and he came to an abrupt stop. What Curtiss said to Kelly afterwards was in private. He did complete his training though. But he was soon killed, we heard, in a foolish maneuver. He thus gained the distinction of having Kelly Field named after him.

March, 1911, (L to R): Greer, Cooper, St. Henry, Purington, Shakelford, Carl Adams, Beck, Walker, Mrs. Beck, Ellyson, Witmer and Robinson. (Note Ellyson's pipe - looks like I copied him in my later career!)

Witmer, me and Hallett (in front of shop)

39

Spuds Ellyson was a totally different person - a worker, scientist and engineer every minute while at North Island. He was always with Curtiss, working to perfect a pontoon combination that would result in a successful hydroaeroplane. Curtiss had brought several sets of pontoons from Hammondsport, patterned after Henri Fabre's designs, and they kept moving them about, adding splash boards - all sorts of things. They constantly figured and sketched on almost anything handy - even covering the workshop's whitewashed walls with designs and calculations. Finally, they came up with a main float about 5 x 6 feet x 14 inches deep, with a hydro-surface bottom, and a smaller float forward. The following happened as recounted by Curtiss in his 1912 book:

"When we brought the machine out on the 26th day of January I felt that we ought to get some results. There were no crowds of people present and there was no announcement of what was about to happen. I had not expected to made a flight, but climbed into the aviator's seat with a feeling that the machine would surely rise into the air when I wished, but that I would only try it on the water to see how the new float acted. Lieutenant Ellyson spun the propeller and I turned the machine into the wind. It ploughed through the water deeply at first, but gathered speed and rose higher and higher in the water and skipped more and more lightly until the float barely skimmed the surface of the bay. So intent was I in watching the water that I did not notice that I was approaching the shore and to avoid running aground I tilted the horizontal control and the machine seemed to leap into the air like a frightened gull. So suddenly did it rise that it quite took me by surprise.

But I kept the machine up for perhaps half a mile, then turned and dropped lightly down on the water, turned around and headed back to the starting point. The effect of that first flight on the men who had worked, waited, and watched for it was magical. They ran up and down the beach, throwing their hats up into the air and shouting in their enthusiasm.

I now headed about into the bay, in the direction of San Diego, and rose up into the air again even more easily than the first time. I flew for half a mile and turned twice to see how the machine would act in the air with the clumsy-looking float below it. The naval re-

pair ship Iris caught sight of me as I went flying by and sent its siren blast far out over the water, and all the other craft blew their whistles, until it seemed as if all San Diego knew of the achievement. Satisfied that it was all right, I landed within a few yards of the shore, near the hangar."

That day, Curtiss had just invented the first 'practical' seaplane - which he called a *hydroaeroplane*, and sometimes an *aero-hydroplane*. It's advisable to comment here on the term 'practical'. Not quite a year earlier, on March 28, 1910, Henri Fabre was first to fly off water at Port de la Mede, Martigues, France, in his *"Hydravion"*. However, his craft, with its large, fixed rudder, had little maneuverability. Like the early Wright craft, it was primarily a pioneering achievement.

In the work on the hydroaeroplane, Curtiss and Ellyson used the excellent facilities of the Baker Machine Works. They now had Bob Baker and one of his young employees, George E.A. Hallett, build a new concept they'd designed. It was a single, scow-type pontoon 12 feet long, 2 feet wide and tapered up in front and down aft from a depth of a foot. Curtiss was so impressed with Hallett's handiwork that a strong bond developed, and he soon joined Curtiss for a long and eventful career.

George Hallett and new single pontoon

Curtiss now fitted on this new single pontoon and eliminated the forward float. *On February 1, 1911, he successfully flew this system, found it far superior to the double-floats and continued its use for six years.*

Hydroaeroplane development - photo sequence:

1: Two-float version

2: Into the water (note folded innertube wingtip floats)

3: Afloat (note Witmer, left)

4: The original two-float hydroaeroplane

5: Single-float version - Curtiss observing balance

6: Single-float version - Curtiss and St. Henry

7: About to takeoff!

8: In flight - San Diego harbor

9: Spectators - Spanish Bight

But the Navy wasn't satisfied with an aeroplane that could only land and take off from the water; they wanted one which could operate from shipboard by being hoisted to and from the water. The USS Pennsylvania was now in San Diego Bay, and Curtiss was determined to demonstrate this desired capability while it was available. He revised the hydroaeroplane, turned its engine around so that its propeller would be pulling, tractor-fashion, rather than pushing, and removed the front elevators, relying solely on the rear ones.

Curtiss was a remarkable and resourceful man in many ways, but there was one thing he could never do: calculate the center of gravity of his aeroplanes. We always had a length of 4-inch drainpipe to place under the center skid or pontoon, rolling the plane back and forth to locate the point of balance. But for some reason or other this hadn't been done with this modified tractor-hydroaeroplane. In fact, the plane hadn't even been test flown when Curtiss had everything arranged for a demonstration to the Navy.

On the back of a mechanician wearing hip waders, he was carried to the gently rocking plane, then taxied from shore and gunned the engine. After a run that was far too long, the plane lifted free of the water and was airborne. But something was wrong; it was flying with its tail low and only about 35 feet in the air, and try as he might, Curtisss couldn't get the tail up. The only thing to do was to decrease the power and settle back to the water, which he immediately did. But the ever-ready photographer did get his picture in the air. Curtiss was still a long way from the cruiser, but instead of heading back to camp he proceeded on to the ship, taxiing the rest of the way.

Curtiss and the plane were hoisted aboard by a lifting cable and, after a brief congratulation from Captain Charles Pond, he was lowered back to the water. The engine had been fitted with a special crank allowing Curtiss to start the engine without the aid of a mechanician, and then he taxied all the way back to the camp, ending his now-historic feat. The photograph of the plane's one leap in the air, plus Pond's report to Captain Chambers in Washington, won the day for Curtiss. *That February 17th is an aviation milestone.*

46

Curtiss - ready for the USS Pennsylvania 'flight'

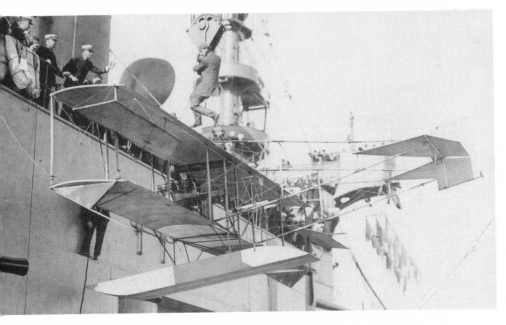

Curtiss - being hoisted aboard

Now, in less than a month, Curtiss had perfected his hydroaeroplane - *the seaplane* - and the shipboard version to the Navy's satisfaction. Next, he used the new single scow pontoon to make an aeroplane that could operate off of either land or water. He attached retractable wheels to the pontoon, and on that craft's first flight he took off from Spanish Bight, circled a couple of times and then landed on the camp's runway. We all rushed over to the plane and I recall Curtiss saying:

"Now if we could just take off the wings and drive this thing down the road, we'd really have something!"

It was Sunday, February 26, 1911.

He called this new version the *"Triad"* because it operated off land, water or in the air. *It was the first "amphibian".* One of Curtiss' stunts was to take off from the bight, fly over to the Hotel del Coronado, land on the beach, have lunch with his wife and then fly back to the camp.

Triad - Hotel del Coronado in background

Charles Witmer, one of the civilian students, became a great buddy of Ellyson's. They were seen so much together that they earned the tag, *"The Gold Dust Twins,"* after the popular powdered soap brand - or was it because Witmer had been an Alaskan gold miner? Once, when Curtiss was working on the new pontoon, he asked Witmer to accompany him aloft in order to observe how it behaved upon water contact, and the only place for Charlie to sit was upon the pontoon. To get into position he had to crawl under the wing and through a maze of wires and struts. Curtiss then took off and came in for a test landing. He misjudged his height and hit the water with a terrific smack, splitting the pontoon wide open and causing the plane to sink immediately to the bottom. Being in Spanish Bight, the water was quite shallow, only about 4 feet deep, and Curtiss simply stood up on his seat and didn't even get wet. But where was Witmer? We started to get worried, and Spuds was tearing off his clothes and rushing for the water when Charlie suddenly popped up like a cork. Even though a good swimmer, he'd had a devil of a time fighting his way out of that underwater cage.

Witmer later flew with the Curtiss Exhibition Team, and also spent a couple of years in Russia accompanied by Hugh Robinson with George Hallett as mechanician. They demonstrated the hydroaeroplane at Sevastopol in 1912 before the Grand Duke Alexander Michaelovitch, president of the Aerial League and a member of the Imperial Aero Club of Russia. The Czar's Navy then purchased several, and by 1914 over half of Russian naval aircraft were Curtiss. Witmer's own aviation career continued for many more years.

Ellyson, the other Gold Dust Twin, due to his proficiency, unbounded enthusiasm and determination, was deemed by Curtiss to be a "practical aviator" on March 31, 1911, *the United States Navy's first aviator.* In 1928 Ellyson was lost while flying a Loening amphibian from Norfolk to Annapolis. He and Curtiss were very close, lifelong friends.

I was then attending high school while at the same time trying to be around Curtiss' activities as much as possible. Between all of my dashing about, I still found time to observe the activities at the camp of Harry Harkness, the other North Island tenant. His three Antoinette monoplanes, the only ones in America, were a design evolution of the Gastambide-Mangin aeroplane (page 18) by Leon Levavasseur, a fine artist as well as a brilliant engineer of both motors and aircraft.

Ellyson and Witmer - "The Gold Dust Twins"

Me (top), Witmer and Ellyson in "Lizzie" - 1911   51

WALDO: PIONEER AVIATOR

Once aloft, an Antoinette flew very smoothly, but was very tricky to handle. It was even-odds whether a flight would finish without some sort of damage. Searching for a more rugged, flightworthy aeroplane, Harkness had Charles Walsh build him a Curtiss-copy, which he then gave to his chief mechanician, John Kiley. It flew better than the Antoinette, and far better than Walsh's hapless monoplane.

Curtiss and Harkness aeroplanes, North Island, March 1911

Me in an Antoinette

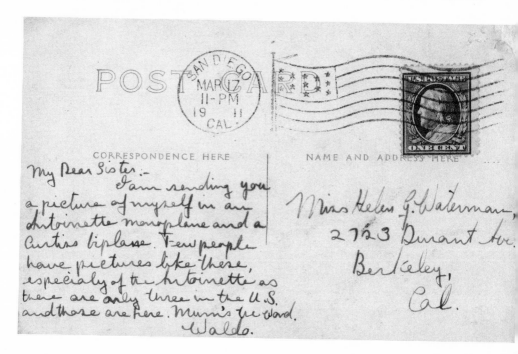

My Dear Sister:—
I am sending you a picture of myself in an Antoinette monoplane and a Curtiss biplane. Few people have pictures like these, especially of the Antoinette as there are only three in the U.S. and those are here. Mum's yr'dear.
Waldo.

Miss Helen G. Waterman,
2723 Durant Ave.
Berkeley,
Cal.

Spring was at hand, and the ice on Keuka Lake was breaking up. Curtiss had accomplished his four objectives: the seaplane, the ship-board seaplane, the Triad and the training of the first contingent of military students (done gratis to encourage the development of military aviation). Therefore, he packed-up to return to Hammondsport, very pleased with North Island and planning to come back that following winter. When he departed at the end of April, he left Charlie Witmer in charge, with instructions to turn the keys over to me when he and his mechanician, John Cooper, left on their exhibition tour.

Witmer - May 1911 (USS Pennsylvania, background)

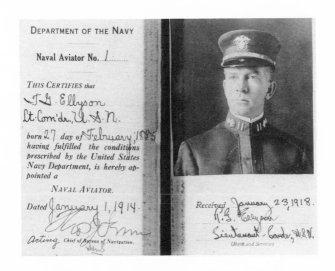

Naval Aviator No. 1

Because of Curtiss' activities at North Island, he was unable to attend the permanent presentation of the Scientific American Trophy in New York on March 29th. Charles Munn, doner of the trophy and publisher of *Scientific American,* in his speech said:

"Mr. President, Mr. Toastmaster, and fellow members of the Aero Club:

I feel sure that we all sincerely regret that it has not been possible for Mr. Curtiss to be present with us this evening and to receive in person the Scientific American Trophy.

I think that this trophy may be regarded as a sort of milestone. Incidentally, it was given by the donors with the object of fostering the art of aerial navigation. In view of the development which has taken place in the art during the past three years, this trophy may properly be regarded as a milestone which has marked, year by year, the progress which has been achieved. When we hear, day after day, of extensive cross country flights of aeroplanes carrying eight, ten and twelve passengers, and when we have seen aeroplanes rise to a height of two miles above the surface of the earth, it is hard for us to realize that the minimum conditions of competition for the trophy during the year 1908 was only one kilometer, or a little over half a mile straightaway. Mr. Curtiss won the trophy for that year by covering this distance and a little more, making in all a flight of about one mile and a quarter.

During the next year the distance was, with a good deal of trepidation, increased to a minimum of 25 kilometers in a closed circuit. Mr. Curtiss won the trophy for 1909 by covering this distance and making, all told, a flight of about 25 miles.

The committee having charge of the arrangements decided to make the condition for 1910 a minimum flight of 50 miles across country. Upon the earnest solicitation, however, of a prominent official of the Aero Club, who had recently returned from Europe, the minimum distance was reduced from 50 to 40 miles.

We all know how gallantly Mr. Curtiss won the cup for the third time by his memorable flight down the Hudson River from Albany to New York. He made the best long-distance record of the year in the first lap of this flight, by covering a distance of 71 1/2 miles, between Albany and Poughkeepsie.

54

THOSE EARLY YEARS

We all have a feeling of endearment for the old historic river which passes by our city. Three names will always remain associated with the history of the river--that of Hudson, the explorer; that of Robert Fulton, the introducer of river navigation; and that of Glenn H. Curtiss, the birdman.

On behalf of the Aero Club of America, as custodians of the trophy, I have the honor to present to you, Mr. Post, the representative of Mr. Curtiss, the Scientific American Trophy, for permanent possession, and I feel sure that it will always be associated by the winner with that historic flight down the Hudson River, and it will furthermore have a special interest as being the first trophy ever offered in this country for aerial navigation."

Scientific American - April 8, 1911

Collier Trophy (won twice by Curtiss - see page 72) Awarded annually "for the greatest achievement in aviation in America, the value of which has been demonstrated by actual use during the preceding year"

55

Shortly before Curtiss left North Island, Witmer and Cooper assembled an aeroplane from the mass of parts lying around the camp. It had a Curtiss 50-hp 4" x 4" engine, double-surface wings and, initially, the Curtiss butterfly tail and single-surface front elevator. However, following those day's 'cut and fit' methods, the front elevator was soon eliminated, simply leaving the outriggers and crossbar, which then came in handy as a level reference. As you looked forward, it would give you your relative position to the horizon, indicating if you were slipping, climbing or descending. It was a complete attitude instrument in one very simple device.

The carrying of a passenger was still a very novel and 'iffy' situation, primarily due to the tender balance of the aircraft and the low horsepower of the engines. However, after Curtiss had gone, the few of us still hanging around started pressuring Witmer, a two-month flying veteran, for a ride, and he finally relented to giving us landlubbers a thrill. We rigged up a 'passenger seat' by wiring a plank across the lower wing's leading edge, beside the pilot's seat, and stretched a wire from the front landing gear fork to the outer strut for a foot rest. We drew straws, and Kiley drew first; myself, second; and John Cooper, third.

After a breathless Kiley landed, I clambered aboard - very excited but acting oh so calm. During the flight I was both sightseeing and carefully watching Charlie's every movement. They hadn't yet removed the front elevator, so I watched its movements as well as the fore and aft motion of the control column. For the aileron movements, Charlie leaned from side to side, operating them with the distinctive Curtiss shoulder-yoke control. It was this control which permitted Curtiss pilots ("operators") like Lincoln Beachey to appear as if flying ("driving") hands-off, whereas in reality they had complete control with their knees holding the wheel, and their shoulders controlling the ailerons. The only surface that I couldn't easily observe was the rudder, but I knew when it was being moved because of Witmer's rotating the wheel atop the column.

The flight only lasted a few minutes. We climbed to an altitude of 300-400 feet, and made a couple of circuits over the camp, taking off going west and landing headed east as there was almost no wind. Between this flight and all that I'd already learned, I was almost prepared for my own flying.

The French, according to *Scientific American*, April 22, 1911, had developed passenger carrying to an extraordinary degree:

> *"On March 23rd, above the aerodrome of La Breyelle, at Douai, M. Breguet made a flight with eleven passengers, or, including himself, with twelve people in his biplane. Rising into the air without any perceptible difficulty, he made a straight-line flight of 5 kilometers (3.1 miles) at a speed of 90 kilometers (55.9 miles) an hour. The weight of the machine complete was 600 kilogrammes (1,322 3/4 pounds), and the live load transported was the same, so that a total weight of 2,645 1/2 pounds was carried through the air at express train speed for a distance of over three miles. The average weight of the passengers carried was 50 kilogrammes (110 1/4 pounds). We believe that this is the first time on record when the live load carried has equaled the complete weight of the machine."*

Breguet at the wheel of his biplane, showing 10 passengers.
The eleventh passenger, a boy, is hidden from view in the photograph.

57

In those grasscutting days, the landing and takeoff were not nearly the things they are today. One made so many abbreviated ones that they became routine long before you actually flew. The real test was one's ability to complete a 180-degree circuit, taking off from a certain spot and then landing at the same spot. When you could do that you were considered an *"accomplished aviator."*

In mid-May, Witmer and Cooper headed "back East", Lizzie was dismantled and stored in a hangar, and I was given the keys. But Witmer and Cooper weren't together long - by the time they reached St. Louis, Cooper had been enticed away by another exhibition flyer, and George Hallett received the chance of a lifetime - a telegram from Charlie requesting that he join him as his mechanician. George joined Witmer, learned to fly at Hammondsport that summer, and later went to Russia in 1912 where he first met Igor Sikorsky. In 1914 he helped build the huge flying boat, *"America"*, for which he was designated copilot. The Great War interrupted that venture, but he had a fabulous career with the Curtiss organization, lasting for many years.

That spring a couple of other exhibition flyers came to San Diego from Santa Ana, 100 miles north. They were Glenn L. Martin and Beryl Williams, and with a Curtiss-copy biplane they put on an exhibition at the Coronado polo field. It was pretty much of a flop because of the one that Curtiss had put on in January, and also because of all the other flying going on around North Island; but at 50 cents admission they did make gas money. Since I had the use of Sigmund's 2-cylinder Buick, I got acquainted with them by driving them between Coronado and the U.S. Grant Hotel, where they were staying.

My school chum these days was Johnnie Day, a bit younger than I. His father was the Reo automobile agent and the president of the Home Telephone Co., one of the earliest dial systems. Johnnie was wild about flying and pitched-in to help me with my various projects. When school was over we gathered-up our camping gear, plus a 22-rifle and a shot gun for rabbit and quail shooting. North Island, before Curtiss' arrival, had been John Spreckles' private shooting preserve; there were thousands of rabbits. But we had more than hunting in mind, I must confess, because we also took along 10 gallons of gasoline and a gallon of Mobil-B oil!

With Lizzie sitting there in the hanger it didn't take much to tempt me. Johnnie said, *"They didn't tell you you couldn't, did they?"* and I agreed that no great harm would come by readying her for use. I was in charge, wasn't I? Thereafter, every morning and evening when the wind was feather-quiet, I'd spend an hour-or-so chasing Lizzie up and down the runway. I even got a few feet off the ground after the first few runs. Then, with Johnnie's imploring matching my increased confidence, we rigged a passenger plank-seat, like on Witmer's plane, and I took him for a ride. He was sure it was a flight, insisting that we were airborne, though I was sure we weren't.

When I'd rigged Lizzie I'd carefully set the throttle block to preclude getting airborne too early - like Ellyson's "first flight". I made many passes back and forth across the field, each time slowing the plane by slipping from the seat, bracing myself against its wing and framework, and using my legs and body to brake. It was a practice which I'd watched the other students do so as not to slow down too soon, thus getting a longer run. Also, one wanted to avoid pushing all the way on the right foot pedal. This was tied to the brake shoe on the front wheel, and you'd run the risk of flicking the emergency switch, killing the engine and necessitating the bother of starting it up again. However, you had to learn which foot to push, for the left pedal was the throttle control! It wasn't much different, though reversed, from today's automobile brake and accelerator pedals. I soon was proficient at stopping, and then picking up the front wheel and turning Lizzie around.

With the throttle set so that I couldn't fly, I didn't think to look down during the first few flights, always peering about 100 yards ahead. But one day while making a high speed run, I glanced downward. I was airborne by at least a couple of feet! From then on I tried to keep Lizzie in the air, and I released the throttle block in order to get all the power possible. I then tried the much desired, all-important circuit of the field. When the conditions of wind and air and engine performance were just right, I completed a few partial ones of around 120-degrees, principally in the westerly part of the island where the grade of the terrain made turns to the left easiest. *By June 28, 1911, I figured I'd mastered Lizzie enough to have successfully soloed.*

The engine was needing an overhaul and wasn't putting out enough horsepower to make complete 180-degree turns, and I've always felt that it took more skill on my part accomplishing what I did with the engine in

59

that condition. However, I could never really call myself an *'aviator'* until I'd flown a circuit. So, being young, determined and impetuous, I decided to take Lizzie's engine home, overhaul it, and then come back to the island and try again.

Johnnie and I bolted the engine to a wooden pallet and carted it home in a horse-drawn wagon. Just when I was all set to disassemble it, a telegram arrived from Curtiss instructing me to ship it to Hammondsport. Darn! Looking back on that incident I've often wondered who alerted Curtiss to the fact that someone was flying at his camp. Possibly it had been his mother or half-brother, Carl, living then in Coronado. But whoever it was, Curtiss must have reasoned that the flying would stop as soon as the engine was shipped, and it surely did. Whenever an engine had previously been shipped from North Island - usually to a stranded exhibition flyer - it had gone by Wells Fargo. So this time, after packing it in some heavy oak planks, I called them and shipped it freight collect. I've ruminated since about Curtiss' reaction when that heavy crate arrived. It must have cost a lot, but he never said a word about it.

They immediately put it into Hammondsport's Lizzie, foregoing its much-needed overhaul. It soon broke a connecting rod which pierced the crankcase and then broke the crankshaft, in effect, demolishing it. I've never been particularly proud of my activities with that engine. I was only 16 at the time and might be excused for my youth. But, I did get in an awful lot of flying that I surely wouldn't have otherwise!

Speaking of that engine, it was one of Curtiss' earliest. It was a vertical 4-cylinder with a 4" bore and 4" stroke. It developed 25-hp at 1300 rpm, quite a high figure then. It had valve-in-head, copper-jacketed cylinders and force-feed lubrication from a camshaft-mounted pump with the oil forced through the hollow shaft to the bearings. The water pump was also integral and mounted on the camshaft. An enclosed gear-driven Bosch magneto charged the ignition. The entire engine, including the pumps and magneto, weighed approximately 175-pounds. It was the great grandaddy of the famous Curtiss OX-5 V8's, early versions of which were efficient enough to propel a large touring car at over 20 miles-per-gallon in 1912.

60

Curtiss engine - early 1911

The very first 4-cylinder water-cooled Curtiss engine was installed in the Aerial Experiment Association craft, the first plane to be sold by Curtiss and flown by Charles F. Willard. It had a 3 3/4" bore x 4" stroke. After this one engine, *all* Curtiss engines up to the summer of 1911 were 4" x 4". About then Curtiss came out with 4" bore x 5" stroke for both four and eight cylinders (and a few six's). In 1916 he increased the bore to 4 1/4" on the 0XX-6 only.

(As I'm dictating this, I pause - for passing in front of me is the massive USS Enterprise in the channel between my home on Point Loma and North Island. It's headed from San Diego Bay to the ocean, and I can't but muse on what Eugene Ely did so long ago - contrasting that with this huge piece of weaponry gives me the shivers.)

61

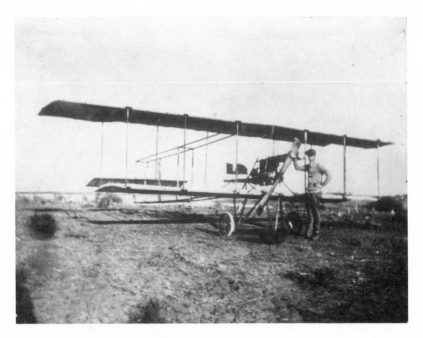

Waterman tractor aeroplane - North Island - February, 1912

Even though my Lizzie flying days were now ended, I was, in my eyes, an aviator with many more options. It was still summer vacation; I had the use of the Cameron engine; and an almost completed tractor-bi-plane. With the assistance of Johnnie Day and Gladys Waters (whose mother ran the apartment where Curtiss' students stayed), we worked to ready it for flight. Some photos may show it with a Farman-type tail, but I soon changed it to a Wright-type. That may clear up any confusion in studying the design. Gladys had become enthralled with Curtiss' dashing flying students, and she was a very willing helper, accompanying us to North Island to do the sewing on the wing fabric, and I must confess that she was my first high school romance. We never got to do much actual flying, though, before school started, and I left the plane at the camp, tinkering with it and getting in a bit of very cautious flying later that fall.

It was early September when I received a letter from Curtiss advising me that John W. McClaskey, a retired Marine officer, would be arriving to open the school October 20th for the 1911-1912 winter session. In my answer I advised him that everything was OK, and that Harkness wouldn't be there this year.

McClaskey soon arrived, and we didn't hit it off at-all-well, he being a gruff, almost deaf ex-Marine and me, in his eyes, being but a 17-year-old kid. I toured him around the camp, opened everything up for his inspection, and gave him the keys. Later I found that few people got along well with him. He was hard to adjust to, but in a few years we'd be the best of buddies.

Among the new crop of students were: Dunford, an Englishman; George Capitsini, a Greek Army Captain; J. G. Kaminski, Polish; a turbanned Mohan Singh; K. Takeshi from Japan; plus several Americans: William Hoff of San Francisco, S.C. Lewis of Chicago, J.B. McCalley of Harrisburgh, Charles W. Shoemaker of Olean, New York, Lansing Callan, Carl Sjolander and Rutherford Page. Also, F. J. Terrill of Springfield, Mass; R.E. McMillan of Perry, Iowa; C.A. Berlin of Centralia, Washington; and M.M. Stark of Vancouver, B.C.. One of Curtiss' early woman students, Julia Clark, would arrive later, along with several American military students. In a month McClaskey, Lewis, McCalley and Shoemaker qualified for their licenses. McCalley even astonished Curtiss, by doing a series of figure eights, remaining in the air longer than any other graduate, and speeding more than a mile-a-minute!

(l-r) Barlow, Kaminski, Smith, Davis, Russell, Singh, Callan, Clark, Dunlap, Takeshi - May 1912

63

Curtiss Aviation School - North Island - January 1912 (note Curtiss, left)

*Students (l-r): Stark, Berlin, McMillan, unknown, Spalding, Callan, Kaminski, Takeshi, "Bi
Maroney (mascot), Maroney, Terrill, Kondo, Singh, Dunford, Park, Capitsini, Clark and Dav*

Curtiss and McClaskey - January 1912

Julia Clark and Bob St. Henry - February 1912 (she was soon killed at Springfield, Illinois, during an exibition)

Mohan Singh - January 1912

John McClaskey - March 1912

65

McClaskey brought with him a new, more powerful 40-hp engine for Lizzie, plus two of the latest Curtiss V8-powered biplanes for the more advanced students.

While he was getting the school organized, I was making short flights with my tractor biplane. But Walsh's Cameron engine was underpowered (though not as bad as the Speedwell), overheating and losing power, forcing me to land. It seemed that the bane of my flying was underpowered engines!

During the time that I was trying to stay aloft longer, the Navy arrived at North Island. Captain Chambers had found enough funds to equip the Navy with three aeroplanes, and in late January, 1912, they set up their camp just north of the Curtiss camp, next to the old marine railway. They had the *A-1*, a Curtiss hydroaeroplane with a new 75-hp V8 engine; the *A-2*, a second Curtiss, a new 60-hp landplane; and a Wright Model C-H hydroaeroplane equipped with a vertical 4-cylinder engine and Burgess-built floats, the *B-1*. It was essentially a Model B Wright rigged-up as a hydroaeroplane. The A-1 was flown by Spuds Ellyson and John (Jack) Towers. The Wright was flown by their commanding officer, John Rodgers, *"scion of one of the most famous lines of American seaman"*, and the junior officer, Ensign Victor Herbster. Their complement was rounded-out by Lt. Holden Richardson, a naval constructor studying float and hull design.

It is quite a credit to Captain Chambers that he accomplished the assembling of this group - working from his musty quarters in Washington in a 'ship' navy. He assumed his vague responsibilities on September 26, 1910, and nurtured naval aviation through its first three formative years as the *"father of US Naval Aviation."*

Richardson and Towers in the A-1 - North Island, February 1912

Winter Training Grounds Curtiss Aviation School
SAN DIEGO, CALIFORNIA.

NORTH ISLAND IN SAN DIEGO HARBOR

1,000 acres of level sand without a tree or building to interfere with flying. Undoubtedly the best grounds for aeroplane flying in America, if not in the world. Delightful and perfect climatic conditions. Leased exclusively for

The Curtiss Aviation School and Experimental Grounds

Opened October 20th, 1911, Season 1911-12, under the direct supervision of GLENN H. CURTISS, assisted by Lieut. J. W. McCLASKEY and staff of aviators. Among the prominent aviators trained at these grounds are: Lieut. T. G. Ellyson, U. S. N., Capt. Paul W. Beck, U. S. A., C. C. Witmer, Hugh Robinson, R. C. St. Henry.

TUITION applies on purchase price of aeroplane. All classes filling rapidly. Get our proposition and booklet "TRAINING" to-day.

THE CURTISS AEROPLANE CO, HAMMONDSPORT, NEW YORK.   Sales Agents and Foreign Representatives The Curtiss Exhibition Company, 1737 Broadway, New York City

North Island, before being filled-in to Coronado   Aircraft - March 1912.

It should be noted that during this time several names for aircraft changed. Hydroaeroplane became *"seaplane"*. And, it soon had to be differentiated from the term, *"flying boat"*, which meant something quite a bit different. A seaplane simply had the capability of flying from the water and was typically a land aeroplane equipped with floats. A flying boat was exactly what the name implied: its hull was a boat with space for the pilot, passengers, cargo and sometimes even the engine, as in my 1913 design.

Several historical references state that January 10, 1912, is the date when Curtiss first successfully flew a flying boat. However, I was there at North Island when he was trying these experiments, and no such feat occurred. True, they shipped out a new tractor twin-propellered flying boat from Hammondsport - still calling it a *"hydroaeroplane"* - but it did not fly. It was so out of balance that it needed a man standing on the rear of

67

its hull to keep the bow from submerging. There's a photo of McClaskey acting as the balance weight. They then spliced on a longer nose section which Baker's fabricated, but it still didn't do the job. Curtiss did make some highspeed runs, but the hull design wouldn't break free of the water. I recall seeing that hull discarded on the beach near the camp. They didn't even take it back to Hammondsport, *where that spring and summer of 1912 they were finally successful in inventing the flying boat - Curtiss' "Flying Fish" with its single-step hull.*

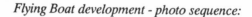

Flying Boat development - photo sequence:

1: North Island, January 1912

2: V-8 engine installed

3: North Island - McClaskey, with foot on stern (!), Callan, right

4: Hammondsport - "First direct-drive flying boat", May 1912

5: Ellyson and almost the final version, July 1912

6: Pilot, passenger and "man in a bathing suit", July 1912

7: Curtiss and Captain Chambers, September 1912

70

8: Racing - Lake Keuka - two flying boats and a hydroaeroplane, October 1912

An article in *Scientific American*, August 3rd, 1912, about The Curtiss "Flying Boat" stated:

"Since he closed his camp and aviation school at San Diego last spring, Glenn Curtiss has been steadily at work at his home in Hammondsport, N.Y., making further improvements upon his hydro-aeroplane. The result of his recent experiments is shown in the photographs reproduced on this page, which give a good idea of his latest combined boat and biplane, known as the Curtiss "Flying Boat."

This boat is a single step hydroplane, 26 feet long, 3 feet wide, and having sides 3 feet high. It is surmounted by a regular Curtiss biplane, having planes of 30-foot spread by 5 1/2-foot depth between the planes. The planes contain a total supporting surface of about 320 square feet, and support, when in flight, a total weight of about 1,000 pounds. As many as four people can be carried comfortably. One of our illustrations shows a man in a bathing suit lying on the deck of the boat behind the planes in addition to the pilot and passenger in front.

The power plant consists of an 80 horse-power Curtiss 8-cylinder, V-type engine and single propeller mounted high up between the main planes at the center. The motor is mounted sufficiently high to provide a liberal clearance between the end of the propeller blades and the boat, the propeller being just back of the main planes, as usual.

Above the papered hull of the boat, at the rear, is a vertical fin terminating in a large vertical rudder. The tail is placed about half way between the boat and the top of this fin, and extends out on each side of it. The horizontal rudder consists of two hinged flaps at the rear of the two halves of the tail. No front elevator is provided, so that the pilot has a clear view in front over the spray hood that is fitted. The balancing planes are at the rear, half way between the main planes. Inclined cylindrical floats are fitted below the ends of the lower plane in case the machine tips in making a quick turn on the water.

This new flying boat of Curtiss's makes aviation perfectly safe, as one can travel 50 miles an hour on the surface of the water, or 60 or more miles an hour a few feet above the surface. It will open up to

71

the motor boat enthusiast heretofore unnavigable streams. In fact all the unused canals and shallow rivers of the country can be skimmed over...with complete safety by the yachtsman-aviator."

It was about this time that Wilbur Wright died, marking the end of the Wright's creative contributions to aviation. Thereafter Orville did little but wreak havoc with litigation over patent rights. This finally subsided when a patent pool was established during the Great War. But Orville Wright never was friendly to Curtiss, rebuffing his every overture for compromise, and as the years passed it was Curtiss, *an early associate of Alexander Graham Bell,* who became the great force in American aviation, pushing always for new achievements. Curtiss was one of only a rare few to win *twice* the coveted *Collier Trophy* - in 1911 for the Hydro-Aeroplane and in 1912 for the Flying Boat. It's a sad commentary in our history that there should have been such a schism between these great, yet strangely similar men. Businesswise, the real parallel lay between Curtiss and Henry Ford, a Curtiss admirer who also had had patent problems. Curtiss was, in reality, *"The Henry Ford of Aviation."*

Curtiss and Henry Ford - Hammondsport - 1914

Curtiss - Wright competition in advertising - 1912

Aircraft - March 1912   *Aircraft - March 1912*

Vic Herbster and I, being closest in ages, became great pals. He'd just completed his flying lessons, soloing in a Wright, and was very encouraging of my biplane efforts. Watching all of the trouble that I was having in simply staying airborne, he reasoned that I could benefit from a ride in the Wright, a two-seater. In those days there were hardly any rules governing the use of military aircraft - it was left up to the pilot whom he wanted to take up. Thus, Vic and I made quite a few flights together, usually experimenting on one idea or another. One was trying-out a bomb dropping device I dreamed up - and then we thought that it'd be great to take a self-photograph of us flying with the camera mounted on the plane.

Richardson had designed a new set of floats ("boats") for the Wright, fabricated in Philadelphia by the Navy, and had them installed for testing by Rodgers. They were interested in the comparative planing properties between the Richardson and Burgess floats. After Rodgers had spent about an hour doing landings and takeoffs, he brought the B-1 in for Vic and I to use.

I'd borrowed a camera which I attached to the outer right strut, near the top wing, focused upon the two seats, with a string tied to the shutter. Also, I had a Brownie No. 3 Folding Camera with which I planned to take several shots while flying. When the mechanicians had gassed-up, they carried Vic and then me piggyback to the plane. Getting positioned wasn't very easy because you had to work your way through the rigging to your seat. When I was all set, after starting the engine Vic signalled for the men to push us away from shore.

Starting a Wright engine was a bit unusual. First, the exhaust valves were relieved so that, under no compression, the pistons ran freely, permitting the propellers to be set spinning by hand. Then the valves were tripped, causing compression and the resultant starting of the engine. The pilot's sole engine control was a lever which had a wide range of ignition-timing settings: retarding the spark slowed the engine and advancing it speeded it up. There wasn't any carburetor; the fuel was metered and injected directly into the intake manifold. By and large the whole arrangement was simple and worked well, especially considering the array of chains and gears used for transmitting the power to the two propellers.

A light westerly breeze was blowing as we taxied into the bay. When well clear of shore, Vic advanced the spark all the way, the engine roared, and we started accelerating across the water. Though I wasn't conscious of it, we weren't gaining speed anywhere near as fast as we ought to have, at least not as well as Vic was used to with the Burgess floats. After a very long run we sluggishly lifted free, and as soon as we had some altitude Vic commenced a wide, sweeping turn to put us over the Navy's hangar and above Spanish Bight, in the right spot for taking the photograph. All during this time I was clutching the camera between my legs while following through on my dual control, though not exerting any pressure upon it.

When we'd reached the photograph spot, Vic banked so that the camp would be in the background, and I got all set to trip the shutter. He had put the plane's nose down in order to gain speed for the bank, but when he then attempted to raise it again, it wouldn't respond.

Instead, it kept going lower and lower. We were now in quite a steep dive toward the water and try as Vic might, he couldn't get the plane to respond to the controls. We were getting mighty close to the water when Vic hollered, *"CRASH!"*, a needless alerting of our dire predicament!

We hit the water at about a 45-degree angle and I never felt water so hard - it was like hitting a brick wall! The water joltingly brought us to a stop, but in the process the nose submerged and we flipped over on our back. The water was cold, but I wasn't yet thinking of that since I was underwater, upside down, in a crazy maze of wires, struts and wings. We'd crashed in the mouth of Spanish Bight, where the water wasn't very deep, and the plane was cocked upside down, resting on its top wing, possibly being floated by the floats. Vic rapidly managed to get free and surfaced, while, Houdini-like, I was still trapped below. Vic told me that he was getting very worried when I finally broke water, gasping and darn happy to be alive.

After climbing up on the floats, the first thing we noticed was Curtiss' launch rushing our way with him in its bow taking photos of the downed Wright machine. When he was close he asked us if there were injuries. Vic answered that we were OK. At that, instead of helping us, Curtiss moved around to get a shot of William B. Atwater in a Curtiss hydroaeroplane heading our way, with us in the foreground! When Vic saw what he was doing he became furious, and when Curtiss had finished taking his photographs and asked if we'd like a lift to shore, Vic retorted, *"No sir; we'll swim rather than ride with you!"*

75

Atwater and Perkins taxiing-by Wright B-1 wreck - March 1, 1912

The hydroaeroplane was being taxied around us by Atwater and his mechanician, Si Perkins. Atwater and his wife, one of the first husband-wife flying couples, were being taught by Hugh Robinson, a close associate of Curtiss for many years. (In May, 1912, the Atwaters introduced the hydroaeroplane to Japan.)

The Navy's launch, a single lunger, finally reached us after a long, cold wait. They'd had a tough time getting it started as it'd backfired, breaking the arm of a seaman. Upon arriving, they passed us blankets and some hot coffee while tying the belly-up Wright to a couple of other boats. Boy, it was sure a mess when they beached it because they had to rip most of the skin fabric in order to drain off the water. However, it was eventually repaired and flew again. I don't know of its final demise except that its engine is now *"the oldest original piece of naval aeronautical equipment in existence."*

A grim Ensign Herbster (note cork life preserver)

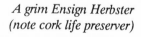

Crash scene - I'm, hatless, standing, center - (Curtiss' photograph)

They hustled me right into Lt. Richardson's tent to warm up and change into some dry clothes, and while I was doing this I plunked a can of beans on the stove. Shortly there was a big 'blopp' and beans spattered everywhere, especially on Richardson's dress uniform hanging beside the stove. I'd forgotten to punch a vent hole in the can!

"Officer Country" - USN - North Island - February 1912

The San Diego Union, Sunday morning, March 3, 1912, headlined:

"WRECKED AIRSHIP WITH MEN ON TOP AND FLYING BOAT AND LAUNCH GOING TO RESCUE"

> *"A capsized hydro-aeroplane, with two men clinging to it, and a speedy hydro-aeroplane rushing to the rescue was the sight that thrilled people along the water front yesterday morning. Ensign V. D. Herbster and Waldo Waterman, in a Wright aeroplane, with Burgess hydro attachment, were the victims of the accident, and Aviator W. B. Atwater in a Curtiss hydro-aeroplane was the rescuer."*

Here's how the Navy's log of that flight No. 105 described it:

> *"Machine at 100 ft. elevation, struck by gust on right wing. Headed down but did not answer warp nor vertical rudder; did not answer horizontal when 20' from water. Probable cause: water in boats; more in left than right. Damage: 48 ribs broken; 1 spar; two front drags; 2 pontoons buckled; 1 tail; 1 perpendicular; 1 foot rest."*

The mystery of our crash was finally solved when it was learned that Richardson's floats were about half-full of water. Apparently Rodgers' trial landings had opened the float's seams, and once they'd shipped water there weren't any interior compartments or bulkheads to contain it. Therefore, when Vic had nosed-over, the water had rushed to the front of the floats, making it impossible to right the aeroplane again. All very logical and simple, and it was a lesson well-learned by Richardson, for he then designed the hulls of the Atlantic-spanning NC's, working with his fellow officer Jerome Hunsaker and Curtiss' Garden City engineering facility ("NC" = Navy Curtiss). Richardson also piloted NC-3, the flight's flagship carrying Jack Towers, the Commanding Officer, but they didn't have the honor of completing the flight. That went to the NC-4 and Albert Read.

Ensign Victor Herbster and I had been responsible for wiping-out one-third of the Navy's airforce that March 1, 1912, a feat of which we were not particularly proud.

Two months later the Navy left North Island, moving to the Naval Reservation across the Severn from Annapolis. It would be several years before they returned, eventually to make it into one of the world's great-

78

est aviation facilities following its purchase by the U.S. Government in 1917. In the meantime, the Army Signal Corps arrived in 1912.

US Army Signal Corps, and Curtiss Aviation Camp, North Island - January 1913

Before the Navy left there was another interesting incident. Just prior to the Navy's arrival, on November 5, 1911, Calbraith Perry Rodgers, 32 years old and 6' 4" tall, *"The Bird Man Who Conquered a Continent"*, had completed the first transcontinental flight. He had flown from New York to Tournament Park, Pasadena, in 49 days, suffering at least 19 crackups in his Wright-EX *"Vin Fiz Flyer"*, advertising a grape soda-pop. John Rodgers, Cal Rodgers' double-cousin, had taken a leave from the Navy, accompanying him in a special railroad "Aeroplane Car". In February, Cal - still sporting a partial cast and recuperating from his last smashup - came to visit John at North Island. He had just been a participant in the third Dominguez Air Meeting, January 20-28, 1912. Cal had never flown a Wright *hydroaeroplane*, but since his *Vin Fiz* was a much-repaired Wright (only two parts were original and unbroken at the completion of his record flight) he was certainly familiar with the way one flew. But cousin John had never flown a vertical bank in the Wright and didn't know how to perform one.

The two cousins went up together with Cal instructing John on how to do this maneuver, but both were large men and they overloaded the plane so that it didn't respond well. Upon landing, Cal then went up alone - a civilian in a Navy aeroplane - and effortlessly demonstrated ver-

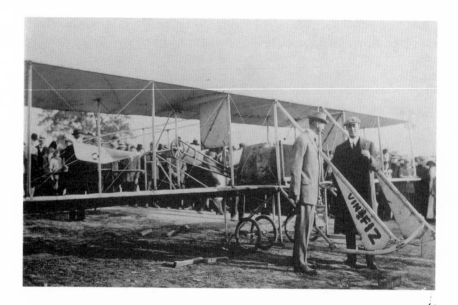

John (left) and Cal Rodgers - Wright-E-X "Vin Fiz Flyer" - 1911

tical turns to our amazement as we watched from the ground. It was a great show by an aviator who had but six hours flying prior to his cross-country epic. He was now a very fine pilot, and I was greatly saddened when he crashed to his death in the surf off Long Beach, California only two months later. Twelve years later John almost met a similar fate in that same Pacific Ocean. But, he was finally successful, *flying* 1,970 miles, *drifting* a further 450 miles, and completing his own epic journey in the PN-1 by being *towed by a submarine* the remaining distance from California to Hawaii. John was killed in a crash in 1926.

*Rodgers' crash
Long Beach
April 3, 1912*

80

Blanche Scott and Glenn Martin - Dominguez 1912

Aircraft, March 1912 reported the following on the third Dominguez Air Meet:

> "The Los Angeles Meet....was a great success, both financially and from an exibition standpoint. On the first Sunday of the meet it is estimated that fully 30,000 people paid admission to the field...
>
> The sensational flying...was done by Lincoln Beachey, Phil Parmelee, Weldon B. Cooke, Farnum Fish, W. H. Hoff and Glen Martin, who carried off the honors for the entire week. Blanche Scott also flew for over twelve minutes on every day of the meet but one.
>
> The speed, altitude and figure eight contests were closely contested for by Lincoln Beachey (Curtiss 1912 biplane) and Phil Parmelee (Wright Model X.)"

Blanche Scott - First American Aviatrix (taught by Curtiss)   81

As I mentioned, while the Navy was still at North Island I was busy trying to fly my tractor biplane, and having troubles because the 25-hp Cameron engine was overheating and losing power. This aeroplane's design, completed when I was still 17, was somewhat unique and deserves comment. It had a tail section closely resembling the Model B Wright, a landing gear like the French Nieuport, and a central landing skid from one of Harry Harkness' cracked-up Antoinettes. Its wing configuration was unusual, with the top wing considerably wider than the bottom, thus lessening rough landing damage and making for a stronger structure. No other planes used this concept before 1911, and I've often speculated that when Curtiss obtained the services of Douglas Thomas from Sopwith and had him design his Model J, Curtiss' first tractor aeroplane - *which was then combined design-wise with his 1914 Model "N" Military Tractor, producing the first of the legendary JN series* - that they must have gotten the JN *(Jenny)* unequal wing configuration from my original design. Additionally, there were few planes in 1911 using tractor propellers - what there were were mostly French - and I was thought quite radical for this design. I reasoned that it was simply the best way to do it.

Me and my "Tractor" on lot in back of home - Hawthorn and Albatross - 1911. Tail was changed before flying.

Just the day before my mishap with Herbster, on Thursday, February 29th, one of California's winter storms hit the field. The lashing wind and rain totally demolished my biplane, rolling it into a sad heap of rubble. About the only thing undamaged was the engine, which I soon returned to Trepte's. Sadly, there thus wasn't any Waterman design to catch the eye of Glenn Martin when he visited Beachey at the camp in March.

Waterman Tractor Aeroplane
February 1912
(also, see page 62)

Cameron engine
in my "tractor"

In April, a second pair of exhibition flyers arrived at the polo field thinking that they could stage a money-making exhibition. One was Horace Kearny, flying a Curtiss-copy powered with an 8-cylinder Hall-Scott engine; and the other, Farnum Fish, *"the world's youngest aviator"* at 18, flying a Wright Model B. An inheritance had provided for Fish's flying lessons and his aeroplane, and he'd just flown at the third Dominguez Air Meet.

83

Glenn Martin, John McClaskey, Lincoln Beachey and Henry Kleckler
North Island - March 1912

But as exhibition flyers, they weren't doing too well. The Curtiss and Wright troupes were garnering most of the business, and they suffered a 'poor gate' as had Martin and Williams the year before.

M. Kondo (Japan), Kearny, McClaskey, Fish, Julia Clark, I. D. Spalding, Callan & T. Gun
Coronado Polo Field - April 7, 1912

84

Following their unsuccessful show, these renegades, without an invitation, hopped across Spanish Bight, landing at Curtiss' field. They then proceeded to solicit passenger rides, flying students, anything to make a buck. This didn't set at all well with GH, particularly since Fish's Wright could make some maneuvers not attempted by his flyers. Curtiss began simmering, and this led to a heavy jawboning session with Fish and an ultimatum from GH that, unless he packed-up and was gone in two hours, he'd personally *pitch his Wright into the bight!*

Fish shrugged, turned to his mechanic, Al Hazard, and instructed him to load everything up, including an extra 5-gallon can of gas. After topping-off the plane's tanks, Fish took off heading north. About three-and-a-half hours later GH received a call from a reporter in Los Angeles wanting more details about *"one of his aeroplanes that has just completed the first flight from San Diego to Los Angeles."* Obviously, this was Fish's Wright, and it made Curtiss even madder because several of his aviators had attempted that feat and none had succeeded.

Farnum Fish
Dominguez
1912
Note Wright
control system

Kearny, on the other hand, was permitted to hang around because his equipment was Curtiss-type, and he'd started negotiating for a new Curtiss in which to attempt an overwater flight from Los Angeles to San Francisco. In the meantime, he was earning money by giving rides and lessons, but his plane's two rear tires wore out at about the same time, threatening to put him out of commission unless they were replaced. He spied the two (Palmer-Goodrich) tires in my biplane wreckage and 'without your leave' helped himself. A couple of days later I recognized them on his aeroplane. Immediately, I let him know that I didn't appreciate it much. At that, he told me that he'd pay for them as soon as he had some cash, and then he asked, *"How about taking a ride with me?"*

Horace Kearny - Curtiss-copy with Hall-Scott V8 - Coronado - April 7, 1912

Well, of course rides were highly desirable, and my demeanor immediately relaxed as I clambered aboard the small jump seat beside his. We then took off for a circuit over North Island which was about the hairiest aeroplane ride that I've ever had. The plane was so underpowered and sluggish that Kearny had the elevator control column all the way back during the whole flight. This position presented far too large an angle of attack and slowed the plane down so that we were flying on the verge of a stall the entire time. Kearny didn't seem fazed - he must have flown that way all of the time - but by the time we landed I was almost too weak to walk away. Later I reasoned that Kearny's flying was much like his flamboyant manner - he never did pay for or return the wheels.

Several months later *"Sure-Shot"* Kearny took delivery of his Curtiss A-1 hydroaeroplane, powered with a new 80-hp V8 engine and fitted with oversized fuel tanks. On December 14, 1912 he took off from San Pedro Bay with Chester Lawrence, an adventurous reporter, as his passenger. Lawrence held a 5-gallon can on his lap and a bicycle pump for pumping the gas into the tank as it ran low. Heavily laden, they planed across the bay, slowly rose skyward, circled and headed northwest, disappearing into the early morning mist. About 20 minutes later they were heard over Santa Monica heading out to sea, and that was the last sight or sound of them - *not even a trace was found as they became the first of a long, woeful list of ocean-daring airmen.*

There were many deaths suffered in those faltering years. By mid-1912, at least 155 men and three women had been killed in airplane accidents in Europe and the United States. Possibly the greatest loss was felt when the two Wright exhibition teammates, Ralph Johnston and Arch Hoxsey, died within weeks of each other late in 1910. A tragedy hitting closer to me happened during the third Dominguez Air Meet. Two pilots, Rutherford Page and Lincoln Beachey, both of whom I knew, raced identical Curtiss'. The race would therefore be won by the more skillful pilot, and there was little doubt in anyone's mind who that would be - Lincoln Beachey. Page was killed trying the 'impossible,' and this tragedy, hitting so close to Beachey, might have been a factor in his decision to give up flying a short while later because so many were being killed while trying to emulate him.

Page's wreck Dominguez 1912

However, Beachey didn't quit for long.

WALDO: PIONEER AVIATOR

The following is from *Aero*, March 30, 1912:

"Lincoln Beachey is on vacation. From the first of January, 1911, to the first of January, 1912, Beachey was busy continuously, flying on an average of four days each week, covering a territory from Maine to California and from British Columbia to Porto Rico. "I am going on a vacation," he announced when he walked into the Curtiss company's office in New York a few days ago, and I do not want to see or hear of a machine while I am resting. I am going to take a steamer tomorrow, but don't know where I am going. I will be back in New York May 25 and ready for another year's work. Good bye."

I'd first met Page when he was a student at North Island. Also, I'd known Beachey since his many visits there, polishing to perfection his ability to fly an aeroplane as no one else could. A good description of what Page must have encountered is, also, from *Aero*, March 30, 1912:

"Hoff Describes His Accident

There have been many different reports as to the cause of my accident, so am sending you a few lines in regard to same. I don't remember anything that happened on that day so we will take the words of the aviators who were there at time.

The accident happened in a race in which Beachey, Parmelee and myself were entered. We started from the center field of a mile track, Beachey being the first to leave the ground, followed by Parmelee. A minute later I followed right behind him, which was my mistake, for, having an 80-horsepower Curtiss, I overtook him before the turn. I was overtaking him so fast as to be 25 feet behind him before I realized it. I, at first, thought of passing underneath, but at this time we would have been over the automobiles and Parmelee was so low I would not have been able to clear the heads of the people. So I tried to get over him and in doing so I climbed at too steep an angle which killed my speed ahead. Then I got in the back wash of Parmelee's machine and at the same time received a side thrust from behind the grand stand. Not being high enough to work, my right hand plane struck the ground and we rolled over several times before stopping. The re-

88

sults were a jaw broken in two places, a dislocated shoulder, broken nose and broken pelvis bone.

I have the helmet to thank, as I had a slight concussion and the helmet had a hole in top and split on the side.

I wish very much to thank the Curtiss Exhibition Company and the aviators present, as they made a purse of $395 for me.

Excuse the appearance of this letter as I am on my back and writing upside down.

When I am well I am going to start a school here in San Francisco.

William H. Hoff"

In 1915 Claude Grahame-White wrote:

"One danger dogged the progress of the pioneer aviators in all their flights. It was the danger that some part of their craft would, when they were in the air, collapse and send them reeling to the ground. That peril is fortunately a thing of the past; thanks to the experience of builders, our craft will to-day survive the onslaught of a gale. But in those days, when what may be called the details of security were reckoned by rule of thumb, the pilot of an aeroplane needed to be a man of exceptional nerve; for besides facing the ordinary dangers of flying, he always had haunting him the dread that a plane or spar would buckle, and send him hurtling to earth."

There were many foolhardy and daredevil young men flying aeroplanes in those years, and the statistics of deaths were staggering for so few flying.

"The years 1910, 1911 and 1912 were the Bonanza years of aviation. In frail machines, the pilots rode to quick fame, quick riches, and, too often, to quick death."

Horace B. Wild

One of the more poignant episodes happened in 1912 when J.J. Frisbie was killed in a Curtiss at Norton, Kansas, *having been driven to fly in unsuitable weather by the jeers of a hostile crowd* (Jane's 1913).

89

FATAL AEROPLANE ACCIDENTS.

Statistical table compiled by Automobil-Welt up to December 13th, 1911, which makes a very interesting study for the thorough student of aircraft.

The 93 fatal accidents occurred with ..	Per Cent. of Victims Killed in Flying		12 Passenger Flights ended Fatally for			In 12 Passenger Flights were Killed		No. of Flights Terminating Fatally	No. of Aviators Killed who had Not Pilot Certificates
	Alone	With Passenger	Pilot and Passenger	Pilot only	Passenger only	Pilots	Passengers		
(In two cases type was unknown)	81	19	7	3	2	10	9	93	16*

Monoplanes Total 38 Name	15 Blériot	3 Antoinette	2 Nieuport	2 R.E.P.	2 Valkyrie	——— 1 each ——— Dorner, Deperdussin, Lilienthal,† Leforestier, Moisant, Oertz, Pietschker, Pilcher,† Pischoff; Poulain, Queen, Russijan, Sommer, Wiesenbach.

Biplanes Total 52 Name	10 H. Farman	8 Wright	5 Sommer	4 Aviatik	4 Curtiss	3 Savary	2 Voisin	2 Curtiss copies	———1 each——— Albatros, Astra, Baldwin, Bristol, British Army, Breguet, Caudron, M. Farman, Fernandez, Hartle, I.A. M.C., Lière, L.V.G., Marra, Short (Grace).

Countries.	France	America	Germany	England	Italy	Russia	Austria	Spain	Belgium	Holland	Luxemburg	Bulgaria	Siberia	Switzerland	Algeria	China	Brazil	Peru	Unknown
Per cent. of victims belonged to	34	15	15	12	8	5	–	3	2	1	1	1	–	1	–	–	1	1	–
Country of origin of machine	53	12	14	7	1	–	3	–	–	–	–	–	–	–	–	–	–	–	–
No. and country where accidents occurred	32	16	14	8	6	5	1	1	2	1	–	–	1	1	1	1	2	–	1

	America	Italy	England	Germany	Russia	France
Ratio of No. killed to No. of holders of pilot certificates ₰ =	12 (74‡) = 17·1 per cent.	7 (45‡) = 15·5 per cent.	9 (110‡) = 8·2 per cent.	11 (135‡) = 8·14 per cent.	3 (55‡) = 5·45 per cent.	27 (500‡) = 5·4 per cent.

* Including 3 killed on gliders. † Gliders. ‡ The figures in brackets give the number of certificated pilots up to the end of October, 1911. ₰ Those who were killed while flying without pilot's certificate, or as a passenger, or in glider experiments, have been omitted. Their numbers are: France, 7; Germany, 4; America, 3; England, 3; Russia, 2; Italy, 1.

Aircraft - March 1912

I never would be what one might call a reckless or "fancy" flyer. Whether this was due to my basic nature or the fact that I survived that 1910 crackup with permanent reminders, I do not know. It could have been because of mother's good wisdom adroitly delivered through the advice and counsel of Glenn Curtiss. He dissuaded me from the exhibition circuit, which I sorely wanted to do, by saying that with my demonstrated talents in design and engineering I should pursue a career in aeronautical engineering. This reasoning made sense to me, for I thought that there should be more to aviation than breaking one's neck.

It was now the spring of 1912 and I was just completing high school. With college in the offing, GH suggested that I attend Massachusetts Institute of Technology. It was then called *"Boston Tech,"* until the school's move across the Charles river from Boston to Cambridge in 1916. Curtiss understood that it was the finest school in the country teaching aeronautics. At this time there was no such thing as "aeronauti-

AERO

Directory of Aviators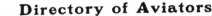

Fair Secretaries Use AERO When Advertising Exhibitions

I want to compliment you on AERO. It has been of considerable value to me during the last few months in arranging for our meeting.— JOHN T. STINSON, Secretary Missouri State Fair, Sedalia, Mo.

I find the Aviators' Directory of value when planning exhibitions. No person interested in aviation can afford to be without AERO.—A. G. RIGBY, Secretary Buchanan County Fair and Racing Association, Independence, Iowa.

THE AMERICAN AVIATORS Inc.
Now Booking exhibitions with Wright Aeroplanes and Burgess Hydroplanes. Permanent address: Memphis, Tenn.

HARRY N. ATWOOD (Burgess Wright.)
Address: Clayton & Craig Aviation School, 15 Harcourt St., Boston.

HILLERY BEACHEY
Beachey-Heimann Biplane (Now Booking)
Address: 1122 Washington Avenue, St. Louis, Mo.

TOM W. BENOIST (Biplane.)
Permanent address: 6664 Delmar Ave., St. Louis.

JOHN D. COOPER
Licensed Pilot
Texas School of Aviation
Address: Care Southland, Dallas, Texas.

THE CURTISS AVIATORS (Curtiss Biplanes.)
Now Booking.
Jerome S. Fanciulli, Mgr. Ex. Dept., 1737 Broadway, N. Y.

DE VAUX AVIATORS
Now Booking (Curtiss Biplane)
Address: 66 Fulton St., San Francisco; 942 S. Grand Ave., Los Angeles.

FARNUM T. FISH (Wright Biplane.)
Address: 2120 Union Ave., Los Angeles, Cal.

HOWARD GILL
Pilot's License No. 31
Holds American Endurance Record
Address: AERO, St. Louis

C. GRAHAME-WHITE (Nieuport and Bleriot.)
Address: Grahame-White Aviation Co., Ltd., London Aerodrome Hendon, England.

WILLIAM H. HOFF
(Flying 75 H. P. Curtiss Model D.)
Address: 4409 24th St., San Francisco, Cal.

ANTONY H. JANNUS
Licensed Pilot No. 80. (Benoist Biplane)
Address: 6628 Delmar Boulevard, St. Louis, Mo.

HORACE KEARNY
(Flying Curtiss Biplane) Licensed Pilot No. 82.
Address: AERO, San Francisco, Cal.

J. C. (BUD) MARS (Now Booking Season 1912)
Address: 17 North LaSalle St. Chicago, Ill.

DIDIER MASSON
(Now Booking Engagements) Aero Club of France License No. 12.
Ivan R. Gates, Mgr.
Address: Care California Aviation Co., 743 Gough St., San Francisco

L. MITCHELL
Pilot's License No. 51. (Wright Aeroplane and Burgess Hydroplane.)
Permanent address: Care American Aviators, Memphis, Tenn.

NATIONAL AVIATORS (Now Booking)
Address: National Aeroplane Co., 2023 Michigan Ave., Chicago.

PHIL O. PARMELEE
(Flying Wright Model X Biplane.)
Address: Aero, San Francisco or University Club, Los Angeles.

HUGH ROBINSON
(Flying the Curtiss Hydra- aeroplane on land and water.)
Permanent Address: 1737 B'dway, New York; AERO, St. Louis.

CAL. RODGERS (Transcontinental Flyer)
Maryland Hotel, Pasadena, Cal.

CHARLES F. WALSH (Curtiss Biplane.)
Permanent Address: 1737 Broadway, N. Y.

LESTER WEEKS (75 H. P. Gammeter Biplane)
Address: Portage Heights, Akron, Ohio.

HORACE B. WILD
Licensed Aeronaut. Expert on all Type of Aircraft and Motors.
Address: 130 Auditorium Hotel, Chicago, Ill.

Exibition Circuit Aviators - Spring 1912

cal engineering". The country's first degree was awarded at Columbia in 1910 to Grover Loening, after he virtually created his own course material. MIT was the first school to award a Masters degree and a PhD, to Jerome Hunsaker in 1912 and 1916. Hunsaker taught aeronautical engineering there off and on for 40 years, becoming the recognized dean in this field. (In 1974, Jack Carpenter, with myself, attended The Early Birds meeting in Boston - and listened-in on an informal discussion between me, Loening and Hunsaker.) But my family's finances and traditions precluded my going to Boston. The decision was made for me to enroll at the University of California at Berkeley that fall.

Chapter 2

1912-1917

College Years and The Great War

IN late August 1912 I entered the University of California at Berkeley, as a student in mechanical engineering bent upon becoming an aeronautical engineer. Eighteen years old, I was a partially disabled veteran of four years in aviation and a pilot of limited experience. As soon as my class schedules firmed-up I started scouting around to see what was going on aviationwise in the San Francisco Bay area. San Francisco, *The City,* was then the center of business, industry and culture for the West. Miraculously, the terrible devastation of the 1906 earthquake had disappeared and it was booming on the grand scale that it had reached over a half-century earlier during the era of the Comstock Lode.

Only a couple of miles from the Berkeley campus was the Hall-Scott Motor Car Co., Curtiss' main competitor in manufacturing aircraft engines. And, on the peninsula south of San Francisco the Christofferson brothers had started an aircraft factory just a few months earlier, which was incorporated in 1913.

92

That fall my nose stayed close to the proverbial grindstone as I acclimated to the college routine and the shock of classes that were much tougher than I'd ever imagined.

I surely was happy when Christmas vacation came, and I headed home to San Diego and North Island as fast as I could go. A few of the old gang were there from the previous year, and a lot of new people. This was Curtiss' third year at North Island. McClaskey was still there, with a new head mechanic, Jake Bailey, whom I got to know quite well during my brief visit. Jake had had an accident that left the fingers of his left hand pressed hard against the palm. He could just barely hold a chisel or file with that hand, doing most of the work with his right hand, but never the less was a very fine mechanic. He was very intelligent and later became chief of engine overhaul for the Army's Rockwell Field, and later for Mather Field near Sacramento.

When the vacation was over (January, 1913) I went back to school determined to build another aeroplane. At that time there was a lot of publicity about the upcoming *Panama-Pacific International Exposition* at San Francisco, and I figured that a flying boat would be just the thing for ferrying folks across the bay to the fair. I'd have plenty of time for this rather ambitious project; the fair wasn't to be held until 1915, so I had two years to complete it. (The Loughead brothers, native San Franciscans, got their start from the money they made from their first aeroplane, a three-place hydroaeroplane used for passenger flights at this same exposition.)

It wasn't long until I'd completed the design, incorporating features that were quite advanced and sophisticated. Up to that time practically all (Curtiss or Curtiss-copy) flying boats had scow-type hulls; mine was to have a "V" bottom and a hydroplane step, a design common years later.

The Waterman Flying Boat, was also to have two tractor (pulling) propellers mounted on the front of the wing, chain-driven from the engine within the hull, much like the Benoist flying boat. I showed these designs to my instructors, and after some hassle they agreed to give shop credit to any students that I could get to help me - provided that I found my own work area and supplied my own materials.

The university's newspaper carried an article about my flying boat plans with the result that I got a call from Walter Seaborn, Berkeley's city clerk. He was very interested in the project and seemed to be the answer to my every problem, promising financial help, a place to work, and best of all, a Hall-Scott engine. He arranged for us to use the shops at Berkeley High School and I organized the several students that had 'volunteered' to work with me. They included Wesley Smith (later a pilot, instrument-flying pioneer and preliminary researcher with TWA and Goodyear in the development of the wing leading-edge de-icer boot), Harold Crowe (later a VP of Air Associates, the largest aircraft retail parts distributor in the country), Alexander Blume, H.W. Cochran, M.E. Taylor and C.J. Erickson.

Everything was soon moving along nicely, and between my studies and the work on the flying boat I had little time left for part-time work. When summer vacation arrived we'd finished framing the hull and had started applying the planking for the skin covering. We left it like that, planning to resume work in the fall. I then got a full-time summer job at Hall-Scott, and in the course of things got acquainted with the bosses, Elbert (Al) Hall and Lee Scott. Al Hall was one of the country's greatest engine designers and would soon be primarily responsible for the Liberty engine. One day I was telling him about the Waterman Flying Boat, how well we were progressing, and how enthused we were to be getting the use of a Hall-Scott engine because of the Walter Seaborn relationship. *"Because of what?"* he said, and dumbfounded I then learned that he knew nothing of this arrangement!

It turned out that Seaborn had been too darn optimistic regarding his abilities to procure an engine from Hall-Scott, and when this all finally came to light it spelled 'doom' to the flying boat project. True, both Al Hall and Lee Scott knew Seaborn, but they knew nothing about our project and had never considered lending us an engine. Seaborn had simply led us on that he had it all committed! Years later I'd have no trouble

94

Aircraft
March 1912

getting Hall-Scott engines, but that was long past the opportunity for college heroics.

For the rest of the summer I mulled over the dilemma that this new revelation posed. By the time school opened I'd decided that it'd be foolish to try and carry on the project lacking that most important engine commitment. We set the flying boat aside, still hoping that something

95

might turn up that would enable us to complete it, but that never happened. All that's left are some photos showing what some college kids were trying to do. Our efforts happened at about the same time that Glenn Curtiss and John Porte were making the *"America"* for Rodman Wannamaker - the first of the great Curtiss ocean flying boats.

Waterman Flying Boat hull - Berkeley High School - 1913

After working full-time that summer at Hall-Scott, I now became a 'steady' part-time worker weekdays after school and Saturdays. When Christmas vacation finally arrived I again hightailed-it for home and North Island, naturally expecting to spend most of my three weeks at the Curtiss camp. As usual there were lots of new faces and a new man, Theodore C. Macaulay, was in charge of the camp. I was glad to see that Jake Bailey was back for another session and he told me that he'd see what he could do with Macaulay to line up some work for me.

Aerial acrobatics (aerobatics) were all the rage then, and Lincoln Beachey was the best there ever was in *fancy flying*. Orville Wright had called him *"The greatest aviator of all"* in testimony of his superb and hard-won skill, and in 1945, pioneer aviator Guy Gilpatric wrote:

> *"I have critically observed the work of some thousands of joystick virtuosi here and in Europe in the thirty years that have passed since Beachey's death, but for my money he remains what his twenty-four-sheet posters proclaimed him to be: "The Greatest Of Them All." Thirty years and two world wars have brought many improvements to airplanes, but when I say that Beachey's flying has*

96

never been surpassed, I say it without reservations of any kind. In his old eighty-horsepower Curtiss pusher, designed by rule of thumb and built like a bird cage, he did things which no other man has ever done in the latest products of wind tunnel, slide rule and million-dollar factory. Beachey's forte was his ability to come close to things without hitting them. To do loops and flip-flops high in the air requires no great skill, but to fly between trees so close together that the machine must be banked sixty degrees to pass through, is flying of the most divine order. Another of Beachey's caprices was to fly around a half-mile race track and flick up the dust with his wing tip on the turns. This was a matter of half an inch; another half-inch would have tripped the plane and spattered Mr. Beachey all over the homestretch.

For a couple of seasons, Beachey teamed up with Barney Old-field in a racing stunt that was a corker. Oldfield would drive his Fiat Cyclone or his front-drive Christie Special and Beachey would stay no more than a foot above him all the way around the track. Call me a liar if you will, but these old eyes have seen Beachey rest his front wheel on Barney's head while both plane and car were doing better than sixty miles an hour. His flight down Michigan Boulevard, Chicago, eighteen inches above the fear-frozen traffic, will probably never be duplicated in the history of the world."

In September 1913 Beachey had just learned that the great French pilot, Adolphe Pegoud, had supposedly been the first to loop an aeroplane. That news almost drove Beachey crazy as he muttered *"Why hadn't I thought of that?"* (Although few knew it, in Russia young Lt. Petr Nikolaevich Nesterov had looped his Nieuport-4 over Kiev on August 27, 1913, and was *"placed under arrest for 10 days for endangering the Czar's Imperial military property."*) Beachey was not to be outdone. He immediately had his biplane

97

Lincoln Beachey
Dominguez - January 1912

modified and strengthened, and performed his first loop over North Island on November 18, 1913, only about a month before my arrival. From that moment on the loop was standard fare in his act and would be bally-hooed far and wide by Bill Pickens, his superagent. Pickens was also Barney Oldfield's publicity manager, and later became Ormer Locklear's huckster.

Beachey toured the country from one corner to another, daily earning from $1,000 to $1,500 for doing five or six loops. He once did over 50 consecutive loops catering to the roar of the crowds. Beachey invented the *"Vertical Drop"*, *"Dutch Roll"*, *"Ocean Wave"*, *"Turkey Trot"*, *"Figure Eight"*, *"Death Dip"*, *"Coney Island Dip"*, *"Spiral Glide"* and other death-defying stunts common later. But by mid-1914 looping had begun to pale; the automobile-aeroplane race was the rage. Oldfield and Beachey *each* had earnings that year of around *$250,000!*

Beachey - Automobile-Aeroplane Race - Dominguez 1912

Naturally, every other exhibition flyer wanted to have a looping airplane, and since Beachey had done it first at North Island, Macaulay was determined to have a looper. The ill-fated Kearney had traded in his Curtiss-copy for a Curtiss hydroaeroplane, and Ted Macaulay had acquired the trade-in for his personal use. Jake lined me up working on its conversion. Already several pilots had been killed trying to duplicate Pegoud and Beachey, primarily because their planes weren't structured for looping stresses. It was a failing that Macaulay impressed upon us should never happen with his aeroplane!

After working on the plane for two or three days I could see that I'd never be able to complete the job before heading back to college. I told

Macaulay that he'd better get me someone to work with that could finish the job after I left. Ted replied that there'd been a young fellow looking for a job, offering to work for only $10-a-week and some flight instruction, and I told him that he ought to get him. He called the chap who then reported for work the next morning. Darned if it didn't turn out to be Bert (Bertrand) Acosta, a kid that I'd had a brief encounter with back in the fourth grade. It went like this:

Bert had entered school in midterm and was assigned a seat near me, in the rear near the window. One day the teacher looked up and saw Bert's jaws moving as if he were chewing gum, a forbidden sin. As was the custom when anyone was caught doing such a dreadful thing, the teacher picked up her ruler and walked down the aisle, prepared to give the offending student a good swat. She said "Bert, spit it out!" and Bert sure did spit it out with a great big splatt! It wasn't chewing gum, but tobacco that he was chewing, and for that he was immediately marched down to the principal's office. That's the last I ever saw of him around Middletown Grammar School.

That initial employment of working on Macaulay's plane was the spark, apparently, that ignited the dramatic flying career of Bert, for he became one of the great pilots of the era. It was said of him that *"he can feel airplanes."* Throughout his flying career he was famed as a maverick, *"Peck's bad boy of aviation"*, a dashing Romeo and lady's man. By 1921 he had won the Pulitzer Race and was Curtiss' top test pilot. In 1927 he was Clarence Chamberlin's copilot, flying a Bellanca for an endurance record, and also flew with Richard Byrd across the Atlantic in the "America" (a Fokker trimotor, not the original Curtiss "America"). This flight climaxed when Bernt Balchen took the controls from Bert's exhausted hands and successfully landed the plane in the Normandy surf. *(Regarding Byrd, whose first fame was due to his "first flight" over the North Pole in 1926, his pilot then was Floyd Bennett who later told Bernt Balchen that this claim was false, a fact confirmed by Balchen, later Fokker's chief test pilot and performance engineer, knowing the elapsed time, distance, and cruising speed of Byrd's Fokker. See Oceans, Poles And Airmen, Richard Montague/Random House, 1971; Arctic Ocean*

99

Map, National Geographic Magazine, *Feb., 1983; and William Davis's article in the* Boston Globe Magazine, *Feb. 1, 1987.)*

In mid-January, 1914, I had to return to school, and left Bert to finish up the job on the looper. Macaulay then took it on a Curtiss exhibition tour, but I don't think he ever did any looping because it still wasn't designed and built for those stresses. Macaulay became a colonel in The Great War (World War I) and later returned to San Diego where he became active in civic work and was one of those responsible for Reuben Fleet's massive move of Consolidated to San Diego in 1935.

Back at Berkeley I was at loose ends now that the flying boat project had been scuttled. Casting about for things to do, I became acquainted with Adolph G. Sutro, the grandson of the genius that had conceived the draining the Comstock Lode tunnels under Virginia City. Sutro had a double-tractor hydroaeroplane which he kept in his own hangar at a marina near where the Panama-Pacific Exposition was to be held. He already had considerable background in aviation. In 1910 he'd worked with the Wrights in their plant in Dayton, and in 1911 he'd accompanied Bob Fowler in the first westcoast-to-eastcoast flight. They had started in Los Angeles October 20, 1911 and finished at Pablo Beach, Florida, February 15, 1912, over three months after Cal Rodgers' flight. This experience enabled Sutro to build his own plane which was basically a Wright derivation except that it was a tractor-type and had a top wing longer than the bottom wing - very similar to my own 1912 wing configuration.

Most of my spare time that spring and summer was spent laboring on Sutro's plane. I completely reworked the structure and replaced the piano wire rigging, which was badly corroded by the damp and salty San Francisco air. There must have been 100 or more wires - one tedious and

Me, around 1914 - 1915

100

This picture shows Robert G. Fowler in his Wright biplane *en route* from the Pacific to the Atlantic Ocean. Seated by his side is Edward R. Shaw, who took some remarkable pictures with his moving picture machine throughout the journey.

Aircraft - March 1912

painstaking job that I was sure glad to finish! Sutro then used this plane to qualify for his FAI license. Because they'd just started making a distinction between seaplanes and landplanes, he ended up being issued Hydroaeroplane Certificate No. 1 in 1913, even though all of my friends from North Island days could have qualified in 1912.

I still needed part-time work when this job was completed and in addition to keeping my hand in at Hall-Scott, I worked for the Paterson Airplane & Supply Co. in San Francisco. Here I helped overhaul the 80-hp Hall-Scott powered tractor hydroaeroplane that Roy Francis had used the previous summer in the Great Lakes "Reliability Cruise".

In August of 1914, the European war erupted just as I was about to enter my junior year at Cal, and like most Americans I had only casual interest in that affair. Later, though, while visiting Beachey's San Francisco Marina camp at the 1915 Panama-Pacific International Exposition I bumped into J.W. McClaskey, the ex-Marine that had run the Curtiss camp in the spring of 1912. (San Diego also had its Panama-California

101

Exposition in 1915). He was now Major McClaskey, having returned to active duty as a recruiting officer in San Francisco. Our initial relationship had never been what you'd ever call 'warm', but now we immediately had a strong bond of friendship - like two lost souls *from the good old days* meeting in a strange land. I soon saw "Mac" in a different light and began to appreciate what Curtiss must have known when he put him in charge at North Island. We became very close friends.

That spring of 1915 Mac and I saw a lot of each other while spending as much time as possible around Beachey's camp. Since both he and I were considered part of the Curtiss inner circle, we were always welcome. Beachey, for $1500 a day, was defying the laws of chance and physics as he thrilled the thousands of transfixed spectators. We, too, were amazed and fascinated by his aerobatics in his *"Little Looper"*, a beautiful Gnome-powered Curtiss-type biplane that Glenn Martin had built for him. Taciturn and moody on the ground maybe, but once the nattily attired Beachey took to the air he earned the admiration of us all.

He had a new sensation that spring - the *"Lincoln Beachey Special"*. It was a monoplane, 80-hp Gnome-powered, which the Eaton brothers had built for him in Los Angeles. It was surely a beauty; very advanced and similar in design to the craft that Pegoud had been flying around the United States. Though it had been designed and powered for vertical climb - *straight up* - one look told me that it wasn't meant for looping like the Little Looper. It was more like a sleek racing aeroplane.

However, apparently Beachey thought otherwise. At 3:30 PM on March 14th, after doing his standard fare in the Little Looper, he took off in the Special. He flew out of sight across the bay, climbed to around 6,000 feet, and then reappeared, performing one loop and starting another. However, for some reason he stopped when only half through it, swooping in a long spiral to about 1,000 feet where he started banking for a turn. Then a wing failed - and as the sleek craft fell faster and faster, the other one was seen to collapse. Lincoln Beachey and his wonderful new monoplane dove into the bay beside the city of his birth only 28 years earlier. He wasn't killed outright but drowned while frantically trying to disengage himself from the harness that held him in three places in that cramped cockpit.

It was a sad and somber crowd leaving the fair that day.

102

Article on Beachey's crash - 1915

Earlier Beachey had written:

"The Silent Reaper of Souls and I shook hands. Thousands of times we have engaged in a race among the clouds--plunging head-long in breathless flight--diving and circling with awful speed through ethereal space. And, many times, when the dazzling sun-light has blinded my eyes and sudden darkness has numbed all my senses, I have imagined him close at my heels. On such occasions I have defied him, but in so doing have experienced fright which I cannot explain. Today the old fellow and I are pals."

103

After the crash speculation held that this 'different' aeroplane had caused him to misjudge speed. Its aluminum body and windshield created an environment new to Beachey and made him unable to "feel the wind" as when normally flying body-exposed.

I wasn't there to witness that final show, but soon I heard the news, which had spread like wildfire. I recalled Mac telling Beachey the first time he saw that monoplane, *"You certainly aren't going to dive or loop that thing, are you, Linc?"* Beachey replied, *"I think it'll be OK.....as long as I don't pull it out too tightly."*

This accident saddened both the general public and we in aviation, for Lincoln Beachey had been an idol. Heretofore, he had always flown aircraft designed for his fanatic determination to push things to the limit. It was hard for me to reconcile: he had lost his life, and we had lost Lincoln Beachey - just as we'd lost the many other daredevils that had tried to emulate his singular mastery of the air.

We set about doing a postmortem on the Special. The Eatons had made an extra set of wings, and with his military connections, Mac got permission to take them over to Mare Island Naval Shipyard for structural testing. Being a budding engineer, I assisted Mac and Arthur Mix, Beachey's top mechanic, in suspending a wing so we could sandbag-load-it to the point of failure. The wing collapsed under the equivalent load of 4 G's (four times the weight of gravity). This was a figure far too low for an aerobatic aircraft, confirming Warren Eaton's plaint that the plane had never been designed for such use.

Warren Eaton later became one of my best friends. As an *Early Bird* president, he was the architect of the original *Early Bird Plaque Program* and honored me in officiating at the dedication of one of these plaques at Albatross and Maple Streets, the site of my first glider flight.

The exposition couldn't mourn Beachey for long; it still demanded exhibition flyers to

My Early Bird plaque - San Diego

thrill the estimated *two million* fairgoers. One was Art Smith, flying a Curtiss-copy powered with a 6-cylinder engine built by Charles Kirkham, an engineer of such talent that Glenn Curtiss, who continually sought out the best brains for his engineering organization, soon hired him. Smith, billed as the *"Human Comet"*, became very popular with his night flying exhibitions, twisting and turning with bright-colored flares on his wing tips that scorched the sky and belched great clouds of smoke. After the fair Art toured Japan with his mechanic, Al Menasco. Although suffering a crackup or two, the *"Smashup Kid"* returned home with a chest full of medals and honors.

Having been beaten by "Vin Fiz" Rodgers, Bob Fowler was still trying for records - and he'd just set one of *flying nonstop from the Atlantic to the Pacific.* It was a dubious distinction since he had merely overflown the isthmus of Panama, but it did get him 'star' billing at the Orpheum Theatre. I well-remember sitting in its rococo majesty while the lights dimmed and his plane's engine started barking and shooting out jabs of flame. The audience thought this simple show just grand, and he was quite the temporary hero. After the show I went backstage, met Fowler and began a lifelong friendship. We'd both be heavily involved in making Jennys for the war two years later.

Fowler's "Atlantic to the Pacific" flight - 1915

Another man that I had some contact with was Frank Bryant. With Roy Francis, he had a twin-tractor biplane that was sort of a Wright-hybrid but more flexible in its handling. I'd first met him at North Island in 1912 when he'd inspected my tractor biplane. He was a very unusual aviator who could seemingly get into almost any airplane, regardless of the seven or eight different control systems then used, and do a very capable job of flying. This unique ability didn't apply to most pilots, and caused many to come to grief.

By this time the Christofferson brothers were getting a handsome reputation due to their advanced designs for both flying boats and tractor landplanes. This was augmented somewhat by the publicity of Silas Christofferson's daredevil flying. He had flown an aeroplane off the top of an office building in Portland, Oregon and in 1914 became the first to fly nonstop from San Francisco to Los Angeles. The brothers were building their aircraft in a small factory in Redwood City, a town about halfway down the San Francisco peninsula. The Army Signal Corp's Aviation Section had expressed considerable interest in the latest Christofferson model, in which they'd altered the control system, changing it from the customary Curtiss shoulder-yoke to the French Nieuport system in which the ailerons are controlled by the foot bar and the rudder by the lateral motion of the stick. While Silas was demonstrating the plane in 1916, he lost control, crashed and was killed. The Army then lost interest in the plane, the young company's financial backers backed out, and the remaining brothers were left with little option but to hit the exhibition trail again. A couple of years later I'd be managing their former factory, but no longer under the Christofferson name.

Throughout this period I was having my own financial problems of figuring out how to stay in college, and was constantly involved in some sort of part-time work. My steadiest employment was with Hall-Scott, and they went out of their way to help me by assigning me long-cut lathe or milling jobs. On these, I could set up the machine and then do some homework while the cut was being made. Eventually I became a full-time Hall-Scott employee, in June of 1916 (as a junior engineer instead of a machinist) and I never did get my college degree.

In all of my gadding around the Bay Area I was having to cover a lot of ground - much of it by ferry, for this was long before the great bridges (including the Joseph Strauss-Clifford Paine colossus of 1937, *The*

106

Golden Gate Bridge). So I acquired a 1909 air-cooled Franklin, starting a college fad when I cut it down to the appearance of a racing car *"just like Barney Oldfield!"* "Old Frank" served me well from 1914 until late in 1917, and was my 'courting vehicle' after I met the lovely Carol Coulter. We'll hear more of Herbert Franklin, and of John Wilkinson and G.E. Franklin's engineering genius later in our story; suffice it to say that their engine and auto innovations were among the greatest in American industry.

The war news from Europe was becoming more and more strident. In addition to reading about it in the papers, I was personally aware of it when several Cal students left to enter the fray through Canada. The tempo at Hall-Scott kept increasing, for tremendous strides were being planned in aviation and they were naturally involved in the government's warmup for war. I was now 22 years old, and as a 'red-blooded American' with almost a college education and experience as an aviator, I was itching to join the flying part of the war.

In the spring of 1917, when America finally entered the struggle against the Kaiser, I immediately hightailed-it to the Army's Rockwell Field to enlist as an aviation cadet. About the first thing they threw at me was the physical examination, and it was a terrific shock to learn that I was considered unfit because of my busted-up ankles. The aviator, then as now, was thought of as a 'superman', a perfect physical specimen, though in Russia the legendary Alexander de Seversky had lost a leg on his first fighter mission. After he recuperated (with special Czarist permission) he went on flying to complete 56 more missions. But that was Russia, not an idealistic America just entering the battle.

Well, I wasn't going to let some Army doctor 'count me out' without a fight, and I went to see an old San Diego neighbor, Thurman Bane, then second-in-command at the field. But even he couldn't get the powers-that-be to relent one iota. I wasn't ever going to become a dashing military aviator! Major Bane was helpful, though, in another way. He told me that the University of California was establishing a preliminary ground school for West Coast aviation cadets, and suggested this for my contribution to the war effort. He then set up interviews for me with some of my old professors who were administering this new program.

I went right back to Berkeley and was immediately hired as the head of the Department of Theory of Flight, Aviation School, Signal Corps,

U.S. Army. (This was before the aviation section was separated from the Signal Corps and renamed "Air Service.") Similar Schools of Military Aeronautics were established at Cornell, Princeton, University of Illinois and the University of Texas. A new class of cadets would start weekly for a six-week course of instruction in the Theory of Flight, Powerplants , Meteorology and Navigation, Radio and Communications and Military subjects. Afterwards, they'd proceed to Army flying schools located at Rockwell Field, Mather Field and March Field (near Riverside) and further east to fields like Kelly Field in Texas.

It was mid-June, 1917 when I assumed this new responsibility, and shortly thereafter I entered into another, more lasting, relationship as well. Since 1916 my mother and I had shared an apartment in Berkeley. In the same building lived one Carol Coulter and her mother. Carol was a native of Nevada, but had spent most of her younger years in San Francisco. In the natural flow of things, she and I became acquainted, and then very friendly as we zipped all over in Old Frank. We were married on June 30, 1917, just as I was beginning my new position at the School of Military Aeronautics. A year later, on June 8, 1918, we were blessed with our first and only child, Jane Gardner Waterman. The generations would unfold as Jane later briefly attended Berkeley's sister university in Los Angeles, UCLA, before helping me out in my business. She married Adrian Blackwell and, in time, made the newlyweds of 1917 grandparents with two lovely daughters, Carol and Nell.

For those first few weeks at the school I was very busy organizing study material which hadn't ever been taught before. I was the *only* instructor on the entire 15 member staff that had had any previous flying experience, so I was literally 'plowing new ground' as I shook-down into the routine of teaching and administering the instructors under me.

The first few classes of cadets were of a very high caliber. Many were college graduates, and almost all had at least a year or two of college, which was fairly unusual in those days. They were the 'cream of the crop', both mentally and physically, of the cadet program. Several come to mind now: *Corliss Moseley*, first to win the Pulitzer Race in 1920; *Jack Macready*, who with Oakley Kelly first flew nonstop across the country in 1923; *Harold Harris*, setter of speed records, a top Army test pilot at McCook Field in the early 1920's and the first American to use the new

Me and Carol, my bride-of-a-week - Berkeley - July 1917
(plane is a Martin with Hall-Scott A7A)

pack-type parachute in earnest; *Lowell Smith*, who with John Richter set an endurance record in 1923 and who led the epic first around-the-world flight in 1924; *Jimmy Doolittle*, pioneer in 'blind' flying, racer, earner of an MIT doctorate in 1925, the first to perform an outside loop in 1927 and the leader of the famous Tokyo Raid in 1942; and many, many more. We'll touch upon several of their careers as my story unfolds.

After around six months of teaching 500 to 600 cadets I began to pale on the job. The tedium and monotony was just not my bent, and the steady decline in the overall quality of the cadets was getting me discouraged. I was suspicious that many were there in preference to being drafted. My biggest challenge seemed to be in trying to instruct the instructors. This was not an altogether satisfying experience, though the subject of Theory of Flight could well be taught without actually flying if

I had done my job well enough. In addition to that chore, I was also doing quite a bit of classroom instruction in rigging, aerodynamics, nomenclature for aeronautics (when I prepared probably the first such glossary of aeronautical terms) and the history of flight (a fairly short subject then!).

As the year was drawing to a close, my disenchantment with the job was pretty complete, and I started looking around for something more interesting and challenging.

(Note: What to call the aviator at the controls slowly evolved - from *operator, driver, or sky pilot*, to finally, today's *pilot*.)

Chapter 3

1918 - 1922

Building Jennys for "Over Here" and Thereafter

IN 1917, when America had entered The Great War, the U.S. "ranked 14th among the nations of the world in aviation." The Army had 55 airplanes: four old, 51 obsolete. The Signal Corps Aviation Section had 65 officers; 'aviators' numbered 35, but only five were fit for combat. The Navy had 38 aviators; the Marines, five. Since the Wrights' flight in 1903, only about 200 American aircraft had been built, mostly Curtiss or Curtiss copies. In 1916 the U.S. aircraft industry had produced only 64 planes. By contrast, in 1914 when World War I began, France had 780 military and 1,000 private planes; Germany had 560 military and 450 private planes (and 18 dirigibles); and England had 225 military planes and about 150 private planes.

Following the arrival of a British-French aviation mission, the American General Staff and the Aircraft Production Board called for the construction of 22,500 aircraft and engines - an unheard-of quantity. $640,000,000, a fantastic sum for those days, was appropriated on July 24, 1917 to initiate one of the largest armament programs in history.

The war was spawning tremendous aviation activity.

111

There were new companies starting up all over the country to produce the plane, *the JN-4, or "Jenny"*, that the Englishman, Douglas Thomas, had helped design for Curtiss. It was selected to be the backbone for the American training effort. One of the local companies was the *United States Aircraft Corporation* in San Francisco. Their factory was the old Christofferson Aviation Co. in Redwood City, about twenty miles down the Peninsula from San Francisco. They had a government contract for 100 Jennys, and when I contacted them I found that Beryl Williams was in charge of production, the same fellow that I'd met in 1911 when he and Glenn Martin had put on their unsuccessful airshow at the Coronado polo field.

I was initially hired as purchasing agent. My office was in San Francisco, but I was on the road all over Northern California for much of the time. My job was semi-engineering, which necessitated close study of the Army's drawings and specifications, and then a lot of scouting around to find raw materials, parts and suppliers capable of making the special items. I had to do negotiating too, for the company was underfinanced and we needed to persuade vendors to give us good terms and credit.

112   *United States Aircraft Corporation - Redwood City - 1918*

Manufacturing Curtiss Jennys - 1918 - (note 90-hp OX-5 engine)

To maximize our purchasing power, we formed a loose alliance with the other Jenny builders in the area: Fowler Aircraft Co. in San Francisco and the Liberty Iron Works in Sacramento. With Fowler's contract for 50 planes, Liberty's 300, and our 100, quite a few parts could be made in common. We at U.S. Aircraft agreed to be responsible for all of the production stamping dies for the fuselage; they, in turn, were to supply other components. Therefore, in addition to close liaison with both Fowler and Liberty, I had to coordinate with several small stamping and forging firms throughout the Bay Area on theirs and our behalf for the production of not 100 but of 450 aircraft. Additionally, for our own contract I set up several subcontractors whose products would be hauled to Redwood City for the final aircraft assembly.

Beryl Williams was busy at Redwood City with his crew of ex-carpenters and an odd assortment of mechanics, setting up the jigs for the assembly of the fuselage and wings. Everything that was fabricated and as-

113

sembled, including all subcontracted items, such as the gas tanks made by the local lamp works, had to be inspected and approved by the Army's Bureau of Aircraft Production, insuring that quality standards were met.

Although I wore the title of purchasing agent, my work was very diversified, involving engineering and management. The company's president had a new Dodge (introduced in 1914) which he turned over to me for calling on the various suppliers, and even for transporting smaller parts. I was really on the move, and it was interesting work, especially after the tedium of teaching.

All wasn't going easy, however, for we three manufacturers. There were frequent problems with the Army's inspector, and the Bureau would shut the production line down until they were corrected. Liberty evolved a procedure to alleviate this problem. They hired the inspector and put him in charge of the whole shebang, and he went on to do a very capable job! In fact, this fellow, Harry Wetzel, stayed in the business and later became general manager of Douglas where he was responsible in great measure for the tremendous success of that company

Fowler had a devastating setback because of a bad fire, had to shut down and went through a reorganization. It emerged as the Howell & Lesser Co., and completed its original 50-unit order plus an additional contract for 75 more Jennys.

I'm very proud to say U.S. Aircraft was the first of the three companies to complete and deliver an airplane. We also were first to complete our 100-plane contract, but we had our share of troubles too; ie: when we'd finished our first couple aircraft, the engines hadn't arrived, so they were shipped over to Berkeley to be used in the rigging lab at the pre-flight school, augmenting the two Martins already there.

Beryl Williams was having troubles with the Army inspector and decided to follow Liberty's example and hire him. It turned out to be a mistake. This chap had previously been a Canadian flyer who'd cracked-up and was unable to continue flying. However, very little was known about his background, and shortly after he was hired we were dumfounded to discover one Monday morning that the safe's entire cash payroll had been cleaned out. And, he'd disappeared with the company's Dodge, to-boot, probably for Canada - we were never able to catch him - and his theft was a major financial blow to the company. From then on I spent much of my time in Redwood City helping Beryl straighten things out. It wasn't long before I'd been promoted to chief engineer, and then to general manager when Williams had to be let go due to a drinking problem. I was then responsible for the final completion of the initial contract, and the negotiation of a follow-up contract.

Once in management I learned a lot about people. One of the more interesting areas in the plant, supervised by the wife of the Woodworking Department's foreman, was the wing shop. Here, the seamstresses sewed the wing fabric and finished the skin by applying an acetate dope which both strengthened and shrink-tightened the fabric. Redwood City was a small town then, and most of these women were local housewives with local prejudices. When a woman from San Francisco's notorious Barbary Coast was hired, she was ostracized by being given the job of applying the dope. Well, anyone who could stand those fumes for eight hours was pretty tough, and after this woman quietly stuck it out for a week she earned the grudging acceptance of the rest of the women and a more pleasant job.

But our biggest problem was money, not people. We started out under capitalized, planning to amortize the die costs over at least 1,000 planes. Thus, when we ended-up with only 425, the company was severely strained. The original promoters had no illusions about a long life for their 'war baby' but they never dreamed that we'd be in-and-out of the war so fast. I was negotiating the follow-up contract when the Armistice was declared on November 11, 1918.

In less than two years the United States had grown from an airpower of virtually zero. At the war's end in Europe the U.S. had 45 squadrons, 740 airplanes and almost 800 American military aviators who had accumulated an impressive flying record of over 35,000 flying hours. There were over 10,000 American aircraft, most still in the United States. The meager officer corps had swollen to over 27,000. The growth had been both dramatic and unprecedented, and was to cause monumental postwar readjustment problems.

So the war was over, and it was truly quiet on the Western Front. We had completed our first major order, but we hadn't yet finished the accompanying order for 40 sets of spare parts, and were given only until December 1st to do so. With everything else being cancelled, I well-remember working until almost the stroke-of-midnight, November 30th, getting the final wing skid formed-up and into its crate - all under the scrutiny of the Bureau's inspector.

115

The company was finished at about the same time. With too many bills, it went broke at the end of 1918, and I was appointed liquidator by the receiver in bankruptcy, charged with wrapping everything up as best I could for the benefit of the creditors.

After first taking inventory, the appraisers came in and set prices. I then undertook selling as much off as I could, eventually even the factory itself. This job stretched on for nearly a year, and in the process I went to most of the military fields in the West trying to peddle our inventory. I wasn't very effective, as there was too much surplus already on the market, but I did make a lot of good contacts. During the war the Navy had returned to North Island, setting-up an Air Station next to the Army's Rockwell Field. I made a trip there, hoping to drum up some business, but as usual I wasn't very successful, though it did give me an opportunity to visit old friends in San Diego.

Heading back to the Bay Area, I stopped to see what was going on around Los Angeles, and found most of the civilian aviation activity at Venice, a small town on the Pacific Ocean lying west of Los Angeles and just south of Santa Monica.

"Venice has a long and turbulent history. It was developed in 1905 by a rich Eastern cigarette manufacturer named Abbot Kinney who envisioned a town of canals and beaches in the spirit of Venice, Italy. Early Venice had (16) miles of broad (4 feet deep by 40 feet wide) canals, gondolas, opera houses and Italian gothic facades (and a sixty-piece Italian orchestra). Simultaneously, Kinney recognized the commercial value of honky-tonk and imported the entire midway from the Portland World's Fair. He built a 1,700-foot pier and furnished it with amusements, including three roller coasters. Mary Pickford, Charlie Chaplin and Mae Murray had summer mansions here, and by 1920 Venice had become the most prosperous seaside resort on the West Coast."

Marcia Seligson, N.Y. Times, March 1979.

Crawford Airplane and Supply, located there, was buying-up surplus aircraft materials, and after spending time with them and some other local outfits I learned of an opportunity to build a personal airplane for a prominent business man, L. (Leslie) C. Brand, president of Title Guar-

116

antee & Trust Co. in Los Angeles. He lived in Glendale, and I worked-out an agreement with him for a Hisso-Jenny (a Jenny powered with the 150-hp Hispano-Suiza engine, far more powerful than the Curtiss OX-5 90-hp engine). I then leased quarters from Crawford, and headed home to San Francisco to wrap-up the liquidation.

Carol, little Janie and I then were living in a small apartment in a home shared with another young couple. The husband was an insurance man and a part-time inventor. He was working on a new type of timing device for the Ford Model T and had an excellent shop in the basement which I could use. At this time (1919) I was just beginning to be intrigued with vertical lift. Since this was four years before Juan de la Cierva's first autogiro, and almost twenty years before the first practical helicopter, I was plowing some new, very rough ground. Whenever I had time I tinkered with this idea, testing the feasibility of building a full-scale machine in order to obtain data on lift efficiency and propulsion. At this early age, suitable power plants were lacking, and like many others, I designed my concept around two Model T engines. First, though, I built a small paddlewheel-type unit to ascertain what aerodynamic forces could be produced. I rolled it around on a walking beam with a balance scale mounted in the system so that for various speed and horsepower inputs I could compute the theoretical lifts. I worked a great deal on this idea over the years, have a patent disclosure on the concept, and hope that someday it may result in a significant aeronautical advance.

Back in San Francisco I apprised the bankruptcy trustees of the hopelessness of getting any more money out of the remaining assets, and with their approval I closed things down, loaded the remaining inventory in a railcar, and headed for Southern California. Having few funds, I arranged to pay for this material with the earnings from my new Venice venture. The railcar was loaded with about everything left in the plant: patterns, jigs, templates, and a miscellaneous array of Jenny parts. I had virtually everything needed to start another aircraft factory!

When the boxcar arrived in Venice we unloaded almost everything into my new quarters, except the wing tables and jigs which we stacked outside. It was getting into the fall of 1919 when my new *Waterman Aircraft Manufacturing Co.* started hiring its factory crew. Several I'd known before or had worked for me at Redwood City. Carl Spangenberger had been Howell & Lesser's fuselage department foreman and later became

117

noted for co-designing the Guiberson diesel engine, one of the few successful diesel aircraft powerplants. Ray (Goldie) Goldsworthy was a recently commissioned Army pilot needing a civilian job in order to effect his release from the service. Wally and Otto Timm were capable and already well-known, and Clarence Prest and Fred Schuman rounded-out the group. I thought that it was a damn good crew - and we soon started work on Brand's plane.

The Hisso-Jenny was somewhat different from the normal Jenny. In addition to its more powerful engine, which was placed differently owing to its greater power and weight, it had ailerons on both upper and lower wings like the "Canuck", the Canadian Jenny. But I figured that I'd have little problem fabricating this airplane with my stock of Jenny parts and fittings. Wright Aeronautical Company was making Hispano-Suiza engines, on license from the French, for around $5,000. With Brand supplying the engine and the propeller, I contracted to build the complete airframe for $3,500.

Brand had one of his Title Guarantee employees, Elon Brown, a recently released Army aviator, keep an eye on our progress during the plane's fabrication. It quickly became apparent that he knew little about aircraft construction. His ignorance presented few problems, though, except for a time or two when he tried bluffing, making things a bit sticky.

After about six or seven weeks' work, we completed the plane, painted the name *"Mono Eagle"* on the side of the fuselage and took it over to Venice Field - which was controlled by my landlord, Harry Crawford. In the meantime, Brand had constructed a fancy Moorish hangar matching his lavish "castle" in Glendale, and had put in his own private airstrip.

The Mono Eagle was named for Mono Lake, near where Brand had a summer camp that he wished to fly to. This brackish and desolate lake is at 6,400 feet elevation and the largest within California. It sits about half-way up the state, just north of the Owens River Valley where the controversial Los Angeles Aqueduct began. Because of this 300-mile-or-so distance, we'd installed an extra-large belly gas tank. However, I had some misgivings about the plane's ability to handle this difficult run unless it was reasonably loaded and very well flown. I was also apprehensive about Brand's small flight strip and still didn't know how good a pilot Brown was going to be.

118

Waterman Aircraft's first product - 1919
Goldsworthy, Spangenberger, Schuman, Wally Timm, Crowley and me

Putting my fears and misgivings aside, Brown and I took a test flight and found it one beautifully handling aeroplane. Brand immediately wanted Brown to fly the plane over to the Los Angeles Country Club on Wilshire Boulevard and land on the fairway so that he could show it off to his golfing buddies. Brown did, but with near-disasterous results.

As planes then didn't have brakes, Brown miscalculated his landing and kept rolling right into a newly-planted rose garden - with skads of stakes supporting the plants. They made a virtual sieve of the lower wing! It was a sad sight, for that plane had been perfect and painstakingly finished. I sent Jack Crowley, my paint and dope man, right over to the country club and he spent the next couple of days patching up the damage, after which Brown flew the now-scarred Mono Eagle over to its new home in Glendale.

By this time I was finding that my quarters at Crawford's a bit tight. After looking around, I found a new space in a garage-type shed adjoin-

119

ing Herb Wilson's place on Washington Boulevard in Santa Monica, about a mile north of Venice. Herb Wilson was then busy building an OX-5-powered biplane. Both Herb and his brother, Al, were Venice-area pilots with Al becoming the more famous of the two - perhaps I should say notorious as we'll see later.

It wasn't only the tight quarters that prompted this move. I was also finding that I didn't like the way Crawford did business, and I'd already had one confrontation with him. I'd made a deal to exchange a set of Jenny fittings for a month's rent, and his idea of a 'set' didn't jibe with mine. I hoped that my new quarters were going to be more compatible.

And, I wasn't alone in having problems with him. During this period Crawford attended an Army surplus sales where they were auctioning a dope shed, a 50 x 50-foot building used for painting and doping aircraft wings. The bid was for the unopened building, including its contents and Crawford was the high bidder. The next day when he arrived to dismantle it and truck it to Venice, they opened it up to find a brand-new Liberty-engined DH-4 airplane!

Testimony later indicated that at the time of the auction the shed had only contained the normal doping materials. No one was ever able to prove just how that gem of a DeHaviland got in there, except to assume that some enlisted personnel had been bribed to push it in that night. In any event, Crawford made his claim to the plane stick and later sold it for about 100-times what he paid for the shed. Wisely, the Army never again permitted him to bid.

The word was getting around that I had probably the best supply of Jenny fittings and parts available, and my old friend, Warren Eaton, came over to see my stock. Following Lincoln Beachey's tragic death, Warren had become chief engineer at St. Louis Aircraft Co., who built 450 Jennys by war's end. He was now chief engineer for Chaplin Airdrome, owned by Sydney Chaplin (Charlie's half-brother) and Emory Rogers, one of my Berkeley students and scion of the Rogers Silver family. Their airfield was 'out in the country' among open fields, an occasional house or barn and oil derrick, on the southwest corner of Wilshire Boulevard and Crescent (now Fairfax) where the "Miracle Mile" is now. In addition to having the Los Angeles agency for Curtiss aeroplanes, Chaplin was carrying-on an airline to Catalina Island; and a charter, flight instruction and exhibition business.

120

Of course, whenever there was any demand for movie flying they had an excellent 'in' as well. At this time though, the movies were just beginning to discover the potentials of the airplane and stunting.

Curtiss wasn't building any more Jennys. (In fact, they were trying to buy them back from the government in order to salvage what little post-war business there was.) So it was virtually impossible to obtain any, and almost none were owned by civilians. Cecil deMille had about the only one I knew of. What you typically saw was the Canadian JN-4, the Canuck. They were almost identical to the Jenny but had a level motorbed, rounded rudder, and ailerons on both top and bottom wings which made them more sensitive to roll maneuvers. In fact, they were very similar to the Hisso-Jenny, and most of their parts were readily interchangable with Jenny parts (though there was enough difference to give me problems on some later conversions).

After Eaton saw what I had and learned about the fuselage and wing jig tables over at Crawford's, he offered me a handsome profit on the lot and we made a deal. However, a couple of days later Herb Wilson was trying to solder a fitting too close to some doped fabric and his place caught fire. He was totally burned-out and my stuff stored next door suffered some water damage too, so I had to make an adjustment with Eaton. They then loaded the truck and headed to Crawford's for the jigs and tables, before returning to Chaplin Airdrome.

And I soon had new evidence about how difficult Crawford could be. When Chaplin's truck arrived to pick up the tables and other gear, Crawford stopped them, claiming that I owed him $50, a substantial sum then. I had to put up twice that amount, $100, in order to get the stuff released to Eaton, and then I started looking for a lawyer.

The deal with Chaplin had been a financial lifesaver. But that $100 was a whale of a lot of money to me, and even though Crawford often bragged that his lawyer brother, Sam, had never lost a case, I was determined to get back what I knew was mine. One of my friends recommended his lawyer, a fellow named Jerry Giesler. I surely didn't know that he was a big-time Hollywood lawyer with fees ranging into the thousands of dollars. (One of Giesler's celebrated cases was his successful defense of Charlie Chaplin against Mann Act charges.) Giesler carefully listened to my $50 problem, and then explained that court commitments would keep him from personally handling my case, but that an associate would be able to help me. This chap, Leonard Comegys, didn't even have an office or desk - I found him sitting at the big table in Giesler's law library. After an introduction I explained my problem to him, and he agreed to represent me.

In those days there was only the Justice Court and the state's Superior Court, and Comegys did a fine job winning my case in the Justice Court. Crawford was pretty upset that Sam had let him down, and insisted upon appealing to the Superior Court. I now had to put up twice the bond, $200, in order to retain possession of the jigs and tables. When the case got to the Superior Court it seemed to drag on interminably. Comegys kept telling me that the court's docket was so full that he was having trouble getting a hearing. Finally, about two years and at least two financial cliff-hangers later, the case was heard, and we won it hands-down. I then learned that Leonard had just passed his bar exam. Without this he couldn't have appeared before the Superior Court - the true cause for the delay. I've chuckled over that many times since, but it surely gave me problems then.

As Comegys and I were leaving the Hall of Records, we bumped into both Crawfords and their witness, Fred Schuman, my ex-employee. Sam said to his brother, *"You might as well pay Waldo his $50; we can't carry this any further."* Harry grumbled, pulled out a big roll from his pocket, and as he was counting out the $50 said, *"Waldo's witnesses got up and lied, and our witnesses got up and lied, and Waldo's were better liars than ours - so here's your $50, Waldo."* That was the way Harry thought and did things, but I still did business with him from time to time because, well-known as the *"aircraft junk man of Southern California",* he had many hard-to-get items.

It was now 1920, and the aircraft industry that had exploded literally from nothing during the war now found itself virtually back to nothing again. With its back to the wall, it faced a public that only knew the airplane as a tool of war, or a plaything of the barnstormers. It was unthinkable to consider flying as a means of transportation, for the planes of that era were erratic in performance and deadly in failure. There were no airlines, no airports, and the "aerial mail" was in its faltering pioneer stage. Then, to top all of this off, the country entered the "primary postwar depression." It wasn't

122

*a very good time to be attempting a living from aviation. Only 302
American aircraft were built in 1921.*

Helping me to survive during these very lean years was some business
I did with George Stephenson and his Pacific Airplane & Supply Co., lo-
cated at 3rd and Sunset in Ocean Park, between Venice and Santa
Monica. Involved in general aircraft remanufacture, repair and servicing,
Stephenson bought the remaining U.S. Aircraft inventory of nuts and
bolts, paid $2,000 and earned me a very welcome $200 commission.

Prowling around for work, I met a fellow named Wylie, the owner of
an Army Martin-S seaplane that'd been converted to a landplane. He
kept his plane in a small hangar on the south side of the trolley tracks at
Venice Field. *The main hangar for this field was on the north side of the
tracks, in a small, triangular area facing on Washington Boulevard, (southwest of the intersection of Washington Boulevard and Venice Boulevard),
but the main flying field was south of the Pacific Electric tracks (with
Kinney's canals to the west), extending southwesterly towards Washington
Street and the marshland that is now the giant Marina del Rey complex.*

One day there were several of us hanging around Wylie's hanger discussing the flight that Brown was about to make flying Mr. Brand up to
Mono Lake. Wylie's Martin had a 125-hp Hall-Scott A5A, a fairly powerful engine, so I suggested that Wylie, myself, Wally Timm and Goldie
Goldsworthy rig the plane so that we could all fly over to Glendale and
watch him take off. The Martin had two cockpits, and we wired a 12-
inch board across the longerons in the front cockpit for Wally, Wylie and
myself to sit, squeezed into the front cockpit. Goldie, as pilot, taxied the
plane to the east end of the field so we'd have a good long run, and we
took off. The only problem was that none of us had bothered to think
about the weather, and when we got airborne we found ourselves in a
solid overcast. We couldn't see the ground from any height at all. We
kept hoping that the fog would blow or burn off, but naturally, it didn't.
It was still fairly early in the morning, however, and the western breeze
off the ocean hadn't come up. In fact, the fog kept getting lower, forcing
us down, and Goldie realized that we were out on a limb. Pushing our
luck, he swung back over the marsh, heading in for a landing. With all of
the extra weight aboard, he misjudged it, came in too fast, and kept rolling and rolling until we were past the west end of the runway, nearing the

123

trolley line. Finally, with no option left, Goldie kicked the rudder hard, abruptly turning the plane, and with a crunch we piled into the railroad embankment at around 15-mph.

With no impediments like seat belts, we three passengers were thrown helter-skelter but fortunately we suffered only a few bruises. However, the plane was one broken bird with its propeller shattered and its fuselage twisted and crumpled, particularly in the rear section.

Being the main instigator of this great idea, I assumed the responsibility for fixing up the Martin. I couldn't do the job for free, but for as little cost to Wylie as possible. We took the wings off, left them in his hangar, and carted the fuselage over to my place on Washington Boulevard. Using mainly Jenny parts in the reconstruction, I learned that seaplanes had a lightly-structured tail section since they were not subjected to landing shocks and I therefore strengthened Wylie's plane as I rebuilt it. At the end of a couple of months hard work I had his plane better than new, redeeming myself somewhat for one of my more hair-brained ideas.

Although we never did get to see Brand's first takeoff, I'm sure he didn't miss our presence. He grew to like his new aeroplane, having Brown fly him all over Southern California where most of the air fields then were military and welcomed civilian flyers. Brand became well-acquainted with several Army pilots and was envious of their Liberty-powered DH-4's. The 400-hp Liberty engine was much more powerful than his 150-hp Hispano-Suiza, but unavailable to civilians. Brand really began coveting one. He told me that if he could ever lay his hands on a Liberty that he wanted a bigger and better aeroplane built around it.

When the U.S. entered the war in 1917 we didn't have a single dependable engine of over 200-hp. (The best was the Curtiss-R used on the largest Curtiss planes. It was similar to the OX-5 in appearance, but differed considerably structurally and had a 5" bore and a 7" stroke.) Therefore, the Bureau of Aircraft Production assembled the country's top engineering talent to design a new engine that could be mass-produced for the war effort. Al Hall of Hall-Scott and Jesse Vincent of Packard holed-up for 48-hours in Washington's Willard Hotel and designed the superlative Liberty engine, soon designated the "U.S. Standard Aircraft Engine." The original design was a V8 of 300-hp, but this was soon enlarged to the standard V12 of 400-hp. *This engine was the*

124

first to surpass the weight-to-horsepower record that Charles Manly estab-
lished in his superb five-cylinder radial, redesigned from Balzer's rotary,
and used in Langley's Aerodrome in 1903. It had weighed 2.4 lbs. per hp,
developing 52.4-hp at 950 rpm.

It's my opinion that the Liberty design was about three-fourths Al
Hall's and one-fourth Jesse Vincent's. Many of the basic features of a
previous Hall-Scott engine (patterned after a Mercedes powerplant)
were incorporated in the design, but Packard's publicity got Vincent the
lion's share of the credit. The biggest innovation in the Liberty over the
old Hall-Scott was the use of steel cylinder forgings with welded water
jackets rather than cast iron. Ford was assigned the job of supplying
these steel cylinders to the manufacturers producing these engines in
these volumes: *Packard (6,500), Buick & Cadillac (2,528), Lincoln*
(6,500), Ford (3,950), and Nordyke & Marmon (1,000).

20,478 Liberty engines were produced, but only about 200 powering
DeHavilands ever got to the front before the end of the war. Naturally
an awful lot of Liberty engines later hit the surplus market. I always preferred the Ford-manufactured ones, thinking them best and Packard's
poorest.

At about the same time that I was completing Wylie's fix-up job
Brand learned that Liberty engines were soon to be released to civilians
for $2,500 apiece. They'd cost the government around $7,000. He immediately took steps to get one while discussing with me the new airplane
that he wanted.

During the war, the French had sent an Aviation Mission to the
United States and one of its members, Captain G. Lepere, designed an
airplane far-superior to the DH-4. Packard built 27 of these LePeres before war's end. The Army used them in the early 1920's for several
speed and altitude records, and for development work on exhaust super-
charging and de-icing. They were an excellent design and well-recom-
mended by my Berkeley students now flying for the Army: Jack
Macready (who flew in one to 38,704 feet of altitude), Harold Harris,
and the very tall and skinny Rudolph "Shorty" Shroeder (who first set altitude records in the LePere in 1920). Therefore, I recommended the
design to Brand, stating that if he could use his Army contacts to get a
set of plans from McCook Field (now Wright-Patterson) in Dayton that
I'd customize them for the plane he desired.

Brand soon got the plans, and I revised them, adding four feet to the wingspread, widening the fuselage to accomodate two passengers comfortably in the rear cockpit, and enlarging the fuel capacity for his Mono Lake trips. I then found a new and better location than my garage-type shed - a building at 3rd and Sunset in Venice, just across the Santa Monica line, and across the street from Stephenson's Pacific Airplane & Supply. This was very handy for parts and supplies, even engine parts because Stephenson's had the Hall-Scott agency. We always had a good and cooperative relationship.

Otto Timm was now working for Stephenson as his top trouble shooter and technician, but continued to help me whenever I needed his expert craftsmanship. During the war Otto had been a civilian senior flying instructor at Rockwell Field. He had tried aircraft design and building, and had even designed a 5-cylinder air-cooled engine. He would soon leave the area briefly (1922-1923) for the Midwest where he gave a young Charles Lindbergh his first airplane ride. Otto was very capable in virtually every aspect of aviation.

The first man that I hired for building Brand's new plane was Clarence Deyette, in my book the finest aircraft woodworker in the country. He'd started with Boeing & Westervelt in Seattle, had drifted south, joined our Redwood City operation during the war, and had then come to Southern California. I hadn't been able to find him for the first Brand plane but was surely glad to have him now. Our association would continue, off and on, until late 1937.

We had a major problem building this LePere-variation because almost everything had to be custom-fabricated from raw material; there wasn't anything standard except the nuts and bolts. To this day many people think we'd simply taken a surplus Army LePere and modified it, though we did closely follow the original plans and drawings.

One of our knottiest (pun unintended) problems was making and forming the plywood veneer skin for the fuselage. We had to build our own plywood press, 25 feet long by four feet wide: no simple task. We then laid-up three plys, mahogany and poplar. The forward section had to have an additional ply of each wood, making it 40% stronger and thicker. The bulkheads were made of 7-ply and the wing rib formers of 1/8-inch, 3-ply, neither of which was commercially available. This was a

Third and Sunset - Venice - 1920 (note young Thurlow, right)

rather complex and painstaking procedure and fully utilized Deyette's woodworking skills.

We started producing the plane's structure as soon as I'd assembled all of the raw materials: steel tubing, lumber, fabric, and a myriad of other items. My crew all pitched-in making benches, racks, shelves and jigs. We had scant enough tools, and when it came to making the spars and similar parts we took them to a nearby planing mill. Wanting to make this airplane a showpiece, I nickle-plated all of the exposed fittings and gave the mahogany fuselage a glistening piano finish. We even woodgrain-painted the metal parts abutting the mahogany. The art of acetylene welding was just developing and I got Otto Timm to use this new technique on the exhaust manifolds and fuel tanks, even though it wasn't specified in the drawings.

Starting a Liberty engine was a tough job. It took a chain of at least three or four people hand-in-hand, cranking it by pulling the propeller. I figured this chore would be pretty difficult in the boondocks where Brand would be flying, so I installed an electric starter. It was one of the first in an airplane and made it easy to start those 400 horses by simply pressing a button. We had the best automobile custom upholsterers do a super-deluxe job on the cockpits using the finest English whipcord and

127

Waterman Type 3 L-400 Airplane

The latest product of the airplane manufacturers of Southern California is the Waterman three place De Lux airplane recently completed and tested at Venice by the Waterman Aircraft Manufacturing Company, a description and general specifications of which appear below.

General Specifications

Motor, 400 H. P. Liberty.
Weight, empty, 2800 lbs.
Weight, loaded, 4135 lbs.
Useful load, 1335 lbs.
Speed, max., 126 M. P. H.
Speed, landing, 45 M. P. H.
Speed, cruising, 105 M. P. H.
Climb, 10,000 ft. in 8 min.
Ceiling, pilot only, 30,000 ft.
Ceiling, one passenger, 25,000 ft.
Ceiling, two passengers, 22,000 ft.
Loading, per squ. ft., 8.9 lbs.
Loading, per H. P., 10.3 lbs.
Spread, upper and lower, 43 ft. 6 in.
Chord, 5 ft. 6 in.
Total lifting area, 475 squ. ft.
Wing curve, R. A. F. 15.
Gap, 5 ft. 1 in.
Stagger, 26 in.
Dihedral, none.
Sweep back, none.
Range, full speed, 500 miles.
Range, cruising speed, 600 miles.

AREAS

Ailerons, 4 . . . . .60 squ. ft.
Elevators, 2 . . . . .25 " "
Hor. Stabilizer . . . . .18 " "
Fin . . . . 5 " "
Rudder . . . . .13 " "

WEIGHTS

Fuselage, complete with seats, tanks, controls, instruments and accessories . . . .   700 lbs
Motor complete with ignition battery and prop. . . . .   880 "
Radiators . . . .   125 "
12 Gal. water. . . . .   75 "
Tail surfaces . . . .   90 "
Self starter and battery. . . . .   85 "
Landing gear . . . .   135 "
Wings, struts, ailerons, fittings and wires . . . .   710 "

Total weight, empty, ... 2800 lbs

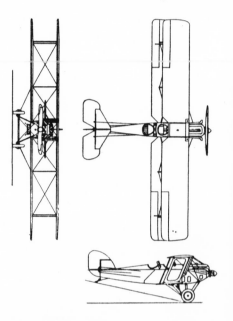

WATERMAN TYPE 3-L400
WATERMAN AIRCRAFT MFG CO
VENICE, CAL.

THE ACE
September 1920

French plush with carpets of velvet. And, we fitted the nonbreakable windscreen with sidewings, just like a sporty runabout. One other item drew quite a bit of comment: *"although nobody has ever complained of the dust above the clouds, the plane is equipped with a cellarette (that will defy government detection), just for such emergencies."* This was at the height of Prohibition, mind you!

128

One of our toughest problems was how to get enough gas aboard for the round trip to Mono Lake. We finally accomplished this by a rather ingenious but complicated 135-gallon fuel system. The system had a large tank in the LePere's center section, extra tanks feeding into this tank, and overflow provision between the tanks if one had a temporary excess of gasoline. It required that certain valves be turned off and on as one tank was emptied and another cut in. Just above the pilot's head was a gauge so that he could easily see what his fuel situation was. The transfer of fuel to the main tank was powered by tiny wind-driven pumps located in the plane's slipstream under the fuselage.

We were doing a very careful and painstaking job and I was particularly touchy about the finish, not only making it perfect but keeping it that way. We had a rule in the shop that no one carried any tools in his hip pockets because of the possibility of scratching a finished part of the plane. One of our employees was Lawson Thurlow, the son of my insurance agent who came to work for me when high school had let out in June. He was crazy about aviation and willing to work for almost nothing as the shop's 'gopher' (go-get-this and go-get-that) and general cleaner-upper in order to be around airplanes. One day after cleaning up in the cockpit he was climbing out when I heard an awful 'screech'. Lo and behold, a screwdriver in his hip pocket had just scored a big gash in the fuselage's piano finish. When he realized what had happened, he burst into tears and hightailed-it for the door. Mad as hell, I was right behind him when he hollered *"I quit, I quit!"* as I bellowed out louder *"Like hell you do - you're fired, you're fired!"*

(I didn't see much more of Lawson until 1938 when I attended the fancy affair celebrating Howard Hughes' round-the-world flight, and there sharing the hero honors was Lt. Thomas Lawson Thurlow, the flight's copilot and navigator. He was now a pilot and one of the Army's best navigators, and had taken leave to accompany Hughes. I was quite impressed with how far Hughes had come as a pilot, remembering that when we first met while filming *"Hell's Angels"* in 1929 he'd had several close scrapes with the rotary-powered Thomas-Morse. I was pleased when he said, *"Please remember that I am but one of five persons who made that trip, and being taller than any of the others, kept getting in the way and making a nuisance of myself. If you must praise any one individual, raise your shouts for Wiley Post, for by flying around the world alone in*

129

the time he did, and with but one eye, he made the most amazing flight that has ever occurred. I don't see how he ever did it. All pilots feel as I do about Wiley. He was a real hero." Thurlow was sharing in the country's excitement over this feat, *adulation rivaling Lindbergh's.* It was wonderful to see him so happy at one of the memorable peaks in a man's career, and I was deeply saddened to learn of his fatal crash several years later.)

After much work we finally got to putting the finishing touch on Brand's new airplane - his family's coat of arms on the fuselage. We also painted the plane's name, taken from the breath-taking Tioga Pass over the High Sierras between Mono Lake and Yosemite Valley. Brand knew his plane henceforth as the *"Tioga Eagle"*, whereas I termed it the *Waterman Model* 3L-400 (three-passenger, LePere, 400-hp).

And soon we had a pilot for this new ship. He was Gilbert Budwig, a former Air Mail pilot, barnstormer, and a fine, experienced pilot that also had done some test piloting for Loughead. After I hired him I put him to work on the complex fuel line installation on the Tioga Eagle, and later I had several flights with him in his Jenny to improve my own piloting skills. It wasn't long before "Bud" or "Buddy" (as we called him) suggested that he'd make the 'right' pilot for Mr. Brand and his new airplane. I thought that this would be a good idea - particularly because of his familiarity with the Liberty engine acquired while an Air Mail pilot. *(By the end of 1920, the Air Mail was being flown completely across the country; New York, Cleveland, Chicago, Omaha, Cheyenne, Salt Lake City and San Francisco.)*

Brand's *"Winged Palace"* was completed the end of July, 1920, and we took her over to Venice Field to put the wings on and do the final tune-up. Mr. Brand wanted a christening for his new plane, *"the most luxurious and modern plane ever constructed....equipped with a 400 hp Liberty motor, the first to be installed in a privately-owned plane",* so there was a band and many dignitaries assembled. A lovely Miss Mary Margaret O'Keefe of Moberly, Missouri, a houseguest of the Brands, christened *"...thee Tioga Eagle...with a perfectly good bottle of champagne."* I had thought it only right to wait for the new owner before turning the engine over for the first time, so when everything was all set I climbed into the pilot's cockpit and went through the starting procedures. I stepped on the starter button: it turned over a few times, went *"whoop, whoop, whoop"* and backfired. I tried several more times, getting nervous and sweaty, but the damn thing still wouldn't start. Boy! Was I embarrassed. Though disappointed, Brand was a good sport about it. The band and all the people finally went home, leaving me there dejectedely trying to figure just what-the-hell was wrong with that blankety-blank engine. I had certainly learned a lesson!

We went to the log book that'd accompanied the engine from Ford's factory. It showed that it had been assembled, run for ten hours on a test stand, completely disassembled, inspected, reassembled and run for another hour. It had then been packed for overseas shipment. Well, after a great deal of fiddling it became obvious that something was very wrong with the timing. After tearing into the engine *for three days* we finally found out that the left bank was advanced 60-degrees and the right bank retarded 45-degrees! How this engine had ever passed the indicated log inspections is a mystery. It was perhaps typical of some of the monkey business that went on in wartime production, about which there had been quite a scandal.

Anyway, after reengaging the valve gearing we finally got it timed properly and it ran like a jeweled railroad watch. Bud got into the pilot's cockpit and I in the sumptuous passenger compartment - much too nice to be simply called a "cockpit" - and away we went on the first flight. We took off in the usual manner from Venice Field, flying west towards the ocean where we then usually turned south. In the middle of the turn the engine started cutting out like it was going to stop, and we were over a swampy area with no place to land. Bud worked feverishly on the various fuel controls and, thanks to his knowledge of how they worked he was able to figure out a combination that got the fuel flowing. (Later we analyzed the trouble. We depended upon gravity feed to move the fuel from the top center-section tank to the carburetor, which was below the tank and considerably forward. However, the rapid acceleration of the plane would overcome the force of gravity, and stop the fuel flow.) By figuring out how to apply double-pressure to the system, Bud had succeeded in forcing the fuel through to the engine. But he'd caused so much pressure to build up in the tank that it was swelling like a pregnant pup and was spraying gasoline all over me. This added pressure was also enriching the fuel mixture in the carburetor so that the engine was belching raw flames from the exhaust. Damn, I was sure we were going to catch fire!

131

Waterman Type 3 L-400 "Best California Made Airplane" 1921

132   *"Brand's Winged Palace" - passenger compartment, left;
pilot's cockpit (note: coat of arms; pilot's fuel guage)*

Tioga Eagle - Brand Aerodrome - 1920 (note Moorish-style hangar)

Bud kept his cool and did a beautiful job of manipulating the various valves and controls while landing. As we touched down he cut all the switches, I had the fire extinguisher ready, and we piled-out as soon as we stopped, expecting that at any moment the plane would go up in flames. Luckily, nothing happened and after the engine cooled down we made corrections to make damn sure that it wouldn't happen again.

The *"finest plane in America"* (valued at $30,000, a princely sum then) was soon delivered to a very proud Leslie Brand, and on April 1, 1921, he threw quite a party, *"attendence via aeroplane only,"* at the L.C. Brand Aerodrome:

> *"The L.C. Brand Aerodrome is located along the foothills between Glendale and Burbank about five miles north of the Mercury-Rogers Field at Hollywood. The field is 1,800 feet long. To enter, glide over small trees at the foot of the field and land on "T" towards the hanger. D.H.'s can cross the trees low at 85 miles per hour without danger of over-shooting."*

133

Everyone came by air including a fellow named Hamelin by parachute. I flew with Barney Oldfield as my passenger - *it was his first airplane ride!*

After a couple years of flying the Tioga Eagle, Brand presented it to Lowell Smith in recognition of his commanding the *"First Around-the-World"* flight in 1924. Lowell had been one of my students at Berkeley and it seemed fitting to me that he be awarded a Waterman airplane, even though the planes the Army had used were Douglas World Cruisers.

The fear of fire that Bud and I had experienced was most terrifying to aviators in those days. Being in an aircraft on fire was the same as being burned at the stake. The flames quickly engulfed the wood, cloth and dope fuselage, leaving only two choices, jump or burn.

The solution was a parachute. Grant Morton made the first parachute jump from an aeroplane, a Wright, at Venice in 1911; "Tiny" Broadwick was the first woman to parachute from an aeroplane - in Los Angeles in 1913. Leslie Irvin, the pioneer Los Angeles exhibition parachute jumper, working with an Army group headed by Floyd Smith at McCook Field, perfected the back-pack chute in 1919 from the earlier concepts of Leo Stevens and Charles Broadwick. The Army started using chutes at McCook Field in 1921 as a result of an order from Colonel Bane. One of my Berkeley students, Harold Harris, was the first to use one there in 1922, escaping safely from an out-of-control Loening PW-2. But parachutes in civilian hands were extremely rare until the early Thirties.

Therefore, with an airplane that could become a fiery holocaust in seconds, and parachutes either too rare, novel or expensive ($350), we ended-up having a tremendous respect for fire. Many people thought that the all-metal planes were fire safe, but the first ones we saw, the German Junkers, easily caught fire because of ruptured fuel lines. They had fuel lines located in the bottom of the fuselage, and if the plane made a belly landing, the friction and sparks would ignite the fuel. Cecil deMille had had his share of problems with an early version of this plane.

When I first arrived in Venice Field in 1919, it was the first major airfield around Los Angeles. Crawford was assembling airplanes there from a great collection of parts, and also had a crude passenger-carrying business with Frederic "Doc" Whitney as his pilot. Rumor had it that Doc was 'well off', but this was not true. He was self-taught and, because of

134

his age and having to wear glasses, hadn't flown in the war; Doc and I were to become very close friends. Also, there was Edward (Red) Unger who had been a noted balloonist and parachute jumper. He lived in a small trailer near the field with his two young daughters and an older son, Ivan (a Hollywood stunter-to-be) for whom he was both father and mother. Being an ex-balloonist, he was good at sewing their clothes, a necessity for that vocation. Red was quite a ballyhoo artist and sold the tickets for the Crawford-Whitney flying enterprise. He also had a Graflex camera and would take a photograph as the passengers alighted, all goggled and helmeted, from their exciting flight. Most folks that'd paid $5 for the ride would also cough-up an extra $2.50 for the picture.

Venice Field soon became the center of barnstorming and carnival-flying, and because of its nearness to Hollywood was the birthplace of movie stunt-flying. One of the first movie pilots was Frank Stites, a pioneer pilot from 1911 Dominguez days who was killed on March 16, 1915, while stunting for Universal Film Company. Later, more-foolhardy movie stunting evolved from Ormer Locklear's suicidal antics first demonstrated when he had climbed out of the cockpit of his Army biplane in 1917. He was then severely remonstrated by his superiors (just like Petr Nesterov), but soon went on to wingwalking and many other stunts until his fatal crash near deMille Field No.2, August 2, 1920.

As the word got out about the money to be made doing stunts for the movies and newsreels, skads of broke daredevil pilots headed for Venice Field. There was always a bunch hanging around, ready and willing for a price to do almost anything they or someone else dreamed up. Almost every pilot was expert at the standard fare of aerobatics: loops, barrel rolls, falling leafs and spins, including virtually all of Beachey's repertoire (page 98). But it was a select few that excelled at real stunt flying, the kind that'd get the audiences squealing and hanging on to their seats.

The best of these was Frank Clarke, whom Al Wilson and Swede Meyerhoffer had taught to fly just a year-or-so before I arrived in Venice. Frank became a legend, and his stunting and hair-breadth scrapes with death were almost too perilous and spectacular to believe. Frank and the others, in addition to the then common wing walking, always had some new variation or stunt to try, such as plane changing. Imagine two planes flying so close together so that a man could clamber from one to

135

another - with no parachute! *Once, the the changer, Al Wilson, slipped and was free-falling through the air, and Frank dove his plane under him, catching Al on his top wing.* Another of Frank's tricks was to take off solo, and then leave the cockpit and scramble over the plane from end to end. Frank got his nickname, "Spooks", from the rigging of his Canuck (Canadian JN4) with hidden controls - he would disappear deep into the cockpit and the plane would appear as if it were flying itself. Frank failed in one trick - trying to catch a plane while running on the ground - but he was successful in changing from horse to plane, plane to car, and plane to train. And, once he even landed his biplane on a moving train.

Hollywood - plane to car - ca. 1921

Possibly his most foolhardy stunt was for the 1921 movie *"Stranger Than Fiction"*. The producers wanted him to fly off of a building in a chase scene. (Silas Christofferson had first done this in 1912, flying a Curtiss-copy off Portland's Multnomah Hotel; and Ormer Locklear did it in 1920 in the movie *"The Skywayman"*, flying off of San Francisco's St. Francis Hotel.) For his stunt Frank had me rework his Canuck by installing a more powerful engine, a Hall-Scott Liberty-4, and strengthening the entire airframe for stunting and rigorous aerobatics. The plane was then dismantled and carted to the top of the new Pacific Electric Railway Building, 13-stories tall in downtown LA, where it was then reassembled. With the law literally on Frank's heels trying to prevent this stunt, he took off on a special 100-foot wooden ramp. My heart skipped a beat as he dipped out of sight for a couple of seconds before gaining enough airspeed to swoop away over the city and back to Rogers Field.

In 1927 Frank planned to fly a J5-powered Fisk International, the "Miss Hollydale", in the Dole "Pineapple Derby." It was a hapless entry as he failed to make the start, but that may well have been a lucky break! From 1927-1929 he was Howard Hughes' chief pilot for the filming of *"Hell's Angels."*

Also around the field were many others, each a character in his own right: Joe "the flying tailor" Hoff, who'd built Frank Clarke's first plane and was later killed in a crash; Al Wilson's brother Herb; B.H. DeLay; Al Johnson; Al Kennedy; Howard Patterson; Mark Campbell; Otto's brother Wally Timm; Art Goebel; Eldred Remlin; Ray Robinson; Howard Batt; Frank Tomick; Mark Owen...gad! so many, and so many more that I've forgotten. What a gang of flyers they were!

Orvar S. Thorsen (Swede) Meyerhoffer was one of the most interesting characters. He was a very rough and tough fellow, and quite a lady's man from all the tall tales he spun, *("I've had 27 cases of the 'clap', and got over every one - except the first.")* Swede had been a well-known aviator since 1911. During the war he'd been flying for the Loughead brothers in Santa Barbara when they built their large F-1 flying boat, which John Northrop helped design. This was only the second airplane built by Loughead, but from the way they advertised it you'd have thought they built dozens. After the war Swede had landed his flying boat, with *"Swede"* painted on the bow, at North Island after interfering with the military's flying operations. They were so mad at him that they wouldn't even help him fly it off, making him dismantle it and truck it away.

Soon after, he headed for Venice Field to continue his escapades. The largest Easter Sunrise Service in Southern California was held at Mount Rubidoux near Riverside, and I remember Swede returning from

137

what he considered a very successful expedition. He swooped down upon the assembled multitude just when they were reciting the Lord's Prayer, sending them cowering and terrified in all directions. He was immensely proud of that.

Swede's mechanic was Jimmy Hester. When he turned the propeller to start the Hall-Scott A7A engine Swede would always say, *"Hang onto it, Jimmy; it won't hurt you,"* scoffing at the danger inherent in this operation. For a husky man, turning-over an engine this small was no great chore, but as I've mentioned, a larger engine would take a chain of several men to turn the prop over. On March 20, 1920 Swede found himself without Jimmy around, and he was pulling his engine over alone. Swede slipped just as it started and the propeller blade struck him, spelling *'finis'* to the man whose slogan was *"Flyers may come, flyers may go, but the Swede goes on forever."* Swede was then with the Gates Flying Circus, and after the mishap this message was wired to the San Francisco home office: *"Swede cranked prop. Prop killed Swede. Send new prop."*

Another flyer, Clarence Prest, who'd worked with me on the first Brand plane, had a small biplane named *"Poison, Dose One Drop"*. It was an exhibition job powered with a Gyro rotary engine which used about a gallon of castor oil an hour. At $5 per gallon, Clarence didn't do much flying. One day in 1920 we passed the hat and raised enough money for him to give us a demonstration of his fine airplane. Upon completion of the show, he landed, hit a soft spot in the field and flipped the plane onto its nose. I guess you could say that it'd had its 'one drop', and it wasn't so 'poisonous' after all.

Of course, during this period I was doing quite a bit of flying but nothing that could be described as daredevil. In fact, on January 23, 1921, I instigated through our Aero Club of Los Angeles one of the first complaints against *reckless aerial driving* when Peter Manshauer was hauled in and fined $50 for stunting too low over Venice. I guess I still remembered my 1910 crackup and had learned my lesson. Anyway, I was too busy with Brand's Mono and Tioga Eagles and other odds and ends to worry about breaking my own neck. Quite a bit of my time was spent in making engine changes, usually installing a more-powerful engine in place of the Jenny's OX-5 (90-hp), such as the Hall-Scott L-4 and L-6, and eventually the Liberty V-12s.

138

*(l-r) Me, Goldie Goldsworthy, Frank Clarke, Jimmy Hester, Wally Timm,
Joseph Hoff, Prest - pilot, Swede Meyerhoffer, Harry Sperl, Al Wilson,
George Stephenson, Otto Timm and Mark Campbell*

Sometime later (1925), a stunting group called *"The Thirteen Black
Cats"* flew out of Burdett Airport on Western Avenue & 102nd Street.
Mark Campbell was one of their luminaries. Working primarily for Fox-
Movietone Newsreel, they were ready and willing to take on most any
stunt for a fee - from a $1,500 mid-air collision down to a mere $75 for
nosing a plane over on its back upon landing. Each member had to have
made at least one parachute jump in order to qualify, and one chap,
Freddie Osborne, had an inspiration as to how he would make his jump.
A mechanic and an avid motorcyclist, he strapped on his chute, climbed
on his motorcycle and raced down Wilshire Boulevard to where it dead-
ends at the palisade dropping a couple-of-hundred feet down to the
beach. As he hurtled into space, he pulled the ripcord and his chute
opened just as he'd planned. The only problem came in landing when he
alit astraddle the Pacific Electric Railroad's power lines at the bottom of

139

the cliff. *(In those days Southern California had an excellent commuter trolley network in "the Big Red Cars" of Henry Huntington's Pacific Electric Railway, a thousand mile system covering virtually all of the LA Basin. It was put out of business by the illegal collusion of General Motors, Firestone and Standard Oil just after World War II.)*

Al Wilson had been flying with the "Hollywood Set" since 1917, about when Harry Crawford had obtained a British-bound Jenny that had been dropped into New York's harbor. Crawford reconditioned it and sold it to Cecil deMille. (Cecil B deMille *"founded Hollywood"* in 1913 when he made *"The Squaw Man"*, the first feature-length film.) DeMille, having the only privately-owned Jenny in the country, enlisted Al as his instructor and pilot, and proceeded to establish deMille Field No. 1 at Crescent (now Fairfax) and Melrose, just south of Hollywood. (We'll discuss more about deMille later.) I'd first met Wilson in 1919 while I was still trying to peddle the U.S. Aircraft surplus. Al later had Otto Timm build him a replica of a 1911 Curtiss pusher which he used in sham dogfights at the 1928 National Air Races in Los Angeles, where one day he was tangling with a Pitcairn-Cierva autogiro and got sucked into its whirling blades and crashed to his death. I was not particularly distressed, other than the shock of watching it; we'll learn more later about my dislike for Al Wilson.

Also around Venice Field were a couple of men that had been among the few enlisted pilots in the Army: Frank Tomick, *"one of the shrewdest pilots on the West Coast"*; and John Montijo, the instructor that first soloed Amelia Earhart. John would do some designing and building of airplanes, and later would lose his life while flying the air mail over the Rockies. John's son would be a student of mine, circa 1940, when I would be teaching again.

Crawford turned the operation of Venice Field over to B.H. DeLay, who had gotten another movie mogul, Thomas Ince, to sponsor him and the field was named Ince Aviation Field in 1919. (Ince was then one of Hollywood's greatest, and in spite of the troubles that he and William S. Hart would have he was sharing the spotlight as a "director-general" of Triangle Film Corporation with D.W. Griffith and Mack Sennett.)

DeLay was crippled (it looked to me as if he'd had polio) and his father always helped him in and out of his plane. He was in the passenger-

140

carrying business, and on days that business was brisk, he seemed to sit in that cockpit for hours. Being crippled didn't affect his ability to fly, though, but it occasionally slowed down some potential customers.

In 1923, after Ince's death, Venice Field was closed down and DeLay moved over to Santa Monica's newly named *Clover Field*. Frank Clarke had done a lot of flying in *"Jail Bait"* (so-named because of Chaplin's Mann Act charges), the first octagon-fuselage OX-5-powered plane built by Ed Fisk. It was a beautiful airplane which he could really make perform, though he never owned it. Apparently DeLay thought he could fly it as well as Clarke, for he bought Jail Bait and in July, 1923, took it up. But he wasn't the pilot that Frank was and proceeded to pull the wings off, killing both himself and his passenger, Ruel Short.

With their none-too-powerful OX-5 engines and amply-buttressed frameworks, Jennys and Canucks were the ideal airplanes to nurture the birth of barnstorming and wingwalking. Their birdcage, or cat's cradle, of struts, wires, king posts, braces, wings, landing gear spreader bars and wing skids meant that there was rarely a spot without a grip - although hardly discernable to the open-mouthed viewers on the ground. The unique juxtaposition of the Jenny and hundreds of itching aviators looking for something *"after they'd seen Parree"* created a part of *"that crazy age"*, luminescent though brief. We'll never see anything like it again.

This epoch of the *"take any chance, do any stunt"* flyers was gaudy, thrilling and unreal - *"It was an occupation of few veterans."* In 1923 there were 85 killed and 162 injured while barnstorming or stunting. Parachuting and low-level acrobatics were the most dangerous. The early movie flyer was often assigned unconscionable stunts to perform as his life was considered cheap. I lost many friends, their last flights often ending on the cutting room floor. A typical example in 1932 was *"The Lost Squadron"*, starring Richard Dix that advertised: *"Facing a flaming death...for $50! Real war heroes fight the gory BATTLE OF HOLLY-WOOD. Once he risked his life for his country...now he takes the same deadly chances to give you a moment's thrill!"*

One of the best-known pilots was Dick Grace. He was good, but not as good as Frank Clarke, and survived almost forty deliberate, controlled crashes. Grace conceived the *"Squadron of Death"* with about twenty-five Hollywood stunters, eighteen of whom were eventually killed, and

141

four who would never fly again. *Between 1925 and 1930 almost 50 aviators were killed while stunting for the movies.*

And so from memories that are now very quiet and somewhat sad, for each of those fellows had a tremendous spark for life and many were dear to me, it is time to talk of things on a broader scale.

What was to be called Clover Field in Santa Monica (named after Lt. *Greayer Clover,* a World War I flyer killed in France) started out being used by flyers while Venice Field was still in its heyday. It was part of the Garland farm used for growing hay, in the southeasterly corner of Santa Monica. There was a windbreak of tall eucalyptus trees (which look so native in California but were imported from Australia) along the north and east boundaries, which shortened its usefulness as a landing field. But there was still plenty of room for the airplanes that we were then flying. At certain times of the year there was a huge haystack smack in the middle of the field which would disappear when the balers came, but it certainly provided some interesting incidents.

Early in the 1920's Catron & Fisk, with Otto Timm as their chief mechanic and test pilot, built a triplane at Playa del Rey powered by three modified and lightened Ford Model T engines - a favorite powerplant then. They transported it to a crude hangar by the eastern windbreak at Clover Field for its flight testing. There wasn't any graded runway, just the normal farming ground which was standard fare in those days. After they got the plane assembled, Otto proceeded to give it its first test flight. As he started his takeoff roll, the machine seemed to be very sluggish and had trouble lifting from the ground. Well, Otto must have been so engrossed in trying to get airborne that he forgot about the haystack. He ran pell-mell into it, banging up the triplane and his own dignity, too.

The gang at Venice Field was a wild lot, and Clover Field often played a part in some fine, sometimes bizarre amusements. One of their favorites was to take a good looking gal for a plane ride, and then all of a sudden have engine failure conveniently over Clover Field. They'd have to make a 'forced landing', but they always seemed to have enough propulsion remaining after touching down to make it to the haystack - preferably the southwesterly side, completely hidden from the roads bordering the field. Frequently we observed, after they'd made their 'engine repairs' and returned to Venice Field, that the young lady had wisps of straw in her hair and sometimes clinging to her dress.

142

While getting ready to build Brand's Tioga Eagle I was scouting around and spotted a skeleton of an airplane under construction in a backyard. I got out of my car, and closer inspection revealed that it was being expertly built from Jenny parts and custom-fabricated members. I figured that here was a hidden talent that I was not availing myself of, and knocked at the door. I learned that it was being built by a young chap that drove a milk route in the wee-morning hours and worked upon the airplane the rest of the day. His name was L. Morton Bach. I gave the housewife my card, requesting that he drop by my place and talk to me about work. A couple of days later Bach showed up, and I hired him for fabrication on the fuselage fittings of the Tioga Eagle. After two or three weeks, though, I was disappointed by the amount of work he finished and began to think that the 30 cents-an-hour I was paying him was being wasted. I often observed him looking over drawings other than the ones he was supposed to be working with, and I should have realized that he was only studying things in order to do a better job - but living up to my *'slave-driver'* reputation, I fired him. He then went across the street to Stephenson's and became a valuable employee working under Otto Timm. *Six years later I'd be working for Morton Bach!*

Shortly after I'd seen Bach's fuselage framework, Clarence Prest also spotted it. He, too, contacted Bach, but with the idea of mating a newly-designed wing that he'd built to Bach's fuselage. This they did, making their *"Polar Bear"* plane. They then took off on a barnstorming trip ballyhooed as *"Mexico-to-Siberia"*. They started from Tijuana in July 1921 and flew north to Canada and then towards Alaska and Siberia. When they took off Morton didn't know how to fly, so they rigged the plane with controls in each cockpit and Clarence taught Mort as they went along. Somewhere in northwest Canada they crashed their airplane, and when they returned to Southern California, even with no *"Siberian Gold"* they'd still had one memorable expedition!

Meanwhile, Cecil deMille's Mercury Aviation Co. established a second airfield, naming it deMille Field No. 2. It was located just north of Wilshire between Crescent (Fairfax) and La Cienega - just across the street from Chaplin Airdrome.

Around this time I became an active member of the Aero Club of Southern California, with George Harrison, secretary, and K. Turner,

143

president, both ex-balloonists and avid aviation boosters. (I was later a director, and chairman at one time or another of the Industrial Committee - the aircraft manufacturers.) At one of our early meetings Neta Snook, a flying instructor working out of Kinner Aeroplane and Motor Corporation's airport in south Los Angeles (at Long Beach Boulevard, west side, and Tweedy Road, now in South Gate), brought a young student, Amelia Earhart, to introduce her to us. This young lady had first gotten the flying bug while watching an exhibition in Long Beach.

I was quoted in Amelia's *First Flight,* page 39, saying about her instructor:

> *"In those days we were not quite sure as to whether 'Snooky' was a man or woman, as few of us ever saw her except in a pair of dirty coveralls...she was one of the first women to take up flying after the War."*

At another meeting Doc Whitney suggested *a feature race between identically Curtiss OX-5 - powered planes* for our second airmeet at the new Beverly Speedway (a board race track southeast of the intersection of Santa Monica and Wilshire Boulevards).

> *A comment on board speedways. These wooden race tracks were banked as much as 52-degrees, permitting much higher speeds than a track like Indianapolis which had a less-than-10-degree bank. However, there was the danger of going over the top! The first board speedway was the Playa del Rey Motordrome, south of Venice, where Roehrig, Masson and Walsh flew in 1910 (page 33).*

This idea was immediately accepted for it was felt that a race between specially-built planes would be spectacular. Emory Rogers had Otto Timm start designing a plane for this race - the *"Pacific Standard C-1"*. He was in good position to do this for he had now bought George Stephenson's Pacific Airplane & Supply and also Chaplin Airdrome. (Sydney Chaplin's time was now being devoted almost exclusively to his brother's interests.) At the same time, Captain Lionel Briggs, deMille's Mercury Aviation manager, contracted with me to build a plane to beat Rogers.

144

*The deMille-Mercury "Gosling" - Waterman-built, OX-5 powered
and capable of 146 mph - 1921*

Therefore we were a pair of across-the-street rivals: deMille and Rogers on Wilshire; and in Venice, Waterman and Pacific squared-away across Sunset Avenue. The newspapers reported our progress:

> *"...great aeronautical mystery prevails at Venice...the windows of each factory have been painted and employees of each plant are forbidden to enter the other. The cause of the vigilance is that within each factory a special racing monoplane is being constructed...both to embody novel constructional ideas...capable of flying at more than 120 miles an hour."*

Other planes being readied for the race included a triplane built by Venice's Catron & Fisk, a rebuilt Ed Fisk biplane and the *Polson Special* that Thor Polson built for Long Beach daredevil Earl Daugherty.

Our work went earnestly on - and as we were nearing completion, I felt sure that we had a winner because I'd sneak-timed the Rogers plane and calculated that ours was about 5 mph faster.

145

Eldred Remlin, then flying for Mercury, was selected as the pilot for our plane named *"Gosling"*. This name evolved from an earlier deMille venture, *one of America's first airlines.* In 1919 deMille imported two German Junkers all-metal transports and initiated *"aero passenger service"* between Los Angeles and San Diego. These Junkers - with *"Goose"* painted on their wing - had been tagged *"Tin Geese"* long before the Ford-Stout trimotor *"Tin Goose"*. Even though there wasn't any similarity between my racer and the Junkers, deMille considered them part of the same gaggle.

"Gosling" with me and Eldred Remlin - July 1921

The race was to be during Elks Week, July 16, 1921, and everyone's eyes were on our two racers. Before the race there was the usual death-defying aerobatics by Frank Clarke in his Waterman-rebuilt Fokker and Earl Daugherty in his Nieuport Special, plus several other hair-raising aerial sideshows.

146

Neta Snook and Amelia Earhart and her "Kanary" - July 16, 1921
(Note Lawrance 3-cylinder radial engine)

Amelia Earhart was there with Neta Snook and the plane she bought while still a student pilot, her yellow *KinneR Airster*. Amelia, in her new sporty patent leather coat, hadn't yet bobbed her hair. It was still in the fashion of the day, very long and held in control by a hairnet. She wouldn't be licensed by the NAA as a pilot for another two years. Later, I'd become intimately acquainted with her "Kanary" - to my chagrin - as we shall see.

The Curtiss Cup Race was the main attraction. It was a two mile course with two pylons, one in the center of the speedway and another a mile outside, but still in full view of the grandstands. The racers zoomed off, going first around a "scattering pylon" dreamed up by Doc Whitney in order to "separate the men from the boys" - a system later adopted for all closed-course racing. It quickly became apparent that our Gosling and the Rogers plane were well-matched. However Emory Rogers was

147

AERIAL AGE WEEKLY, July 25, 1921   463

THE WATERMAN RACING MONOPLANE

THIS machine was designed and built to compete in the coming Los Angeles Speedway races to be held on July 10th, and therefore only three factors were taken into consideration in its design. These are: As fast a machine as possible with a stock OX-5 motor, a machine with as great a visibility as possible and at the same time one that would handle well on the sharp turns. The resultant design has therefore not been one of particular beauty or graceful lines nor one of low landing speed or great climb. However, after due consideration of the various types, it was decided to build a machine of the parsol monoplane type with a thin wing section.

In order to completely streamline the required motor, it was necessary to build a fuselage of porportions larger than the orthodox. In this particular instance, however, this has become a very desirable feature, as the large keel area has proven to be indispensable in making a sharp turn at a high speed. Below are the general specifications of the machine:

General Specifications

Curtis OX-5 .... 90 h.p.
Weight, empty .... 885 lbs.
Useful load—pilot, 10 gal. gasoline, 12 quarts oil, 245 lbs.
Speed (maximum) .... 130 m.p.h.
Speed (landing) .... 60 m.p.h.
Speed (cruising) .... 110 m.p.h.
Load per sq. ft. .... 11.1 lbs.
Load per h.p. .... 12.5 lbs.
Spread .... 21 ft. 9 in.
Chord .... 66 in.

Total lifting area .... 112 sq. ft.
Wing curve .... U.S.A. 15
Stagger and sweep back .... None
Range (full speed) .... 120 miles
Range (cruising speed) .... 135 miles

Area

Rudder .... 5 sq. ft.
Fin .... 1½ sq. ft.
Ailerons .... 16 sq. ft.
Elevator .... 10 sq. ft.
Horizontal stabilizer .... 12 sq. ft.

Weights

Fuselage complete with tanks, seat, controls, instruments and accessories .... 224 lbs.
Motor complete with propeller .... 405 lbs.
Radiator .... 23 lbs.
Water .... 28 lbs.

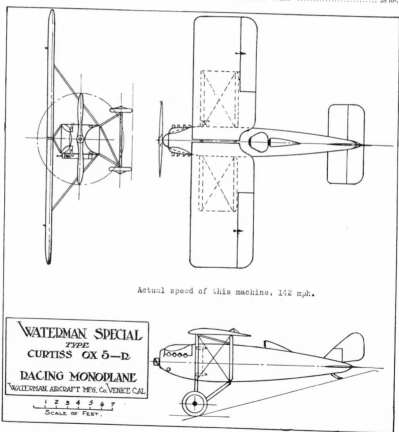

Actual speed of this machine, 142 mph.

WATERMAN SPECIAL
TYPE
CURTISS OX 5—R.
RACING MONOPLANE
WATERMAN AIRCRAFT MFG. Co. VENICE CAL.

1 2 3 4 5 6 7
SCALE OF FEET.

taking the pylons much tighter than Remlin and was stretching his lead a bit each lap on the turns. Whether this was the fault of Remlin or my plane I do not know. But the result was that Gosling, despite being faster (with a top speed of 146 mph), was losing ground steadily. At the end of the 15 laps we'd lost and were sorely disappointed. But in that day's Aerial Transport Race to Oceanside and back, 111 miles, Gosling proved its stuff by winning going away (but the Pacific plane was not in this race).

Cecil deMille used Gosling in several movies and then sold it for a token $50 to Art Goebel, later the winner of the "Pineapple Derby", who named it "Lightning". But it did not fly well since it no longer had the proper engine and propeller, and he soon resold it.

Art Goebel and "Lightning" (ex-Gosling)

After Gosling I was primarily involved in reconstruction and altera- tion jobs for either Pacific Airplane & Supply or Hall-Scott. Hall-Scott had acquired several German Fokker D7's, considered to be the hottest wartime fighter. 142 came to the United States as a result of the Treaty of Versailles - *the first time a specific war machine was ever demanded,* and many were later collected for the filming of *"Hell's Angels"* in 1927. But now Hall-Scott figured that they were an excellent demonstration airplane for their engines and I reworked one by installing a Hall-Scott Liberty-6 and adding a second cockpit, at about the same time I re- worked Frank Clarke's Canuck for the Railway Building sequence.

Sometime earlier a prominent jeweler, A.L. Markwell, propositioned that he would buy the first twin-engine OX-5-powered plane capable of carrying six people, even with only one engine. We all took a whack at this deal, but I could never get a written contract so I never speculated on it. However, George Stephenson did. He had Otto Timm design and build the airplane, but their *"Pacific Hawk"* could barely keep aloft on two engines, let alone one.

The typical situation then was noted by an Army Air Service performance report on a new twin-engined bomber of 1920 in which it was solemnly set forth as a result of thorough going tests that *"the ceiling with one engine has been determined to be 4,000 ft. below sea-level."*

Hall-Scott decided that this plane would be a good demonstrator and had me rebuild it, installing Liberty-6's. For the final proving flight Frank Clarke, Lee Scott, E.H. Baxter and myself clambered aboard. We climbed perfectly to 5,000 feet for the altitude test and then went out five or six miles over the ocean, when Frank suddenly discovered that we were almost out of gas. By now we were down to around 1,000 feet and he simply cut off one of the engines and easily flew the plane back to Venice Field, even circling once before coming in for a beautiful landing.

The plane, though, never quite met Markwell's stiff requirements and the project petered out. The last time that I saw it, it was abandoned to one side of Rogers Field, disintegrating, with its engines removed.

Stephenson also had me do some work on a couple of Standards. They'd sold one with a Liberty-6 to an Oklahoma Indian that appeared to have 'all the money in the world'. Everyone thought that his tribe had struck oil. Anyway, I was working on his plane but he never got to fly it. He was picked up as one of the most wanted men in the country. All those 'barrels of money' had come from a Texas train robbery! It wasn't long before the Federal marshalls trucked the plane away, too.

The other Standard I worked on was for Richard Burke, a young man who wanted it for commuting between his Pasadena home and his elegant 'cabin' in the mountains at Big Bear. We'll hear more about him.

During this period a wealthy young sportsman, David Davis, contacted me. He and Donald Douglas had formed a partnership to construct an airplane that Douglas had designed for a nonstop transcontinental flight. This airplane, to be called *"Cloudster"*, was already well-

150

along in its construction at this time but they needed additional space. Their original quarters in Santa Monica were very cramped, and they thought that they might use some of the extra space I then had at Third and Sunset. But I discouraged the idea, feeling that I had well-enough with my own operations and I didn't want to become involved with anyone else. I've ruminated many times over this episode. If I'd taken Davis up on his proposition it may well have led to some interesting things, seeing just where Donald Douglas was to go in later years!

The work that I had done in rebuilding the Pacific Hawk had taught me about planes of this type, with the result that Cliff Durant contacted me to design a twin-engine plane for his Durant Aircraft Corp. in Oakland. Cliff, the son of William C. Durant (founder of General Motors), was a famous race car driver in addition to being a sportsman aviator. I'd completed his plans, sending them and my bill to him when another much greater opportunity appeared.

The Navy was about to issue a design competition for three new torpedo planes, each from a different manufacturer. After corresponding with my old friend Holden Richardson, now in charge of aeronautical design for the Navy, I started preparing my concepts. I had most of the preliminary layouts completed when I had a chance to hitch a ride to the Bay Area and collect the $50 that Durant still owed me. At that time we were living in a small bungalow on Washington Boulevard in Venice. After packing my bag for several days of travel, not knowing for sure just when I'd be heading back home, I kissed Carol and little Janie goodby.

Upon arrival in Oakland, Durant immediately paid me and I then decided to head for Washington to pin-down the Navy contract. I hurriedly wrote Carol, gave her my itinerary, enclosed Durant's check and after mailing the letter took the train east.

In Washington I met with Richardson and several Navy individuals to get the rules, specifications and procedures right. Just when I was ready to leave for home I ran into Corliss Moseley, another of my Berkeley students. He had won the first *Pulitzer Race* (1920), and was thus posted to the staff of the legendary Billy Mitchell. General Mitchell led our airmen in the Great War, was Assistant Chief of the Army Air Service and a strident voice for 'air power' and an independant Air Force. *He had just demonstrated its potentials (July 1921) by bombing and sinking the*

151

"unsinkable" German battleship Ostfriesland in only 25 minutes with a flight of Martin bombers.

Mitchell's staff, 1920: (l-r seated) Maj. Van Nostrand, Lt. Col. Sherman, Mitche, Lt. Col. Hartney, Capt. Corliss C. Moseley. (standing) Lts. Wheeler and Olmstee Capts. Miller and Wright, Lt. Schneeberger.

Actions of this type were not endearing Mitchell to the "old brass" and he was definitely *a burr under their saddle*. At this time, though, he was the most influential man in military aviation. Moseley told me that I was *playing for peanuts* with the Navy in comparison to a much bigger Army contract being set up at McCook Field. He also told me that Mitchell and his staff were taking the train that evening for Dayton and that it would be a good idea if I were on it, too.

I raced back to my hotel room, packed and, luckily, caught that train. I soon located Moseley and he introduced me to General Mitchell. The General and I then had a long conversation. He was fully aware of my activities and was fascinated with the LePere-variation that I'd built for Brand. He considered me to be a fully-qualified aircraft manufacturer, and he went over in detail the forthcoming contract for 200 Thomas-Morse MB3A pursuit planes. Fifty of these were already being manufactured by Thomas-Morse, and it was Mitchell's intention that 200 more be built by two to four different manufacturers, thus giving work to a broader segment of an industry then starved for work. These potentials dazzled me, having been building only one or two planes at any one time for the past year or two. A 50-plane contract was unheard of - and it surely was a helluva lot more than three Navy planes.

152

At McCook Field I was given every courtesy - being almost part of Mitchell's entourage. Then, I also discovered that my old friend, Colonel Thurman Bane, was chief of the Army's Experimental Station there. I was given access to anything about the Thomas-Morse I needed to know and I carefully studied the prototype, figuring its reproduction costs.

When I'd learned all that I could after three or four days, I decided to hurry home and prepare my bids. I bade Mitchell, Bane and Moseley goodby - but only after suggesting to Moseley that it'd be better for me to take his curvaceous lady, the *Pulitzer Trophy*, home with me rather than his railway expressing it to California. This most prized of trophies met with great acclaim upon arriving with me in Los Angeles.

It is a sad commentary that Ralph Pulitzer withdrew this trophy, so linked to Billy Mitchell, following his court-martial in 1925 which was a result of Mitchell's "final straw" statement about the Shenandoah tragedy - damning the military's administration. With Mitchell gone, no further government money would be spent on racing aircraft, thus eliminating this racing trophy.

However, when *"Lady Pulitzer"* and I arrived home in Venice she was surely more welcome than I! Golly, did I ever get a tongue-lashing from Carol - *"...just what nerve did you have leaving me and Janie for a month without any money and not even telling me where you were going!"* I listened in shocked disbelief as she recounted how the only way she knew where I had been was the arrival of parcel post packages full of my dirty laundry - from San Francisco, Washington, and even one from Dayton! I was dumfounded at such accusations for I had sent her the letter with an itinerary and the $50 check! Well, the whole thing was finally solved when, weeks later, the letter arrived, redirected by the dead letter office; I'd addressed it to Washington D.C., not Washington Boulevard in Venice!

It would be quite a spell before I'd be in Carol's good graces again. She and Janie were forced to eat chipped beef because they were fundless and accorded limited credit at the nearby grocery, and to this day creamed chipped beef is a forbidden dish in our home!

Now, as I proceeded to lay out my plans for bidding the Army's contract, I had a few moments to rethink my acquaintance with Billy Mitchell. While at McCook I'd been with him quite a bit and had watched him fly several different planes. I was greatly impressed with his ability to handle virtually any type of aircraft. He insisted upon personally flying every new plane, whether it was a Martin bomber or a little 3-cylinder Sperry Messenger. And whenever he got in an aircraft, you knew that he was the man in command and would do the flying. He left a wonderful impression upon me as a man not only with great flying skill, but also great intelligence and military astuteness; *he spelled out the Pearl Harbor scenario in the '20's almost exactly as the Japanese would do it in 1941.* I thought of him as a pilot's pilot in much the same way as *Aero Digest's* Frank Tichenor did when he wrote, *"He has done more for the cause of aviation than any other man in the nation's history except for the Wright Brothers."*

I put together bids on the Thomas-Morse in quantities of either 50 or 100 planes, disregarding a bid on the entire 200-plane quantity because of Mitchell's admonition that the Army did not intend to give the entire order to only one company. Then, while awaiting the outcome of the Army bid, I proceeded to prepare my concept for the Navy torpedo plane. I completed the specifications and three view drawings preparatory to submitting them, but held off doing so in anticipation of the Army order. It so happens that I still have those Navy drawings and the plane that I designed was very similar to those submitted by Douglas and Martin. Theirs, however, had 'stick & wire' fuselages whereas mine had welded tubing; and I planned to use the 600-hp Packard engine rather than the 400-hp Liberties. Also, my design had the torpedo carried within the plane's belly and released by clamshell doors.

I never submitted my Navy bid, though, and sometime later the Navy awarded contracts to Bill Stout (for an all-metal design) and to both Douglas and Martin. This Navy order was Douglas' start into much greater things. I have always felt that my design would have been one of those chosen - if only I'd submitted it.

Obliquely, I feel that I was somewhat instrumental in getting Donald Douglas underway. *In anticipation of receiving the Army's contract, I had worked with Mr. Fisher, deMille's business manager, lining up financing commitments. Then, to my utter dismay, when Boeing took the entire 200-plane contract I had the commitments but nothing to work on. These sources of funds then shifted over to Douglas and his principal backer, Harry Chandler, owner of The Los Angeles Times, and Douglas Aircraft*

154

was soon building their first military airplane, the Douglas DT-1 Navy tor-
pedo plane.

Regarding the Army contract which I'd put all of my eggs into, it turned out that I was low bidder on the 50 and 100-unit quantities. *But I didn't bother bidding the entire batch of 200, which Bill Boeing did - bidding $1,448,000 for the lot, or $7,240 per airplane. He was therefore substantially lower per plane than my lowest bid. The savings was enough so that the government elected to get as many planes for their dollar rather than spreading the business around as they had first planned. Boeing, with this largest of postwar aircraft contracts, was able to discontinue making furniture and devote his company's total energies to aircraft production.* Today Boeing and McDonnell Douglas are the two giants in the industry, slugging it out in a multi-billion-dollar market. Inadvertent as it was, I surely helped them get started. What a rueful thought that is!

During this 1920-1921 period few of us had any idea that the aircraft industry would someday grow to its present size. Those days were so very lean that no one could make any money out of aviation. We all lived by our wits and expected that anyone working for us would do likewise. Our employees would work for nothing or next to it just for the privilege of being around airplanes. At Waterman Aircraft Manufacturing Company I paid from nothing up to 65 cents per hour to my top man - except for Otto Timm. He got $1 because he usually worked on a specific job, and he had a speciality of oxy-acetylene welding (plus the fact that he supplied his own tanks and materials) so he could demand the higher pay. Clarence Deyette also was so skilled and resourceful that he, too, earned $1 an hour. However, this was balanced-out by several of my employees earning only 35 to 40 cents an hour - due in part to the scarcity of work combined with their fervent desire to build airplanes. There are people around, particularly those that later worked for more successful aircraft builders (Douglas, Boeing and Ryan, for example) who feel that they were underpaid in those days. But they forget that the reason any of us, including the bosses, were able to stay in business was because none of us earned much more than a living wage. It was the only way the industry survived those very skimpy years.

With the loss of both the Army contract and the Navy's developmental award, I was left with few options or potentials. The funds and resources of Waterman Aircraft Manufacturing were about nil. Later it

155

was written that *"all but a few dedicated men stuck to their trade of building airplanes during the lean 1920's,"* and they were certainly starting to lean heavily upon me. Down but not quite out, I was casting about for some way to keep my hand in aviation and food upon the table.

In those days Southern California, outside of Los Angeles proper, was one huge orange grove, and the grower's worst fears centered upon a citrus crop's killer - frost. The only way known then to combat a freeze was smudging. Containers filled with fuel oil were placed by the hundreds throughout the groves and then ignited when there was a possibility of a temperature drop to freezing. It is hard to imagine, but the air then became full of thick, black, oily smoke. If a breeze came up, smudge could cover the neighboring communities, leaving a residue of black film over almost everything and even filter inside homes if the occupants forgot to close windows. This could pose a public relations problem of almost insurmountable proportions. We'd just had one of the worst freezes on record which had resulted in a great amount of fruit and tree damage, and a terrible hue and cry from the communities where there had been a lot of smudging. The farmer was damned if he did smudge and doubly-damned if he didn't - for he'd then probably lose both his trees and his crop.

There was a move to outlaw smudge pots which prompted me to do some thinking on the problem. It was well-known among the ranchers that there was rarely frost damage if even a slight breeze was blowing. Though it wasn't well understood at the time, freezes occurred when there was a temperature inversion: a condition when the air is warmer a few hundred feet up than it is at ground level. If there was a bit of wind these two layers of air would mix, raising the ground temperature above freezing. But if there was no wind there was danger of a freeze, necessitating smudging.

One day at the field the idea of using airplane propellers to stir the air and create a wind was suggested. That idea fascinated me, and, combined with what I'd learned about the subject, I determined to do something about it. I got Chase Story, a custom propeller manufacturer, to work with me. Chase was feeling the economic pinch, too, for an awful lot of surplus propellers were hitting the market and he was enthusiastic about the possibilities. He worked with me, but we weren't partners: he

156

was working as my employee for $50-a-week, a wage which he was very happy to receive. Together we built a model of what we considered to be an ideal apparatus. It could be cheaply built from surplus aircraft materials, and would, theoretically, raise the temperature to above freezing in a grove of approximately 10 acres.

We then made arrangements to demonstrate our model to a group of ranchers in Covina, a small town about 25 miles east of Los Angeles. They'd been brutally hit by the last freeze (citrus growers, usually having groves of 10 to 20 acres, are called ranchers in California - where any property of an acre or more is often called a "rancho"). Chase and I set up our demonstration in the ballroom of the Elks Hall. We inflated toy balloons with gas, tied to each one a weight sufficient to keep it only a foot or two off the floor, positioned them throughout the room, and then put the wind machine in the center of the room. When we turned the machine on, the wind would cause the balloons to drift away. When they came to the edge of the room they would then rise and drift toward the center of the room - where the machine was - and then fall to their original position. We repeated this cycle over and over again, with the ballons being successively sucked-in and blown-out. The demonstration was successful to the tune of around $3,000 being collected which enabled us to build a full-scale unit.

Chase and I then moved to Covina, and 'camped' in the rear of the blacksmith shop that was fabricating the unit for us. After quite a search we decided that the best place to set up the machine was in a 20 acre grove a couple of miles west of Covina, owned by Irvin Reynolds, the local Buick dealer. For most of the summer we worked together setting up the citrus *"Heat Mill"* at Reynold's, and a second one for a walnut grove. The one for walnuts worked by blowing the air along the ground and under the trees rather than over and down as with the citrus. We also took advantage of some new knowledge gleaned from the ranchers. When there was a freeze and no apparent wind, as a matter of fact, there was always a very slight drift from the northeast. We, therefore, relocated the Heat Mill from dead center to the northeast quarter of the grove, thus ensuring more even coverage.

When we completed these units, I proceeded to draw up the ideas and concepts, and I was awarded a patent on the *Waterman Heat Mill* in 1924.

157

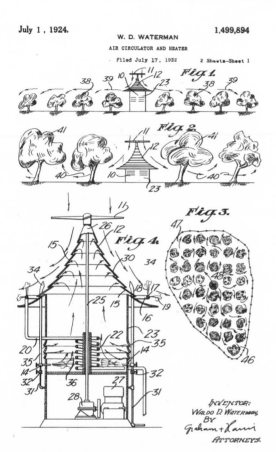

July 1 , 1924.

W. D. WATERMAN

1,499,894

AIR CIRCULATOR AND HEATER

Filed July 17, 1922

2 Sheets—Sheet 1

Citrus "Heat Mill" Patent

Walnut "Heat Mill" - 1922

Since I was now spending almost all of my time in Covina, we decided that we ought to live there. We moved into a small house in an orange grove near the center of Covina with Janie, who had just turned five. We thought about *how wonderful it would be to live in an orange grove,* but soon learned otherwise! The house was smack-dab in the middle of the grove. They had only removed four trees to make room for it and one could almost reach out any window and pick the fruit. *Hah!* An orange grove is a farming operation; it needs cultivating, often, with the resulting roar of the tractor, the rattle of the cultivator - dust, dust, dust! Then they've got to irrigate every couple of weeks, so there are water trenches running all over the place - mud, mud, mud! Then add spraying, pruning, fumigating, and picking. Well, once was enough of such an earthly paradise. Oh! I almost forgot to add the joys of smudging.

During this time, 1922, an uncle gave me $1,000 and it didn't all go into the Heat Mill operation. Ever since the war the only way to get a Jenny was to buy one from Curtiss who had repurchased many from the government while trying to stay solvent with what little postwar business there was. They were selling them for $3,000 to $4,000 apiece. But there were hundreds still gathering dust in the Army's warehouses, and finally these were offered for sale on a sealed bid basis. On the rumor that they would go for $500 each, I sent my 20 percent deposit ($100) to Washington. But when the decision was finally made, they were to be sold for any and all bids over $400. So just to be sure I wired for permission to pay the balance when I got delivery.

My approval came, and Chase and I immediately headed in his Model T for Rockwell Field where we were among the first buyers to arrive. I got the pick of the lot and selected a Howell & Lesser second-contract airplane. Chase helped me assemble it, and then he headed home by car as I proudly flew my spanking new OX-5-powered airplane to Irwin Reynolds' hayfield south of Covina. Shortly after this, Chase went back to Los Angeles. With everything on the Heat Mills set up and waiting, there wasn't anything more to do until the frosts came.

Now that we were living in Covina I felt confident that we'd soon prove the worth of the Heat Mill concept. It was only a matter of time until we would cash in when *our* crop was saved while others were being lost to the frost.

159

But now I wouldn't have to sit around waiting for the eventual success - I had an airplane! Soon I was carrying out the basics of barnstorming, taking passengers and sightseers for their first airplane rides ($5 for ten minutes), doing aerial photography (a favorite of local real estate developers) and a whole spectrum of things that we'll shortly touch upon in more detail.

Now, with aerial transportation, trips out of town became more frequent. Irvin Reynolds and I had both attended UC Berkeley, and the biggest thing that any Cal man wanted to do was to see archrival Stanford beaten. This annual contest is one of the oldest, bitter and largest attended conflicts in college football annals, replete with the most spine tingling of all college yells, *"Give 'em the axe, the axe, the axe!"*...The Axe Yell.

*Barnstorming over Covina
in my new Jenny*

Irv agreed to supply the game tickets and pay for the gas while I supplied the transportation - my Jenny. This trip was quite an expedition for 1922. We had to stop several times in each direction for gas, and there weren't any landing fields as such. One typically landed in a hayfield near a road, and even if there was not a soul in sight, almost as if by magic there would be people around your airplane in five minutes, seemingly springing right out of the ground (see next page). Around Venice, Los Angeles and the larger towns, the airplane was a common sight but 'out in the sticks' the airplane was still a very unusual contraption. Thus you could always count upon getting assistance, gas or overnight accomodations when you dropped down at some rural field.

Using the "iron compass", the railroad, we flew north, first to Bakersfield, then to a pipeline station at Mendota (35 miles-or-so west of

160

ge Carpenter

Fresno) and then San Jose, landing at each place for fuel. This year the game was being played at Stanford's huge new stadium, completed just the year before and one of the largest ever built. Therefore we made our final landing at a field in San Carlos that I had known while at United States Aircraft. As usual, the game was a razzle-dazzle affair; the enthusiasm and tension in the packed stands was almost electric. The final score was the best for a Cal man - we tromped Stanford 28 to zero in winning *The Big Game!*

Being November, it was awfully cold on the return trip over the Tejon Pass (el. 4144). Irv and I, having drunk too much hot coffee in Bakersfield, were getting very, very uncomfortable. The combination of the coffee and cold temperature dictated that I land very soon or we were going to pee in our pants. Even without the relief tubes common today, I had never done such a thing. But, trying to find a place to land over "The Grapevine" (named because of the road's innumerable switchbacks) was tough to do, and it wasn't until near Saugus that I found an open field. We both clambered out of the plane and started working our way through the many layers of clothing we were wearing. There were no zippers then, just a godawful lot of buttons, plus the newspapers we used for insulation. We were about set to relieve ourselves when I noticed a half-dozen people watching us. Damn! Fumbling a bit, we weren't able to complete our mission. But since we'd warmed up we were able to hold on until we had been driven into town to the local 'hotel' where we finally were able to solve our problem. This episode made me a bit wiser, and I started carrying a milk bottle in the plane on long jaunts. This was a far better container than the brown paper bag a buddy of mine once used with apparent success until he proceeded to dump it over the side and the slipstream caught the saturated bag, bursting it and drenching him!

161

During this time Carol, holding Janie on her lap, and I would often take the Jenny on flying trips, usually to San Diego where my mother was still living. On one of these we decided to placate our neighbors' often-voiced fears about the dangers of taking Janie with us and relieve the burden of an increasingly cramped cockpit. So we left her with the folks in Covina when we took off for a day's round trip to San Diego. It was late in the afternoon when we returned to Covina; the sun was just setting over the Puente Hills; and we were very surprised to see such a large crowd awaiting us, including the folks we had left Janie with. But we couldn't spot Janie, and the long faces on our neighbors told us that something was wrong. Well, it turned out that she and their little girl had been rough-housing on the bed and Jane had taken a tumble, breaking her collarbone. Yep, it was surely too dangerous to take Janie flying, but it was apparently more dangerous at home!

Another time, while my mother was visiting us we were discussing the possibility of Janie going home with her for a visit. I couldn't understand Janie's excitement, so I asked her. She replied, *"But Daddy, I'm going to ride on a railroad train; that's why!"* To her, flying was 'old hat', but riding on a train was the most wonderful thing she could imagine.

And there was the time that we visited my uncle, the one who gave me the $1,000. He was visiting his wife's relatives in Newport Beach, about 30 miles south of Covina, and we flew there, landing on the beach in front of their house. After a short visit my uncle wanted a ride in the Jenny. I bundled him up with a helmet and goggles, put him in the front seat, and we took off for a 15-minute flight. Upon landing we were greeted by the local police who insisted that I was breaking some sort of law and that I would have to accompany them to the police station. I surely didn't know what laws I might be breaking, and I could tell they weren't sure either. But, they figured it was something that had never happened before and must, therefore, be illegal. At the station I was accused of conducting a passenger carrying business without a license. Boy! I had a terrible time explaining to them that it was my uncle whom I'd been carrying, and that he hadn't paid for the ride (unless you could consider that it was his money that had bought the airplane). They finally let me go; guilty I appeared, but innocent I was. This is one of the very few scrapes I've had with the law, but it is typical of the problems that gypsy barnstormers had in those days.

162

Chapter 4

1923 - 1927

The Big Bear Airline, Barnstorming
and My Airmail Scandal

NOW having my own Jenny I was flying around quite a bit, and on one of my jaunts landed in Ontario. My arrival must have reminded them about discussions I'd had earlier with their Chamber of Commerce concerning the possibilities of moving my aircraft manufacturing from Venice to Ontario. The talks had been progressing nicely until a damn fool barnstormer swooped into town to hustle some dollars. He was racing a high-speed passenger train and his Jenny was sucked into the vortex of the train, crashed, and killed his young lady passenger. This tragedy dashed any hopes of support for an aircraft activity, and our discussions had petered out.

Anyway, a group contacted me to complete a Jenny they'd bought and to teach them how to fly it. There was a barnstormer strip at Ontario and they wanted to experience what Thomas Funderburk said so well:

"The pilot listened to the sound of the wind in the wires and knew his speed without guessing; he felt the sun and the wind on his cheek and from that knew his bearing and whether or not he was flying cleanly, without skidding or slipping. He felt a sense of oneness with the machine that was an extension of his brain and hands and feet. His limitations were the machine's limitations. It would take him as high as there was oxygen to breathe, and it would dance there, over all but the highest clouds. He could dive and zoom, loop and spin, and feel a harmony with the wind, and a closeness to the elements over which he triumphed. The realization of his oldest dream came and went in a day, and we shall never have such wings again." (The Fighters, Grosset & Dunlap, 1965, by permission)

The flight strip - a good one - was just east of town, between the Southern Pacific and Union Pacific railroad tracks. It was about 150 yards wide at the east end, a couple of miles long, and around 50 yards wide at the west end. It was owned by the Union Pacific and rented out for vegetable farming during the spring rainy season. For the rest of the year it was vacant and ideal for the barnstormer.

The key members of the flying group were all prominent Ontario individuals; a lawyer, the Buick dealer, Ford dealer and Chevrolet dealer. Just like me, they'd bought a surplus Howell & Lesser Jenny from the Army at North Island. Theirs, however, wasn't completed and they needed help. After some haggling we reached an agreement that would get them a flyable airplane, flying instruction, and keep me close to my Covina Heat Mill project. Flying the commute between Covina and Ontario wasn't economical (Ontario is about 15 miles east of Covina, 36 miles east of Los Angeles), so I also made a deal with the car dealer members of the group each to loan me a car for a week at a time.

We moved their incomplete Jenny to a vacant barn near the Ontario strip. Then I set to dope, varnish and enamel the wings; assemble all the mechanical parts; and finish it for flight. It took about three weeks. We then towed the glistening Jenny to the strip, where we'd made an arrangement with the farmer to abandon his crop for 1,000 feet at the east end. This was more than enough room for a Jenny's takeoffs and landings. I took her up for a test flight or two, and then started teaching my pupils.

164

These flights caused quite a stir in town as flying was still new and daring, and this was a project involving prominent local citizens.

Our schedule had me taking one of the group for flight instruction each morning. This left me with afternoons free to work on the plane, and to fix and tidy up what was starting to become a useful facility. Those afternoons weren't very renumerative, though, so I suggested that if the group would provide the materials, I'd construct a hangar for little cost. They liked this and offered me any additional help I'd need.

Before starting the hangar, though, I thought it wise to contact the Union Pacific so that our building investment would be protected. I negotiated a lease for the eastern 3,000 feet of the field at the normal agricultural rates. This was all done in my name because the group was gun-shy of any financial responsibility beyond their immediate goals. In those days anything related to flying was nigh uninsurable and carried on under a 'buyer beware' basis, though most barnstormer passengers were probably unaware of this. Anyway, people didn't sue at the drop-of-a-hat as they do today, and we never had many problems. Otherwise, litigation probably would have put most of us out of business and aviation would have waited many more years to grow.

Along this line, several years later (1930), the president of United States Aviation Underwriters wrote to "All Licensed Pilots":

> "We appeal to you now because we believe that safety in aviation is dependent almost entirely upon the common sense and experience of pilots as a whole, not only the pilots now actively flying but also those pilots holding executive positions in the industry. Certainly until the engineering laboratories can produce something radically different from the present airplane, the safety of the machine must continue to rest in the hands of the pilot. And just as certainly, we believe, it is the actual flying experiences of the pilots that must shape the course to be followed if safety is to be attained."

I now designed a 55 by 40-foot hangar and started work on it as soon as the lumber and corrugated steel arrived. A lad named Louis Morrow, crippled with a club foot, hung around every minute he was off from school, and soon became a ready helper when we got into building the hangar. He was a very willing worker, and was soon charged with gassing the Jenny and checking the oil and water. His only pay was an occasional ride and eventually some flight instruction, although his disability probably kept him from ever getting his official pilot certification. Several times, however, he flew with me as my mechanic.

As I'd planned, when the hangar was complete there was room for both their's and my Jenny and I moved my plane over from Covina. Now I had a much better opportunity for personal enterprise: carrying passengers and prospects to mountain real estate developments, aerial photography, leaflet throwing, banner towing, flight instruction, etc. These were some of the many things that the barnstormer and entrepreneur of the air did to earn a buck in the early Twenties.

However, few of us made much money or were steadily employed as barnstormers, and I could foresee that as my students became more flight proficient my teaching income would lessen. Something else had to be found to generate income.

Because one of my best sources of money had been the conversion and sale of surplus aircraft, I thought that this would be a good line to pursue. Now, however, there were no more bargain-priced Jennys available, but there was to be an auction of 50 Boeing-C seaplanes at North Island. They had more wing area than a Jenny (495 square feet), and of course, had no landing gear except pontoons. Overall, these were very good airplanes with but one problem. Their engine, a Hall-Scott A7A 4-cylinder of 110-hp occasionally caught fire from broken fuel lines. This was caused by excessive vibration and I knew that it could be corrected by simply replacing the original propeller with the smaller Jenny prop. The engine would thus rev faster and smooth out. The only remaining problem was economic, for the Hall-Scott used more oil than the OX-5 engine, but one could learn to live with that.

These seaplanes were knocked down to a ridiculous figure by a San Diego surplus dealer. The Navy's full page ads, offering them for $2,000, quoted their original cost of $10,250 each. He was selling them for *$250* apiece, but even at that price wasn't finding many buyers because about the only place a seaplane was useful was in Alaska. However, I had an idea for modifying them into land planes, and therefore persuaded each member in the Ontario group to buy one after conversion. For $550 they would get a completed biplane, and I would be left with the tidy sum of $350 per plane to cover my labors and a nice profit. (I only paid *$150*

166

each for these sea planes - after making a deal for six - plus $50 apiece for hauling to Ontario, a total cost of *$200* each!)

Manufacturer: Boeing Airplane Company, Seattle, Washington.
Type: Training seaplane.
Accommodation: Two pilots.
Power plant: One 100 hp Hall-Scott A-7A.
Dimensions: Span, 43 ft 10 in; length, 27 ft; height, 12 ft 7 in; wing area, 495 sq ft.
Weights: Empty, 1,898 lb; gross, 2,395 lb.
Performance: Max speed, 72·7 mph at sea level; cruising speed, 65 mph at sea level; climb, 23·5 min to 5,000 ft; service ceiling, 6,500 ft; range, 200 st miles.
Serial numbers:
   C: A147–A148, A650–A699.

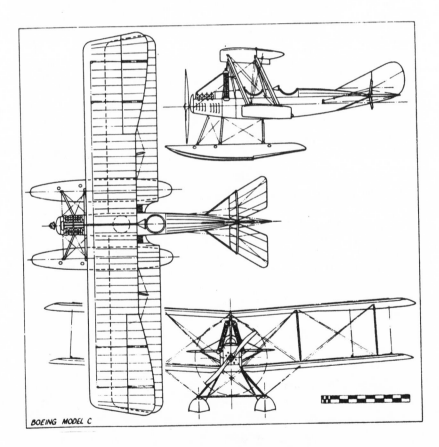

Technical Data - Boeing Model C Seaplane

167

These Boeings had much better equipment than the Jenny: a magnetic compass, an airspeed indicator, a compressed air self-starter and code radio equipment. Except for the radio, all of these features were useful. Especially nice was the self-starter which eliminated burdensome or ofttimes dangerous spinning of the prop, providing that the pilot had pressured the air tanks before he killed the engine.

Four of the Boeings were for the group and two for myself. Their conversions then supplemented my income for several months. This was in addition to the extra money I made teaching their owners how to fly them because they differed somewhat from the Jennys. They had a wheel-type Deperdussin control rather than a stick, and a Farman-type tail skid which made for a slightly changed landing technique. When I had converted Wylie's Martin-S back in Venice I found that the fuselage for a seaplane wasn't well structured for tail stresses, and in order to take the bumps and jolts of landing I devised a tail skid borrowed from the early Farmans. The front landing gear, with wheels replacing pontoons, was basically normal, and the final effect of the airplane was quite pleasing. The engine, though totally different from the OX-5, wasn't of much concern to the owners because they left its care totally up to me.

We now had quite an operation going: a 3,000-foot-long airfield, hangar, two Jennys and six Boeings. Things were moving along very well, and with high hopes for the future we incorporated *Ontario Aircraft Corporation* with me as general manager. I was 31 years old.

While completing the Boeing conversions and teaching their owners to fly them, I also barnstormed a bit and carried out some general flight instruction. One notable student was Fritz Secor. Along with his brother, they used all the spare cash from their jobs at the Hotpoint plant (started in Ontario) to learn to fly. Fritz was a fine student and became a natural pilot, especially at aerial mapping, and was a longtime friend.

With things going so well, Carol and I decided to move from Covina to Ontario. We didn't like our orange grove home, and being tied down by the Heat Mill I was dependent upon the next frost in order to demonstrate its potential. Waiting for a frost in Southern California is like waiting for the ground hog to come out of his hole; you know that he will, but only he knows when! So, I had left instructions with Reynold's mechanic on exactly how to operate the Heat Mill when the next frost

168

hit. Incidentally, I'd replaced the Hall-Scott A7A with a more powerful 6-cylinder Union dirigible engine which was better suited to this job.

I got this Union engine from the Army Air Service Balloon School at Ross Field in Arcadia, where Santa Anita Racetrack is today. They had a large hangar and winching trucks to raise these observer-carrying captive balloons *("Elephants")* to an altitude of around 4,000 feet. Though ballooning was a dying art, it was always interesting to fly by a balloon field and see them in the air as there was little else in the skies then.

This diversion was not without its peril. One day I was flying my Jenny from Covina to deMille Field No. 2, scanning *The Saturday Evening Post* which I often did because flying was pretty monotonous and there was rarely any other aircraft anywhere close. I happened to peek over the side. Gads! I was over the balloon field and the soldiers around a winch truck were frantically waving, trying to tell me that there was a balloon heading my way. If I had hit its cable, this tale would have ended. I pushed the panic button, made a hard split-S turn and looked for that balloon. Sure enough, there it was, 400 feet below me. I've always felt that was one time when my invisible copilot was helping me!

When negotiating the purchase of the Union engine, I'd stopped by the balloon school to see the commanding officer, Lt. C.P. Kane. His clerk told me that he was 'out flying,' so I said, *"Thanks"*, and started to leave. But he said, *"Oh, you can see him; he's just down in the hangar."* This stopped me cold. When I drove into the hangar I saw a small one-man balloon tethered about ten feet off the floor with Lt. Kane sitting in it, reading. I began to wonder what 'flying' consisted of in The Balloon Corps, but I had been told he was flying, and I guess he was.

Kane and I discussed our business, and I then left, muttering to myself. In those days Air Service flyers had to get in *flight time* every 90 days to qualify for 50% additional pay for *"the hazards of flying."* In this case, Lt. Kane qualified by sitting in that balloon for eight hours on the last day of a 90-day period. Then, on the next day he repeated the performance for the following 90-day period. Thus, he had to go 'flying' only twice a year for a 50% raise in pay!

George Carpenter, Arcadia California, 1919

169

Balloons weren't the only things that one had to watch out for then. During the 1923 Los Angeles County Fair at Pomona (about six miles west of Ontario), I was towing an advertising banner and flying low over the fairgoers. I had equipped my Jenny with an exhaust-powered horn that made a hellava racket and thus got a lot of attention. All of a sudden the Jenny veered hard to the right, and as I searched frantically for the trouble I saw a rope stretching taut across the right wing. Thankfully for me and the crowds below, it broke and I was able to straighten out and avoid a crash. As I looked back, I spied two very-large advertising kites with big banners streaming from them. One was now settling back to earth. I realized that I had neglected to keep a sharp eye out for aerial obstacles, and once again my invisible copilot had saved me.

I immediately headed to Ontario thinking that I'd damn soon hear from the kite flyer, and I surely did, in no uncertain terms! He arrived steaming, claiming that I had damaged his equipment to the tune of $100. Well, I'd done some thinking about this problem and I countered by berating him. I told him that if he knew the law he would have had warning pennants every 50 feet along his kite line; and that he, not I, was the violator of the state aviation laws! If he wanted to pursue the matter any further, I would file a complaint and he would undoubtedly be fined a considerable sum.

My bluff worked, for in spite of there being no such law the kite man calmed right down and left as I heaved a sigh of relief. Interestingly, in some defense of my ruse, the state soon had a law virtually the same as what I had dreamed up!

About this time, early 1924, there were rumors in aviation circles that the Post Office Department would soon be calling for commercial operation of several new airmail routes. Initially using Army equipment and pilots, the Post Office had been carrying *"Aerial Mail"* since May 1918. By 1920, it had painfully grown to a transcontinental route, but now with civilian pilots, from Hazelhurst Field at Mineola on Long Island to San Francisco, with major intermediate stops at Cleveland, Chicago, Omaha and Salt Lake City. My college chum, then Lt. J. Parker Van Zandt of the Army Air Service, wrote: *"There is a revolutionary fact abroad in the land; aircraft have gone to work. And the nation is waking to find itself fast-wedded to a new handmaid of progress - the United States Transcontinental Air Mail Service."*

170

With war-vintage, Liberty-engined deHaviland DH4 biplanes, this service was pioneering but not very reliable. If the contents of an air-mailed letter was important, one sent a duplicate by rail, for the chances were only 50-50 that the *"Aeropost"* letter would get there. Even if it did, though, it didn't beat the train by much because the airmail still had to go by rail to the transcontinental route cities. For instance, airmail from Los Angeles went first by train to San Francisco, then by air to the East.

I decided that the best way to find out about these commercial air-mail rumors was to go to Washington, D.C., where I met with Harry S. New, the Assistant Postmaster General. He told me that the Post Office was anticipating proposed legislation, the *Kelly Bill*, and had lain out feeder routes into the main transcontinental route which the Post Office would still retain. These feeders would be awarded to bidders of demonstrated capability. Of these routes, Route CAM-4 (Contract Air Mail), Los Angeles - Salt Lake City, interested me and I vowed to get it. I headed home, planning a program that would prepare Ontario Aircraft Corp. to be a qualified bidder for this major venture. The key to my bid would be the enlargement of the corporation into an airline, and not just for the postal business.

Ontario is far enough inland to be considered fog free (smog was unknown then), and it seemed logical that as air service grew into Los Angeles that it could become a major alternate landing field whenever other airports in the basin were 'socked in'. As many air travelers know, even today with instrument flying Ontario is often used when Los Angeles International (LAX) has zero visibility.

Also, a few months before my Washington trip the possibility of air service to Big Bear presented itself. I had run into Richard Burke, who had a fancy retreat in the mountains at Big Bear Lake. It was about 100 miles east of Los Angeles if one flew, but an awful lot longer and tougher if one drove the twisting and precipitous mountain roads then. Remember, Richard had bought a Waterman-modified Hall-Scott L6-powered Standard biplane from Pacific for the trips to his cabin. Since he was still a novice pilot and the flight to Big Bear was tricky even for experienced flyers, he asked me to accompany him there, both to assess the feasibility of flying into the mountains and to judge his piloting.

We flew from Rogers Airport (now moved to the northwest corner of Western Avenue and El Segundo Boulevard), refueled at Ontario, and came in over Big Bear looking for the best place to land. A lovely pine-bordered meadow east of the lake was apparently the spot for Burke's houseman was waiting with the Ford Model T that Richard kept there. When we arrived at the cabin I thought to myself that this was really the way to 'rough it.' It was two stories tall, built from two-foot-thick logs and sumptuous by any standard. One night in these spectacular surroundings filled my mind with ideas for providing air transportation to the many people that were waiting to share this experience.

Big Bear Lake is about 20 miles east of much-smaller Lake Arrowhead, and this two lake area was becoming very popular. It was one of the few places that people in Los Angeles could really be in the majestic high mountain country. Big Bear lies just to the north of San Gorgonio Peak, at 11,502 feet the tallest mountain in Southern California. The altitude at the lake is 6,750 feet, well-over a mile high.

However, getting there wasn't half the fun. There was only one very rough road connecting the two lakes, and only two routes directly to Big Bear. The most popular was east from Redlands, a town about 80 miles from Los Angeles. This road was torturous, a series of sharp switchbacks so narrow that it was one way going up certain hours, down others, and toll to boot. The other way into Big Bear was a ninety mile trip out of San Bernardino. You went north through the 4,000-foot-high Cajon Pass, a long, tough grade for cars both then and now. Then you entered the Mojave Desert, 'high desert' of 3,000 foot elevation, and drove to the town of Victorville. Then it was through the Lucerne Valley, and finally you climbed the Cushenbury Grade into Bear Valley. Either one of these routes was tedious, demanding on your nerves, rough on your car and took several hours. Air service into Big Bear looked to be a natural.

So with Harry New's good counsel, an excellent facility at Ontario, and now a place to go which would provide rigorous flying experience, I started promoting the airline idea. We figured that there would be a good passenger business, considering the hardships of the roads. And, the folks living at Big Bear were enthusiastic about the prospect of more tourists and customers for their real estate developments. During this time California was in the midst of a real estate boom rivalled only by Florida's land bubble. My associates in Ontario also thought this was a capital idea, warmly endorsing it because they didn't have much desire anymore for flying their Boeings and saw the airline as an easy way out.

172

Under the aegis of the Ontario Aircraft Corp. we formed the *Ontario-Big Bear Airline,* and through our lawyer, Archie Mitchell, enlisted a prominent judge, J.R. Pollock, to be its president. I then set about selling stock to finance the airline.

We converted my two Boeings to land planes that could carry four passengers and the pilot. These larger and heavier loads required more powerful engines, and I located a couple of Renault 160-hp engines for the job. However, I wasn't very good at selling stock and had to borrow $1,000 from Richard Burke to pay for them and complete the plane alterations. I hired Otto Timm to assist me, and because of the hopes we had for the airline he moved to Ontario, planning to be a permanent employee. In the Midwest in 1912, Otto, flying his Curtis-copy had been known as *"the Boy Wonder Flyer."* After leaving Pacific Airplane and Supply he had just spent a year-and-a-half with Ray Page's Nebraska Aircraft Corp. in Lincoln where as chief engineer he made a conversion on a Hisso-powered Lincoln Standard similar to what we planned.

To modify the Boeings we removed the front seat and gas tank, enlarging that space to accommodate four passengers, two abreast. We took the wingtip floats and hung them as gas tanks from the top wing, traded wheels for pontoons, put on the Farman-type tail skid and installed the Renault engines. Finally, I test flew the plane with a full load of passengers and found it to handle and fly very well. We then christened the first Boeing *"Daddy Bear"*.

"Daddy Bear" - Big Bear - 1924

173

I worked out an arrangement with the Motor Transit Co. in Los Angeles for their stages, or buses, to carry passengers to Ontario; Big Bear Airline would then carry them to the mountain resorts. The ticket that a passenger purchased at the bus terminal (Sixth and Los Angeles Streets in Los Angeles) covered both the air and ground transportation; this was very unique and *the first of its kind*. We also had an arrangement with Big Bear Estates for transporting prospects to their lot development.

Motor Transit Co. and Ontario Aircraft Corp. to Big Bear 1924

For the maiden flight of the Big Bear Airline I invited Ontario's Mayor Ball, plus a leading minister, the newspaper editor and the Ontario Hotel manager to be our first four passengers. We planned to fly them to Big Bear for lunch at the Big Bear Lodge. While they were enjoying the mountain delights, we would then fly the lodge owner's daughter, Sandy, and three leading Big Bear citizens down for lunch at the Ontario Hotel. This would be quite a feat, for in those days it took around five hours just to drive one-way, and we would be flying round-trip in a bit over two hours.

174

We took off from Ontario shortly after 9 AM on Sunday, April 26, 1924, for the 68-minute inaugural flight, which was very smooth and uneventful. Upon landing we were met by Al Brush, Big Bear Lodge's owner, and a group of excited local residents. Al then took the Ontario foursome to lunch as his honored guests, and I took off with Sandy and the others. We landed at Ontario after another good flight, and following a warm reception were escorted to the hotel for a luncheon.

Everyone was very impressed with the airplane as modern transportation.

At about 2:30 PM, we took off again, and had flown through the Cajon Pass when, all-of-a-sudden the engine sputtered and died over the Lucerne Valley. I went into a cold sweat. But since I had planned the route in such a way as to have a place to land almost anywhere, I started a 'dead stick' glide near Box S Springs. However, there wasn't any way of determining the wind direction, so that when we landed the plane made a wrenching ground loop (abrupt swing-around) and blew-out one of the tires. Everyone was a little stunned, but all were safe and unharmed.

I couldn't fix the tire there, and I surely couldn't risk taking off with a load of passengers on only one tire. The road passes right alongside Box S Springs, and fortunately a car headed to Big Bear was soon loaded with three more passengers squeezed in for the few remaining miles.

I was left cussing to myself - *"Hell!"*, I was swearing out loud! I discovered that the engine had stopped because gunk in the converted wingtip floats had clogged the fuel lines. It was a simple matter to blow out the lines, but it was a bit trickier taking off on one tire. Since I couldn't replace the tire at Big Bear, I went the long way back to Ontario, gingerly landing there in late afternoon. Fortunately the lines hadn't clogged again. So, after replacing the tire, draining and cleaning the tanks, and checking all the fuel lines, we were ready to take off on schedule Monday morning.

It wasn't a very auspicious start for the airline.

And the second day was even worse. I took off with two passengers, one a stockholder who was in love with Sandy and was hoping not to have to come back that evening. The other was a San Bernardino businessman named Miller who frequently made trips to Big Bear in connection with his wholesale produce firm. This trip up was uneventful; we ar-

175

rived at the lake around 10:30 AM, gassed-up, had lunch at the Lodge and loaded for our 2 PM takeoff. Since the minister had already come down by car, there were three seats available for the return trip for the remaining folks that I had taken to Big Bear the day before.

The day, though, was windy, hot and dry. It was a *"Santa Ana"* condition which occurs in Southern California several times a year and is caused by a pressure differential between the Los Angeles Basin and the surrounding high deserts. The hot desert winds are superheated when they rush through the passes and canyons, such as the Santa Ana Canyon. They cause all sorts of inconvenience and irritation, both physical and psychological. To the flyer they spell loss of lift, plus the sirocco-like gusts can be tricky and very dangerous. Arch Hoxsey was the first to experience the bedevilment of Santa Ana's during the second Dominguez Air Meet. They would also plague Carl Spatz and his *"Question Mark"* flight almost three decades later, and in 1975 they caused near-disaster to Malcolm Forbes and his ballooning.

However, I didn't think that the winds were severe enough to delay our departure and took off with Mayor Ball, the editor, the hotel manager and Mr. Miller as passengers. But I knew that we were in trouble as soon as we were clear of the meadow and committed to flight. The air was turbulent and lacked the solid feel of good, cool, stable air. It was tough, deciding whether to make the normal wide circle going through the desert pass over Whiskey Springs, or to go the shortest course, straight across the lake and over the dam, above rough, forested terrain.

I chose the normal course because if we could gain enough altitude we could proceed on the planned route, and if we didn't, I would be in the best position to land back at the field. Well, *Lady Luck denied me!* As we were making the wide, sweeping circle to the left, the bumpy air intensified. I was unable to climb more than 50 feet above the lake. And then, all of a sudden, a hard downdraft hit us and we crashed into the lake.

Wrestling my way out of the cockpit, I made a fast head count. Everyone seemed OK and accounted for except for Miller. He was nowhere to be seen. Only the tail of the plane was afloat, and I frantically dove into the passenger compartment, but try as I might I couldn't locate him. Mayor Ball, who was around 80 years old, had apparently wrenched his back. He and the others were soon picked up by people in skiffs and fishing boats and rushed to shore. The three shaken and sodden passengers were soon dry and calmed down, with the mayor bedded-down in the Lodge. I stayed with the plane, futilely searching for Miller, hoping for the miracle of seeing him turn up alive. It was a couple of hours before we were able to hook a line to the wreckage and drag it ashore. Still no Miller.

Miller's body was recovered the next day, and the cornoner's inquest revealed that he had not drowned but had apparently died of a heart attack when he plunged into the very cold lake waters. We later learned that he had been imbibing a bit at the Lodge while recounting the adventure of his flight, and this drinking could well have contributed to his plight when we crashed. Fortunately for me and the airline, we were held blameless in his death and there was never any legal action taken, possibly because this was at the height of prohibition - and bootlegging.

Nevertheless, this was a terrible shock because it was the first time anyone had been injured or lost while flying with me. Also, it surely didn't help the airline much. The publicity was very damaging to our fledgling enterprise with several stockholders wanting to call it quits. But we decided to keep moving ahead and rushed the conversion of the second Boeing, this time semi-enclosing the passenger cockpit. About ten days later we had number two ready to fly, naming it *"Daddy Bear II"*. Just prior to the crash we had also completed another conversion, a Thomas-Morse Scout which I made into a two-seater for the carrying of either cargo or a passenger. I used it immmediately for an emergency flight, taking respiratory equipment to the doctor at Big Bear treating Mayor Ball, thankful to have the opportunity of giving any help I could. After resting a bit, the other passengers had gone back to Ontario by car. They expressed no ill feelings and even spoke highly of the care and efforts that I had made. Small solace! I will always remember that day.

We thus had to complete a third Boeing conversion so we would have two airline planes after the loss of Daddy Bear I. This extra and unanticipated expenditure almost exhausted our funds. We also had far fewer passengers than we had projected since there was a natural hesitancy to ride with an airline having our record. Cutting costs to the bone, I had to lay off Otto Timm. He was damn unhappy about it and insisted upon severance pay. I didn't have any cash and finally agreed to give him the second Union dirigible engine instead (which I was holding as a spare for

177

the Heat Mill). This ended the only argument that Otto and I ever had in a friendship that endured for many years. (Otto, along with his brother Wally and Jack Gardner then formed Timm Airplane Corporation on San Fernando Road in Glendale.)

Before Otto left he helped me build a contraption that was both airboat and snowmobile. Most of the resorts at Big Bear were about three miles down the lake from the airfield, and I dreamed-up this *"Hydroglider"* as a novel, fast and hopefully profitable way of carrying people around the lake. We built it out of salvage from the wreck of Daddy Bear I, old Boeing seaplane parts, a Hall-Scott engine, pontoons, and a steering rudder that would work both in air and water. It was some machine! When we first put it in the lake and revved-up the engine, the propeller gave us plenty of push, but the pontoons weren't the proper design to get the craft planing properly. So, we rebuilt the hull with a large step; she then proved to be very fast. This craft was similar to the airboats one sees today in the Everglades. Ours, however, would carry its six passengers over water in summer and on ice and snow with skis in the winter. It was very popular, and we found it profitable enough to employ an operator for it in the winter when the airline wasn't flying. On ice it could attain chilling, thrilling speeds approaching sixty miles an hour.

Waterman Sled - Me, left and Carol, far right - 1925

178

Movies with the Sled - Me at the wheel - Big Bear 1926

Business was very slow that spring because of our rocky start and we decided to fly weekdays only if we had a minimum of two passengers. Our weekend schedule was flown regardless of passenger load. In order to have a good case for the pending Post Office route-bidding we registered our scheduled service with the California Railroad Commission, as there was nothing else to supervise airlines then. We published a fare of $17.50 one-way and $30.00 round-trip. The dovetailing of bus and airplane passengers with the Motor Transit Co. worked fine. This same concept was used later when Transcontinental Air Transport used planes during the day and trains at night to rush its passengers coast-to-coast in as little as 48 hours, depending on the weather (see page 246).

During the summer season several of the lake resorts helped promote the airline and tourist business by buying our tickets and either reselling them to their guests or sometimes giving them away. In those days there was still a lot of hunting around Big Bear, and one day a local guide wanted me to fly an illegally-shot buck out for him since the game wardens were checking autos. I wasn't very happy about this, but he, among others, had been so helpful during our first months that I figured it might be a way to reciprocate. I said, *"OK. Load the buck a half-hour before the flight in the front seat where it won't be seen, and I'll take it down."*

179

At flight time I headed for the plane. Standing there, holding a give-away ticket, was the game warden. Apprehensively I looked into the cabin, under and around the plane. There was nary a dead deer in sight; it had disappeared in much the same way as the 'underground telegraph' had warned of the warden's trip. I whistled a sigh of relief, collected the tickets and loaded the warden and the other passengers for the run to Ontario.

During the mid-1920's Big Bear was a favorite destination for the wealthy Southern Californian sportsman and quite a few adventurous Hollywood stars. This was the time of *"The Roaring Twenties"*, *"flaming youth"*, *"the speakeasy"* and *"The Jazz Age"*, and movies were enjoying fantastic, unparalleled popularity. Stars like cowboy actor William S. Hart *("America's First Hero"),* Douglas Fairbanks, Mary Pickford and Harold Lloyd were earning salaries of $10,000 a week or more - virtually untaxed - working for directors like Cecil deMille. Since our operations were based at Big Bear Lodge, the lake's best resort, I met and flew many of these people. Two that became close friends were artist Clyde Victor Forsythe and actor Reginald Denny, a veteran of the Royal Flying Corps. and an avid flyer at the peak of his movie career who later became involved in the aircraft industry. Denny was first known as one of the screen's best comedians, but with the coming of sound he became a fine character actor with his impeccable English accent.

Clyde Forsythe was creator of the popular comic strip *"Joe's Car"*, syndicated by the New York World to over 300 newspapers nationwide. His cartoon character, Joe Jinks, often rode with me because many times I was included in the strip. *Waldo Waterman was now a cartoon character!* Clyde persuaded me to use my name, *Waldo*, as he did in the comics, rather than the W.D. that I had typically used. He said that Waldo was distinctive, and that it would give me much better publicity. So, from then on Waldo it was.

Not merely a cartoonist, Clyde (Vic) was also a fine and well regarded painter of desert scenes. He had encouraged young Norman Rockwell when he was just starting, and became his close friend. We met Rockwell when Carol and I visited the Forsythe's at their luxurious San Marino home. By the late 1920's Rockwell had already achieved fame and fortune due to *The Saturday Evening Post* covers, though his earliest illustrations were for *The Youth's Companion.*

180

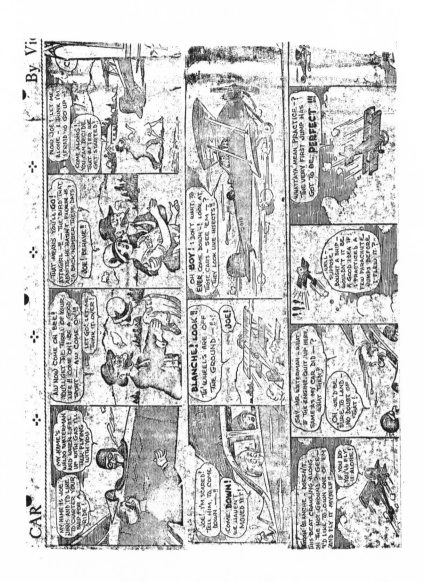

Joe's Car - By Vic Forsythe - I'm a cartoon character! - Los Angeles Express
1925 (note the 4-passenger airline Boeing)

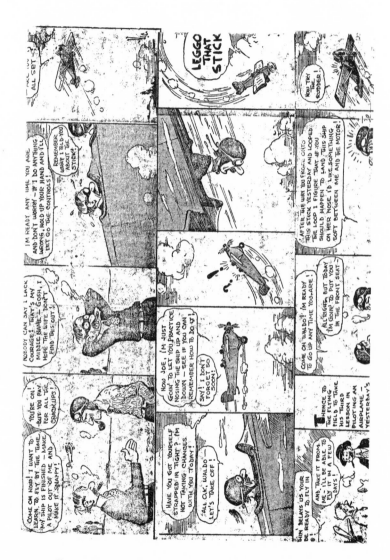

I'm teaching Joe Jinks to fly - in the comics - 1925

Another interesting character around the Lodge was Roy Thatcher, an ex-shipyard worker from Long Beach who'd had a penchant for drinking a bit much. Upon sobering-up he sometimes found that he'd invested in some wild scheme or other. One day he awoke to find that he had bought some apparently worthless land on Signal Hill near Long Beach. He couldn't unload this dirt on another sucker, and he soon woke up another morning as a millionaire. His land turned out to be smack-dab in the middle of *the richest oil field in the world in 1921*, as described by Lockwood in the *Los Angeles Times:*

> *"Any lingering danger of gasoline shortages in Los Angeles vanished after the massive oil strikes at Huntington Beach in 1919, and at Signal Hill and Santa Fe Springs in 1921. By 1923, Huntington Beach produced 113,000 barrels a day, Santa Fe Springs, 32,000 barrels, and Signal Hill, 244,000 barrels"...1/5 of the world's oil production at this time."*

Signal Hill - World's richest oil field - 1926

183

The boom was so great on Signal Hill that one could read a newspaper, day or night, from the light of the burning gases; and the wooden drilling derricks covered the hill like a dense forest.

Roy became a big spender and everyone was handy when he was spreading it around. He often chartered the airboat to give kids exciting rides on the lake, but I never did much flying with him.

My best and staunchest friend was Richard Burke, the man who first introduced me to Big Bear. He always helped bail me out whenever I'd run out of money for some scheme or other; he kept his guest quarters and Model T always at my disposal; and his caretaker and housekeeper accorded me his hospitality even when he was home in Pasadena.

The activities of the airline, the airboat and the airsled, plus sundry charters and plane conversions kept me going financially through the balance of 1924 and all of 1925. We may not have been rich; but Carol and I, along with Janie, were leading a different, exciting life and were making the acquaintance and friendship of many fascinating people.

I continued to give flying lessons with one of the original two-place Boeings. It now had a more conventional rear tail skid, not the Farman type. One day a rancher from nearby Chino came to the field and asked in broken English if I would give him some instruction. He said he'd done some flying and just wanted a refresher course to get the feel again. This was an old gag used by individuals who thought they could fly with a minimum of instruction to save some money. So I took his statement with a grain of salt. But, immediately after we had cleared the field and I signalled him to take over I knew that he *had* done a lot of flying! We landed after a couple of circuits and I told him to take her up alone as he could fly as well as I. Later we had quite a talk; he turned out to be Julius Schroeder, a German World War I ace with several Allied planes to his score. He served as technical adviser when Howard Hughes filmed *"Hell's Angels."*

There's another fellow that I met in this era and what I know of him makes an interesting interlude. One day in 1925 a Louis Babbs came to the field and wanted a 20 minute 'sample' of a dual flight lesson. For this I charged $5. I always instructed from the front seat, and had a rear view mirror so that I could observe the activities of the student. Much to my surprise, Babbs was paying no attention at all to the controls or to what

184

the airplane was doing. He was just sitting there looking around at the view. When we got back on the ground I explained to him that I didn't think he'd ever make an aviator and discouraged him - something almost unheard-of in those days.

Now there's a gap in the story. By the late 1920's Babbs was claiming to be a movie stunt man, an aviator, and that *Waldo Waterman had taught him to fly*. He then had joined-up with a carnival as a motorcycle stunt rider putting on a hair-raising act. He married a member of the troupe with no legs, also a stunt artist, who rode with him - just hanging on with her arms around him.

We move on to December of 1932 for more of Babbs. I was a TWA copilot assigned with pilot Olsen to fly a Ford trimotor to Riverside on a movie charter; I recall that we were just to be 'background'. The story entailed the hero-aviator to stop a racing locomotive and thus prevent a catastrophic accident; but hero-aviator didn't see the railroad sign, hit same, and sheared off one side of the plane's wings. The plane - one built by Ed Fisk for Vic Fleming in 1922. And the pilot? You guessed it - *Louis "Speedy" Babbs,* and he flew it well and to the script, crackup and all.

These two events were the only times I ever laid eyes on him, though I have some recollections about his wild escapades after that. I felt sure that if he persisted in this type of activity he would soon meet his Maker. I certainly wouldn't question that he'd broken 56 bones in course of his career!

During a quiet spell in the spring of 1925 I took a four-passenger Boeing on a barnstorming trip, hoping to raise some much-needed cash. Young Louis Morrow went along as my mechanic and we headed for Barstow (around 75 miles northeast of Ontario) where there was a small landing strip at the base of a mountain. My aunt Abby was there trying to establish a model farm on some Mojave River bottom land a couple of miles from this strip, where I'd 'vacationed' in 1910. We flew over and spotted the strip. Boy, it was a tough one. We made a rough landing and finally stopped by running into a pile of brush, with no damage, luckily, and Aunt Abby's foreman met us in an old truck and drove us over to the farm. Called *Waterman Ranch,* it was the last vestige (other than an abandoned mine) of *Waterman Station,* the empire that my grandfather built in the 1880's.

185

Cotta Forsythe and me, and the barnstorming Boeing, but with the later Waterman-Salmson eng

At the farm they were raising alfalfa. I walked over a couple of long strips of it and it looked OK to land on. The three of us, the foreman, Louis and I, went back to the plane, unloaded and lightened it and pushed it up the hill to get as much runway as possible. Louis and the foreman were taking the gear over to the farm while I took off alone. But as I landed the wheels dug in, and the plane flipped over! The alfalfa field had looked fine, but the strip where I landed had just been irrigated!

So here I was, alone, strapped in, upside down, but uninjured, and the only damage to the plane was a broken prop, pretty typical then.

We flipped the plane upright, got a new propeller and some tools from Ontario, and soon had everything repaired. We then took off for Randsburg, about 50 miles northwest of Barstow. It was one of the few mining towns still active in California, and had a big cash payroll. I shrewdly planned our arrival on payday. But as we flew over the landing

186

strip adjoining their baseball diamond I saw it was too tight. To shorten our roll I tried sideslipping, and I still didn't make it. We were still rolling and the baseball backstop was getting mighty close. I tried to ground loop; the landing gear collapsed, and there we were on our nose again! This time, in addition to the broken propeller we had to fix the landing gear. Carol had to come and drive me back to Ontario to get all of the repair materials, and by the time we had the plane fixed up the payroll had all gone to the local saloons, ending that barnstorming trip.

Helping with the survival of the airline were a couple of very profitable movie contracts, one with Victor Fleming, a close friend who was later credited with the final direction of *"Gone With The Wind."* He was doing a movie at mile-high Lake Arrowhead involving a "Forest Patrol" seaplane and asked me to rig-up a plane with pontoons to fly off the lake. So we reconverted one of our Boeings to a seaplane and trucked it to the lake. There was some question whether we could land or takeoff on Arrowhead because it is far smaller than Big Bear, but I did prove that the plane would operate well at altitude off a small lake, and I also got my picture taken in movie makeup!

The movie, *"Mantrap"*, starred Clara Bow, the *very sexy* flame-haired *"It"* girl, Ernest Torrence and Percy Marmont. At this time 19-year-old Clara Bow was the No. 1 Movie Star of the era (John Gilbert was her male counterpart, then under contract for an unheard of $1,500,000 per year). She was the *"hottest movie representative of Flaming Youth."* The story of Clara Bow 'taking on' most of the 1926 or 1927 USC football team - including young Marion Morrison (John Wayne) - is well-known; whether true I don't know. But I do remember once she was on Fleming's lap and he was rubbing her as he told me she was the "best lay" ever. In the script I doubled for the aviator who was the prey of the vamp "Alverna" played by Clara Bow - and at just the crucial moment, darn it, my doubling ended! Thus ended my first encounter with the torrid and loose-living world of off-screen Hollywood. *Wow!*

We then trucked the plane back to Ontario, and made the seaplane a land plane again.

Another Hollywood assignment I had was for Henry King, the Fox director. Known as *"the flying director"*, he was an aviation buff and we became well-acquainted, often crossing paths when he flew his Waco biplane. He was directing the very popular comedy duo *"Potash and*

187

Clara Bow in "Mantrap"

Los Angeles Times - July 24, 1926

188

Me - in the movies! Boeing seaplane, Lake Arrowhead - 1926

The "Mantrap" Boeing - note "Richfield Gasoline"

189

Perlmutter" in one of America's favorite serials, originally from *The Saturday Evening Post* and already on film for a decade. In this movie *"Partners Again"*, he needed some snow covered mountain backgrounds. Due to the rigorous demands of our airline, Waterman aircraft were getting quite a reputation for high altitude performance. Thus, Henry had me do the flying for this spectacular high Sierra filming. I made many flights with ace cameraman Ray June. Later the plane was trucked to the studios for closeup work with the stars, George Sidney as Abe Potash and Alexander Carr as Mawruss Perlmutter.

Unlike *Mantrap,* in King's serial I did engage in a bit of 'acting', though certainly not enough to be called an actor! Of course, this was all before 'talkies.'

Somewhat later, when Howard Hawks was filming *"Dawn Patrol"* in 1930, he used two of my two-place Boeings (one the same plane that Schroeder had flown) because they resembled 1917 German fighters. They flew in a scene showing two of vonRichthofen's fighters scrambling and being shot down just after their takeoffs. The planes were cleverly set up so that they took off, reached an altitude of 50 or 60 feet, and then nosed-over and crashed - all with no one aboard. I watched these premeditated crackups with both awe and sadness, for that was the end of two spunky Boeings. However, they lived on celluloid much longer than I ever suspected. For, when Hollywood remade *"Dawn Patrol"* a decade later (1938), starring Errol Flynn and David Niven, darned if they didn't use that same scene again. And that's still being shown on TV today!

Among my other activities, I became a radio personality with my own aviation program on KHJ, a top Los Angeles station. This evolved from a program aimed at youngsters called *"Uncle John".* Uncle John Daggett had me on to talk to the kids about flying and aviation. After a few programs I was introduced to an older fan, a financier who loved to fly. He chartered my services several times for sightseeing flights with Uncle John and his friends around Southern California, even once flying over Mt. San Gorgonio. During 1926 I had become such a 'steady' on the program that I started my own program, though catering to an older, adult audience and patterned on my Berkeley teaching of 1917. I was able to liven things up a bit with personal anecdotes, but since this was long before tapes and 'recorded transcriptions', occasionally Carol would have to stand-in and read my script for me. One time she did this while I

190

was *on location* at Lake Arrowhead for the *Mantrap* filming, preparing yet another anecdote!

Regardless of my reputation for high-altitude-performing aircraft, I knew that they were still marginal, especially when flying over 7,000 feet with a full passenger load. I had started with the Boeings and their 110-hp Hall-Scotts; then I installed the 160-hp Renaults, and still I needed more power. About the only other engines we had after World War I were the Liberty and the rough-running Wright copy of the Hispano-Suiza. The fine air-cooled radials (evolutions from the French 200-hp *Anzani* radial of 1915) hit the market in the mid-1920's; Wright's 200-hp J-4 *Whirlwind,* designed by Charles Lawrance, in 1924 for $5,000; and Pratt & Whitney's 425-hp *Wasp,* designed by Fred Rentschler and George Mead, in early 1926 - for a hefty $7,500 each. These two engines, originally aimed at the military market, were totally out of my reach.

But a third engine looked more promising for me. Towards the end of the war the French firm, *Societe des Moteurs Salmson,* developed a fine water-cooled radial that weighed about the same as the Renault but developed 260-hp. (In 1918, Americans flying Salmson 2-A2's shot down Hermann Goering, the leader of Jasta 27 flying his all-white Fokker D-7 in the Richthofen Geschwader "Circus".) Scouting about, I found a new Salmson at Weber Showcase & Fixture Co. in LA. When I went to see it I met Al Menasco, Weber's chief engineeer who had been with Art Smith on his exhibition tour in Japan in 1916. Though not a pilot, Menasco was a top-notch mechanic temporarily out of aviation. Smith had died Feb. 12, 1926, in Ohio while flying the mail for National Air Transport, and Al was working to dispose of the 125-or-so surplus Salmson engines that Smith had purchased as an investment. Menasco and I worked out a deal for my trying out one engine; the rest were stored in Dayton. If it proved satisfactory I would be able to use several more.

I installed the Salmson in an airline Boeing, but before I was able to fly I had to find a reverse-turning propeller because this engine rotated a direction opposite to American engines. I lucked-out by finding some four-bladed props that had been on Liberty engines installed as pushers on the Curtiss HS-1L flying boats. The reverse of a pusher on an American engine equalled a puller on a French engine!

Being a good scavenger, I located another Salmson that Universal Studios had been using in a wind machine. They were unhappy with it

191

TABLE III.—PRINCIPAL CHARACTERISTICS OF SOME TYPICAL AIR-COOLED AIRPLANE ENGINES, 1928

Manufacturer	Model	Rated		Type	Number of cylinders	Bore, inches	Stroke, inches	Compression ratio	Propeller gear ratio	Number of valves per cylinder	Weight, pounds	
		Horsepower	Revolutions per minute								Total	Per horsepower
Fairchild-Caminez (A)	447-C	135	1,000	Radial	4	5 5/8	4 1/2	5.2	Direct*	2	360	2.67
Warner Aircraft Company (A)	Scarab	110	1,850	Radial	7	4 1/4	4 1/4	...	Direct	2	270	2.45
Wright Aero. Corp. (A)	Whirlwind C	220	1,800	Radial	9	4 1/2	5 1/2	5.4	Direct	2	510	2.31
Wright Aero. Corp. (A)	Cyclone	525	1,900	Radial	9	6	6 7/8	5.3	0.5†	2	760	1.45
Pratt & Whitney (A)	Wasp B	450	2,100	Radial	9	5 3/4	5 3/4	5.0	Direct	2	660	1.47
Pratt & Whitney (A)	Hornet	525	1,900	Radial	9	6 1/8	6 3/8	5 1/4	0.5†	2	750	1.43
Curtiss A. and M. Co. (A)	Chieftain	600	2,200	2-Radial	12	5 5/8	5 1/2	...	Direct	4	900	1.50
Allison Engineering Co. (A)	Liberty A.C.	410	1,800	V-45°	12	4 5/8	7	5.3	0.6†	2	1,000	2.44
A. D. C. Aircraft Ltd. (B)	Cirrus II	75	1,800	Vertical	4	4.33	5.12	4.9	Direct	2	285	3.80
De Havilland (B)	Gipsy	85	1,900	Vertical	4	4 1/2	5 1/16	5.0	Direct	2	280	3.30
Bristol, Ltd. (B)	Cherub III	33	2,960	Flat	2	3.54	3.8	5.5	Direct	2	95	2.88
Bristol, Ltd. (B)	Jupiter VI, A.M.	440	1,700	Radial	9	5.75	7.5	5.3	0.5†	4	720	1.63
Bristol, Ltd. (B)	Mercury (racer)	800	2,500	Radial	9	5.75	6.5	...	Direct	4	680	0.85
Armstrong-Siddeley (B)	Genet	65	1,850	Radial	5	4	4	5.2	Direct	2	200	3.08
Armstrong-Siddeley (B)	Jaguar III	385	1,700	2-Radial	14	5	5 1/2	5.0	0.657†	2	800	2.08
Lorraine-Dietrich (F)	100 CV	100	1,350	Radial	5	4.92	5.51	5.0	Direct	2	331	3.31
Lorraine-Dietrich (F)	230 CV	230	1,800	Radial	7	5.31	5.90	5.0	Direct	2	575	2.50
Anzani (F)	6-80	80	1,500	2-Radial	6	4.13	4.92	5.1	Direct	2	225	2.81
Siemens & Halske (G)	Sh 11	96	1,750	Radial	7	3.94	4.72	...	Direct	2	333	3.47

(A)—American (B)—British (F)—French (G)—German

* Each cylinder fires every revolution, therefore equivalent to a reduction gear of 0.5 ratio.

† Made in both direct-drive and geared models—weight given is for direct drive.

The Airplane And Its Engine - Chatfield and Taylor - McGraw-Hill - 1928

TABLE IV.—PRINCIPAL CHARACTERISTICS OF TYPICAL WATER-COOLED AIRPLANE ENGINES, 1928

Manufacturer	Model	Rated		Type	Number cylinders	Bore, inches	Stroke, inches	Compression ratio	Propeller gear ratio	Number valves per cylinder	Weight, pounds	
		Horsepower	Revolutions per minute								Total	Per horsepower (rated)
Curtiss A. & M. Co. (A)	OX-5*	90	1,400	V 90°	8	4	5	4.9	Direct	2	377	4.2
U. S. Government	Liberty 12-A*	420	1,700	V 45°	12	5	7	5.4	Direct	2	875	2.08
Curtiss A. & M. Co. (A)	D-12-D	435	2,300	V 60°	12	4.5	6	5.3	Direct	4	680	1.56
Curtiss A. & M. Co. (A)	Conqueror	600	2,400	V 60°	12	5 1/8	6 1/4	5.8	0.6†	4	755	1.26
Packard Motor Car Co. (A)	3A-1500	600	2,500	V 60°‡	12	5 3/8	5 1/2	5.5	0.507†	4	760	1.27
Packard Motor Car Co. (A)	3A-2500	770	2,000	V 60°	12	6 3/8	6 1/2	5 1/4	0.506†	4	1,160	1.51
Packard Motor Car Co. (A)	X Racer	1,250	2,700	X	24	5 3/8	5	....	Direct	4	1,402	1.12
D. Napier & Son., Ltd. (B)	Lion 11B	470	2,000	W-60°	12	5 1/2	5 1/8	5.8	0.658	4	966	2.06
D. Napier & Son., Ltd. (B)	Racer	875	3,300	W-60°	12	5 1/2	5 1/8	10.0	0.765	4	930	1.06
Rolls-Royce Ltd. (B)	F-12	490	2,250	V-60°	12	5	5 1/2	6.0	0.552	4	865	1.77
Rolls-Royce Ltd. (B)	Condor III	670	1,900	V 60°	12	5 1/2	7 1/2	5.3	0.477	4	1,320	1.97
W. Beardmore & Co., Ltd. (B)	Cyclone	950	1,350	Vertical	6	8 5/8	12	5 1/4	Direct	4	2,150	2.27
Farman (F)	18-W I	550	2,800	W-40°-I	18	4.33	4.92	6.0	0.393	4	820	1.49
Hispano-Suiza (F)	12-M	500	2,000	V-60°	12	5.12	6.69	6.0	Direct†	2	882	1.76
Hispano-Suiza (F)	12-N	650	2,000	V-60°	12	5.9	6.69	6.0	Direct†	2	1,000	1.54
Lorraine-Dietrich (F)	450 CV.	450	1,850	W-60°	12	4.72	7.08	5.5	0.647†	2	850	1.89
Lorraine-Dietrich (F)	650 CV.	650	2,000	W-40°	18	4.72	7.08	6.0	0.647†	2	1,190	1.83
Junkers (G)	L-5	280	1,500	Vertical	6	6.3	7.48	5.5	Direct	2	705	2.52
B. M. W. (G)	VI	600	1,500	V-60°	12	6.29	7.48	5.5	0.626†	2	1,120	1.87
F. I. A. T. (I)	A-S3 (racer)	970	2,500	V-60°	12	5.71	6.88	6.0	Direct	4	920	0.95

(A)—American (B)—British (F)—French (G)—German (I)—Italian

* Obsolete—in use but no longer manufactured.

† Made in both direct and geared models. Weight given is for direct drive.

‡ Made in both upright and inverted models.

because they thought it required very expensive castor oil. I knew otherwise, for it was a radial, not a rotary engine, and so I bought it cheaply. It was in A-1 condition, and I now had a reserve Salmson.

With this more-powerful Salmson-powered plane I figured to make money by taking sightseers four-at-a-time instead of the conventional one-by-one. Chino looked like a good bet to try this out. It was a small farming community about five miles southwest of Ontario that had many migrant farm workers. When they were paid they were great spenders until their money was gone. I arranged for a ticket seller to meet me at a hayfield in Chino on payday. This fellow was an auctioneer and had worked with me before. He could sure huckster tickets!

The field was small, but the Salmson yanked the plane off the ground with its four passengers, easily clearing the tall eucalyptus windbreak at the west end. However, I had to be sure the engine was warmed-up, running smooth and revving fast or those trees could be a real bother. We were doing a land office business; I'd already carried two or three loads for ten-minute rides at $2.50 apiece. It looked like we were going to make a bundle. There were about 25 field hands waiting patiently for what was probably their first airplane ride, and I could see more coming from across the fields. I was giving her the gun for the next takeoff when, suddenly, all hell broke loose. The big four-bladed prop shattered and flew in all directions. Luckily it hit no one. I never knew why it shattered: whether someone threw a rock or it sucked-up something from the uneven hayfield or what. But when the propeller goes on a radial, it's virtually a deathknell for the engine too. With a broken prop, the imbalanced crankshaft takes a terrible racking. The crankcase usually breaks the engine mounts off and the engine drops out of the plane. This can mean disaster if one is in the air. But in my case we were fortunately still on the ground when the engine tore itself loose, dangling only by the ignition and water lines.

I was in quite a fix, but I surely couldn't see refunding the money to that lineup of passengers. I got a friend to rush me by car to Ontario, and I flew the other Boeing back to Chino. Since this one had the Renault engine I thought it wise to take only two customers up at a time, but even then I just barely cleared those trees. During the ten-minute flight I decided that it was simply too dangerous for this small field. It was heartbreaking when I gave the rest of the paid-up customers their

193

money back. Discretion may well be the better part of valor, but it certainly left me feeling poorer that day.

But after my taste of the Salmson, now, more than ever I knew that the future of aviation lay with new, powerful and sophisticated air-cooled radials like the Whirlwind and the then-rumored Wasp. I also knew that I had to have more powerful engines for the airline, especially if we won the Post Office airmail competition. With my limited means I couldn't dream of spending $5,000-and-up for a new Wright engine, but I did have two Salmson radials, though water-cooled (and one in pieces in a basket), and an idea entered my fundless brain.

I had studied the Whirlwind carefully, and piecing my Salmson together I saw that I could probably convert it from water-cooled to air-cooled, like the Wright engine. Also, since I had a lead on over 100 of these engines, if I were successful in making the conversion I should be able to make a good business selling them nationwide.

I took a combustion cylinder from the damaged engine and stripped the steel water jacket off. I then made some copper fins and brazed them to the cylinder in a manner similar to the Whirlwind. It made a very handsome piece of machinery, and I polished it until it shone. Like a good promoter, I took this gleaming cylinder to Al Menasco. He was impressed, and also liked my idea for the disposition of the remainder of Art Smith's Salmsons. Working through him I negotiated a six month option to purchase the lot at $90 each, providing I worked hard on a program that would sell the whole batch.

Waterman Engine cylinder detail

I fabricated a complete set of nine cylinders with the copper cooling fins, rebuilt the Salmson and christened this now air-cooled radial the *Waterman Engine*. I made one other change. The original engine used 'rat trap' valve springs which could be troublesome. I replaced these with standard Liberty engine valve springs by using extended valve stems, thus lessening potential valve problems. I figured that these modifications cost around $400, and with the original cost of $90, the total was around $500 each. I planned a selling price of $1,000 apiece, a figure which would return a good profit and be way below the price for a virtually comparable $5,000 Whirlwind. I then installed the new Waterman radial in an airline Boeing.

We had enjoyed so many courtesies from Clyde and Cotta Forsythe that I was hard put figuring out how to reciprocate. Clyde was a golfer, and a good one at that; he even did a monthly golfing cartoon for a leading New York magazine. There was a new golf course, The Parkridge Country Club in Corona (15 miles south of Ontario), that was hoping to attract flying golfers with their new landing strip, and Carol and I invited the Forsythes to join us as the first golfers to use this unique service (November, 1925). We all piled into the the Waterman-Salmson powered Boeing and flew off to Corona. Upon landing we were royally entertained by the club's management, played a round of golf, and took off for home. It was a lot of fun, though I'm a lousy golfer!

Flying golfers! (l-r) Clyde, Carol, Me and Cotta Forsythe

195

After initial discussions with Menasco about obtaining financing, I flew to several local fields to generate interest in my engine. Interest I got, but few potential orders. I realized that I'd have to go 'back East' to find customers. It was now the summer of 1925.

On one of my demonstration flights I landed at Clover Field to see Bach Aircraft Co. Remember, several years before I had fired a young Morton Bach when I thought that he was thinking too much and working too little on Brand's Tioga Eagle. After that, he built up a sizable business setting-up and rigging Jennys. He charged a nominal fee, but got the Jenny packing crates which he then used to build a couple good hangars. (Planes became nicknamed *"crates"* from this Jenny period.) His business enlarged into general aircraft maintenance and repair and some passenger carrying in his Standard named *"King Tut"* (whose tomb had just been discovered in 1922). He also designed and built a very sweet Rhone-powered biplane. By the time I visited him he was preparing to build another design. *It was a trimotor; compact, very fast, and a good load carrier.* His sales manager, Wilbur White, was raising financing to put this pace-setting plane into production.

Outrigger engines for the Bach *"Air Yacht"* were to be two Kinner 5-cylinder 100-hp radials, which Bert Kinner had developed from the pioneering 3-cylinder Lawrance engine used on the Airster. The main center engine was to be a Wright J5 Whirlwind. However, after Morton saw my radial perform and compared prices against his limited means, he placed an order with me. The Waterman engine was going to power what was designed to be the *world's fastest transport.*

In the meantime the Post Office Department called for bids on the first five feeder lines: the fourth, CAM Route 4, Los Angeles - Salt Lake City, which I wanted. Bid opening was to be September 15, 1925. I immediately started pulling together all the data and information, including a description of the planned aircraft and how it would be modified to comply with the postal requirements. I anticipated using the airline Boeing, converting the passenger cabin for mail, shortening the lower wing and installing a Hall-Scott L6 instead of the Renault engine. Later I would install the Waterman radial. I worked very hard on this bid preparation and at the same time scouted around to see what the competition might be up to. All I could find out was that there were three or four groups planning to bid. None had any operating experience, and only

196

one looked to be a possible threat - a syndicate headed by a Byron L. Graves and tied-in somehow with the Ford Motor Company.

Graves was Ford's Southern California regional manager, and a long-time associate of Henry Ford. He was a nice guy to meet. He would be very pleasant, smile, offer you a cigar and later send you happily on your way. Then you started to realize what had happened; he had told you nothing but you had told him a lot!

His company, *Western Air Express,* had some other pretty high-powered talent associated with it: Harry Chandler of the *Los Angeles Times,* James Talbot of Richfield Oil, and a Harris Hanshue, a famous ex-race car driver who was going to manage it.

There were some things that I didn't know, and when I started having trouble raising financing these became apparent. For one thing, Graves' boss was an aircraft manufacturer. Henry Ford was now in business with Bill Stout producing the Stout 2-AT all-metal monoplane, powered by a single Liberty engine. Ford was anxious to sell this plane to these new airmail contractors, and this explained why Graves played such a strong role in organizing Western, both in its inception and its financing. Also, as you recall, one of my original Ontario associates was a Ford dealer who was having difficulty getting Model T's because the factory couldn't keep up with the demand. He told me that he couldn't openly support my airmail endeavor, and furthermore, he was told by Ford that unless he subscribed for at least $5,000 in Western stock he would find far fewer Model T's coming his way. Apparently this was 'standard procedure' for Ford. And to-cap-that-off, the tremendous influence of the Harry Chandler made it impossible for me to even raise Ontario Aircraft Corp's modest $50,000 goal.

The details of this story later became known to me because Graves, Hanshue and Stout were all close associates of mine further into my career, as we'll see.

I was spending a lot of time pounding-the-pavement looking for money, and in figuring and refiguring our proposed bid. I began to understand why people like Chandler and Ford were interested. The potential profits looked fantastic.

One day at Big Bear I got a ride back to Ontario with my old friend, Corliss Moseley, and his wife. On the way down we talked about my plans for the airmail bid, and when we arrived home I asked them in to

197

meet Carol and have lunch with us. When we got into the house, my papers were laying about, and we got into further discussion about my ideas and figures. I showed Moseley my plans for the mail planes, and he seemed very interested. He surely was! Weeks later, to my dismay, I found out that he was to be *chief operations manager* for Western, working directly under Hanshue!

After leaving the Army Air Service, where Moseley had been in charge at Clover Field, he'd commanded the California Air National Guard at Griffith Park in Los Angeles. He had used Guard planes and pilots to survey the way to Salt Lake City, establishing a route and locating emergency landing fields. Later, when Western had the route, only ex-Guard pilots or those having the blessing of Harry Chandler were chosen. Little credence was given for any other experience.

Nevertheless, I went doggedly ahead figuring the fantasies of postal largess. I could only rely on the Kelly Bill and its stipulation that the maximum a carrier could receive would be four-fifths, or 80 percent, of the postage paid. Though inexact, I figured that there were typically 40 letters to the pound, at 10 cents apiece, equalling $4. The top bid, then, couldn't exceed 80 percent of $4, or roughly $3.20 per pound. Said another way, if each letter's postage was 10 cents-per-ounce, then the carrier could get up to 8 cents-per-ounce. I spent many hours estimating expenses and laying out projections of what I thought the traffic would be and what it would bear, and finally arrived at a bid figure of 7.31 cents-per-ounce, or 73.1 percent of postal revenue. This would generate profits of over $2,000 per-month with the absolute minimun of 150 pounds each-way. Profits went to over $10,000 per-month when the weight of the mail was only doubled to a still conservative 300 pounds each-way, a sum far too heady for contemplation!

I submitted our bid, and when they were opened in Washington on September 15th I was excited to learn that we were low bidder. The only other bonded bidder, Western Air Express, had bid the maximum 8 cents.

And there was more bad news for Western. They learned that their Stout airplane was unacceptable because it had a poor altitude capability. They then immediately amended their bid, substituting the new Douglas M2 biplane. One good reason for this was that the Stout 2-AT was a dog at anything over 5,000 feet, and this route flew a lot higher than that. But

198

the main reason was probably that Douglas and Chandler were buddies and major Los Angeles businessmen. *Ironically, Harry Chandler had first gotten interested in aviation in connection with my preliminary financing plans for the Thomas-Morse MB3 Army contract, which I'd lost to Boeing. He had then underwritten Douglas' financing for the Navy's torpedo plane which I had decided not to bid on.*

Whatever the reason for the plane switch, apparently Henry Ford was really burning. When Graves went to his office the next day he found another man sitting at his desk. Just as he was about to throw this fellow out Graves was handed a telegram telling him he was fired, signed "Henry Ford"!

But being the low bidder, I felt that I had the world by the tail; that the award was almost mine as I hit the pavements again, feeling sure of finding financing.

However, I was about to learn the hard way about politics and big business. Western had been able to raise over $300,000 while I was still struggling for $50,000. Western had no operating experience, no equipment, no airfield; I had all of these. Western was high bidder; I was low. But, on November 7, 1925, Western Air Express was awarded *CAM-4,* Los Angeles - Salt Lake City; the result, I understood, of a $25,000 Washington lobbying effort involving William MacCracken.

In retrospect it is interesting to see the calibre and resources of the other various CAM route-bidders. Route *CAM-1,* New York - Boston, went to Colonial Airways. This group included Connecticut's governor, a Boston banker, a Rockefeller, Vanderbilt Whitney and young Juan Trippe *who had promoted and helped create the Kelly Bill through his well-placed Yale connections.* Route *CAM-2,* Chicago - St. Louis, went to Robertson Aircraft Corp. owned by war flyers Frank and Bill Robertson. This was a shoe-string affair with a young just-commissioned ex-barnstormer, Charles Lindbergh, as their chief pilot. Route *CAM-3,* Chicago - Dallas, went to National Air Transport, organized by an ex-Assistant Postmaster General, a Chicago banker, Whirlwind designer Charles Lawrance and Philadelphia's G.T. Ludington. Route *CAM-5,* Elko (Nevada) - Pasco (Washington), was given to Walter Varney's Varney Air Service, Ltd. This was a 'boondocks' route for which he was the sole bidder.

At this point, I'd like to digress to talk about aviation organizations, since I was involved with many. And, my involvement led to a job possibility with the Department of Commerce.

The Aero Club of France had been founded in 1898 for ballooning. The advent of balloon races then caused the formation of the *Federation Aeronautique Internationale* on October 14, 1905 as a governing body for the licensing of all those either competing or exhibiting in the air. In the same year, the *Aero Club of America* was formed as this country's representative of the FAI, and it licensed many balloon pilots prior to 1909, just as in Europe.

Frank Lahm, a young U.S. Army officer, became interested in ballooning while in France and entered the first *Gordon Bennett* Balloon Race in 1906. (Prior to 1906, the Gordon Bennett - *The Paris Herald* - races were Europe's premier *auto* races.) He won it and thus did with a balloon what Glenn Curtiss would be first to do with an airplane in 1909. Lahm then became the first Army man taught to fly by the Wrights, and thus the *first designated aviator in the U.S. Army.*

The First International Air Meet was held in France's Champagne region at Reims in 1909, and the most sought after prize was the Gordon Bennett Cup for the fastest laps around a closed course. All the great French aviators were entered in this event: Bleriot, Latham, Paulhan, Farman, Voisin; and one lone American, the motorcycle speed king from Hammondsport, New York, Glenn Hammond Curtiss. Curtiss won that race and the Cup, flying at 46-1/2 mph. He thus firmly earned his niche as the most popular American aviator: both on the Continent, where the Commission Aerienne Mixte gave him the No. 2 license, alphabetically after Bleriot; and in America where the Aero Club likewise bestowed upon him license No. 1. This triumph, closely following his Scientific American achievement, had put Curtiss in a position which would infuriate the Wrights and which was compounded further by their patent litigation.

Therefore when I met Glenn Curtiss and became his unpaid employee in January of 1910 I was realizing the dream of every sky-struck American boy. Curtiss generated tremendous awe and hero worship throughout his lifetime. After Lindbergh flew the Atlantic and was just becoming a legend in his own right, Ralph O'Neill (New York, Rio and Buernos Aires Line - NYRBA) remembers that, more than anything else, "Slim" Lindbergh wanted to work for the Curtiss organization.

200

At that time, the FAI system of licensing was the only recognition or authenticated evaluation of a pilot and his skill. Yet it didn't mean anything more than the fact that a pilot had passed a certain number of quite simple flight tests. If a pilot was not going to race, compete or exhibit in a certified meet or exhibition, then an FAI license was of little value to him or her. However, the FAI license was used by many of the flying schools as certification of their graduates' flying abilities. I remember a professor from Los Angeles, Harry LaVerne Twining, and his assistant, Warren Eaton, coming to North Island in 1911-1912 as official FAI observers. They were requested by Curtiss to pass upon the proficiency of his students; therefore you'll find that all Curtiss School graduates are listed as FAI licensees. I was frequently asked to be a pylon judge, certifying that the student didn't cut into the pylon air space, though I never had occasion to have an FAI license myself.

It wasn't until 1927, following the Air Commerce Act of 1926, that there was any official Federal legislation of aviation activities, such as pilot licensing. Shortly after World War I a group of us pilots began to realize that a self-governing body should be developed in order to try to control harem-scarem flying, best or worst exemplified by Ormer Locklear. We formed the *Professional Pilots Association* with the idea that the term 'professional' would denote flying as a profession, just like the practice of medicine or law. (Sometime later, 1930, another group of pilots around Chicago led by my old student, David Behncke, organized what evolved into the *Airline Pilots Association,* later affiliating with the American Federation of Labor).

The first president of our association was Gilbert Budwig, with Howard Patterson as secretary. We had about 20 members. For membership a pilot had to have flown for at least four years and, most crucial, another member had to have no fear of flying with him while having no access to the controls! In actuality this requirement was rarely enforced, but it was an implication that had to have full accord from all of our members. There were many 'devil take the hindmost' pilots that were automatically ruled out for membership, and those of our members who barnstormed, full or part-time, were well-advised that at no time could they perform aerobatics while carrying passengers for hire. We well-knew that we had to erase the reckless and hazardous flying image before the public would start to accept aviation as anything but a fool's plaything; as a barnstormer, even Lindbergh had been known as *"The Flying Fool"!* I was personally a leader in this 'crusade' and lodged one of the first complaints against a stunting pilot in 1921.

Earl Daugherty of Long Beach was a fine pilot in our group, while at the same time being an irrepressible daredevil. With Frank Hawks he performed the first aerial refueling; he was also married in the air - oh, he had a list of stunts with no end. For several years he served as my vice chairman of the Aero Club's Trade Committee. In December of 1928, though, he finally paid the price for disregarding our rule about stunting with passengers. He tore the wings off his plane, and all were killed. *Earlier that year Helen Carpenter took her three children, Win, Alice and two-year-old Jack, for a 'free' real estate promotion ride with Daugherty, something that their father, upon learning of it, really exploded about!*

For the most part we were self-governing, trying to control Southern California aviation activities with a conservative approach. It was not an easy chore. After Dave Behncke got his group going we corresponded, hoping to merge our two organizations because our aims were common though our methods a bit different. We were never able to work this out, though I sure tried during my presidency following Patterson's. Boyd Montieth Shelton followed me as president, and thereafter, the organization seemed to go downhill as it became more and more 'weekend' flyers, dimming our professional image.

The organization eventually quietly folded its wings. But not before we had established a code regarding ceilings, visibilities, safe routes and aircraft airworthiness which were extensively adopted into the Department of Commerce's Aeronautics Section when it was set up to administer a new Federal Act in 1926. This law provided for the appointment of an Assistant Secretary of Commerce for Aeronautics and the establishment of a bureaucracy to regulate all interstate aircraft activities. Its jurisdiction included: licensing and inspection of all pilots, the approval of all aircraft engineering and design, the layout and lighting of airways, and the certification of airports.

202

Arrest 219 Pilots for Air Traffic Violations

TWO hundred and nineteen pilots were arrested for breaking traffic rules of the skyways during the last year. Their offenses included taking-off or landing at airports in the wrong manner, low flying over congested areas, stunt flying with pay passengers, dropping heavy objects, carrying explosives, flying without a license, carelessness, and flying an overloaded machine. One pilot was caught smuggling aliens into the country in his machine.

Frank Tichenor of *Aero Digest*, then the leading aviation magazine, editorialized the desirability of getting a well-qualified professional pilot into this new Assistant Secretary position. Our Professional Pilots Association thought that we should recommend a candidate for the final selection by Commerce Secretary Herbert Hoover. A major meeting was called - the largest turnout ever with over 150 Southern California aviators attending. The ramifications of this most important appointment were thoroughly discussed. The conclusion of the meeting came with a resolution being passed that *I should be our candidate.*

Although I was well-known throughout the West, I figured that I needed much more national exposure. Coming in late July 1926 was the *"On To Denver"* race, a very popular affair. It was held each year to a different 'on to' city with aircraft handicapped according to engine displacement and the distance flown. To participate in this race, only to Denver, I figured I'd need the smallest displacement engine I could find. Scouting around, I located the KinneR Airster that Amelia Earhart had first bought, used, for $2,000.

I'd first seen it when she and Neta Snook had it at the Elks Week races at the Beverly Speedway in 1921 (see page 147). Like I, Amelia had been fascinated with its engine, a Lawrance L2, 3-cylinder of only 60-hp. It was the primitive first in the line of American radial engines developed by Charles Lawrance that led-up to the famous Whirlwind. Its horsepower certainly seems puny when compared to the heights that radial engines achieved - in 1949 the Wasp Major developed *3,500-hp* from four banks of seven cylinders, 28 in all.

Unknown to me at the time - until much later, 1975 - after Amelia sold the plane its new owner cracked-it-up, killing both himself and his luckless passenger. Thus, when I located the Airster and made a 50-50 deal with its owner for the proceeds of the race, it had been completely rebuilt. *But it still had that original engine.*

I thought that I had the ideal aircraft, tailor-made for this race. And I hoped by winning it I would get enough publicity to influence Hoover's appointment.

I took the little plane out to Ontario to prepare it. Trying to figure the most advantageous starting point, I finally selected San Francisco. I'd then simply follow the well-marked transcontinental Post Office route to Salt Lake City, and then "On to Denver". I took off early on July 28th

203

KinneR Airster at start of "On to Denver" Race - 1926

headed for San Francisco through the San Joaquin Valley. About halfway along I noticed that the oil pressure had suddenly gone down. This, of course, meant that the engine wasn't being properly lubricated. I immediately made an emergency landing on a dry lake near the Shell oil pumping plant at Cheney, about 50 miles west of Fresno, sorely perplexed by this problem.

I'd flown for three-hours and-twenty-minutes and had covered 250 miles - damn good time. After landing I checked everything out but could find nothing amiss. In fact, the engine seemed to be very well lubricated as it was even splashing a bit of oil, but not enough to indicate any damage. At any rate, I made several adjustments and took off again, this time rolling the plane over on its back thinking that would break an air lock or maybe cure whatever was out of whack. No such luck. I landed again, and with the help of Shell's H.W. Gray went over everything again. Again I took the Airster up, and still couldn't fathom the trouble.

After landing the second time I chanced to grab the tip of the propeller, pulling it forward rather than in a circular motion, and found that I could move it about three inches fore and aft. For that, there was only one explanation: the crankshaft was broken! Few people would believe that I had two successful flights with an engine which had a completely

204

broken crankshaft, but that was certainly the case. Later, when we disassembled the engine, we found that there was a complete break in the shaft across its rear cheek. The jaggedness of the break had let the shaft still turn the accessories, but the oil was being pumped through the crankshaft and diverting into the open crankcase, thus showing zero pressure.

The broken shaft threw me totally out of contention, and feeling mighty low I called Carol to bring the car up to Cheney via Fresno. I then took the wings off, tied them to the fuselage, hooked the tailskid to the car's luggage compartment and towed the whole shebang back to Ontario. This sort of thing was getting to be an old story with Carol as twice before she'd had to do the same thing when I'd had trouble with the Boeings. The sort of mechanical problems that caused these aborted flights were more normal than not, and we thought little of breakdowns other than their being a damn nuisance. That was the mechanical 'state-of-the-art' in the 1920's. *Lindbergh's flight would really be the first to demonstrate the engine reliability that we were just starting to get in the latter part of that decade.*

Thus my plans were killed for winning the race and the follow-up transcontinental trip I'd planned for the appointment. I wasn't able to pursue the matter aggressively - though it probably wouldn't have made any difference. Hoover ignored the aviation community and appointed Bill MacCracken, a Washington attorney. He did a fair job until 1929 when he left government, but in 1934 he got some bad publicity because of his collusive role in the *"Air Mail Scandle"* (see page 199).

(The Federal Government had just established full recognition of aviation by appointing the "Big Three" Air Chiefs. In 1926, Edward P. Warner, professor of Aeronautics at M.I.T., was named Assistant Secretary of the Navy for Air; F. Trubee Davison was named Assistant Secretary of War for Air; and William P. MacCracken, Jr. was appointed as Assistant Secretary of Commerce.)

The Department of Commerce soon started their program for licensing pilots, setting up six districts throughout the country. They initially trained their inspectors in Washington. Each inspector was then sent

(l-r) Edward P. Warner, Charles Lindbergh, William MacCracken and F. Trubee Davison - Washington Post - July 3, 1927. Save for the "eastern establishment" I might have been sitting there! - Or was it because Hoover was a Stanford graduate?

Warner, the Navy's Air Secretary, was the first to know Lindbergh, having met him upon his triumphal arrival in Washington on the USS Memphis, June 11, 1927. The Spirit of St. Louis was then "erected" at Anacostia Naval Air Station under Warner's overall supervision, assisted by Ken Lane and Ken Boedecker of Wright Aeronautical, the engine's manufacturer. Note Warner peering into the Spirit's cabin.

206

into the field with instructions to license all eligible pilots, and one of my old Berkeley students, Walter Parkin, was sent to Southern California. Here I was in reverse again! One of my students was inspecting me. When Walter arrived in Ontario he had already inspected several pilots in Los Angeles, and we laughed about the peculiar situation. He said, *"Waldo, well, I at least have to say that I saw you fly - so get in the plane and circle the field once and we'll write you up."* This I immediately did, getting license number 417, but one of our more swashbuckling pilots didn't fare so easy. He decided that he'd do a stunt landing for Parkin, impressing upon him with just how wonderful a pilot he was. But he misjudged his height, his plane stalled and he made such a hard landing that its landing gear collapsed right in front of Walter. He got his license, all right, but hotshot Earl Daugherty was the laughing stock for quite a while.

Several other organizations had their origins at about this time. One, the Air Race Association, was formed to bring the National Air Races to Los Angeles in 1928. This association, later reorganized as the Air Industries Association, periodically put on static aviation shows. I was a vice president and very active in it until we finally disbanded.

Also at about this time the *National Aeronautic Association* (NAA) was formed, replacing the now outmoded Aero Club of America. NAA chapters were established throughout the country with our Southern California group, of which I was president in 1937, becoming the largest.

Since my earliest days I'd always been an active participant in the various groups I was affiliated with. For instance, while president of the Professional Pilots Association I served upon the committee that recommended the location for Los Angeles' municipal field - *Mines Field,* which was just south of where Venice Field had been and is now Los Angeles International Airport (LAX). We were severely criticized for that selection because of the intermittent fog there. But the public didn't realize that instrument flying would soon be common, greatly lessening this problem in favor of the other obvious advantages of this site. In addition to our site recommendation, we recommended that Cliff Henderson be the field's first general manager.

So with my hopes for the Commerce job dashed and the air mail route awarded to Western Air Express, I was feeling pretty down-in-the-dumps. Virtually all of my plans and long preparation had simply van-

207

ished into graspless air. When the airmail contract fell through, all of my credibility in Ontario went too, so I decided to close the airline as it wasn't setting any success records. (True, later I could get some solace from the *"Air Mail Scandal"* - but that wouldn't be until Hearst's young Fulton Lewis Jr. broke that story in 1934.)

Then, to-top-everything-off, the Heat Mill project fizzled as well. I'd had one of Reynold's mechanics tending the machine and was away when the first freeze hit. The unit had run for 10-1/2 hours when it threw a connecting rod through the crankcase, and the resulting backlash sheared-off the long propeller shaft, stopping everything. As the Union engine normally used one-gallon-of-oil-per-hour, and we had a 10 gallon oil reservoir, it became apparent why the engine ran dry. There was little I could do to convince the growers that the fault lay with a stupid mechanic that failed to add oil! They figured that if one of Reynold's mechanics couldn't operate it properly, neither could they.

My idea was a good one, though, and after my patents expired this type of frost prevention became widely used. It was a rueful thought for my pocketbook but, I guess, a considerable contribution to the good of the citrus industry.

After liquidating the Ontario Aircraft Corporation and the Big Bear Airline, as the *Waterman Aircraft Co.* I moved with two of the four-passenger Boeings to Clover Field, then the top airport in the West, to continue the passenger-carrying and charter business However, I soon found that the Boeings, which had been just fine out in San Bernardino County, were totally out-of-date in sophisticated Santa Monica next to the latest creations of Ed Fisk and Donald Douglas. Business was very scarce, and my only hopes for making a few bucks seemed to lie in drumming-up more orders for the Waterman engine.

However, at this time I had my own radio program on KHJ which was earning some money. To lick my wounds over the loss of the airmail bid, gather some interesting material for the program and perhaps find some buyers for the Waterman engine, I hatched a new scheme. I would 'survey' the newly-awarded airmail routes, following-up on an article "Government's Air Mail" by J Parker Van Zandt in *National Geographic Magazine,* January 1926. I wrote Assistant Postmaster Harry New with this proposition. With formal permission he soon authorized me to ride on all of the new CAM routes on the condition that I would give him a full report of my findings.

Therefore, in the fall of 1926 I left Los Angeles, suitcase and specifications for the Waterman engine in hand. It was the start of a six-week's odyssey that covered over 6,800 miles upon eleven different lines - quite a feat then. I flew first with Western Air Express, *CAM-4,* in a Douglas M-2 mailplane to Salt Lake City, an uneventful trip. (WAE's first scheduled trip had been April 17, 1926.) Then, because I wasn't authorized to ride the Post Office's own planes on the main transcontinental route, I caught the train to Chicago.

There I connected with National Air Transport, *CAM-3,* for the run to Dallas. The only place for me to ride was in the mail compartment. They removed its triangular cover and I curled-up with the mail sacks. This was an interesting journey in more ways than one. As the plane made its stops enroute - Moline, Illinois; St. Joseph and Kansas City, Missouri; Wichita, Oklahoma City and Fort Worth - there were usually two-or-three sacks put-on. Always one with a heavy brass padlock contained the registered mail, and the rest had only lighter steel locks. A corresponding number of sacks were typically put-off. Sitting there with my knees under my chin I had little else to do and nothing to watch, so I began to get curious about why those bags seemed so lightly loaded. Feeling them carefully, I was surprised and wryly bemused to discover that each appeared to contain only *one* letter!

By this time the rules had been changed from the time of my bid, and the mail was being paid for by the pound, including the sack and the lock. Registered mail required the additional 'protection' of the much-heavier brass lock. I later learned that at least one CAM operator had ordered its employees to mail one registered letter at each stop. This created a lucrative built-in volume and revenue far in excess of the actual postage paid. This was one item that was surely going into my report to Harry New.

It was certainly postal larceny, and unnecessary when one considers the legitimate earnings possible by playing within the rules. Harris Hanshue later told me that Western Air Express (WAE) had been hauling loads of around 500 pounds between Los Angeles and Salt Lake City, grossing $1,500. With costs of only $350 per-trip, they were thus netting one-way profits of approximately $1,150. This gave them a very tidy net of around $60,000-a-month!

Will Rogers, "the patron saint of aviation", was an avid aviation booster and early user of air transportation. He flew the only kind of air transport available then - the mailplanes. He once commented, *"While you are talking about progressing aviation, don't overlook...Western Air Express. One year and a half ago, they started with only 20 pounds of mail. Today, in here packed around me, is 550 pounds."* *("They didn't put stamps on him, but he paid for his own weight as if he were a package.")*

As my sojourn progressed, I became more and more disenchanted with my mode of travel. I was further aggravated by the fact that I didn't have a parachute whereas the pilots usually did. Finally, though, I rationalized that most of the time we were flying under such a low overcast and there wouldn't have been enough room for the 'chute to open even if I'd had one.

Upon returning to Chicago, I was scheduled to fly to the Twin Cities, Minneapolis-St. Paul, on *CAM-9*. Charles Dickinson, the luxuriantly-whiskered grand old aviation booster, had initially started this service. But terrible "Siberia" weather and too many crackups forced him to relinquish the route to a new company, originally organized by Bill Stout, called Northwest Airways. Dickinson was truly one of the patriarchs of American aviation. Though in his seventies, he was instrumental in founding *"The Early Birds"* - *"An Association of Oldtime Airmen"*, the most exclusive 'club' in aviation. *Each member must have soloed prior to December 17, 1916.* I have been involved with The Early Birds almost from their inception. The organization was first conceived in Chicago in 1928 by P.G.B. "Spud" Morriss, R.C. "Tex" Marshall, Ben Foulois and John Nichols, in addition to Dickinson.

Northwest had just assumed the route on October 1st, and I was to be their *first* passenger. They didn't own any aircraft and had borrowed a Travel Air from National for this inaugural run. My pilot turned out to be Dave Behncke, mentioned earlier. Our flight to St. Paul, with stops at Milwaukee and La Crosse, was normal, and we landed just before noon. I was hosted at lunch by the line's vice president and operations manager, Colonel Louis H. Brittin, and then we loaded-up for the return run. We landed at Milwaukee after dark, picking up Charles "Speed" Holman, the line's second pilot and operations manager, who later won the

210

Thompson Trophy in 1930. Speed crammed his way into the front cockpit with me and the mail sacks, making for a pretty rugged but thankfully short trip into Chicago. I then bid Dave and Speed a warm goodby.

It was again the train to New York because of those darn Post Office rules. And then I connected with Colonial Air Transport, *CAM-1,* for the run to Boston via Hartford, flying in a Wright-powered Curtiss Lark biplane. *The "Aviation Route, NY-B" started at Hadley Field, New Brunswick, N.J. (70 miles southwest of New York City) and ended at "East Boston Airport", now Logan International. Airports enroute included Bethany, CT., Hartford, CT., Dudley and Framingham, MA. The route was marked by twenty-one 24-inch beacons, one every 10 or 15 miles.* In Boston, I met briefly with Sumner Sewall, the district manager in his office-shanty (leaning against the National Guard hangar) and after an overnight stay took off in the morning for the return to New York, this time in a Fokker Universal. (I wouldn't return to Boston until 1974 for our annual Early Birds gathering.)

I then made a quick round trip to Washington D.C. and Norfolk, Virginia, on Philadelphia Rapid Transit Air Service, a passenger line using the new Fokker F-VII trimotors. Since they didn't have an airmail contract, this trip was a courtesy of Mr. J.A. Queeney and Lt. Victor Bertrandias, who was on leave from the Army to organize the lines flying personnel.

The Wright Engine Builder August 1926

Prominent figures in the aeronautical world at the inauguration of the Philadelphia Rapid Transit Air Service between Philadelphia and Washington.

Reading from left to right: Mr. A. H. G. Fokker, Secretary of Commerce Hoover, Admiral Moffet, Chief of the Bureau of Aeronautics, Mr. E. T. Mitten, Chairman of the Board of the P. R. T. Company, Mr. J. W. Drake, Assistant Secretary of Commerce, Mr. J. A. Queeney, President of the P. R. T. Company, Mr. E. P. Warner, Assistant Secretary of the Navy for Aviation, Mr. F. T. Davison, Assistant Secretary of War for Aviation.

211

(Tony Fokker, the Dutchman that designed Germany's best World War I fighters, was now building aircraft in the United States as well as in Holland and continued doing so until his death in New York in 1939. We'll hear more about him.)

Then it was the train, again, to Cleveland to catch *CAM-6,* Ford Motor Co., (managed by Shorty Schroeder), flying in a Stout 2-AT monoplane into Detroit. From there it was Ford again to Chicago on *CAM-7* on the *first* Ford-Stout 3-AT *"Tin Goose"* trimotor.

The nearer to Chicago we came, the more apprehensive I got regarding the next segment of my journey. That was to St. Louis with Robertson Aircraft Co., *CAM-2,* and just the past week or so I'd read about one of their pilots losing his *second* mailplane on November 3, 1926. What made it worse was that he had bailed-out each time. I was scared stiff that I would draw this fellow who was so quick-on-the-trigger. In fact, he held the American 'record' for bailing-out - *four times* - something that earned him scant praise from the rest of us pilots. *For it was then the common belief that you rode your plane down under all but the most final of circumstances.* Of course, we weren't too knowledgeable about each of his jumps, and from what I've learned in later years it appears that each was warranted.

It was just after daylight when I arrived at Checkerboard Field, the air mail station at Maywood Illinois. I was met by a tall, slender chap about 24 years old who looked like he knew his way around airplanes. As soon as we shook hands I knew that he was the guy I feared. *"Hello, I'm Waldo Waterman,"* I said and he replied, *"Hi, I'm Charles Lindbergh."* (The bail-out king!)

> *"Have you got a parachute?" I was gruffly asked.*
> *"No", I said. "I'll risk it without one."*
> *"Put that one on," he said.*
> *"But that one belongs to the pilot," I remonstrated.*
> *"Put it on or you don't fly with me," said Slim Lindbergh.*

Lindbergh was the chief pilot for this struggling enterprise. He then climbed into the D.H. 4's cockpit, and I, wearing a parachute for one of the few times in this long journey, clambered into the front mail com-

212

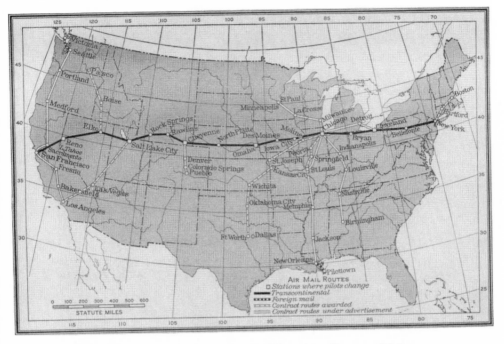

Air Mail Routes - National Geographic Magazine - January 1926

partment. He had it rigged-up with a special seat which he'd first installed in order to give his mother a ride in the plane.

I flew with him to the airmail fields in Peoria, Springfield and into St. Louis where I first made the acquaintance of the Robertson brothers. When I bade Slim "goodby" I had little inkling of his soon-to-be fame or of the circumstances of our next flight together.

From St. Louis I entrained to Albuquerque where I met Colorado Airways, *CAM-12*, who had the route from Pueblo to Denver to Cheyenne. This line had the most rickety equipment that I'd yet seen. On the run to Colorado Springs I flew in a war surplus Hisso-Standard that reminded me of barnstorming days. From there into Denver, though, where I met the line's president, A.F. (Tony) Joseph, I flew in a newer Ryan M-1 monoplane. (WAE took over this route in 1927.)

By train from Denver to Salt Lake City, I again met-up with Western Air Express. My pilot turned out to be Eldred Remlin, who you may recall had raced deMille's Gosling in 1921. WAE was one of the few op-

213

erators requiring that everyone wear parachutes, and as we boarded chutes were handed to me and a young woman reporter doing a story on Western. I put mine on *under* the overcoat that I was wearing. When a mechanic asked me just what I'd do if I had to use it, I said that I'd simply slip the coat off, demonstrating how easily that was accomplished. I noticed that this reporter was taking all this in, wide-eyed, and I could see her making notes about it for her story.

She didn't follow my example, however, and put the chute on over her overcoat. The trip was very smooth until we started running into lower desert air about an hour out, and then it became bumpy and warmer. Casually I started to slip the overcoat off of my shoulders, and I saw a look of consternation on the girl's face. I leaned over and patted her on the knee saying, *"Don't be worried; there's no problem - I'm just taking my coat off because it's too hot."* I've worn a lot of parachutes since that episode, but I've never had to use one.

I finally arrived home, tired and with a suitcase full of dirty laundry. I didn't have any new orders for Waterman engines, but I did have a lot of material for the radio program and some interesting revelations for Harry New.

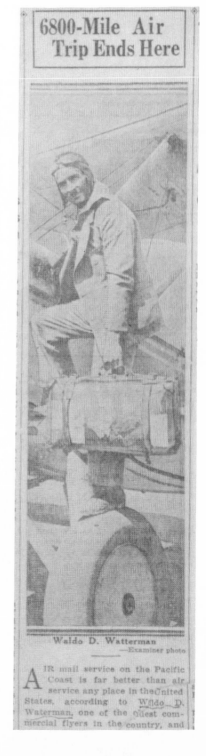

6800-Mile Air Trip Ends Here

Waldo D. Watterman
—Examiner photo

AIR mail service on the Pacific Coast is far better than air service any place in the United States, according to Waldo D. Waterman, one of the oldest commercial flyers in the country, and

Los Angeles Examiner 1926

214

HOW TO ENJOY FLYING

1. *Don't Worry.*

Relax, settle back and enjoy life. If there's any worrying to be done, let the pilot do it; that's what he's hired for.

2. *The Pilot Always Takes Off and Lands into the Wind.*

Be patient while the plane taxis to the corner of the field before taking-off. The luxury of flying doesn't appear until you begin to use the third dimension.

3. *The Pilot Always Banks the Plane when Turning in the Air.*

Just as a race-track is banked at the corners, so an airplane is tilted when making a perfect turn. Take the turns naturally with the plane. Don't try to hold the lower wing up with the muscles of the abdomen—it's unfair to yourself and an unjust criticism of your pilot.

4. *The Atmosphere is like an Ocean.*

It supports the plane just as firmly as the ocean supports a ship. At the speed you are traveling, the air has a density practically equivalent to water; to satisfy yourself, put your hand out the window and feel the tremendous pressure. That ever-present pressure is your guarantee of absolute safety.

5. *The Wind is Similar to an Ocean Current.*

At flying levels it is usually as regular as a great, smooth-flowing river. You can study its direction by watching the shadows of clouds on the country below, or the smoke from chimneys. Once in a while the wind is gusty and rough, like the gulf stream off the coast of Florida. These gusts used to be called "air-pockets," but they are nothing more than billows of warm and cool air and nothing to be alarmed over.

6. *The Air-Pressure Changes with Altitude.*

Some people have ears that are sensitive to the slight change in air-density at different altitudes. If so, swallow once in a while, or breathe a little through the mouth, so that the pressure on both sides of the ear-drums will be equalized. If you hold your nose and swallow, you will hear a little crack in your ears, caused by the suction of air on the ear-drums. Try it.

7. *Dizziness is Unknown in Airplanes.*

There is no discomfort in looking downwards while flying because there is no connection with the earth; only a sense of confidence and security, similar perhaps, to what birds feel. Follow the route on the map, and identify the places you pass. Owing to the altitude, you may think you are moving very slowly, although the normal flying speed of the plane is 95 miles an hour.

8. *When About to Land.*

The pilot throttles the engine, preparatory to gliding down to the Airport. The engine is not needed in landing, and the plane can be landed perfectly with the engine entirely cut off. From an altitude of 2,500 feet, it is possible to glide, with engine stopped, to any field within a radius of 4 miles. Under no occasion, attempt to open the cabin door, until the plane has come to a full stop.

American passenger air travel was beginning a year later:
Air Travel News, December, 1927

Chapter 5

1927 - 1930

Test Pilot, Airline Pioneer & Airport Manager

ALTHOUGH the trip through the airmail routes had given me the chance to interview several manufacturers regarding my engine, I still had no orders other than the single one from Bach. Regardless, I went right to work upon this project - only to have Al Menasco pull-the-rug out from under me, declaring that he wanted the whole thing to himself! Thus, when my option expired he picked it up and, appropriating my idea for modifying the Salmson, formed the Menasco Motors Co. With the financial backing that we'd lined-up for our joint program, Al proceeded to produce his concept of this engine. He figured it would be directly competitive with the Wright Whirlwind if cylinders identical to the J4B's were made for it, so he made new cylinders rather than brazing fins to the originals. This caused his *Menasco-Salmson* engine (Model B2) to end-up selling for $3,250 rather than the $1,000 that I'd planned. As this was still a whale-of-a-lot cheaper than the Whirlwind, it might have worked-out if performance and reliability were comparable.

216

But they weren't. He sold a few of these engines, one to Roscoe Turner and another to Leland Schoenhair for his Ryan M-1. Both of these proved unsatisfactory because Menasco's new cylinders would start coming apart in the wrong places. Also some of the basic weaknesses of the Salmson were emphasized when he tried to crowd too much horsepower out of the original assemblies, far-more than they'd been designed for. The net result was that the Menasco-Salmson was a failure. Although this didn't make me too unhappy, it doomed any other versions of this fine engine. It was too bad; it'd been a damn good idea!

However, with other designs and concepts, mostly borrowed, Menasco went on to build quite a successful engine manufacturing company. It seems apropos that one of his engines was named "Pirate"!

I had now cleared-up my operation at Ontario, and my move to Clover Field wasn't proving renumerative with my antiquated Boeings, so I had plenty of time to spend on the engine conversion for Bach. Shortly after installing my radial in the nose of the trimotor (with smaller Kinners on each side) we found that it wasn't reliable enough, and I was working mostly on it. The Kinners were giving fits, too, even greater than mine, and it finally boiled-down to my total involvement with Bach Aircraft Co. as an experimental engineer and their chief test pilot.

Bach-1 Trimotor

Career changes were also going-on with an old friend, Gilbert (Bud) Budwig. Remember, I'd recommended him as Leslie Brand's pilot for the Tioga Eagle. He'd then found that Mrs. Brand also expected him to act as chauffeur, driving her around in their Pierce-Arrow limosine - and this he'd refused to do. He quit and set-up a business in Glendale for home radios, the latest new-fangled invention. Radio broadcasting was just in its infancy, having begun in 1920 with Westinghouse's KDKA and bursting forth in 1922. By the end of 1922 there were 30 stations; by 1924, 500. Radios were operated by storage batteries: one, two, even three "B" batteries in the living room next to the radio - and these had to be recharged often. Bud was trying to develop a rectifier to convert ordinary household electricity into

217

direct current to eliminate the batteries, and he was finally somewhat successful.

There always was quite a gang of pilots hanging around Bud's shop, and since he made 'bathtub gin' in the back room, I suspect that they were doing a bit more than jaw-boning. However he wanted to get back into flying and I tried to help him in this regard. *Earlier, in 1919, Bud did some test flying for the Loughead brothers. They had started manufacturing airplanes in Santa Barbara in 1916 and built one huge bi-motored ten-passenger flying boat, the F-1, and a couple of Curtiss HS2L's. They then developed a process for making slick fuselages and built a sweet little sport plane, the Model S-1. In addition to being the first aircraft with the Vega-type body, it had a two-cylinder 25-hp air-cooled engine, the Loughead-Stadlman XL-1, when Bud did its testing. Also, it had foldable wings so an owner could store it in his garage, and the lower wings rotated, differentially, as ailerons (for there were none), or together, as an airbrake, upon landing. But there was simply no private plane market then and Loughead had to liquidate in 1921 after building just this one postwar airplane.*

In 1926 Budwig was holding forth with his radio shop cronies when Allan Loughead, looking for backers, brought in the drawings for the first Northrop-designed Vega airplane. Several of Bud's friends saw the design, and one, Kenneth Jay, expressed great interest. He got his boss, ceramic tile manufacturer Fred Keeler, to back this venture. With Keeler's substantial investment, the earlier Loughead operation (or what little there was left of it) was brought to a warehouse-type building in West Hollywood. There, Tony Stadlman (1886-1982), shop superintendent, and young Jack Northrop (1894-1981) set-to-work with a skeleton crew of employees for this new *Lockheed Aircraft Co.,* which was formally organized in December 1926. It had a simpler spelling of the name (after brother Malcolm's popular Lockheed brakes, the first automotive hydraulic brakes, first used by Chrysler).

They proceeded to produce the original *Vega* in 1927. It was an aerodynamic revolution with the patented *Loughead process* for molding a perfectly streamlined monocoque fuselage from thin sheets of plywood veneer. The veneer and a liberal application of adhesive was laid-up in a concrete mold in two lengthwise, mirror-image, segments shaped like the fuselage. Then a rubber air bag was inflated to exert tremendous pressure on the plywood as the adhesive set. This structure was light and

218

very strong, up to its fracture point when it then would shatter in all directions. More importantly, it was so aerodynamically clean that it was unsurpassed for several years and got Lockheed "on the map".

Publicity for the Vega was heightened when George Hearst bought and had his San Francisco Examiner sponsor the first Vega in the fateful Dole *"Pineapple Derby"* to Hawaii. The subsequent loss of this *"Golden Eagle"* apparently did not dim the company's star, for Keeler soon had to move to larger quarters adjoining his factory near San Fernando Road in Burbank (bordered on railroad tracks with an area suitable for flying operations, Burbank-Glendale-Pasadena Airport today). This was early in 1928 and the company prospered to such an extent that Detroit Aircraft bought control in 1929. The stock market crash then doomed this phase of the Lockheed saga, casting the company into obscurity until rebirth in 1932 when Robert E. Gross and partners purchased the assets for only $40,000. By 1961, when Gross died, Lockheed's worth had risen to $500,000,000 and the company employed 60,000 people.

This period of the mid-1920's was one of the most dramatic in the annals of aviation history. Aviation had crawled, walked, ran and was now all set to fly. The public was becoming familiar with names such as Lindbergh, Byrd, Balchen, Chamberlin, Ruth Elder and Nungesser-Coli, many now all but forgotten. One of the most publicized flights (prior to Lindbergh's) was made by Richard Byrd on May 10, 1926 when he flew near the North Pole in the *first Fokker trimotor.* Much to Tony Fokker's chagrin, it was named by Byrd the *"Josephine Ford"* after sponsor Edsel's young daughter After a triumphal return, Byrd, Bennett and Balchen flew the plane around the country. One stop was at Ford's Dearborn Field (then the finest airport in the country - forerunner of today's modern airports) where Ford and Bill Stout were building their all-metal airplanes. The Fokker trimotor was put in the hangar that night, and a bit of hanky-panky went on. While Byrd and his crew were being royally entertained, Stout's engineers scrambled-all-over the Fokker, getting as much aerodynamic design data possible. Even though Bill Stout swore that *"wing curve and all other basic structure had been designed for our ship long before..."* it wasn't long until a very similar Ford-Stout trimotor appeared! Tony Fokker was heard to say that his plane *"gave Ford something more to imitate."*

219

Tony Fokker   *1927*   *Bill Stout*

Tony had a good sense of humor and ribbed Bill Stout about his copying *"Josephine."* Once, during a party when Bill was dancing with his daughter Wilma, Tony sidled-up to him and said *"Bill, I see that you have one of your original designs with you - and I certainly want to compliment you upon such a lovely product."* Tony and Bill had started their sparring a few years earlier, originally over the merits of wood versus metal airplane construction. Stout built the first all-metal American airplane in 1922, the Navy's Model ST torpedo plane (for which I'd planned to compete), while Fokker was a long-time wood proponent, though Stout's *"Bat-Wing"*, America's first thick-wing plane, was of wood veneer. In one of their classic standoffs, Bill said *"You see, any plane built of wood starts getting a disease after six months. That disease is veneer-eal disease."*

Bill also had a great sense of humor and was never afraid of telling a story on himself, a trait that I've always respected in the wide gamut of personages that I've known. Over the years Bill and I were to become the closest of friends. He had the imagination *and* the 'brass' to be successful in many endeavors. For instance, when he was starting the Stout Metal Airplane Co. in Detroit in 1923 he didn't have a dime, so he wrote

220

a series of letters to the *'who's who'* of industry and eventually got to the punchline requesting an, *"...investment of $1,000 apiece, no more"* with the admonition *"...that you'll never see your money again but that you'll have some fun."* Darned if he wasn't successful in raising all the capital he needed, even snaring Henry and Edsel Ford as investors. And, as was Henry Ford's wont, in mid-1925 Ford ventured into the mass-production of airplanes by buying-out all the other investors at double their original investment.

Stout then became general manager of the Airplane Division of the Ford Motor Company. But it wasn't long until Bill also started (along with several of his original investors and independent of Ford) Stout Air Service and the Stout Air Lines between Detroit, Cleveland and Chicago. It was a popular line with an impressive number of innovations.

The Ford organization was very serious about getting into the aircraft industry, witness my run-in with them over the airmail route. They got a few of their larger dealers to establish airlines with Ford-Stout aircraft. One, Jack Maddux, the LA Lincoln dealer, in 1927 set-up *Maddux Airlines* operating in California, Arizona and as far east as El Paso, Texas.

Prior to Maddux there had been several attempts to get airlines going in Southern California. Cecil deMille tried first, forming *Mercury Aviation Co.* in 1919 with Jenny *"air taxis"* running on schedule to Los Angeles, Bakersfield, Fresno, Venice, Long Beach and Pasadena. He then purchased a couple Junkers all-metal transports. This original *"Tin Geese"* service folded soon after *"a goose"* made a particularly messy landing, crashing into the field's outhouse!

In 1922 *Pacific Marine Airways* began service to Catalina Island (which was first served by the *Syd Chaplin Air Line* in 1919-1920 with Curtiss *"Seagull"* flying boats). PMA continued until WAE took it over in 1928, adding a Sikorsky S-38 to their fleet of Loening amphibians.

Also a pioneer was the *Los Angeles - San Diego Airline,* started in early 1925 with 3 Hisso-Standards modified to carry four passengers within a cabin. The founders were B. Franklin Mahoney and T. Claude Ryan. *(The "T" in Ryan's name stood for Tubal, and was a long-suffering issue with him, not unlike "log-head" Loughead.)* They operated from Dutch Flats in San Diego, with J.B. Alexander managing their field at Mesa Drive near Exposition Boulevard (near USC) in Los Angeles. It

"Aerial Service" - joy hop flights in a Curtiss flying boat, Catalina Island, California - 1921

was *"the first regularly scheduled year-round passenger airline in the United States."* They soon acquired a larger plane, the *Cloudster,* the first aircraft built by Davis-Douglas in 1921 (and the first plane to carry its own weight in payload). It had been wrecked and they rebuilt it into a transport with a ten-passenger cabin. The pilot and mechanic rode forward in an open cockpit. This airline suspended operations in mid-1926 after safely carrying over 20,000 passengers. The Cloudster then ferried barrels of Mexican beer and ended its *'rum-running'* with a forced landing in the surf at Ensenada, where it disintegrated.

In early 1927 Ryan sold-out both the Ryan Flying Co. and Ryan Airlines, Inc. to Mahoney. His timing could have been better, as this was just prior to an inquiry from a Charles Lindbergh about building an airplane to fly across the Atlantic!

222

Mahoney planned upon reviving the airline, but after the fantastic publicity caused by Lindbergh decided to stick to manufacturing Brougham B-1's, sister ships of the now-revered *Spirit of St. Louis.*

Lindbergh over San Diego - 1927 (note North Island under left wing)

The aviation picture was dramatically evolving at this time, particularly when it came to long distance flying.

In 1913-14, Glenn Curtiss and Englishman John Porte combined their talents to build the "America" for Rodman Wanamaker - the first flying boat designed to fly the oceans. Though the Great War diverted this project, it served as the cornerstone for the tremendous growth of the Curtiss Aeroplane Company during that war as they built flying boats modeled after the America for the British. In 1919 Curtiss and the Navy's D.W. Taylor, G.C. Westervelt, H.C. Richardson and J.D. Hunsaker created the "NC" Flying Boats, of which the NC-4 was first to cross the Atlantic.

Just a year after Byrd's flight everyone, including Byrd and Charles Levine, was preparing to win the $25,000 Raymond Orteig prize for being first across the Atlantic. *Six men died in the attempt before Charles Lindbergh won it on May 21, 1927* - a date marking the turning point in world aviation.

223

"We" - Charles Lindbergh and "Spirit of St. Louis" - May 13, 1927 - a week before becoming "The World's Greatest Hero".

Rare photo of Lindbergh spinning Spirit's prop, San Jose, Costa Rica, January 9, 1928

From 1927-on anything and everything was thought possible for the airplane, and many things were attempted which should never have been done.

224

From *Aviation*, January 2, 1928:

"Shortly before Aug. 16, there began what might be considered a black period in aeronautics during 1927. James D. Dole of Hawaii had offered $35,000 in prize money to the first two planes to make a non-stop flight from California to the Pacific Islands. Several civilians entered the race which was referred to as the Dole Derby, and due to various reasons, the principal one being insufficient time in which to prepare for the race, two fatal accidents took place before the race was even started, The original date set for the start of the race from the Oakland Airport was Thursday, Aug. 11, but as the result of an agreement between the nine entrants the race was put off until noon of the following Tuesday, Aug. 16. The race was won by Arthur C. Goebel and Lieut. W. M. Davis, U.S.N., pilot and navigator, in the Travel Air monoplane "Woolaroc" (Wright Whirlwind), which covered the distance from Oakland Airport to Wheeler Field in 26 hr., 17 min., 33 sec. Second place winner, and incidentally the only other plane to complete the flight, was the Breese monoplane "Aloha" (Wright Whirlwind), piloted by Martin Jensen with Paul Schulter as navigator, which completed the flight in 28 hr., 16 min. Of the eight planes which started the race, two crashed on the runway of Oakland Airport and three turned back, and one of these restarted two hours later. The plane piloted by J. W. Frost with Gordon Scott as navigator, was never heard from again after it had passed out over the open water of the Pacific, nor was the plane piloted by John A. Pedlar and accompanied by Lieut. V. R. Knope as the navigator and Miss Mildred Doran, the only woman in the race. After turning back from an initial attempt to make the trip Capt. Wm. P. Erwin took off again on the following morning in his plane with the intention of seeking the whereabouts of Frost and Pedlar. Sometime later he radioed word that he was in a spin and going down. That was his last message to the civilized world. As the result of these disasters many and varied protests were filed in Washington against the continuance of trans-oceanic air races, and for a time the former successes were eclipsed by the recent disasters."

One of the original hopefuls in this *Pineapple Derby,* an ex-Army pilot, made a 50% deposit upon a Travel Air J4B-powered biplane which was to be tailored for the race by making it into a *"flying gas tank".* The Travel Air dealer contracted with Bach Aircraft for this conversion, and because it wasn't down their alley, Bach had me take over the job. I began by bulging-out the fuselage, removing the passenger seat, and installing tankage for 600 gallons of gas. I also added extra instrumentation. Though I considered it damn foolishness, I never questioned this pilot's right to risk his neck though I did question his overall flying ability. But this did not prevent me from doing the best job I knew how to do. However, just when I'd completed the job the Travel Air dealer removed the plane's propeller, telling me that the fellow hadn't paid his bill and that he wasn't going to release the plane until he had.

Day after day the plane sat there with the pilot-buyer assuring us that he would soon have the funds in order to gain its possession. Finally, with the race only a week away, to my total surprise I learned that he was in jail. He had been working as a stock broker's clerk, had embezzled the down-payment and was going for the balance when he was caught. He never entered the race, and probably saved his neck because the gas-laden planes built for this race were almost impossible to get off the ground - and if crashed became fiery holocausts.

As noted, two planes did finish the contest: the *"Woolaroc"* Travel Air piloted by Art Goebel, a Hollywood stunter whom I'd never thought much of; and the *"Aloha",* a Breese monoplane piloted by San Diego's Martin Jensen. Goebel had a generous sponsor, Oklahoma oil's Frank Phillips, owner of the ranch that the plane was named after. Phillips also sponsored a second entrant, *"Oklahoma",* and would later sponsor Wiley Post (rumor had it that this caused Goebel some anguish and might have led to one of Post's later problems). Both Jensen and Goebel sensibly had capable navigators, Paul Schluter and Bill Davis, respectively, using good instruments including earth induction compasses.

One of the starters was the *Golden Eagle,* that first Lockheed Vega. With Pilot Jack Frost and navigator Gordon Scott it took off with a roar and soundlessly disappeared into the western haze - *never to be seen again.*

Another plane was a bit more fortunate, the updated Fisk bi-motored triplane, *"Pride of Los Angeles"* (see page 142 for its original version)

226

owned by cowboy actor "Hoot" Gibson. Pilot Jim Giffen splashed-crashed it into the Oakland estuary in a pre-race flight, and Bach then purchased one of the recovered J5-C Whirlwind engines which I later reconditioned for installation on the Bach-1 trimotor.

Will Rogers, aviation's strong proponent, commented *"Every paper is raving about legislation to stop ocean flying because 13 people have been lost - just a fair Sunday's average in auto deaths..."*, but the public soon forced the abandonment of these grueling long distance contests.

The oceans had been dramatically conquered by the airplane, and a new era of aviation achievement dawned. The price had been very great. As I think back upon that period I can only surmise that most of the tragic losses were the fault, not of the aircraft and their engines, but of the foolishness and inexperience of the men who attempted to fly them. These events are but the endless repetition of history, wherein many attempt but few succeed.

It was now the fall of 1927 and I was working virtually full-time at Bach, spending much of my time flying their *"Air Yacht"* trimotor to prospective customers. In September the National Air Races were to be held in Spokane, Washington, and a gang of us headed there, planning to enter the trimotor in the multi-engine transport race with me as pilot. When we were over the San Joaquin Valley (my old nemesis) there was a banging from the center Waterman radial engine. Something was very wrong and we made an emergency landing in a small dry lake bed, rolling into some tule grass with no damage to the plane.

An investigation found that a broken valve had dropped into a cylinder, which did no significant damage but made a helluva racket. We fished the valve up through the valve guide and tied it off. That cylinder was no longer operable, but after plugging the empty intake manifold the engine would operate, though roughly.

At that point Mort and I got into quite an argument over the wisdom of flying the plane loaded with passengers back to Santa Monica in that condition. I stated that I'd neither be a passenger nor fly any passengers, though I would fly it back with only a mechanic aboard. Finally, after more hassle, Mort decided to fly it back himself accompanied by Clarence Trout as mechanic and copilot. The rest of us were left to shift for ourselves by either hitching a ride or catching a bus home.

227

This episode both ended our plans for going to Spokane and spelled the end of Bach's use of the Waterman engine. Bach replaced it with the salvaged Whirlwind. That was a pretty bitter pill for me to swallow, but I went about my job normally, though a bit quieter than usual.

It was shortly after the trimotor was shipshape again that Mort received a call from Charles Eakin in Portland, Oregon, who, with his wife, operated the Pickwick Stages in the Northwest. (We were soon to learn that Mrs. Eakin, like the Aerial Experiment Association's Mable Bell, was a strong voice in the endeavor if not the real power!)

Today's Greyhound buses evolved from the Pickwick line which originated in San Diego using Packard V12's on a stretched chassis carrying passengers from San Diego to Escondido and the Imperial Valley. There wasn't any terminal; passengers were simply picked-up in front of the Pickwick Theatre across the street from the U.S. Grant Hotel. The cigar stand was the ticket office and the name "Pickwick" was simply tagged-on from that pickup location. This service grew eventually to dominate the bus service throughout the West.

The Eakins decided that, if they could get suitable equipment, they would start an airline between Seattle, Portland and San Francisco, with headquarters in Portland. They convinced Bach to make a demonstration flight to the Northwest to ballyhoo the new airline in order to raise financing. I was given this trip assignment.

In 1927 there were hardly any airfields worthy of the name, especially north of San Francisco. The occasional strips were typically just large enough for a Jenny, and there was no weather information except what was supplied to farmers. Under these conditions I slowly worked my way up through central California to Medford, Oregon, and finally landed at a primitive airstrip beside the Columbia River at Portland, where we set up a tent for our hangar. Conditions were miserable. It was raining or drizzling almost every day, and what little flying we did was done under these low ceiling conditions. However, regardless of the weather, we were able to make several flights around Portland and even up to Seattle, and the Eakins assured us that they would purchase five transports.

It was during this visit that I first met Tex Rankin of Portland's Rankin School of Flying and Rankin Flying Service. I gave him his first ride in a large, multi-engine transport, even turning the controls over to him briefly. We became good friends. Tex went on to become one of

228

Me and Bach-1, powered by a Whirlwind and two Kinners, 1927

the country's finest stunt pilots during the 1930's. He once performed an incredible 131 *outside* loops, one a minute for over two hours! (Jimmy Doolittle was first to perform this most-difficult maneuver in May 1927.)

In the late 1920's the looping craze was in full fury. Speed Holman set a (short-lived) world's record for normal (inside) loops, 1,093 in 1928. The ladies weren't left out either when, in 1930, Laura Ingalls performed 980 loops. On another occasion she did 714 barrel rolls. Nesterov, Pegoud and Beachey had really started something!

On our way home from Seattle, near Camp Lewis (between Yelm and Tumwater - Olympia Beer country today), a fast-moving storm caught us and we were hit by unbelievable rain and sleet. Both of the wing engines quit and the nose Whirlwind was losing power. Regardless of the cold, I was sweating as we were in *real* trouble. Thank God, I spotted a clearing among the dense forest, a pasture about a half-mile

229

square. I quickly put her down for a sloppy but safe landing - the kind that *"was good as long as you could walk away from it."* There wasn't even enough power in the iced-up Wright to taxi to the farmhouse, and my passengers had to trudge in the mud across the field. We then hitched the farmer's team to the trimotor, pulling it over beside the barn where inspection indicated nothing amiss other than all of the ice. Then I headed for the warmth of the farmhouse, becoming another of the guests-too-many for that night on this farm.

By morning the storm had passed and the engines thawed out. We loaded-up and headed for our next fuel stop at Salem. Flying over the lovely Willamette River Valley (the real goal of those pioneers on *The Oregon Trail*) was spectacular with the backdrop of the towering Cascade Mountains to the east. We were really enjoying the Northwest for a change. After a brief stop at Salem we took off again, but soon loud banging and severe shaking from the left engine spelled trouble. Although I hadn't planned it, I showed how the Bach could fly and land on two engines as long as the main center one was running well. Upon landing we discovered that the left Kinner had a cylinder head blown off, which would keep us grounded until a replacement was obtained.

Upon calling Santa Monica we were assured that a new cylinder would soon be enroute. It was an erroneous assumption. Kinner didn't have any spares and had to cast and machine a new one: a chore that took them several days. They then shipped it airmail by Vern Gorst's Pacific Air Transport, which had just started, and we surely helped him get in-the-black fast as the postage was $87! We soon had the engine repaired and continued the trip home. It was an impressive flight, following the magnificent mountain ranges of the western slope for virtually the entire distance.

After stops in Oakland and Fresno, we pulled into Santa Monica, very weary but feeling that we'd done a good job. It wasn't long until Bach received the order for the five Air Yachts from the company that the Eakins and their group formed, *West Coast Air Transport Corporation.*

Upon receipt of their order we proceeded to rush the modification of Bach-1, which I'd originally flown north, and the completion of Bach-2 in Bach's location behind Crawford's on Second Street. Following all the engine problems we'd had, a decision was made to use the Pratt & Whitney 450-hp Model B Wasp for the nose position and two 125-hp

230

Siemens-Halske engines in the wing positions. The latter was a German engine that Claude Ryan was promoting. He had flown up to Santa Monica in his Siemens-Halske-powered Ryan M-1 to demonstrate these engines and I'd been quite impressed, particularly with their immediate availability. As a result, Bach ordered two 9-cylinder, 125-hp models for Bach-1; and eight 7-cylinder, 100-hp, engines for use on the following four Air Yachts.

Bach-2 - 450-hp Wasp, center, & two 100-hp Ryan-Siemens - January 1928

I did a considerable amount of test flying with these first two planes. When everything was satisfactory, Morton flew Bach-1 and I flew No. 2 from Clover Field, headed for Portland to make our first deliveries to West Coast, carrying some business-related passengers as well. It was early in 1928, and the trip north took only a couple of days.

The ground facility that West Coast provided at Portland's new Swan Island airport - connected by a causeway to the mainland - was a large circus-type tent partially floored with wooden planks. On the Washington side of the Columbia River was the Army's Pearson Field, commanded by Oakley Kelly, Jack Macready's partner in 1923 when they were first to fly nonstop across the country. In spite of the marginal flying conditions with almost steady rainfall, we were determined to get their service underway as scheduled March 1st when Bach-1 was to make two round-trips daily to Seattle while Bach-2 would make a round-trip every two days to San Francisco.

231

Bach-2 - "luxurious Air Yacht...accommodates ten passengers, and boasts a heating and ventilating system, hot and cold running water - even electric cigar lighters." January 1928

It was soon apparent that Mrs. Eakin was running things, which she did in no uncertain manner! She flatly stated that she was going to show us airplane people just how to run an airline - *"just like Pickwick Stages. That was the only way to make any money."* Of course, as she was a lady I couldn't argue with her much, but it was a tough situation contending with both her and the foul weather!

It was then customary for airlines, if weather conditions precluded flying, to put their passengers on a train for all or part of the journey, at the airline's expense. Thus air fares were fairly high, about twice what they are today. But Mrs. Eakin was determined to offer an airline fare comparable to rail fare - one of Pickwick's success secrets - and she had no thought of paying for any *extra* train fares for her customers. (West Coast's rates were: Portland - Seattle $12 one-way, $20 round-trip; Portland - San Francisco $45 one-way, $80 round-trip.)

232

The BACH AIR TRANSPORT

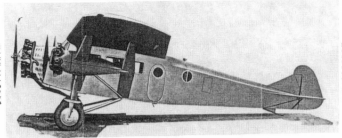

Air Worthiness

Constructed and equipped throughout with the most advanced ideas of the aero-dynamic world, the Bach Air Transport offers the ultimate in safety, economy and comfort in air transportation facilities. While a creation of beauty, yet its ruggedness of construction to meet every flying demand must necessarily bring a feeling of true pride in its performing supremacy.

Appointments

Entire cabin is finished in matched wood. Deep, comfortable, upholstered chairs, heather floor rugs, paneled reading lights, sliding plate glass windows, individual ash trays and electric cigar lighters offer complete convenience. With clock, drinking fountain, hot and cold running water in the lavatory, a subtle luxury is immediately apparent.

VETERAN PILOTS and seasoned air travelers alike, thrill to the exceptional performance and luxury of comfort embodied in the Bach Air Transport. Here, indeed, is to be found rugged, reliable air transportation developed far beyond the present-day standards. Equipped with the finest engines obtainable and control system for two pilots, the Bach Air Transport offers a new note in safety and comfort for its passengers. The cabin includes heating and ventilating systems, toilet and lavatory. The designing and equipping of the cabin was accomplished with but one ideal in mind—and that was to afford the greatest possible comfort to passengers.

AN ENGINE combination unique in aerial transportation with a 410 h.p. Pratt and Whitney Wasp in the bow, and two 150 h.p. motors in the wings, totalling 710 horsepower. The performance of this ship with ONE, TWO or THREE motors is astonishing the aviation world. Speed range from 50 miles to 150 miles per hour, with 120-mile cruising speed. Extraordinary stability under all conditions, together with minimized operating costs are the result of Bach's foresight in the design and construction of this most modern of air vehicles. The Bach Air Transport has a normal cruising range of 500 miles, with seating capacity for 10 persons. Prices and further particulars may be obtained by writing direct to the Bach Aircraft Company, Clover Field, Santa Monica, California.

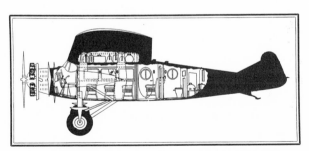

BACH TEN PLACE TRANSPORT

BACH AIRCRAFT COMPANY

SANTA MONICA   CALIFORNIA

On the first morning scheduled for the run to San Francisco there was a very low overcast, with the possibility of worsening weather to the south around Medford and the Siskiyou Mountains where we had to go through a pass. I remonstrated with Mrs. Eakin about starting under such conditions, but she told me that either I'd take off on schedule or I could take the train home and she'd see to the flying herself - period! Well I had to keep in the good graces of the customer so I kept my trap shut, and Tommy Fowler (Richfield's ex-Fokker trimotor pilot), my copilot, and I took off with our load of passengers - giving no hint that I considered it damn foolishness. The weather to the north was fairly clear though, so Mort (with Hershel Laughlin as copilot) took off on schedule via Tacoma to Seattle's Georgetown Field, an hour-and-a-quarter flight.

We were about 20 miles south of Salem, headed for Medford, when the front closed in and we had to grope our way back to Salem. I then put all of the passengers on the train, charging their tickets to West Coast, and Tommy and I laid-over until the next day for the return run. Then in clear weather we flew into Portland to be greeted with the 'cloudy weather' visage of Mrs. Eakin. Boy, was she upset! Trying my best, I couldn't convince her of the wisdom of our deed. But others finally assured her that if anyone could have gotten her passengers through safely, it would have been me.

Well, that helped my ego a bit, but the next morning she was still making things difficult when it came time for the flight. After a bit of discussion she said, *"Waldo, please don't start out and then have to put the passengers on the train again. If there's any likelihood of that, I want you to cancel the flight."* Boy, what a change! The weather looked pretty good and I told her that I thought we'd get through OK. That first trip had sure cleared the air, and she learned that, just as with the early airmail pilots, *the man flying the airplane has to make that final decision.*

In the meantime, Mort and Hershel were keeping to their schedule, thus making Mrs. Eakin happy on that score. Their trip, though, was a snap compared with the San Francisco run. It was much shorter and followed a broad valley the entire distance.

We took off for San Francisco on schedule and had an uneventful 5-1/2 hour trip - no cancellations, no train trips, though I did have to do a bit of low-level, contour flying, which was exciting for the passengers. After scheduled stops at Medford and Corning, California, we landed at

234

Oakland. The next morning we headed north for Portland on schedule with almost a full passenger load (the plane carried eight passengers and a crew of two), again for an uneventful trip, and I continued to fly the route for the next couple of weeks. In the meantime Mort had indoctrinated Laughlin enough to turn the first pilot responsibility over to him, and he returned to Southern California. I soon followed when my copilot, Tommy, took over, knowing the route almost as well as myself. Mrs. Eakin and I both smiled a bit when I bade her a warm good-by.

I mentioned that much of the construction of these trimotors was done in the location behind Crawford's - a location with a considerable degree of historical significance. Originally it was the site where I rented space next to Herb Wilson. Following my move to Third and Sunset, Crawford built a good-sized building on it which Bach moved into when they outgrew their Jenny-packing-crate hangars at Clover Field. After Bach Aircraft moved to larger, more modern facilities at Metropolitan Airport, Lloyd Stearman, Mac Short and Freddie Hoyt moved in. They formed Stearman Aircraft in 1927, which later became a major manufacturer after moving to Wichita. Following Stearman was the Joseph Kreutzer Corp., a division of LA's Buick dealership which became quite active building a small six-place trimotor "Air Coach" powered with three LeBlond engines. This story went on-and-on as this location became the cradle or birthplace of many aviation enterprises.

As a permanent Bach employee, I'd given up my space at Clover Field and had moved my two old Boeings onto a vacant lot next to Bach's factory. My time was being spent in a wide variety of projects involving test flying, engineering and some rebuilding. For one job I rebuilt a cracked-up Fisk International, installing in it the Waterman radial which I had repaired after the mishap in the trimotor. However I was getting more involved in Bach's engineering problems, and it was becoming obvious that the Department of Commerce's Engineering Branch would soon be requiring complete drawings, specifications and stress analysis for all aircraft licensed for manufacture. No one knew what these regulations were going to be, but we all knew that they would be rigid and require strict adherence to ensure the highest degree of safety. All of this was going to require specialized aeronautical engineering - both design and structural - and we were frantically looking for qualified personnel.

235

During my stint with U.S. Aircraft, Carol had stayed with friends in Palo Alto, where Stanford University is located. Their daughter had married Thayer Todd, an assistant professor at the university's propeller wind tunnel. I'd met Todd several times and knew that he had consulted for Vance Breese, builder of Jensen's *"Aloha"* and Herb Thaden's all-metal monoplane. It appeared to me that he would be the ideal man to assume Bach's engineering responsibilities. I then found that Todd was interested, provided that he be permitted to accept a pending position with the Department of Commerce if chosen. Also, he requested that his young assistant, Max Harlow, come with him. Harlow had just graduated in aeronautical engineering and was newly married. After checking this out with Mort, I received the OK to hire them both. It turned out to be a very good decision.

Soon after they'd started working at Bach we discovered that Harlow was the brains and Todd the administrator. So, when Todd was selected for the Washington position we winked as we congratulated him on his good fortune. Before leaving he and Harlow worked-out a tentative submittal procedure for the Department of Commerce which proved very handy later when Todd, in effect, was approving procedures which he'd already set-up. Max's superb engineering submittals resulted in Bach being one of the first manufacturers to win approval for their Air Yacht - *Approved Type Certificate No. 114 in February of 1929.*

This aircraft was a magnificent machine and we were all very enthusiastic about its prospects. It sold for $30,000; its closest competition was Cord's Stinson trimotor at $25,000. Both of these were far-cheaper than the Ford-Stout's $40,000. To demonstrate the Air Yacht's outstanding performance, I flew one over the frigid heights of Mount Whitney, at 14,495 feet the tallest peak in the 48 states, and then down below sea level into the torrid heat of Death Valley - *all in 30 minutes.* It was good for a lot of newspaper copy.

Soon the Air Yacht and I were enlisted to aid the law. We made a fast flight with passenger Dwight Longuevan, inspector of detectives of Los Angeles, to Sacramento in December 1927, regarding the extradition from Oregon of "fiend" kidnap-killer William Hickman. Governor C.C. Young was thus the *"first California executive to sign requisition papers that were brought to the Capitol City by airplane..."* With the signed papers we then flew to Corning, further north, to accept the prisoner from the Oregon authorities.   However, feelings were running so high throughout the state regarding Hickman that *it was feared he'd be dragged from the aircraft and lynched.* At the last minute the decision was made to take him by train to Los Angeles. It was a good move, for each time we landed for fuel we were met by enraged mobs intent upon a lynching, and we had a devil-of-a-time convincing them that Hickman wasn't aboard.

Conduct of this sort may seem strange today, but lynching - the mindless vengence of the mob - was certainly not unknown then. Nationally, "lynch justice" was a shameful statistic, and as late as 1933 a pair of kidnap-murderers were strung-up in the main park of San Jose, California.

The Air Yacht was gaining popularity in other ways, too, as it was the ideal vehicle to take a group on an outing. Clyde Forsythe once borrowed one with my piloting services for an *"air yachting party"* to San Diego, complete even to *"highballs in the sky"* (see next page). Another time Gilbert Beesemeyer, Bach's banker, took some influencial businessmen duck hunting at their Hollywood Rice Growers Association's retreat in Wasco. Even though I'm no hunter, I found it to be a most interesting jaunt with many good yarns told.

One day I received a message to go up to the Bach front office and see Wilbur White. When I walked in he gruffly said, *"Waldo, you're fired!"* Stunned, I stood there, and then noticed a glimmer of a smile on his face. He said that H.J. Heffron, Bach's president (who also headed a real estate company in Hollywood) *"...wanted me to come right over and see him."* Not knowing what was up, I entered Heffron's office about an hour later, and still not clueing me in, he asked me to take a ride with him. We got in his car and drove through the Cahuenga Pass to the San Fernando Valley, then little more than a hot, arid agricultural area. We went to a large bean field, surrounded by alfalfa fields and walnut and orange groves, adjoining the Southern Pacific's tracks to San Francisco. There Heffron said, *"Waldo, what do you think of this for an airport?"* *"OK - but so what?"* I answered. I was then apprised that Heffron's group had options on the land and plans to acquire more surrounding acreage in order to create an *"industrial airport"* - with me as its general manager! I was taken aback, for I far preferred the flying, designing and manufacture of airplanes, but I thought that this might be quite an opportunity as I said, *"Yes sir, Mr. Heffron; I'd like that job."*

LOS ANGELES EVENING EXPRESS, TUESDAY, DECEMBER 13, 1927

'VIC' GIVES YACHTING PARTY, WAY UP AMONG CLOUDS

Airship Takes Crowd on Joy-ride From Los Angeles To San Diego

"I'm going to throw a little yachting party and would like you to be one of my guests," said Clyde Forsythe to eight persons recently.

"Delighted" replied the eight persons in tones of pleasure.

"This yachting party is going to be different," said Mr. Forsythe. "It's going to be up in the clouds." He waved a hand airily up toward the sky. "We're going to San Diego and bark on the Bach air yacht, and it will be some aerial joyride."

And that's just exactly what Mr. Forsythe did—gave the first aerial yachting party in Southern California. You can gamble on Mr. Forsythe doing things differently, for he is the famous cartoonist who as "Vic" draws "Joe's Car" for the Evening Express, and scores of other newspapers, and when he starts out to plan a party he plans one that is a party.

NOTED PILOT

So Mr. Forsythe borrowed the palatial air yacht from the Bach Aircraft Company at Clover field and impressed his old friend, Waldo Waterman, chief pilot for the company, to do the piloting. Mr. Waterman is a noted pilot with 18 years' service to his credit and when he takes up a ship one can feel a master hand at the stick.

And so the party gathered at Clover field and Mr. Forsythe gaily waved the members to seats inside the big monoplane with its three motors, there was the cry of "contact" from Mr. Waterman, and the party sailed away to see what they could see from 3000 or more feet in the air.

Laughing and chatting, the party roared over Los Angeles, spun past San Pedro harbor with its line of grim warships lying below, and crossed over Long Beach and its far-flung oil fields looking like toys. Huntington Beach, Balboa, other coast towns, passed swiftly in review in gorgeous panorama, then the yacht bore to sea and the passengers had a taste of what transpacific fliers experience. Clouds scurried by. The yacht played tag with them at 4000 feet. Fog closed in dense, bewildering to the aerial joyriders, but the pilot calmly roared through it and soon came out into bright sunshine with San Diego in the distance.

SEE LOS ANGELES LIGHT

A short stop at North island the party again boarded the for the return. Coming back Los Angeles it was growing and suddenly the lights of the flashed out, furnishing the air a view of Los Angeles at 300 seldom obtained. Miles and of lights, with tiny automobil low throwing their feeble along the streets. The aeria riders held their breaths in the far-flung scene of brilli

Then the hangars of Clove loomed up and Pilot Waterm the plane down like a feather gathering gloom.

The Bach air yacht is the cabin, passenger-carrying built by the Bach Aircraft pany of Clover field, Santa M The cabin is equipped with lights, lavatory, drinking fo cigar lighters and other co ences. Six persons are seated main cabin, while back of t a two-seated private compar The ship sails without vib and the three motors give a s ness in the air that is remar Ten of the planes have been by the coast company to be service between Los Angele Portland.

By this time deMille's two airfields had been crowded out by the city's tremendous growth westward, in part because of the oil fields first exploited by Edward Doheny. Even today there are oil wells still pumping in Beverly Hills!

Rogers Field also moved, primarily because of Emory Rogers' tragic death in 1921. Emory had been ill; rumor had it that he had a brain tumor which was causing blackouts. As was customary, a little excitement was built-up on Sunday afternoons at Rogers Field to attract onlookers who would then be solicited for rides. On the day of his death, one of Rogers' pilots took the plane up and put on a lukewarm show. As I understand it, Emory then jumped into the plane and proceeded to put on a good show finalized by a *'pylon'* turn at the intersection of Fairfax and Wilshire.

The turn ended in Emory's fatal crash. His plane was a complete washout, hitting the pavement of Fairfax Avenue, about 100-yards north of Wilshire, not far from where Ormer Locklear crashed. No one else was involved.

Although I didn't see this accident, I arrived shortly thereafter and from all reports I received I would now attribute it to a *high-speed stall*. We knew little about high-speed stalls in those days, which later killed famous racing pilots Art Chester and "Fearless" Freddie Lund. One even threatened me in the 1931 Air Transport Race in Cleveland - when Harvey Firestone beat me.

But back to the new airport. I set-up my office in the offices of the three partners, Heffron, McCray and St. John. The first task was drawing up the airport's plans, while at the same time I scouted around pricing acreage near the proposed field. It varied considerably: all the way from the $750-an-acre that we paid for the 250-acre bean field to as much as $4,000-an-acre for highly-improved walnut groves. Today (1974) this same land must be worth $500,000-an-acre. It's where one of Lockheed's main plants is located! All told, we assembled around 400-acres for the main complex with options on several adjoining pieces.

I laid-out two runways intersecting at not quite right-angles in order to have the best wind relationship. They were very commodious, 4,000-feet-long and graded to a width of 1,000-feet, a far cry from the Jenny strips of only a few years earlier. We parceled-off the balance of the property in a wide variety of sizes and shapes to accommodate almost

239

any desired operation or use, and I set-about lining up prospective tenants and buyers. I would tailor a particular parcel to a specific company and then give them a 90-day option, no strings attached, providing they evidenced some interest. It was a very successful technique that got a lot of signers interested in our *Metropolitan Airport* without feeling that they had made an irrevocable commitment. Among the first were two aircraft manufacturers, naturally Bach being one; several 'fixed base' operators; and quite a few individuals including several Hollywood stars. By the time we were ready to break ground we had a potentially thriving facility. My status in the aviation community was a big help because 'real estate broker' was a bad name in Southern California due to all of the flim-flam land deals, and I emphasized that Metropolitan Airport would be a boon to aviation, not simply another property development.

The airport corporation built a combination administration building and control tower, plus a nearby general service hangar. The competition between the oil companies for field locations was intense with Richfield, Union and Standard the principal contenders. While at Ontario I'd gotten almost all of my gas and oil free by simply letting Richfield paint my plane in their colors and put their logo on the tail. It was a common practice, and you'll notice some sort of advertising on many planes of that era, particularly those of 'personage' pilots.

I was successful in signing-up all three oil companies for Metro, but was most interested in working-out something with the biggest one - Standard Oil.

During negotiations with Standard I got Sidney Chatterton, their head of aviation, together with our Lloyd St. John to finalize the deal. To my amazement I soon discovered that St. John then sold Standard a big hunk of acreage several miles further east for their own airport! Boy, I sure muttered a few thoughts about real estate brokers. Standard Oil then got together with Boeing Airlines, predecessor to United Airlines, and created United Air Terminal, which was dedicated May 30, 1930. Later it would be successively called: Union Air Terminal (1934), Burbank Airport, Lockheed Air Terminal (1940), Hollywood-Burbank Airport, and Burbank-Glendale-Pasadena Airport (today).

I'm certain St. John made a handsome commission, but he surely created a competitive monster. Standard and Boeing built a very plush facility - California Mission style buildings with red tile roofs - and they

240

Aerial view - looking west - Los Angeles Metropolitan Airport - January 1, 1930

"The finest airport on the coast" - 1929

242

First registration at Metropolitan Airport - Richfield's Dudley Steele and me - 1928

The Good Year blimp has been around a long time!
(So has Union gasoline.) Metropolitan Airport - 1929

stole some of my prime prospects, including Pacific Airmotive and Jack Northrop's Avion Corporation (which he and Ken Jay formed in 1929 when they spun-off from Lockheed). Well, regardless, I still had enough prospects for a good start at Metro, though not as many as I'd hoped.

In reality, the airport that suffered the most was the new Los Angeles Municipal Airport, *Mines Field.* Bureaucratic red tape had delayed its development so much that Cliff Henderson lost many prospects to these two independent fields. But he did get things moving well enough to commit to holding the *National Air Races and International Aeronautical Exposition there in 1928.*

The National Air Races had been aviation's big annual event since evolving from the first Pulitzer Race at Mitchel Field, Long Island, in 1920, and they really gathered momentum from 1925-on. The last one was held in Cleveland in 1939, ending that wonderful aviation era. Cleveland hosted more races than any other city; but Omaha, Detroit, St. Louis, Dayton, Chicago, Los Angeles, Spokane and Philadelphia were also host cities. Naturally these races attracted the best pilots and aircraft in the country, competing for a variety of prizes and trophies. Most notable was the *Thompson Trophy* (1930-1949). It had replaced the *Pulitzer Trophy* (1920-1925), a casualty of the tragedy of the Billy Mitchell court-martial which had put the 'damper' on government funding for ever-faster aircraft. It was for a 'closed course' race. From 1931-on another prize, the *Bendix Trophy,* was awarded to the winner of a cross-country race ending at the races. *The crowds attending these affairs were huge. In 1928 there were over 250,000 attendees, 763 visiting planes and 5,000 recorded landings. The 1929 Cleveland Races were planned to double these figures.* The spectators invariably got their thrills, often a bit more than the contestants planned, for there were a tragic number of fatal and near-fatal crashes. I attended all but one or two of these events, missing the last one because of my own near-fatal condition.

The first National Air Race held on the West Coast was at Mines Field, now LAX, in 1928, and *Aero Digest's* Frank Tichenor wrote:

"Those Californians had promised the greatest air show ever held in this old world - and they gave us all of that. They picked for it the finest natural setting to be found in their incomparable collec-

tion of such matters and then their human handiwork came pretty close to being fit to match the glories of the Lord's. Paint in your mind the picture of the Sierra Nevada mountains as the background of a magnificent flock of planes, sailing like migrating birds toward an appointed destination. For further background try to visualize such sunrises as you never dreamed about before, such clouds as you did not know that vapor had the wisdom to compose, such gorgeous evening skies as Turner in his painted ecstacies hung above his oil and canvas glories of old Venice, noonday clarity which sparkled as if one might be within a perfect diamond and looking out, a paradisiacal temperature neither hot nor cold, those mountains ever back of all. . . . And then - Where five weeks before had been an oat crop now was a permanent flying field, the perfect product of sheer magic, efficiently laid out, magnificently equipped. Beside it, where five weeks before had been nothing whatsoever, now rose the biggest exhibition building ever erected on the Pacific Coast. Add to these sheer wonders all the others you can think of when your mind is really active and you will have one half of an idea of what the California Air Race Association had done for aviation while nobody was looking. Not a detail missing. Greatest ever. Worthy of the world's newest and perhaps greatest art and industry. Worthy of the Golden State. Worthy of America! Too much praise cannot be given Dudley Steele, Cliff Henderson, Harry Wetzel and others of the dominating spirits in this most magnificent of air shows. We concede the California climate without a single quibble. The Californians were so sure of it that they built their exposition buildings without roofs! After the first day the crowds were - well, they were "capacity", as the theatre-men say - and "capacity" in this case, was darned near all outdoors. Remember, that everyone who went to this astounding exposition had to get there in a motorcar and you will have something to think over. Thursday, Friday and Saturday and very emphatically Sunday the grandstand gates were closed before noon. Air-minded? More so than any other part of the United States. Miss California, ladies and gentlemen, once more takes the rostrum as the schoolma'am of the nation. Ask her your questions about aviation and then listen while she answers.

245

Everybody flies in California. Over thirty landing fields dot the Los Angeles territory alone - all active and conducted as a part of every-day life. In California flying is both a regular business and a popular, accustomed sport. There's no ballyhoo about it. I arrived upon the Coast a few days before the opening of the Show. Impressed by the crowds I saw at the first landing field I drifted to, I remarked that the visitors and contestants for the big show were coming early. The manager of the field (me!) looked at me with a worried and perhaps suspicious eye. Another eastern nut, no doubt, my mind, if any, perhaps affected by the altitude on the way out. What I had thought visiting planes were the machines of regularly operating air-lines and those of habitual resident fliers - Californians who fly as casually as they eat or ride in motorcars. These Californians fly home from their jobs, and then take a turn or two around the home locality. Then they land for dinner, which they eat while the plane stands casually outside as New York suburbanites park their Fords. Having eaten they take another little flight, perhaps two hundred miles or so to play a game of bridge, but more likely a delightful little journey just for the love of flying. In the morning they fly back to business."

I was chairman of the race's Aviation Technical Committee, one of the main operating committees. I also contracted to enter a gag airplane, the *"Air Rail Line"*. This was a takeoff on the service that Transcontinental Air Transport (TAT) was starting to ballyhoo a year prior to its inauguration in mid-1929. *In 48 hours TAT was going to whisk passengers coast-to-coast via airplanes and trains. This service entailed a night train from New York to Columbus, Ohio; then a daylight flight to Waynoka, Oklahoma; then a night train to Clovis, New Mexico; and then a flight into Los Angeles, landing at Glendale Airport, 12 miles east of Metro. In reality it didn't beat the train by that much, which alone took 72 hours, but it was one of the first attempts at coast-to-coast service. Lindbergh associated with it in 1928 and therefore it wasn't long until the "Air Rail Line" was called "The Lindbergh Line". TAT's air-rail service began on July 7, 1929 and operated until the fall of 1930.*

I'd prepared this funny plane by taking one of my old Boeings and revamping it to look like a locomotive. It was complete with smoke

1928 National Air Races, Los Angeles - Exposition Hall and Grand Stand
Aero Digest - October 1928

Chance Vought Corp.   Wright Aeronautical Corp.

Pratt & Whitney Aircraft Co.   American Eagle Aircraft Corp.

"Exposition buildings without roofs!" - over 4 1/2 acres of exhibit space, truss-framed and roofed with translucent fabric.

stack, steam dome, boiler, cow catcher, cylinders and pistons with connecting rods that moved back and forth as the plane taxied. The rear fuselage had a series of painted windows with dummies' heads sticking out, each wearing helmet and goggles. It also had steam and smoke-generating equipment, an exhaust air horn and a locomotive bell. Boy! It was some contraption. If you didn't see it, you could sure hear it!

The Grandstands - National Air Races - 1928

I planned to taxi this apparition back and forth in front of the grandstands, then fly it in front of the crowd (some 40,000 strong), land and have the pilot (dressed as a locomotive engineer) go around the plane with a huge oil can and wrench, taking care of his machine. As I was too busy with my responsibilities to fly the plane myself, I arranged for ex-*"Hell's Angels"* pilot Harry Crandall to fly it. With all of this extra junk on it, the plane was tricky to fly. In addition, it was a 'rudder plane' (meaning that you had to exert an excessive amount of rudder pressure when turning or banking), so I carefully coached Harry on how to handle it. The plane's first takeoff was to be near the infield fence so the spectators could see all of the caricatures and paraphenalia. However, there was a slight crosswind as Harry was taking off, and he lost control and spun into the fence at the far end of the bleachers, wrecking the plane. The announcer, thinking that I was piloting, blared out *"Well, folks, Waldo and all of the other dummies are all right!"* This made me mad-as-hell, but what-the-heck, I had to be the butt of a few jokes once in awhile.

That was the end of the Renault-powered Boeing. The original Waterman-powered Boeing also was soon junked and its engine was sold to John Montijo, the pilot who, with Neta Snook, taught Amelia Earhart to

248

fly. John was at the California Polytechnic Institute (now a state university) at San Luis Obispo (midway between LA and San Francisco) teaching aircraft construction. He used that first Salmson-Waterman in one of his planes, flying it for several years. John was killed in 1935, crashing near Walsenburg, Colorado while flying the mail between Pueblo and El Paso.

This might be a good time to give you an idea of what the airline passenger business was like in those days.

Transcontinental Air Transport (TAT) was a major player and had been started in 1928 by Clement Keys of the "Curtiss-Keys Group", *"the father of commercial aviation"*. (In 1920 Keyes, acting for Glenn Curtiss, bought-out the Willys group's interests and became president of the Curtiss Aeroplane and Motor Corporation.) TAT was affiliated with both the Pennsylvania and Santa Fe railroads. Lindbergh tied-in with TAT after his triumphal cross-country tour, and flying a Curtiss fighter-type plane made a survey of their routes. Keys was instrumental in forming the huge *North American Aviation Co.* - a complex that, in addition to TAT, controlled Curtiss-Wright (merged in 1929), Sperry Gyroscope, Eastern Air Transport and National Air Transport (originally backed by Henry Ford). Keys also owned a large block of Douglas stock.

Another entity, *Aviation Corp. (Avco),* was promoted by Wall Streeter's Harriman and Lehman. In the heady days after Lindbergh's epic flight, they huckstered over $40,000,000 in stock to finance their ambitious plans of buying-up almost every company related to aviation. They eventually had around 80 subsidiaries, including eleven airlines. These included Colonial, Universal, Embry-Riddle, Interstate, Southern Air Transport and American Airways, which emerged as American Airlines. *(Avco's Universal Air Express was the first to complete a transcontinental Air-Rail flight - on June 17, 1929. They used Fokker trimotors, the New York Central and Santa Fe railroads - by rail from NY to Cleveland, by air to Chicago, Kansas City and Garden City, Kansas, and then by train to LA - all in 60 hours!)*

A third passenger carrier, *United Aircraft & Transport,* was the result of the airlines that Bill Boeing built, plus Varney's line. It also had a tie-in with Hartford's Wasp and Hornet engine builders, Fred Rentschler and George Mead, and with Chance Vought. After a proxy fight with

Keys in 1930, United wrested control of National Air Transport from North American. This addition created today's United Airlines.

Thus, North American, Avco and United were the 'big three' holding companies that monopolized the aviation industry.

Of all the airlines, TAT - *The Lindbergh Line* - was probably the most interesting, doing everything in a posh manner in keeping with the flamboyance of the Twenties. For example, they served their dinner meals on gold-trimmed service - earning the additional nickname *"The Gold Plate Line"*. But regardless of the luxury, their cross-country trip was arduous, and only the most daring and adventurous passengers enjoyed it. For a one-way fare of $350, one rode in Ford-Stout trimotors with eleven other passengers on none-too-comfortable seats that hummed and vibrated. The plane's all-metal construction transmitted the engine's labors (and fumes) too well. (Interestingly, the Bach trimotor's all-wood construction was an advantage as it soaked-up and dampened the engine vibrations.) Three of air travels enemies were *fear, fare,* and the all-too-common *airsickness* - after some rough flights it was easiest to hose the plane out! In addition to the din and racket, the heating and ventilation was marginal. In 1927 Mrs. Gardiner Fiske, flying in a Fokker Universal from Boston to New Brunswick, N.J, as one of Colonial Airways' first passengers recalls in the Boston *Globe*: *"It was so cold, we covered ourselves with blankets, and so noisy that we wrote notes instead of trying to talk to one another." (See page 215)*

It wouldn't be long until the public was demanding more comfortable passenger transports, which we'll shortly be at the beginning of.

To carry passengers between plane and train, TAT used a very unique trailer-type van developed by Glenn Curtiss and Carl Adams, originally from Jenny fuselage parts and fittings. It used lightweight (1,200 lbs.) 'stick and wire' construction, covered with aircraft-type fabric and was pneumatically-coupled with an automobile. This *"Aerocar"* spawned, in the 1930's, the Curtiss Aerocar Co. in Coral Gables, Florida who manufactured them as *"revolutionary modes of passenger and light-freight transportation"* and as a home and *"drawing room on wheels."* It *was the predecessor of the Airstream-type travel trailer.*

In May, 1928 Harris Hanshue's Western Air Express, assisted by a Guggenheim grant, acquired three new 12-passenger Fokker F10A trimotors and started a *"Model Airline"* between Los Angeles and San

250

TAT passengers boarding a Ford-Stout trimotor from a Curtiss Aerocar - 1929

Francisco, taking only 3 hours vs. the train's 13 (one-way fare $60). This service was soon to prove successful, far-more-so than TAT's due to their frequent problems in making the connection between plane and train. TAT often left some unhappy passengers stranded in either Ohio or New Mexico. Also WAE's Fokkers were of wood construction and thus more comfortable. This fact foretold great things for Fokker and led to Hanshue later becoming president of Fokker Aircraft Corp. of America, which later became known as General Aviation Corp. and Atlantic Aircraft before merging into North American Aviation. General Motors also had a major stake in Fokker.

By the summer of 1930, 20 of the 25 airmail lines were in the hands of the Big 3. Hanshue's WAE was the only major independent. Hoover's Postmaster General, Walter Folger Brown, wanted to "shape things up a bit" and called a meeting of United, Avco, TAT, WAE, North American's Eastern and Stout Air Lines. This "spoils conference" eventually led to the forced "marriage" (with Brown "holding the shotgun") of TAT and WAE, *forming Transcontinental & Western Airlines, now known as TWA*. Hanshue was dead-against teaming his very profitable

251

line with money-losing TAT, and he later told me that, at the conclusion of one of the more heated meetings, he retorted to Brown *"I think it's a lot of shit. Let's go to lunch."*

Also, added to T & WA was Maddux Airlines and the Aero Corporation. The latter operated Standard Airlines, a small line flying (movie stars) to Phoenix, Tucson, and El Paso from Los Angeles. It was owned by Jack Frye and Paul Richter, who were also the coast's Fokker agents.

Hanshue was made president of the new TWA, which continued to be known as *The Lindbergh Line.* Frye and Richter were installed as vice presi-

Acme

HARRIS M. (POP) HANSHUE
. . . profane, rough-edged President of Western Air l press, is one of the very few legendary figures amo airline chiefs. Proud of the system he built up in the Southwest, he objected stubbornly, but futilely, to me ing with T.A.T. He still nurses a professional distaste his enforced bedfellows.

Fortune May, 1934

dents, and Kansas City was chosen as the main operating base. *The country's first transcontinental-through-service was flown on October 15, 1930, between New York and LA.*

Sometime later Hanshue (apparently one of the few airline executives with much integrity) was forced to resign. He was replaced by "the Mellon crowd's" Richard Robbins, who, in turn, was replaced by Jack Frye, one of TWA's most dynamic top executives. Frye, in concert with Howard Hughes, really shook-up the airline business. Hanshue had then moved-on to Fokker in Wheeling, West Virginia, until both The Depression and Knute Rockne's death spelled the decline of that concern.

Whereas Maddux threw all of their chips in with TWA, a spin-off of WAE still retained an independant airmail run to Salt Lake City and kept their field at Alhambra, in the LA Basin. Calling themselves General Airlines, this operation merged with several other lines, creating what became Western Airlines.

Therefore as a partial summation, here's how our airlines evolved:

United came from Boeing Air Transport, National Air Transport, Pacific Air Transport, West Coast Air Transport, Varney Speed Lines and Stout Air Lines.

TWA was the result of the TAT, WAE, Maddux and Standard Airlines combination. Western Airlines was a spin-off of WAE.

American Airlines came from Avco's original American Airways holdings. The control of Avco was wrested by E.L. Cord from Harriman and Lehman in 1933 after a momentous battle.

Eastern Airlines evolved from Eastern Air Transport, part of Keys' North American Aviation, which went bankrupt in 1933 and thus GM acquired 30% control.

It was the first period of unprecedented growth for the airlines. In 1928 there had been only 50,000 American air travelers. This figure grew to over 165,000 in 1929 and to over 500,000 by 1930, tenfold in just two years! The public was finally finding something useful for the airplane.

Just as these events started to unfold and while I was still at Clover Field, Carol and I thought that we'd be in that area for some time and thus rented a small house in Santa Monica Canyon, a picturesque area just north of Santa Monica. The canyon had two creeks (a rarity), many large oak and sycamore trees, and met the ocean at what is now Will Rogers State Beach, a fine swimming spot. Further up the canyon was the Uplifters Club, playground of many movie people including Will Rogers and his polo-playing friends. He had moved to this area in 1928 - carving out his handsome Santa Monica Ranch as a home and retreat on its 300 acres. Later, we found a beautiful building site on Mesa Road, between the beach and the Uplifters Club, and constructed our first home there. We lived in this unspoiled canyon from 1928 to 1951, and I will always remember it as our favorite place, one in which we considered it a privilege to live.

By October 1, 1928, we had completed several of the main buildings at Metropolitan Airport and opened the field for use, but the official dedication was December 17, the 25th anniversary of the Wrights' first flight. As noted, during the Air Races the Early Birds had just been or-

AIR TRANSPORT GUIDE
Mail   Passenger   Express

Complete schedules for all air transport lines in the United States, such as appear on this and the following page, were published for the first time by any magazine in the August issue of Air Travel News. Since that time three other aviation periodicals have adopted the idea. Air Travel News will appreciate it if operators and others will help us keep these schedules corrected up to date each month.

BOEING AIR TRANSPORT M-P-E   Chicago to San Francisco, 1904 Miles   Contract Air Mail No. 18

Westbound	Mail Close	Leave	Phone	Eastbound	Mail Close	Leave	Phone
Chicago	**6:30**	**7:50**	Wabash 8084	San Francisco, Cal.	6:05	7:00	Kerney 2041
Iowa City, Iowa	**8:40**	**9:40**	425	Sacramento, Cal.		7:45	
Des Moines, Iowa			Maple 707-W	Reno, Nev.		9:00	195
Omaha, Nebr.	**10:30**	12:35	Atlantic 9301	Elko, Nev.		11:00	1553
North Platte, Neb.		2:00	29	Salt Lake City, Utah		**3:05**	Wasatch 5569-3321
Cheyenne, Wyo.	3:30	4:45	656	Rock Springs, Wyo.			
Rock Springs, Wyo.	6:30	7:05	415-J	Cheyenne, Wyo.		7:30	656
Salt Lake City, Utah	9:00	10:20	Wasatch 5569-3321	North Platte, Neb.			
Elko, Nev.	10:45	11:15	1553	Omaha, Neb.	**10:30**	12:30	Atlantic 9301
Reno, Nev.	**1:00**	**1:45**	195	Des Moines, Iowa		1:30†	Maple 707-W
Sacramento, Cal.		**2:45**		Iowa City, Iowa			
San Francisco, Cal.		Ar. **4:30**	Kerney 2041	Chicago, Ill.		Ar. 5:45	Wabash 8084

CLIFFORD BALL AIRLINE M   Cleveland to Pittsburgh, 123 Miles   Contract Air Mail No. 11

Southbound	Mail Close	Leave	Phone	Northbound	Mail Close	Leave	Phone
Cleveland, Ohio		**12:15**		Pittsburgh, Pa.		**2:30**	
Youngstown, Ohio		**1:00**		Youngstown, Ohio		**3:15**	
Pittsburgh, Pa.		Ar. **1:45**		Cleveland, Ohio		Ar. **4:00**	

COLONIAL AIR TRANSPORT M-P   Boston to New York, 192 Miles   Contract Air Mail No. 1

Southbound	Mail Close	Leave	Phone	Northbound	Mail Close	Leave	Phone
Boston, Mass.	**5:15**	**6:15**	Kenmore 4680	New York, N. Y.	2:00	5:00	Ashland 7750
Hartford, Conn.	**6:15**	**7:35**	2-9211	Hartford, Conn.		6:35	2-9211
New York, N. Y.		Ar. **9:15**	Ashland 7750	Boston, Mass.		Ar. 7:50	Kenmore 4680
(Hadley Field)							

COLORADO AIRWAYS M   Cheyenne to Pueblo, 199 Miles   Contract Air Mail No. 12

Southbound	Mail Close	Leave	Phone	Northbound	Mail Close	Leave	Phone
Cheyenne, Wyo.		**5:30**		Pueblo, Col.		**4:00**	
Denver, Col.		**6:55**		Colorado Springs, Col.		**4:50**	
Colorado Springs, Col.		**7:50**		Denver, Col.		**6:00**	
Pueblo, Col.		Ar. **8:30**		Cheyenne, Wyo.		Ar. **7:30**	

FORD MOTOR CO. M-F   Detroit to Cleveland, 91 Miles   Contract Air Mail No. 6

Southbound	Mail Close	Leave	Phone	Northbound	Mail Close	Leave	Phone
Detroit, Mich.	9:50	10:40		Cleveland, Ohio	**2:00**	**3:00**	
Cleveland, Ohio		Ar. **12:10**		Detroit, Mich.		Ar. **4:30**	Cherry 4880

FORD MOTOR CO. M-F   Detroit to Chicago, 237 Miles   Contract Air Mail No. 7

Westbound	Mail Close	Leave	Phone	Eastbound	Mail Close	Leave	Phone
Detroit, Mich.	**12:10**	**1:00**		Chicago, Ill.	7:55	9:00	
(Central Time)				Detroit, Mich.		Ar. 12:00	Cherry 4880
Chicago, Ill.		Ar. **3:00**					

NATIONAL AIR TRANSPORT M-P-E   New York to Chicago, 723 Miles   Contract Air Mail No. 17

Westbound	Mail Close Day	Mail Close Night	Leave Day	Leave Night	Phone	Eastbound	Mail Close Day	Mail Close Night	Leave Day	Leave Night	Phone
New York, N. Y.	Day 10:00	**6:30**	11:00	Night **8:00**	Lexington 8044	Chicago, Ill.	Day 6:30	**6:30**	Day 8:00	Night **8:00**	Harrison 8234
New Brunswick, N. J.			**12:15**	**9:35**		Cleveland, Ohio			**12:15**	12:15	Lakewood 9006
Cleveland, Ohio	2:30	**12:00**	**4:35**	2:30	Lakewood 9006	New Brunswick, N. J.			**4:45**	4:45	
Chicago, Ill.			Ar7:00	Ar.5:35	Harrison 8234	New York, N. Y.			Ar.7:00	Ar.6:15	Lexington 8044

†Not regular stop.

M—Mail.   P—Passenger.   E—Express.   F—Freight.   Time shown is local at airport of arrivals and departures.

Light Face Type—A. M.   **Bold Face Type—P. M.**

NOTE:—"Ask Mr. Foster" Offices handle Pacific Air Transport Tickets.

NOTE:—Varney Air Lines carry bulk of mail from Seattle, Portland, Spokane and Tacoma to connect with Boeing Air Transport

---

Today's airlines came from these airmail companies

AIR TRANSPORT GUIDE
Mail Passenger Express

These air schedules, continued from the previous page, are designed to assist travelers in arranging their itineraries, so that parts of their routes may be covered by plane where the advantages of air travel will result in time saving or in greater pleasure enroute. This department of Air Travel News will be enlarged as added lines and taxi services are established, and will be carried as a permanent feature.

NATIONAL AIR TRANSPORT M-P-E — Chicago to Dallas, 987 Miles — Contract Air Mail No. 3

Southbound	Mail Close	Leave	Phone	Northbound	Mail Close	Leave	Phone
Chicago, Ill.	3:45	5:50	Harrison 8234	Dallas, Texas	7:00	7:45	5-7113
Moline, Ill.	6:50	7:20	Moline 738	Fort Worth, Texas	7:00	8:15	Prospect 2169
St. Joseph, Mo.	10:10	10:20	St. Joe-6-0349	Oklahoma City, Okla.	9:00	10:10	Walnut 4214
Kansas City, Mo.	10:50	11:18	Leeds 1090	Ponca City, Okla.	10:40	11:10	
Wichita, Kans.	12:45	1:18	Market 6185	Wichita, Kans.	11:15	11:57	Market 6185
Ponca City, Okla.	1:40	2:05		Kansas City, Mo.	12:15	1:57	Leeds 1090
Oklahoma City, Okla.	2:00	3:05	Walnut 4214	St. Joseph, Mo.	2:17	2:40	St. Jos. 6-0349
Fort Worth, Texas	4:00	5:15	Prospect 2169	Moline, Ill.	4:00	5:15	Moline 738
Dallas, Texas		Ar. 5:35	5-7113	Chicago, Ill.	Ar. 6:30	Ar. 7:20	Harrison 8234

NORTHWEST AIRWAYS M-P-E — Chicago to Minneapolis, 377 Miles — Contract Air Mail No. 9

Westbound	Mail Close	Leave	Phone	Eastbound	Mail Close	Leave	Phone
Chicago, Ill.		5:50		Minneapolis, Minn.	1:30	2:30	
Milwaukee, Wis.		6:50		St. Paul, Minn.	2:10	2:40	Cedar 5693
Madison, Wis.		7:40		LaCrosse, Wis.	3:30	4:00	
LaCrosse, Wis.		9:30		Madison, Wis.		5:45	
St. Paul, Minn.		11:30	Cedar 5693	Milwaukee, Wis.		6:35	
Minneapolis, Minn.		Ar. 11:40		Chicago, Ill.	5:15	Ar. 7:30	

PACIFIC AIR TRANSPORT M-P-E — Seattle to Los Angeles, 1099 Miles — Contract Air Mail No. 8

Southbound	Mail Close	Leave	Phone	Northbound	Mail Close	Leave	Phone
Seattle, Wash.		11:45*		Los Angeles, Cal.	11:00	12:01	Vermont 4279
Tacoma, Wash.		1:30*		Bakersfield, Cal.		1:30	
Portland, Ore.		7:00		Fresno, Cal.		3:00	
Medford, Ore.		9:30		San Francisco, Cal.		5:00	
Fresno, Cal.		1:15		Medford, Ore.		9:00	
Bakersfield, Cal.		3:15		Portland, Ore.			
		4:45		Tacoma, Wash.		1:30*	
Los Angeles, Cal.		Ar. 6:15	Vermont 4279	Seattle, Wash.		Ar. 2:00	

ROBERTSON AIRCRAFT CO. M-P-E — Chicago to St. Louis, 278 Miles — Contract Air Mail No. 2

Southbound	Mail Close	Leave	Phone	Northbound	Mail Close	Leave	Phone
Chicago, Ill.		5:50	Maywood 4010	St. Louis, Mo.	3:30	4:15	Avery 2725
Peoria, Ill.		7:25		Springfield, Ill.		5:20	
Springfield, Ill.		8:15		Peoria, Ill.		6:10	
St. Louis, Mo.		Ar. 9:15	Avery 2725	Chicago, Ill.		Ar. 7:30	

STOUT AIR SERVICES — Detroit to Cleveland — Passengers only

Eastbound	Leave	Arrive	Phone	Westbound	Leave	Arrive	Phone
Detroit	9:15	Cleveland 10:55	Clifford 0106	Cleveland	9:15	Detroit 10:55	Main 8833
	3:15	" 4:55			3:15	" 4:55	

VARNEY AIR LINES M (See Note) — Salt Lake City to Pasco, 700 Miles — Contract Air Mail No. 5

Westbound	Mail Close	Leave	Phone	Eastbound	Mail Close	Leave	Phone
Salt Lake City, Utah		10:00		Pasco, Wash.		6:00	
Boise, Idaho		2:50		Boise, Idaho		9:20	
Pasco, Wash.		Ar. 6:00		Salt Lake City, Utah		Ar. 2:45	

WESTERN AIR EXPRESS M-P — Salt Lake City to Los Angeles, 600 Miles — Contract Air Mail No. 4

Westbound	Mail Close	Leave	Phone	Eastbound	Mail Close	Leave	Phone
Salt Lake City, Utah		9:10		Los Angeles, Cal.	6:30	7:35	Trinity 6754
Las Vegas, Nev.		2:25	Trinity 6754	Las Vegas, Nev.		10:40	
Los Angeles, Cal.		Ar. 5:25		Salt Lake City, Utah		Ar. 3:20	

PAN-AMERICAN AIRWAYS M-P — Key West, Fla., to Havana, Cuba — Foreign Mail and Passengers
(154 Franklin St., New York)

	Leave	Arrive	Phone
Key West	7:30	Havana 8:40	
Havana	5:00	Key West 6:10	

*Dispatch by train to Vancouver Field.

Art Goebel and me - and the plaque   December 17, 1928

ganized, and a highlight of our dedication was the unveiling of a plaque commemorating both the Wrights and those *"Pioneer Aviators".*

Following the opening, we took scores of folks for rides in the trimotor, and there was a great hum of activity caused by many visiting planes plus all of the 'fixed base' flyers at the field. This airport was then the *finest in the West* and definitely 'the place to be.'

Going out to an airport on a Sunday was a favorite pastime and we always had sizable crowds at Metropolitan. Many were intrigued to the extent of paying for a thrilling airplane ride. I charged $2.50-per-person for a flight in the Bach Air Yacht. It was a chance for folks to experience the thrill and luxury of airline travel, if only for a few minutes.

Shortly after the dedication I received a call from a Robert Adamson inquiring about using the field as a base for some experimental work by the Army Air Service. *They wanted to carry out an endurance flight testing the practicability of aerial refueling, sustained engine operation, and the limits of human endurance.* After looking over our facilities and discuss-

256

Fly with Waldo Waterman! Bach trimotor at Metropolitan Airport - 1929

ing with me what field support they'd need, Metropolitan Airport was selected for the (historic) Army *"Question Mark"* flight. This odd name was the simplest way of putting the Army's quest for new answers to evolving problems - "Question Mark". During the closing weeks of 1928 the Army group arrived, under the command of a Major Carl Spatz. It included a Captain Ira Eaker, Lt. Harry Halverson, Lt. Elwood (Pete) Quesada, Ross Hoyt and mechanic Sgt. Roy Hooe, among others.

257

(l-r) Roy Hooe, unknown, Elwood Quesada, Harry Halverson, Ira Eaker & Carl Spatz

Carl "Tooey" Spatz, under his wife, Ruth's urging, would later add an extra "a" to his name for the sake of pronunciation, which was too similar to the word "spats", a then-fashionable shoe-covering.

During World War II, as General Spaatz, he first commanded the 8ᵗʰ Air Force in England, following General Eaker's initial preparation. Then he commanded all U.S. Strategic Air Forces in Europe while Eaker took command of the Allies' Mediterranean Air Forces, and my Berkeley student Jimmy Doolittle assumed the 8ᵗʰ's command. In the postwar years, Carl Spaatz became the first Air Force Chief of Staff. The friendship I started in that December of 1928 would last until his death in 1974. To round-out this trio of Generals, Pete Quesada commanded the 9ᵗʰ Tactical Air Command and later was Director of the Federal Aviation Administration, and an official with PanAm.

This *Question Mark* group had five planes. The Atlantic (Fokker) C-2A trimotor was the endurance ship, and an extensive backup included two Douglas C-1 refueling biplanes and two Boeing PW-90 pursuit

258

'blackboard' planes. Their fuselages were black in order for messages to be painted in watercolor-white for communicating with the Question Mark crew. The blackboard ships were necessary because there was no inter-aircraft radio then - and ground-to-air transmission was too poor to be used. In addition to these crude messages, the only other means of communicating was by tying letters to the nozzle of the fuel hose. Spatz sent me one in this manner, which I cherish to this day (see next page).

With a goal of establishing a new endurance record, the U.S. Army Air Service Refueling Mission's Fokker took off on schedule, mid-day, January 1, 1929, and continued in uninterrupted flight between Los An-

Fokker (Atlantic C-2A) Question Mark at Metropolitan Airport - January 1, 1929

Douglas C-1 & Question Mark - December 31, 1928   259

U. S. ARMY AIR SERVICE REFUELLING MISSION

PERSONNEL
Major Carl Spatz
Capt. Ira C. Eaker
Lieut. H. A. Halverson
Lieut. Elwood Quesada
Sergt. Roy W. Hooe

Tri-motored Fokker *"QUESTION MARK"*

On Board Question Mark.
LOS ANGELES, CALIF.

January 6 1929

6th Day
9:32 A M.

Metropolitan Airport,
Mr. Waldo Waterman.
My dear Waterman,
The motors are beginning to labor and it is only a question of time until we shall use your landing area. The night lights have been excellent. It has given us confidence to know an excellent airport was beneath us in case of a forced landing. While still in the air the crew want to thank you for the untiring effort you have made and the assistance you have been to us.

Sincerely
Carl Spatz

Refueling the Question Mark - January 1, 1929

geles and Rockwell Field, North Island. It landed almost a week later at Metro, having been refueled 43 times with over 5,000 gallons of gas drained to the Question Mark from the Douglas tankers. During this tricky refueling operation the planes flew approximately 70-mph at only 20-feet-or-so apart; and in addition to gas, food and other supplies were passed. It was a very dramatic episode; not only for the duration of their flight, but also for the sheer logistics involved and the expert flying that was required. The Question Mark's *150 hours and 40 minutes* were also an engineering achievement, for engines then rarely went more than 100 hours before requiring an overhaul.

The crowds around the airport grew each day, and by the time the flight terminated due to an engine malfunction, millions across the country were avidly following the Question Mark exploits. It was terrific publicity for our new airport, putting us 'on the map' immediately.

Because of the success of the project, Spatz was awarded the *Distinguished Flying Cross* - for flying a Fokker in peacetime. During the war

261

he had shot down three enemy Fokkers - which only goes to show you how time can turn around things!

And speaking of 'shooting down', during the flight one incident irritated Spatz greatly. On January 2ⁿᵈ a young lady flying an R.O. Bone *"Golden Eagle"* appeared, but we thought little of her as there were many planes flying in and out of the field, all naturally keeping well-clear of the Army's operation. However, much to our consternation, she started circling the field. Unknown to us at the time, her plane was equipped with oversized fuel tanks, and she was out to set a women's endurance record. I soon determined her intent - for all such records had to be officially attested - when I got Joe Nikrent, the FAI representative, to admit that he'd installed a barograph in her plane, just as he'd done on the Question Mark. Well, when Spatz discovered that there was another plane flying around in his air space he really raised hell, sending me a message to *"Get that damn plane out of there right now!"*

My reply was, *"What do you want me to do; shoot her down?"*

Finally Spatz realized our dilemma, understanding that there was little we could do. That evening, without a refueling set-up, she was forced to land. 22-year-old Evelyn (Bobbi) Trout had established a new record of slightly-over-12-hours aloft - grabbing a piece of the headlines for that day.

The Bobbi Trout affair wasn't the only problem that we encountered. Lt. Howard Keefer, Blackboard Ship No. 2's pilot, was a harem-scarem daredevil. He tried to knock over the control tower almost every time he came in for a landing. He would dive towards it, and then make a zoom skyward and a split-S turn, followed by a snappy landing. Try as I might, I couldn't cool him down. The only man that could, Spatz, was out of reach - so I had to grit my teeth and hope that he wouldn't hit anything.

That reminds me of Maurice (Loop-the-Loop) Murphy - one of the gang that earned his nickname by arriving over a field at around 4,000 feet and then looping all the way down. At the same time that I was test-flying the new Bach in 1928, Murphy, after being one of the many *"Hells Angels"* pilots, was test-flying an all-metal trimotor for George Prudden of Prudden-San Diego Airplane Company. This plane had corrugated Duralumin wing surfaces. These were quite an innovation, and there was a lot of speculation as to whether or not the rivets would keep the skin on during flight. Several of us pranksters put a sackful of marbles into

262

the plane's open wing structure so that when it maneuvered they'd make an awful racket - sounding just like popping rivets. It sure worked! When Loop Murphy took that trimotor up, he came right back down for a very fast landing, no loops or anything, and wouldn't take it up again until he'd discovered what we'd done!

Loop-the-Loop was carrying-on a torrid love affair with the sister of movie star Anita Stewart. She'd arrive at the field in her Chrysler "75" roadster, wait for Murphy to finish his flying, and then away they'd go. Shortly he announced that he was giving up flying to marry this lovely girl, and we all chalked-it-up to love being stronger than flying. However, when Maddux Airlines started flying Ford trimotors, who should

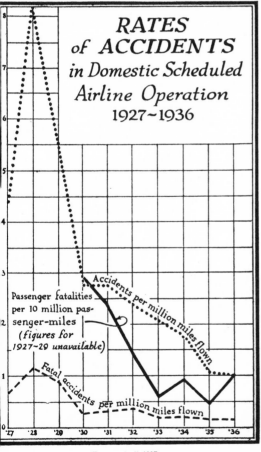

RATES
of ACCIDENTS
in Domestic Scheduled
Airline Operation
1927~1936

Accidents per million miles flown

Passenger fatalities
per 10 million pas-
senger-miles
(figures for
1927~29 unavailable)

Fatal accidents per million miles flown

'27 '28 '29 '30 '31 '32 '33 '34 '35 '36

show-up as one of their pilots but Murphy. He explained by telling us that he had convinced his bride that flying transports involved no risks and was only a routine job. Unfortunately, this wasn't quite the case. In the spring of 1929 Murphy was headed for Phoenix, having just taken off from San Diego, when an Army Boeing pursuit ship started playing tag and doing loops around his "Tin Goose", not an uncommon sport then. The Army pilot shaved one maneuver too close, clipping the transport and causing it to crash with the loss of all aboard - while Lt. Keefer bailed out - catching his 'chute on his plane as he, too, rode it to his death.

But aerial hi-jinks were not then the primary cause of the transport crashes;

Fortune April, 1937

weather and human fallibility were usually to blame. The Lindberghs were great friends of the Maddux's, and Anne Lindbergh was distressed by the "hideous" crashes. One, a Maddux trimotor, crashed on January 19, 1930 at Oceanside. It was enroute from the Mexican playground of Agua Caliente to Los Angeles when the ceiling became 'zero'. Two other transports, one Maddux and the other Western, had also started but had turned back - indicating that most of the accidents were caused by pilot error, much as I had thought about the Dole ocean flight losses.

The Question Mark's flight was the first of many that would either start, end, or be performed at Metropolitan Airport. Notable was Frank Hawks who, between 1927 and 1933, set over 200 records. (He had given a young Amelia Earhart her *first airplane ride* at Chaplin Airdrome in 1920). Late in 1929 "AE" flew a Lockheed Vega at over 180-mph on a 3-km course at Metro, certified by the ever-present Joe Nikrent.

About a mile-and-a-half west of Metropolitan was Caddo Field, the airstrip that young Howard Hughes and his top pilot, Frank Clarke, used for filming the Great War epic, *"Hell's Angels"*. Hughes, then only 24 years old, had already shot most of this movie. But 1928 saw the 'talkies' revolution, and he decided that he'd have to reshoot much of the film, a very costly effort. I had an arrangement with Noah Dietrich (Hughes's right-hand-man for over three decades) to assist Caddo Productions in any number of ways - though I was probably the only pilot around Hollywood that didn't actually fly or claim to fly in that movie! Everybody thought that Hughes was nuts to be pouring so much money - *almost $4,000,000* - into *"Hell's Angels,"* but he was really the squirrel that ate the nuts. It was a whopping success, making him more millions. Even today it is still playing somewhere in the world.

One of the many things that Dietrich had me do was locate parachutes for a big 'dogfighting' scene. I was 'on call' for a flat rate of $10-per-hour and 10-cents-a-mile. On this occasion I had to go all the way to March Field and persuade the Army to lend me 18 chutes. When these were added to Hughes' six, the filming of this dangerous sequence became considerably safer. At this time it was a rare civilian that owned a parachute; they were used almost exclusively by either the Army or airmail pilots.

Another time I drove all over scouting-up Travel Air 2000's, a model closely resembling a Fokker D7. All that I could locate were rented for

264

the film. *In one grand sequence there were 85 aircraft in the air at once, quite a logistical feat.* Hughes spent over a half-million dollars buying, modifying and renting airplanes for this movie.

A German Fokker used in "Hell's Angels"

Frank Clarke as Lt. von Bruen

"Frank Clarke in a real German Fokker D-VII that was actually used during the war as a part of the famous Richthofen's Flying Circus.

Pilot Clarke flew this plane over 400 hours in "Hell's Angels," and five motors were "burned up" before the picture was completed.

The spectacular 10,000-foot dive during the air sequence was performed with this ship."

265

Planning "Hells Angels" Gotha flight scene - (l-r) Harry Perry, chief photographer, Fred Fleck, assistant director, Roscoe Turner, Frank Clarke, chief pilot, Al Wilson, Harry Crandall, my "Air-Rail" plane pilot (kneeling), Roy Wilson, Frank Tomick and Jack Rand.

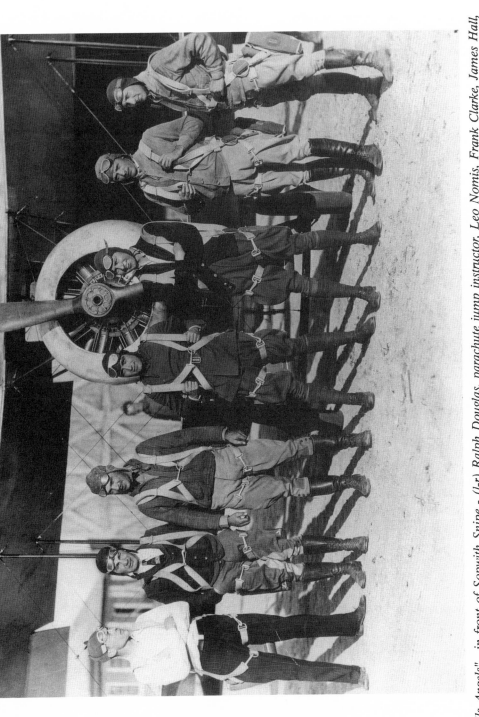

"Hells Angels" - in front of Sopwith Snipe - (l-r) Ralph Douglas, parachute jump instructor, Leo Nomis, Frank Clarke, James Hall, Ben Lyon, Frank Tomick and Roy Wilson.

An aerial "dog-fight" in "Hell's Angels."

Jean Harlow and Ben Lyon in "Hells Angels"

268

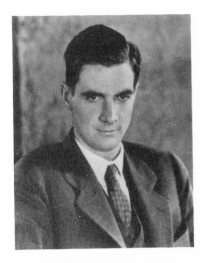

Howard Hughes

When Howard Hughes first came to Hollywood in 1925, he was 20 years old and the sole heir of the family business, Texas' *Hughes Tool Company*. At this time he had an income in excess of $5,000-*per-day*, so what might have appeared as foolish extravagance was 'simply business' to Hughes as he spread his largess around. Naturally, his activities were a welcome 'shot-in-the-arm' to the aviators in Southern California. During the interminable three years that he took to film *"Hell's Angels,"* the $150 to $200-per-week he paid was a meal ticket that few aviators wanted jeopardized, though it has been intimated that some made too good a thing of it. Much of the flying was very dangerous, though, and it's a sad commentary that four lives were lost during the filming.

All movie assignments didn't end sadly, though. Martin Jensen, because of his celebrity status (earned finishing second in the Pineapple Derby) had an unusual contract with MGM in 1927. He built a cage in his Ryan Brougham to transport Leo, MGM's lion, from San Diego to New York. Enroute, near Phoenix, he disappeared, and for a few hours most folks thought it was nothing but a movie stunt. However, when several days went by, there was genuine alarm and a lot of speculation as to whether Martin was eating the lion or the lion was eating Martin. About a week later they were found. He'd had a forced landing in the mountainous desert, and both he and Leo were alive and in fair condition. It was a good story that one could smile about when it was all over.

During this time the City of Los Angeles was organizing the new Municipal Airport at Mines Field (which after 1950 was known as LA International, LAX.) The Airport Committee was conducting examinations for the Director of Airports, and even though I really didn't want the job since I was doing far better managing Metropolitan, plus all of my extracurricular activities, I did relish seeing how I'd stack-up in the competition. The partners at Metropolitan got a bit upset when it was announced that I was an applicant, even though I had told them ahead of

269

time that I had no intention of taking the job. Regardless, I took the examination, and out of the 25 contenders I placed first in both the written and oral sections. However, there was a bonus for military service and so I came in third. In spite of this, Pierson Hall, chairman of the selection committee, wanted me to accept the position, but though flattered, I stood by my original commitment and turned him down.

It was 1929 and we were in the euphoria of possibly the greatest economic bubble in the country's experience; one could be *"on Easy Street"* by playing on margin in the stock market. One day Clyde Forsythe told me that a friend of his at Bailey Brothers (large stockbrokers) wanted an entre into Bach. Thus, I set-up a meeting between Heffron, White, Morton Bach and Bailey Brothers. Then, not coincidentally, a couple of days later, Byron Graves, my old antagonist from the airmail days, showed-up at the field with a friend. He seemed interested, like many others, in the new facility, but especially in the Bach trimotor. Graves introduced his friend, George Holley (of Detroit's Holley Brothers Co., supplier of Ford's carburetors), and I then suggested that if they were so interested in the plane that we ought to take a ride. *"Come on - hop in,"* I said. Knowing of Grave's previous connection with Western Air Express, I envisaged a big order resulting from this demonstration.

As it later turned-out, Graves and Holley were scouting around for Bailey, not WAE. Their enthusiasm led Bailey Brothers to underwrite 250,000 shares of Bach Aircraft, and eventually to Graves becoming Bach's president. As soon as I learned of Bailey's involvement, I reasoned that I was instrumental in bringing it about and that I should therefore have a share of the deal. After some negotiation I was given an option for 3,000 shares at $1-per-share, a sum I didn't have and would have to raise. It was suggested that I see Gilbert Beesemeyer, president of Guaranty Building & Loan in Hollywood and a major Bach backer, who then arranged for my loan with the stock as collateral. Similar deals were also made for Morton Bach and Wilbur White.

Beesemeyer was a great aviation booster in addition to backing many commercial and industrial developments in the area. As his organization was in the heart of Hollywood, many film personalities invested in it. One was Wallace Beery, who kept his Travel Air at Metropolitan. That *"lovable lug"* was very upset when, after the 'crash', Guaranty collapsed along with many financial institutions. Apparently Beery lost a bundle,

270

but he recouped it rapidly as a result of his box office smashes: *"The Big House"* (1930), *"The Champ"* with Jackie Cooper (1931) and the *"Tugboat Annie"* films with Marie Dressler (1933).

I was never able to blame Beesemeyer too much, though, for I always felt that he was doing what he thought was best for the area, not simply for himself. He never lived 'very high', and I'm almost certain that he didn't deserve the jail sentence that he eventually served. I felt that his was but one of the many tragedies in that crazy time.

Anyway, when Bach stock hit the market, it opened at $3-a-share and made me a handsome paper profit of $6,000. I then sold-off enough to repay my note, so that when the bubble finally burst I wasn't hurt much.

Bailey Brothers were also involved with the Kinner Engine Co. Reuben Fleet of Buffalo's Consolidated Aircraft made a deal for 1,000 Kinner engines to be used in a major production run of Fleet-2 biplanes. As part of the deal, Bailey arranged for Fleet to receive an option for 10,000 shares of Kinner at $1 per share. This large Fleet order gave the Kinner stock such a boost that Reuben sold it later at around $6-a-share - in effect, getting his engines cheap and making a tidy stock profit, also.

I also had stock in the Metropolitan Airport venture, but it was never underwritten by a major brokerage house and therefore never broadly held. Although a bit uneasy if the airport failed to meet expectations, I was nonetheless very busy and making good money managing the airport ($400 a month), while also earning commissions on real estate deals at the airport, and a bit more from the test-flying and demonstrating I was doing for Bach. All-in-all, I was flying high and we were living the good life.

Therefore, watching the construction equipment going up the road towards Will Rogers' place, Carol and I decided to build our dream home in Santa Monica Canyon. My mother, now retired as San Diego's outstanding woman architectural designer, prepared our plans, and after clearing it with the directors, the airport's contractor built our home at cost.

During this time, as a possible entrant in the *Guggenheim Safe Aircraft Competition* (won in 1930 by the Curtiss "Tanager"), I dreamed-up a new type of airplane which would have movable wings so that the dihedral could be varied, and filed a patent on it in 1928. I considered it revolutionary enough to create interest, and, hopefully, a business, and

271

after a discussion with Clyde Forsythe I built a small-scale model and prepared a presentation for prospective investors. Figuring that for the engineering, construction and demonstration I'd need to raise $25,000, I had Leonard Comegys prepare a syndication for 25 investors at $1,000 apiece (just like Bill Stout!). I then corralled every likely-looking prospect until I had 23 signed-up. Bob Porter, Kinner's president, threw-in one of his new 190-hp C5 engines for the last two shares. Thus, with the money and engine committed, I then leased part of the second hangar at Metro for building this new plane, which we named the"*Flex Wing*".

Loading-up over a ton of sand (note my high altititude equipment!) - July 1929

Late in July, 1929, I also got into another project: I attempted a new altitude record for multi-engine aircraft, sponsored by both Bach and Union Oil. We loaded an Air Yacht with 1000 Kg. (approximately 2,200 pounds) of sand; Joe Nikrent installed the FAI Richard barograph; and I climbed in for the flight, clutching the oxygen bottles. In 40-minutes I reached 18,000-feet, but it took almost another hour, laboring-away to squeeze 2,000-feet more. Although I didn't see any black spots, I took a few whiffs of oxygen anyway. My method was very basic. I clenched the tube in my mouth and turned the bottle's valve on and off as needed. It wasn't sophisticated, but it worked. Like a toy balloon bouncing against the ceiling, I couldn't go any higher, and I remained there for 15-minutes to permit the barograph to make a definite mark. (I surely didn't want to have a nondiscernable mark - like Arch Hoxsey had when H. LaVerne Twining disallowed it, even after his fatal 1910 crash at Dominguez.) I was shooting for 20,000 feet, and with my two altimeters reading 20,000 and 20,400, I figured that I had established the record - beating (ex-student) Harold Harris' record of 16,732 feet in an Army ship.

Upon landing I was greeted by Mort Bach, Byron Graves (now Bach's president) and excited ground crew members. On August 17, 1929 the record was officially certified by the Bureau of Standards - *20,820 feet*. I was proud of that!

After reaching 20,820 feet - (l-r) Morton Bach, me, Joe Nikrent with barograph, and Graves.

273

Shortly after my flight, Jack Frye and Paul Richter flew a Fokker trimotor in an effort to beat my record. They landed in great glee telling one and all that they had succeeded. Their claim is still remembered, but untrue; their instruments were faulty and the record was never 'official'.

Bach's business was now really booming. One of the local orders came from G. Allan Hancock, an oil developer and philanthropist who donated Hancock Park, including the La Brea Tar Pit, to Los Angeles County. He was the head of the College of Aeronautics in Santa Maria, about 120 miles up the coast from LA. He ordered a special Bach outfitted with a Wasp in the nose and Whirlwind J5s on either side, totalling 800-hp. I was asked to fly it up to Santa Maria and take a group for an orientation flight. Also, I was to help Hancock select the best of his pilots for this aircraft. Carol accompanied me, and at Santa Maria we loaded-up Mr. and Mrs. Hancock, his general manager and three or four of his pilots for a run to Oakland. After a brief stay there, we took off for Santa Maria, and Mrs. Hancock looked out the window and spied the left tire flapping on its rim. Apparently as we had turned prior to take-off, the tube must have pinched, deflating the tire. We were now in a very serious situation. This plane had a very wide landing gear and attempting a landing on only one wheel would be tricky and dangerous.

I decided to fly all of the way back to Metropolitan so we could land in front of Bach's factory. At least, if there was any damage that would be the best place to fix it. I had plenty of time to think-out, the best landing procedure during the three-hour flight to Los Angeles. I'd already made my pilot selection, Pat Fleming, and I had him assist me. We got the passengers belted-in and cushioned as well as possible, except for two or three of the pilots which I had a special task planned for. Finally, as we came in for the landing, everyone was well-coached, but expectant and tense. I was watching the left wheel, keeping it off the ground as long as possible, and Pat was watching the right; he was to apply full brake pressure as soon as it touched down. Just when I saw I couldn't hold the left wheel up any longer, I hollered out "Move!" and the standing pilots quickly moved to the rear to keep the tail from flipping up. The gals let out a shriek as they were the only ones with nothing to do except be scared, but other than that there was no more excitement.

274

Everything worked in unison and we came to a stop as if nothing were amiss at all.

Captain Hancock had quietly taken in the landing preparations, and when it was all over he expressed his 'well done'. From then-on he insisted that I check-out every new pilot before he was permitted to fly that airplane, the pride of his fleet.

Reflecting the hectic activity of the times, *Clement Keys succeeded (with GM's help) in merging the Curtiss Aeroplane & Motor Co. and the Wright Aeronautical Corp. to form the new Curtiss-Wright Aeronautical Corp, in 1929.* This must have galled Orville Wright terribly since he had carried such a grudge against Curtiss for so many years. *Wright had sold out in 1915* and thereafter was never a significant factor in aviation, whereas as early as 1914 the Curtiss companies were worth almost $10,000,000, and the Curtiss name would be a force in American aviation well into World War II. Over the years there were well-over 200 Curtiss aircraft designs utilizing more than 65 Curtiss patents. In 1917 Curtiss had partially sold-out to a group headed by John Willys (Willys-Overland), assuming the 'honorary' position of Chairman. But he kept Curtiss Engineering at Garden City, for many years an innovative organization. I recall Curtiss telling me of his distress over what had befallen the Curtiss Aeroplane Company late in WWI, causing him in 1920 to use a large portion of his substantial profits backing Keyes to buy-back control and 'clean house'. The friendship that I had with Glenn Curtiss was very dear to me - and I was very saddened when he died (of appendicitis) in 1930 at only 52 years of age.

1929 was the headiest of years for aviation. It rocketed to spectacular heights with little to foretell of the woeful depths to come. Avco, United and North American were gobbling-up everything related to aviation. Curtiss-Wright was acquiring airports, including Glendale Airport which they renamed Curtiss-Wright Airport and put Corliss Moseley in charge of. This field, offering service facilities and a flying school among other things, was never very successful, but real estate appreciation would later redeem the investment handsomely.

A principal figure in Avco was Errett Lobban Cord, *"a very foxy tycoon"* who as a teenager got his start in the car business in Los Angeles. Prior to his asociation with Avco, he controlled several companies including Lycoming and Stinson Aircraft. He had established Century Air-

Cord's Stinson trimotor and Century Airline - Glendale, California 1931

lines in 1931, operating out of Chicago, and a short while later, Century Pacific Lines between LA, San Diego and San Francisco, flying Stinson trimotors. Avco (which Cord controlled after 1933) also furnished these planes to several other lines, including Philadelphia's Ludington.

Cord also controlled Auburn and Duesenberg, and in 1928 was developing his radical front-wheel-drive *Cord* automobile with inventor Harry Miller in Los Angeles. (Miller continued and completed the great front-wheel-drive work of John W. Christie and Ben Gregory.) Cord sent Cornelius W. van Ranst, an automotive engineer with Duesenberg, to work with Miller on the car's prototype. (In 1921 van Ranst had designed the famous eight-valve pushrod Frontenac Head, making the Ford Model T a very 'hot' dirt-track racer, and he had also collaborated with Louis Chevrolet, long before GM). Van Ranst was a good friend of Clyde Forsythe, so it wasn't long before I, was hanging around Miller's place quite a bit. *Harry Miller was the finest racing engine builder in the country, thanks in large part to the genius of co-workers Leo Goossen and Fred Of-*

276

fenhauser. (Miller cars won at Indianapolis in 1923, '26, '28, '29 and '30, while Duesenbergs won in 1924, '25 and '27.) The Miller engines later became known as Offenhauser and as Meyer & Drake, with Leo Goossen still the principal designer.

I was one of the first to drive the front-wheel-drive prototype before it was sent back to the Auburn-Cord factory. It was introduced in August 1930, and put into production as the Cord L-29. Though a fascinating automobile, it was never a great success because it was too tough to steer and too expensive at a time when the country was tightening its belt. Around 4,000 had been built when production was stopped in 1932.

Harry Miller had built a prototype aircraft engine for Linc Beachey in 1914-15. In 1929, following the Cord episode, Miller had prospects good enough for he and Gilbert Beesemeyer to get together with Lockheed's Fred Keeler, financier George Schofield and G.E. Moreland, forming the $5,000,000 Miller-Schofield Company. They planned to offer a 130-hp air-cooled horizontal 8-cylinder engine for $2000, but because of the crash this company went bankrupt in mid-1930 - a very short life indeed.

It was while I was managing Metropolitan that I had my greatest involvement with movie stars hangaring their planes there. I saw a lot of Wallace Beery and Paul Lucas, due primarily to a mutual interest in aviation. Others were Ken Maynard, Hoot Gibson and Bill (Hop-a-Long) Boyd - all fellows that preferred to fly rather than ride a horse!

Bach's factory - Metropolitan Airport - 1929

277

Shortly after I set the altitude record, the Bach Company had a terrific tragedy. I was test-flying one of the new trimotors just off the production line - one of eight for Pickwick Airways, just organized to operate between San Francisco, LA and San Diego - and later into Mexico City. I looked down to see a raging fire in the newly-completed second half of the factory. Landing immediately, I rushed over to the inferno. All hell was breaking loose! The whole plant appeared to be exploding in all directions as acetylene gas tanks ignited, blowing-up like bombs.

Luckily no one was seriously injured. The factory was soon rebuilt and producing airplanes again, but in spite of fire insurance the loss was never fully recovered and this turned-out to be the beginning-of-the-end for Bach Aircraft (then under George R. Bury as president).

But as planned, I was to enter a Bach trimotor in the transport race at the 1929 Air Races in Cleveland, August 24 - September 2.

Billy Brock was then at the factory picking up one of the Air Yachts ordered by Schlee-Brock Aircraft Corp. of Detroit, a company that he and Ed Schlee had formed following their record Detroit-to-Tokyo flight in 1927 flying a Stinson SM-1. They were Lockheed's major distributors - and it was quite a testimonial for Bach when they placed an order for 35 trimotors. He also planned to enter the race, so there would be two Bachs competing.

Just before we took off, the first Women's Air Derby (*"Powder Puff Derby"* as it was later tagged by Will Rogers) was flagged-off at Clover Field on August 18th with 19 starters, and my good friend Louise Thaden was the first to finish in Cleveland on the 26th, followed by Gladys O'Donnell and Amelia Earhart - those *"Sweethearts of the Air."*

I took the trimotor east with quite a passenger load: Morton Bach, Max Harlow, Wilbur White, Victor Clark of the Flying Club of California, and Terry deLapp, the *LA Times* aviation writer.

About the only person left at the field was my assistant, Hal Wells, and he reported to the press *"about all the folks had gone to the races, including Victor Fleming and Howard Hughes"*.

Upon arriving in Cleveland, I first flew the Bach as the official parachute jumpers ship, and then entered the multi-engine transport race. With myself flying one Bach and Billy Brock another, our only real competition was the Fokker. Bach had upgraded our engines to a Hornet in the nose and two Whirlwind J6's - a total of 1,100-hp!

> *"Roaring over the five-lap course, a Bach transport defeated the pick of the Eastern-made, three-motored ships in the feature race for heavy passenger planes ... piloted by Waldo Waterman; in a display of speed and remarkable maneuverability the pylons were polished with the speed and agility of a sport plane ... (a) Triumph for the West, the crowning event..."*

Leaving the Fokkers and Fords way behind, it was really a race between Billy and myself. My average speed was 136.4-mph, Brock, 134.5-mph, and the Fokker F-10, 123 mph. I was lucky to come in first and pocket the pilot's half of the purse.

The public was particularly taken by this race. They had never seen planes of this size race around pylons before the grandstands. And they could relate to these planes, for many were just starting to experience airline transportation. The Bach did a superb job of trouncing the competition, and in retrospect I would say that this moment was the *zenith* in Bach Aircraft's fortunes. I still treasure the trophy I won that day.

Just a month-and-a-half later - on *"Black Thursday"*, October 24, 1929 - that awful financial (and social) calamity, *the stock market crash*, became a shuddering reality. Following that moment, it seemed that everything started to crumble. The heady dreams that we had would never materialize. Bach survived the fire but wouldn't weather this jolt. Metropolitan Airport would succumb, too, though it would take longer. Any thoughts of growth and expansion were dashed, not to rise again for almost a decade.

Trophy - "Multi-Motored Ships, 100-mile race - 1929"

The Early Birds
Cleveland Migration 1929
HOTEL CLEVELAND

Wild Fruit Cocktail
Collected from Mexican Jacals
by CONDOR HORACE B.

Waterman Soup
Combined Secretly in 1909 from Balloon Dope Juice,
Shellac Berries, Essence of Petrolatum, Glider Wire Kinks and
Imported Sceptic Ex-Hu-Mat-Ions
by WALDO in Person

Stinson Ap-pear-i-tif
Grown on Breckenridge Field, on the South loop, at Tokio, and
Flavored with Katies, Eadies, Marjies and Jackies
imported from Tennisee (that's a Secret)

Famous Fokker Flutterless Friers
Fetched from far Frankfort for famished fliers from far fields
frantically fearing falseteeth fractured from fierce filets
falicitate FOKKER

Wright Salad
Components Released for first time by ORVILLE
Three struts of Kitty Hawk with half pint of Bicycle Shop stirred
with Printing Press and blended with dope from Lillenthal flavor
with Smithstsonian then remove the flavor.

Coffyn Coffee Cognac
(SANS COFFEE SANS COGNAC)
(BO-COO H2O)
A dark brown taste with odor imported from the mud flats on the
bottom of an F boat by FRANK

HARTNEY CIGARS
Collected by HARROLD and BILL MITCH
in cabbage patches near Chaumont,
soaked with Club Lafayette vinegar

DEPEW SNIPES
DICK and FISH cleaned these and scaled them
They are wrapped in tennis leaves and
filled with Greenland

Early Birds dinner menu, Hotel Cleveland, 1929. Somewhat of a "who's who" of early aviators - Horace Wild, myself, the Stinson clan, Tony Fokker, Orville Wright, Frank Coffyn...

281

When all of this started to happen, I was still in the East following the races and delivering the Bach to Detroit. I didn't have any crystal ball, but I surely had a hunch that something was amiss. I immediately wired Carol not to spend the $50 check that I'd left with her to buy a chow pup from a new litter at Gladys Waters' kennel in La Mesa - remember her? (See page 62.)

Well, I was too late. When I arrived back home, Carol advised me that she'd already spent the $50 for an evening gown which she wore to a lavish party thrown by William Randolph Hearst and his mistress, Marion Davies, at the Ambassador Hotel.

Carol had gone to this bash with our good friends and neighbors, Doug and Marion Shearer. Doug's sister, Norma (1902-1982) was then at the peak of her fabulous movie career. She was one of *"Hollywood's patricians"* and had married MGM's *"little genius"* Irving Thalberg in *"the wedding of the year"* in 1927 (Carol & I were guests). In 1930, she would be one of the first Oscar winners for her performance in *"The Divorcee"*.

Irving Thalberg and Norma Shearer

It was a time of unparalleled, extravagant lifestyle, even for Hollywood. In this context, Carol reasoned it appropriate to spend the $50, but I have always considered it to have been a terrible waste!

Though I missed that particular affair, I had another opportunity to meet Hearst. A couple of years later, Doug Shearer, one of my partners in the ownership of Bach-22, was working on getting Thalberg involved - one way or another - in aviation, maybe even to the extent of his buying our trimotor. Doug called me one day, requesting that I fly the Air Yacht up to San Simeon, Hearst's fantastic hideaway.

This Hearst "ranch", with 240,000 acres stretching approximately 50 miles along the Pacific coast midway between San Francisco and Los Angeles, was then the "most magnificent estate in the Western World". It was a complex of Moorish Castles, dominated by La Casa Grande with a gold and gilded baroque interior that boggled the mind and eye. The richest and most powerful publisher in the world, William Randolph Hearst spent an estimated $1,000,000 annually for over 30 years to accumulate a treasure horde of art, buildings and crafts of old world masters. The "cream" of this bulging collection was assembled and recreated on "The Enchanted Hill". This most fabulous private residence had 38 bedrooms, 31 baths, 14 sitting rooms, movie theater, billiard room, dining hall, assembly hall, and two libraries - over 100 rooms in all. (Now a California State Park.)

I was to fly there, pick up Thalberg's party, and fly them back to Los Angeles. I landed at the small strip near the castle, just below the hill, and was met by a Packard sedan and driver. Ensconcing myself, I was looking forward to the ride up to the "Big House" and a meeting with Hearst. We'd just passed one of the *"Animals Have the Right of Way"* signs, and I was looking at some of the strange animals roaming the fields (Hearst's zebras, now acclimated to California, are still in those hills), when the Packard suddenly turned into what was obviously the hired hands' complex. More-than-a-bit annoyed, I was escorted into a huge farm-style dining room where I would have lunch while waiting for Thalberg's group to finish their visit. I sat down, almost muttering to myself, for this was certainly not the way we aviators were accustomed to being treated. But it apparently was how Hearst did it (though he had obviously been delighted when Paulhan gave him his first aeroplane ride at Dominguez in 1910).

Zebras and Buffalo - Hearst's San Simeon Ranch - 1930

Nonetheless, I enjoyed the meal and the chance to observe how Hearst's help acted towards him. The atmosphere wasn't much different than at military messes, especially the Navy's, for most of the help were Filipinos. I got a kick out of hearing Hearst referred to as *"The Chief"*. It was by either that name or by *"W.R."* that he was known to the people that worked for or knew him well.

I then cooled my heels, tinkering with the plane until about 4 o'clock when Thalberg finally showed-up. After spending some time with him I understood why F. Scott Fitzgerald modeled some of his characters after him - he was quite a dynamic individual. The flight back to Clover Field, the nearest airport to MGM, was uneventful, and though Thalberg seemed to enjoy it we were never able to get him committed to aviation.

Afterwards when I was telling Doug about my treatment he said, *"Forget it, Waldo; Hearst is famous for that sort of thing - don't take it personally."*

284

Chapter 6

1930 - 1933

Depression Clouds the Skies

WHEN I returned from Cleveland in the fall of 1929, the shock of the stock market crash was just beginning to be felt. But I still had my job managing Metropolitan Airport, plus flight testing and demonstrating for Bach Aircraft. So, things hadn't yet slowed me down much. I immediately started rounding up the Waterman Aircraft Syndicate commitments for building the new type of plane that I'd designed, the *"Flex Wing,"* and now I began to feel the first cold winds of the Depression. Collecting that $25,000 wasn't easy, and the syndicate agreement specified that only when all of the shares were committed could I start assessing the members at the rate of 25% per month, figuring that it would take around four months to complete.

One of the subscribers was Maurice Graham, whom I'd known since instructing at Berkeley. He had just been lost while on a Western Air Express mail run between Las Vegas and Salt Lake City. His disappearance touched off one of the largest searches in the West, but after about three weeks all hope was abandoned. Later he was found sitting on a log, frozen to death. He had wandered about five miles from his crashed plane and had eaten half the can of salt-packed tomatoes that he always carried in case of an emergency. I didn't press his estate for his commitment, and in spite of few others trimming theirs because of the general economic uncertainty I was finally able to collect slightly under $20,000.

In a belt-tightening process that the times dictated, the airport directors asked me to take a cut in pay. Instead, I elected to resign in order to devote all of my time to the Flex Wing while taking the same pay from the syndicate as I'd had running the airport. Also, at this time I had a $5,000 windfall from the estate of a wealthy uncle in New York which I eventually sunk into this project.

However, before leaving my job at Metropolitan there was an incident that was quite amusing. It was shortly after the 1929 Air Races when the famed English aviatrix, Lady Mary Heath, showed up in Los Angeles flying her 95-hp Cirrus-powered Avro Avian. It was a plane similar to the one that she'd flown across Africa and had then sold to Amelia Earhart. I had first seen that one when Amelia landed it at the 1928 National Air Races. She flew it from the east coast, and then back again, completing in that sweet little airplane the first coast-to-coast roundtrip flight ever done by a woman. Anyway, Lady Heath wanted someone of prominence to fly the Avian and comment on its characteristics, and I was the one chosen. Just as I was about to climb into its cockpit she tapped me on the shoulder saying, *"I say old chap, may I see your brevet?"* Well, I was taken aback and didn't know whether she wanted me to take down my pants or what - when somebody said, *"Waldo, she wants to see your license."* That was the first time that anyone had ever asked to see my license, and it surely caught me off guard.

The affairs of Bach Aircraft weren't going well and they were having to trim salaries and lay people off, and as time went along I snatched the best of them to help me on the Flex Wing. By June of 1930, the plane was completed, though still uncertified and in an experimental category. I then test-flew it around Metro and garnered quite a bit of newsreel and press publicity.

(I've mentioned "newsreels" a time or two, and those readers of the television age might like to know that in the 1920's, 1930's and 1940's "going to the movies" was a weekly habit enjoyed by almost everyone. For the 25 cents admission (kids a dime) moviegoers typically saw two full-

length features - plus a newsreel that brought to the screen all the important events of the week, a cartoon or two and usually a scary serial. There were even some theaters showing nothing but newsreels.)

The Flex Wing - Waterman 4.C.L.M. (X169W) - Metropolitan Airport - 1930

(Note: Though the news release of August 15, 1930, read "they overcome airbumps much in the manner of shock absorbers on automobiles", in reality, the wings stayed level while the fuselage seemed to ride every bump along the way. Carol and I were both airsick a few times during our trip East).

But back to the Flex Wing. After completing the flight tests and making a few changes and adjustments, I decided to take it to the 1930 National Air Races in Chicago to demonstrate it. The races were to be held at the Curtiss-Reynolds Airport from August 23rd to September 1st, and I was on the daily program to show off the plane's unusual merits. In mid-August Carol and I took off for Chicago, flying in an aircraft still in its experimental stage. It was in fact a prototype from the ground up for it had Kinner's new C5 190-hp experimental engine as powerplant, plus all of the other innovations that I'd built into it.

287

The Flex Wing at the National Air Races - Chicago - 1930

The Flex Wing created quite a sensation wherever we went - because of it's unique variable wing design. In cruising the wings were set at a high dihedral angle, while for landings and takeoffs they were flattened straight-out with no dihedral angle. This ability to change dihedral angle enabled the pilot to adjust the wings' angle of attack to the most efficient aerodynamic position for each respective maneuver, whether landing, taking off, climbing or cruising. No one had ever seen anything quite like this "rubber duck" - *an airplane that could change its shape.* It was similar to the ability of today's supersonic jets to change the swept-back angle of their wings. Our nickname for this plane was *"Flapper".*

The adjustment was accomplished by attaching the wing to the fuselage with a hinge aligned at 30 degrees from true fore and aft, *and* by an oleo wing strut incorporating an airspring-type of shock absorber commonly used for landing gears. Varying the air pressure in the wing strut unit altered the wing dihedral and thus the *"angle of incidence"* desired for optimum performance. Additionally, this arrangement helped absorb a great deal of the shock from rough-air flying, making it more comfortable for both crew and passengers and straining the plane's structure much less, though airsickness sometimes was a problem.

288

Press Release: "Fool Proof Monoplane" - "Closeup of Waldo D. Waterman, inventor, and air operated cylinder-piston, that controlls the raising and lowering of wings which act as shock absorbers to plane." - September 1930

The Flex Wing - N.A.C.A. Langley Field - 1930   289

The key innovation of this invention was the 30-degree nonparallel alignment of the wing hinge which therefore permitted a wide range of 'angle of incidence' or angle of attack (the principal aerodynamic variable.) I was awarded patent No. 1,783,529 (December 2, 1930). (My old friend, Claude Ryan, copied my "Flex Wing" name in 1961 for his unique line of Rogallo-wing craft)

After arriving at the races I flew the Flex Wing every day to show off its unusual features. I also raced a Bach trimotor, the one that Billy Brock had flown at Cleveland the year before, in the transport race. But I wasn't quite so lucky this year and I came in second.

These National Air Races were very major events in those years, on the same plateau with the public as the World Series. They had immense grandstands packed with thousands of spectators, and, naturally, everyone of note in aviation was there, too. Lined up beside my Flex Wing were several other interesting planes and pilots. Next to me was engineer-inventor-pilot (like myself) James McDonnell with his "Doodlebug", a pioneering version of a STOL (short takeoff and landing) aircraft. "Mac" and I got well acquainted, particularly since we were both seeking similar characteristics in private-owner airplanes. Later, though, he was to go in another direction - becoming the head of McDonnell Douglas. In 1932 we would compete in a cross-continent race: Mac in a Great Lakes plane and me in the Flex Wing. We've kept up a friendly relationship over the years. (He died in 1980.)

During the races I also spent some time with Frank Hawks. Known as *"Meteor Man"*, he was an ex-San Diegan and a legend in his own right. He flew up to Big Bear a couple of times before I ventured up there - though he found little to keep him there. Frank set countless records, *probably more than any other flyer*. In 1938 he was promoting the Gwinn Aircar, a competitor then for my Arrowbile, and he flew into a powerline, a much too common pilot's nemesis, and was killed.

Coast-to-Coast in 18 hours, 21 minutes & 59 seconds! February 1929

290

Also at the races was Steve Wittman from Oshkosh, Wisconsin. I'd first met him in 1929 when he had raced his crude looking plane with a Cirrus engine, built by him and his students. It may have been no thing of beauty but it beat everything in its class. Steve had become a regular competitor at the races, and this year he was in his usual winning form. Steve is very active and on the Board of Directors in the *Experimental Aircraft Association*, the largest group of serious aviation buffs in the world.

On the other side of me was a sleek little Cirrus-powered white plane. It was so clean and highly polished that a fly would have slipped off of its surface. It was being raced by Ben Howard, its builder. Its fuselage designation was "Howard DGA", and I innocently asked Ben just what that meant. *"Damn Good Airplane!"* he replied - and it sure was! Its Cirrus engine only put out 95-hp, and I said, *"Boy, it's a beautiful plane; it's too bad that it isn't fast enough to enter in the Thompson Race."* He replied, *"Oh, but I am going to enter that race!"* I kinda laughed, assuming that it was a joke.

Well, that race, the highlight of the Air Races and last on the program, was marred by a tragedy and several other misfortunes. The leading plane, a Curtiss Hawk, crashed, killing its pilot, Marine Captain Arthur Page. As a result, Ben Howard and his DGA "Pete" came in third, a terrific triumph for him. The race was won by Speed Holman - my tight-seat companion on that flight from Milwaukee to Chicago in 1926 - flying a Laird "Solution" and averaging just over 200 mph.

Ben went home to build newer racers "Ike" and "Mike", powered with stronger Menasco engines - and later, the great "Mister Mulligan".

Al Menasco, after doing me in on my Salmson engine conversion - and then jinxing it by his over refinement - stayed in the aircraft engine business. He took another design, the English Cirrus, and turned it upside down so that the cylinders protruded downward from the crankshaft. He installed one of these in a Great Lakes plane that had previously had the right-side-up Cirrus, and the improvement was remarkable. This led Menasco to start producing a quite successful line of engines. These "Pirate" (4 cylinder) and "Buccaneer" (6 cylinder) engines pretty well dominated the lower horsepower racing categories for many years.

Sometime later Menasco conceived of hooking two of his six-cylinder engines side-by-side geared to a single propeller. If one engine quit, the

291

other would then power the plane for a safe landing. This Unitwin installation was made on a special Lockheed Altair built by AiRover (later named the Vega Airplane Co., a subsidiary of Lockheed in 1937). This "flying test stand" was Mac Short's baby and it flew successfully, eventually logging 85 hours. Ground handling problems, however, caused an end to the project. Mac Short later formed Aircraft Components, a company making aircraft stampings which was managed during World War II by Gilbert Budwig as Mac stayed on with Lockheed. It was located at Metropolitan Airport, *starting to be called Van Nuys Airport.*

Another Menasco user was Allan Loughead. He left Lockheed when it sold out to Detroit Aircraft in 1929, before Mac's tinkering with this concept. He then formed Loughead Brothers Aircraft Corp. in Glendale and then, as Alcor Aircraft Corp., moved to the Bay Area. They developed the Alcor Duo-4 and Duo-6, using side-by-side Menasco engine setups. However, each engine drove its own propeller. Their Duo-6 met its demise when Eldred Remlin cracked it up, hitting the newsreel cameras - a damn poor way to get 'good press.' Max Harlow worked with Allan on the engineering of this idea.

As I mentioned, the Air Races climaxed with Page's fatal crash. As this event was last, the clearing of the wreckage delayed for a couple of hours those planes planning to leave. It was getting towards dusk when we finally got the 'green light', and then there was a mad scramble as about 200 aircraft got airborne at once! There wasn't any radio control. There were scores of planes taking off south into the wind at different speeds and different rates of climb, and we were smack in the middle of it. It was pure luck *(and Carol's alert eye that prevented a mid-air collision!)* that there weren't any more accidents. Our own situation was really tricky because we had to turn north to head for Milwaukee, where we were to spend the weekend with friends living in the nearby town of Wauwatosa.

When we finally cleared that thicket of airplanes, we found ourselves in a darkening sky intermittently lit up with a distant thunderstorm. Even though it was in our path it looked to be well beyond our destination. But when we arrived over Milwaukee, with only a few more miles to go, it started raining bucketfuls with thunder and lightning all around. Our friends were waiting for us at Wauwatosa's Curtiss-Wright Field, supposedly with paved and lighted runways, hangar and service facilities.

292

Luckily we found the field, but it was pitch black now; there weren't any lights *as the storm had knocked out the electricity.* The only way I could determine that we were over the airport was by the lightning flashes and by the dim lantern-lit forms of airplanes barely visible through the hangar's windows. The location of the runway was a mystery; all I could do was try to figure where it should be in relation to the hangars. In desperation I came in for a blind landing. It was like descending into a pot of ink - for as we neared the ground all definition disappeared, and all I could do was keep going straight ahead with a mild rate of descent. *Sooner or later I'd either touch down or hit something!*

My unseen copilot was with me again. My guesstimate of the runway's location turned out to be almost correct, but landing on a black asphalt runway on a black night meant that my first awareness of it was when we hit. It was a rough landing and the airplane took a terrific jolt, for I wasn't fully flared, but we were safely on the ground. I then taxied into the hangar with its dry interior and flickering lights. Carol and I were emotionally drained, but very happy to be warmly greeted by our friends.

There had been some structural damage from that rough landing, but soon the plane was jacked up, and after a week of visiting and making repairs, we took off for Cleveland. There, as earlier arranged, I exchanged the original shock struts for the new "Aerol" struts - shock absorbers that operate on compressed air and oil, manufactured by the Cleveland Pneumatic Tool Co.. I found them to perform better both under flight conditions and in cushioning landing shocks.

Next we headed for Buffalo to visit an old friend from the McCook Field days (when I'd been bidding the Thomas-Morse fighter), Major Reuben H. Fleet. "Reub", a resourceful man, after pioneering U.S. Air Mail in 1918, had resigned from the Air Service and later established Consolidated Aircraft Corporation in 1923 in Curtiss' old wartime factory. In short order he'd produced the very successful Army trainer, the PT-1 - which started this firm off to becoming one of the world's greatest aircraft manufacturers. At the time of our visit in 1930 Reub and his associates, diminutive Lawrence D. Bell (Glenn Martin's ex-factory manager) and Isaac M. (Mac) Laddon, were going full bore. They were producing flying boats for Ralph O'Neill's pioneering continent-connecting *NYRBA Line (New York, Rio and Buenos Aires Line)* which Reub had invested in and Pan Am would later wrest away. They were also making newer versions of their trainers. This was my first acquaintance with Mac Laddon, Consolidated's chief engineer, but not my last. It was far more pleasant than my later brushes with him would be.

Consolidated's Fleet Aircraft, Inc. was run by Larry Bell, and was very busy producing the popular line of Fleet Model 2's using the Kinner engines which Reub had made such a good deal for. Reub was also making a particularly lovely airplane that looked like an all-metal version of Lockheed's Air Express. It was called the Fleetster 20 and had originally been developed for O'Neill's NYRBA Line, but was now being offered to other buyers. TWA bought four to use with the Hornet engines from their defunct Fokker F-32s, and I flew them several times in 1933.

While I was managing Metropolitan Airport I had corresponded with Reub, suggesting that our location had a far better climate than Buffalo for the making of airplanes. In response he had come out, looked us over and expressed a keen interest. However, because of his growing flying boat business he needed a near-water location and entered into negotiations with Los Angeles for a site near San Pedro. This never materialized though, and because Fleet had taken his Army flight training at North Island's Rockwell Field he was soon in negotiation for a site on San Diego Bay. In the early Thirties he then secured an attractive option on a sizable acreage of mud flats beside the bay. In 1935, after dredging and filling, they built an excellent factory adjoining a new airport - now known as Lindbergh Field - a perfect place for flying boat development. Thus Consolidated Aircraft followed in Glenn Curtiss' steps. I could only recall my conversation with Curtiss at Dominguez in 1910 and the similarity of it in my correspondence with Reuben Fleet in 1929.

When I'd been planning this trip I'd hoped to stop and see Curtiss as I usually did whenever I was close to Garden City. But he had passed away on July 23rd, just before we left Los Angeles, and therefore I sadly bypassed Curtiss Engineering. After leaving Buffalo we flew across upstate New York and then down the Hudson River, landing at Long Island's Roosevelt Field - where I'd first met Igor Sikorsky and his group of Russian expatriates. There we visited with Leroy Hill (whom I'd first worked with at Hall-Scott) and Harold Crowe, the fellow Berkeley student that had worked with me on the 1913 flying boat project. They had formed Air Associates - a very successful aircraft supply house with nationwide branches, including one at Glendale's Grand Central Airport. We frequently saw each other, and later they would assist me in trying to find financing for the Department of Commerce's Vidal airplane competition. But, that's further into our story.

Next was Philadelphia - and Golly! Anyone that complains about Los Angeles smog should have seen it over the City of Brotherly Love that day. After groping around we finally located the airport, landing to visit Townsend Ludington. He, TAT veterans Gene Vidal and Paul Collins, and Amelia Earhart (who, as Ludington's vice president for promotion, was emulating Lindbergh's association with TAT) were running *the first "shuttle airline."* With the slogan *"on the hour every hour"*, their New York, Philadelphia & Washington Airway was operating between those cities with ten-passenger Stinson trimotors. Ludington Lines, though, would soon be absorbed into Eastern Air Lines.

Pitcairn-Cierva autogiro over Philadelphia - 1931

The autogiro culminated a decade of laboratory work and experimental flying by Juan de la Cierva, whose basic inventions led to today's helicopter.

295

Philadelphia was then becoming the center of rotary-wing activity, due in large measure to Harold Pitcairn's license to manufacture the Cierva autogiro. Both Pitcairn's autogiro and one made by Kellett were familiar sights during the 1930's. They were followed by the vertical lift achievements of Sikorsky, Bell, Hiller, Kaman and Philadelphia's young Frank Piasecki (who started out in a vacant store and ended up selling out to Boeing what is now their Vertol Division). Pitcairn had further developed what is considered the first helicopter design, the German Focke-Achgelis, and all of these various concepts led to Sikorsky's 1939 design of the first modern helicopter. Vertical lift has been one of my particular interests, ever since my first experiments with it in 1919. Somewhat later, in the Forties, I'd do considerably more with it while working with Bill Stout.

Our next stop was Washington D.C. where we were to visit relatives. We landed at Hoover Field, the Capitol's only airport and then simply a flightstrip beside the Potomac River. I was checking in when the airport's manager looked up and said, *"Were you flying NC169W in from Philadelphia just now?"* I said, *"Yep,"* and he then said, *"What kind of a map do you have?"* *"A Rand McNally,"* I replied, for that was all we used then - regular automobile road maps. Only the military had airway maps. He then escorted me over to the large Rand McNally map on his wall, and as he pointed out a large area cross-hatched in red just north of Washington he asked, *"Does your map have this marking?"* *"Yep, it sure does,"* I replied. *"You don't know what that means?"* he said. *"Nope."* *"Well, Mr. Waterman, I think that you should learn to read your maps better because you've just flown over Aberdeen Proving Grounds, and the Army had to stop firing some new antiaircraft guns that they were testing for fear of knocking you down."*

From then on I became a much better map reader - but this sort of thing was typical then. Today it would result in far more than a word of caution, but in those days everybody was learning from a low state of ignorance. We were feeling our way in aviation, and it was this sort of happening which led to today's rules and regulations.

We stayed with my sister Helen and her husband, Marine Colonel G.M. Kincade. Carol remained with them while I went down to the Langley Memorial Aeronautical Laboratory in Virginia (run by the NACA, National Advisory Committee for Aeronautics), in order to carry out the tests on the Flex Wing. This was a result of a meeting that I'd had at the Air Races with Dr. George Lewis, NACA's Director, and of his urging that I bring my interesting airplane to Langley. NACA assigned their chief test pilot, Bill McAvoy, and an outstanding engineer, Fred Weick *(designer of the NACA cowl),* to work on the testing. Devices were installed to record the angle of the wing (in relation to the fuselage) and the amount of motion while performing the whole gamut of maneuvers. Also, recorders measured the amount of control system movement, the air speed, and the acceleration forces imposed upon the aircraft during these maneuvers. With all of this paraphernalia affixed, McAvoy and I flew the Flex Wing from mild to severe maneuvers in order to simulate the sharp-edged gusts as they affected the plane's structure.

Upon the completion of the testing the results showed that this design innovation reduced the structural loads by around 25%. In other words, an aircraft normally having a load factor of four would hence have one of five-and-a-quarter, thus providing far more structural integrity. This sounded like a terrific breakthrough, but unfortunately for me the all-metal cantilever wing was just coming into wide use. It had been invented by the German, Hugo Junkers, and first used on his J1 in 1915. The metal cantilever wing performed in basically the same manner as my Flex Wing when it was designed into the fuselage structure in the same way. That is, as the loads increased, the dihedral increased and the angles of attack decreased. *It therefore doomed my concept to being a one-of-a-kind engineering achievement and, alas, a commercial failure.*

Returning to Washington, I picked up Carol, and we flew for home, following the main highways as was the custom then. I wanted to stop off and see Frank and Bill Robertson, who were Lindbergh's employers when I'd first met him on the Chicago-St. Louis airmail run in 1926. Now located in Kansas City, Kansas, they had sold out their old airline at Lambert Field and started the Robertson Airplane Service Co. (There are two Kansas Cities. The one most people know is located in Missouri and the other one is smaller and just across the river in Kansas. Their airports are opposite each other, too.)

We landed at Kansas' Fairfax Field, and as usual, quite a crowd gathered to look over the Flex Wing. While I was showing it off, all of a sudden a roar screamed out from a high speed plane overhead. It was Jimmy Doolittle flying Shell Oil's Travel Air *Mystery S* and he was head-

297

ing for a landing at the Missouri field. As was common practice, he came down in a screeching dive towards the center of the airport, then he swept upward in a steep, tearing climb. But this time, to everyone's horror, he collided with a National Guard PT-3A trainer. The Mystery S chewed the tail off of the Army plane, and its pilot and student bailed out, drifting safely down as Doolittle nursed his badly-damaged monoplane in for a landing. Being the superb pilot that he was, Jimmy handled things OK af-

Jimmy Doolittle

ter the crash, though I am sure that he must have been quite chagrined. I believe that was the last bit of harem-scarem flying that he ever did.

But it surely left an impression on Carol as she quietly said, *"Waldo, a half-hour ago we were just where that Army plane was - and we don't have any parachutes."*

As we flew further west - following what was to become Route 66 - the weather really started closing in over Oklahoma until there was only 300-400 feet between the ground and the bottom of the clouds. If you were flying today under such conditions, you'd be on instruments. But then, as long as you could clear the clouds and the ground and see reasonably far ahead, you kept on flying. The entire Oklahoma plains area that we were flying over - or maybe I should say *weaving through* - was dotted with tall oil well derricks - and since I could see forward well enough, I was flying a course that was zigzagging between them. However, Carol could only see out sideways - and seeing a derrick go whizzing past the wingtips every few seconds got her to a virtual state of nervous collapse, a condition for which I could hardly blame her. Soon she was strenuously urging that we *land - land anywhere, but land!* Since we were fairly close to Elk City, I headed there.

After landing and tying down the plane securely (neccessary because the winds in that area can be quite fierce, picking up a plane like a leaf), a shaken Carol and I took a taxi to the only hotel in town. I fully expected to take off in the morning, but Carol thought otherwise. She flatly stated that we wouldn't leave until there was at least a 1,000-foot ceiling and five miles visibility.

Passing the time in a small town is quite a trial. There was only one 'picture show', and we had already seen all the movies. However, there was a radio in our room and the World Series was on. Carol hates base-ball, and after having to listen to the games day after day, she vowed that she would never listen to them again. Finally after seven days of tedium, boredom and baseball, the weather lifted, and gratefully we were able to take off. We then made it all the way to Kingman, Arizona, where we spent the night in a hotel next to someone who was either drunk or had a helluva case of asthma. After a sleepless night, we took off in the morning for the last leg into Los Angeles.

Boy! Was Carol glad to get home and out of that airplane - and she flatly stated that she would never again ride in an airplane. And, by golly, to this day she hasn't! (Well, almost! Soon after, I mistakenly coerced her into one more flight.)

In the meantime things were not going at all well for the Bach Aircraft Company. Its meteoric growth in 1929 saw it go from 65 employees to well over 200 and from a 25,000-square-foot factory to one of over 40,000 square feet. It had been producing up to six trimotors a month on its nine-acre grounds, but now it was crippled by hard times. There simply weren't any new orders coming in, and B.L. Graves, the company's president, was desperately trying to raise fresh capital but with little luck. About this time, a prospective Bach investor from the East bought an Air Yacht, and with his pilot, R.S. McCallister (one of the many Hughes *"Hell's Angels"* second-string pilots), they took off on a cross-country demonstration tour. I never thought that McCallister was qualified to fly a trimotor - and he attempted some maneuvers with it that only a much better pilot could have carried off. (Later, Harold Johnson, *"The King of the Tin Goose"*, would perform a variety of amazing acrobatics in a Ford trimotor at air shows, including upside down flying, loops, snap rolls, slow rolls, hammerhead stalls, Cuban eights and whirling spins. He would finish off his display with low-level snap rolls, the last one only about 25 feet off the ground and then three or four screeching loops before sideslipping into a perfect landing.)

It wasn't unheard of, therefore, to do some fairly rigorous aerobatics with the Bach trimotor, too, for it was a very fast, maneuverable and well-built airplane. I often did a few of them, particularly when demonstrating the merits of the plane. But McCallister and his investor-employer went a bit too far one day while showing off the Bach over Roosevelt Field. After several loops they went into a steep power dive,

299

and as they started to pull up, the forces were far in excess of the plane's design limits. They pulled the wings off and killed themselves in a crash. This tragedy, like Fokker's Rockne crash, ruined the reputation of a fine airplane. Coupled with the stock market crash, it spelled the end of the company. It is ironic to think that both Bach and Lockheed were comparable companies then, but in a few years one would be all but forgotten and Morton Bach would be working for the other - in Lockheed's sheet metal department and subsequently as a vice president.

At this time I still thought that the Flex Wing had promise, and upon my return to Metropolitan I started making modifications and completing the government's type certification. Max Harlow, laid off by Bach, helped me complete the drawings and stress analysis. (Max's wife, Evelyn, had been my secretary when I was managing Metro.) Max worked with Ivar Shogran, an old friend from San Diego days, who was my shop superintendent and who'd previously been with Glenn Martin. They made a good team which quickly resulted in the Approved Type Certificate being granted in early 1931.

At that point, without any work to do, I couldn't keep them on the payroll. I helped Max get a job with Kinner Aeroplane & Motors and eventually I got Ivar into Douglas Aircraft - though that was a bit tougher to accomplish. Over a period of several months I kept calling my old friend from Jenny-building days, Harry Wetzel, now in charge of things at Douglas. Invariably he'd say, *"Hell, Waldo, we already have too many engineers just twiddling their thumbs in the drafting room - and we sure don't need one more."* However, by mid-1931 things opened up a bit and Ivar got hired, though his first assignments were very small. It wasn't until the late summer of 1932, when Douglas' fortunes started to turn around upon the receipt of the inquiry from TWA's Jack Frye that led to the DC-1, that more substantial work came to Ivar. He continued with Douglas, becoming one of their top engineers and the *chief project engineer on the DC-8 before his retirement.*

Max worked with Kinner for some time designing several of their new planes. Later, after another of my contacts, he joined *Pasadena City College,* a 2-year junior college ("PJC"), and developed a course in aeronautical design, structures and drafting that became a model for training aeronautical engineers. In fact, many of his two-year graduates were more desired than were four-year graduates of nearby Cal Tech.

300

Max was a great pal of J.B. Alexander, Howard Hughes' chief of aeronautics during the filming of *"Hell's Angels"*. It was suspected that through Alexander some of Hughes' money got into some Harlow projects. Max and his students designed an all-metal four-place plane, the Harlow PJC-1, that was so unique and advanced that it prompted the establishment of the Harlow Aircraft Company in the old Western Air Express hangars at Alhambra Airport. I think that Hughes was behind this venture, for it wasn't long until Harlow Aircraft had purchased the entire airport site, later selling it for a tremendous profit.

The early-1930's was a period of crunch for the fledgling aircraft industry. It had just started to blossom after Lindbergh's 1927 flight, so it was a very brief bloom. It was a period of great change for many companies. Mahoney, builder of The Spirit of St. Louis, made the fatal mistake of dropping the Ryan name and selling out to interests that moved his facility to St. Louis. There, it regained the Ryan moniker but disappeared into the Detroit Aircraft maze. In the meantime, Claude Ryan was keeping solvent by selling the German Siemens-Halske engines, known as Ryan-Siemens, which we'd used on the Bachs. He soon got back into aircraft manufacturing, founding the T.C. Ryan Aeronautical Corporation in 1928. Today it is still an industry name, and Claude is one of my closest friends. (Ryan died in 1982, at 84.)

During those days Detroit Aircraft Corporation seemed like it was bent upon gobbling up the whole aircraft industry and moving it to Detroit, but the Depression thwarted that scheme. As the Aircraft Development Corporation, they'd already backed Ralph Upson in his metal-skinned blimp ZMC-2 project located at Grosse Isle Airport. But, after demonstrating it around the country, there didn't appear to be any future for its unique qualities (though it made over 750 flights before being dismantled 12 years later). Then, with their sacks full of money, they picked up St. Louis's Ryan, as noted above. In mid-1929 they bought control of Lockheed, putting Carl Squier in as general manager, and Allan Loughead bailed-out quite a richer man. Just prior to this, in 1928, Ken Jay and Jack Northrop had left Lockheed in order to form their own Avion Corp., later evolving into Northrop Aircraft.

But in 1931 Detroit Aircraft's stock plummeted from $15 to less th..n thirteen cents a share and they went bankrupt, causing the receivership of Lockheed by Title Insurance & Trust Co. (TI's president in the early Twenties was Leslie Brand, for whom I'd built two airplanes.) Lockheed was now put 'on the block' - lock, stock and fuselage. A syndicate composed of Robert Gross, Walter Varney, Cyril Chappellet and others, bought it. Lloyd Stearman took over as the new president with Carl Squier as sales manager, Hall Hibbard as chief engineer, and Gross in charge of the money.

I could go on and on discussing the people and company changes during this time. There was a tremendous amount of shuffling about, and what was put together one day would, often as not, blow asunder the next. The Depression sometimes made strange bedfellows. For instance, Jack Northrop was first with Loughead, then with Douglas, then back with Lockheed. Then he formed his own company, Avion, which was first a division of United Aircraft and, later, a subsidiary of Douglas again. Finally, in 1939, Jack co-founded today's Northrop Aircraft. In 1925, in Wichita, one company, Travel Air, had Clyde Cessna, Walter Beech and Lloyd Stearman all working together as its officers - each of whom would have their own companies in later years. *It was a time of tremendous personal opportunities - and many, many shattered dreams.*

As the Twenties came to a close, the shocks of that dark October rippled through more and more companies. And, as the hesitant Thirties dawned, there were few aircraft manufacturers surviving those lean years. There was the company that Glenn Curtiss had formed when he spun off from his original organization, Curtiss Engineering in Garden City - and there was Glenn Martin in Ohio, Bill Boeing in Seattle, Bill Stout in Detroit, Reuben Fleet in Buffalo, Claude Ryan in San Diego and, in the Los Angeles area, Donald Douglas at Clover Field and me with the Flex Wing at Metropolitan.

Bach Aircraft went down the long road to oblivion, and I was appointed the liquidator of its assets. It was a task that was taking place time and again nationwide. This melancholy job first necessitated taking an inventory of everything, and then the gradual liquidation of what I could sell. This therefore gave me a temporary base of operations, and I moved my office into Graves' old haunts. They were certainly far more sumptuous than anything I'd ever enjoyed heretofore. Times being what they were, things didn't sell easily, and it appeared that it would be quite a while before most of the stuff was disposed of - so I moved the Flex

302

Wing into a Bach hangar. This saved the rent that I had been paying to Metropolitan and allowed me to fiddle with the plane while I sold Bach's inventory on a contract percentage for the bankruptcy receivers. When I started getting to the bitter end, there were several trimotored transports in various stages of completion which could be purchased very cheaply. So, with some associates, principally Doug Shearer and a few other MGM employees who were all still making good money, we purchased Bach Air Yacht No. 22. It was nearly completed - and we figured to finish the job and then use it for charter work or resell it for a profit. We've already touched upon one of its episodes - the San Simeon trip - and we'll hear of others in a bit.

Metropolitan Airport was one of Hollywood's favorite places for filming aviation-related sequences - and one of these has always rankled me a bit. It was during 1931 and the filming of *"Sky Bride"*, and I'd loaned my Bach president's office to its star, actress Virginia Bruce, for her dressing room. It also starred Richard Arlen and Jack Oakie and was huckstered with these words, *"Love rides the clouds at 200 miles an hour! Cloud-bursting, Heart-bursting daredevils...risking their necks for the love of a beautiful girl!"* As I've mentioned, this office was far plushier than any I ever had - but by the time this movie queen had used it for only three or four days, it was a living mess. My opinion of those beautiful gals surely went down a notch or two.

Robert Coogan, Jackie's younger brother, was in this film - and I was likewise appalled at how his mother yanked and jerked him around, making him do certain things that he should have been trained to do without that kind of urging. It was almost brutal - watching this fat, sloppy woman practically maul this little kid during a couple of sequences filmed around the two Bach trimotors used in the movie. Apparently the boy's father acted the same way. Charlie Chaplin recounts the father referring to Jackie as, *"...the little punk."* Well, that was Hollywood - and I just bit my lip and quietly went about my business.

This period, 1927-1930, saw the three Great War flying movies released. Bill Wellman's *"Wings"*, starring Clara Bow, Buddy Rogers, Richard Arlen, and a young Gary Cooper in a bit part, debuted in 1927 - with the great Harry Perry behind the cameras. *It won the first Oscar in 1928.* In 1930 both Howard Hawks' *"Dawn Patrol"*, starring Richard Barthelmess and Douglas Fairbanks, Jr., and the biggest one of all, Hughes' *"Hell's Angels"*, opened.

303

Clara Bow - "Wings" - 1927

The *"Hell's Angels"* premier, May 27, 1930, was the greatest that Hollywood had ever seen - before or since - and Noah Dietrich had sent me two tickets for this "$100,000" extravaganza. Knowing that it would be a very posh affair with all of Hollywood's 'who's who' attending, Carol and I gussied-up in our evening clothes. I'd just bought a new Chrysler sedan (it cost just under $1900) and Ote Carter, my hangar chief at Metropolitan, dug up a chauffeur's uniform to drive us to the premier.

We got into the traffic early, planning to arrive at Grauman's Chinese Theater before the peak of the crowd. But we soon found ourselves barely moving on a jam-packed Hollywood Boulevard. We inched along close to an hour and the theater's entrance was far ahead, so we began to suspect that we'd never make it on time. *While all of this was going on, overhead the whole fleet of "Hell's Angels" planes and pilots were mock-dogfighting; there were fireworks blazing the darkening sky; and rockets and searchlights intermittently stabbed their paths in the night. It was a fantastic show, and Hollywood was in a frenzy like I'd never seen. The only thing close to what we were watching was the euphoria exhibited at the end of the war.*

While we were still at least a block and a half from Grauman's, Carol and I decided that we'd never make it on time by automobile, and we got out and walked the rest of the way. The largest crowd that I'd ever seen was packed around the theater's entrance, ogling as limousine after limousine disgorged the greatest assemblage of Hollywood stars ever to gather for an opening. *There was Charlie Chaplin, Cecil deMille, Gloria Swanson, John Gilbert, Lionel Barrymore, Jesse Lasky, Maurice Chevalier, Irving Berlin and Jerome Kern among the many, many top personalities that "had" to be there.*

Our decision to walk was a smart one. Ote later told me that it was another hour before he got to the entrance, and then he had to keep right on going, for he couldn't turn off. Los Angeles had turned out 600

304

policemen to control the surging crowds - *one estimate put it at half-a-million fans.*

As we entered the theater's foyer my eye was caught by the picture's beautiful platinum blonde leading lady, Jean Harlow (Harleen Carpenter), holding a huge sheaf of yellow roses which accented her lovely hair. She was wearing a very, very low-cut light blue satin gown, and greeting people with her gorgeous body and gorgeous smile as they entered. She was really a gorgeous gal. Recovering my composure, Carol and I were seated, and before the lights went down, we did a lot of ogling on our own and were even ogled-at a bit ourselves.

Jean Harlow - maybe not a fine actress, but gorgeous, gorgeous!

The lights dimmed at 10 PM and the show started. The first hour was vaudeville, hosted by Frank Fay, and included an appearance by my fellow aviator, natty Roscoe Turner attired in his dazzling 'uniform' of powder-blue tweed jacket, Sam Browne belt, whipcord breeches, shiny boots, white scarf, jaunty military-type of hat and a finely-waxed pointed mustache. He'd just raced a Lockheed coast-to-coast for a new record.

Finally at 11 PM the feature began - starring Ben Lyon, James Hall and that beautiful Jean Harlow. I was already quite familiar with many of the scenes, for I'd either seen them shot or had others tell me about them. One memorable incident concerned a scene with Frank Clarke and another pilot, Earl Gordon. Gordon was to play the part of an aviator that got a bit chicken at times and would refurbish his ardor and zeal with a good stiff drink. In this case Frank and Earl were flying a two-place Fokker - the same one that I'd rebuilt for Hall-Scott a few years earlier - and there was a camera mounted out on the wing focused on only the front cockpit. In this scene Gordon was supposed to chicken out and have to nip the bottle. It was shot a couple of times, but Hughes didn't like the 'rushes' and

305

wanted it shot again - a penchant with him as he sought perfection in this effort. Frank and Earl remonstrated with Hughes, telling him that they could do a more realistic job if Earl could only have real scotch whiskey to drink instead of tea. Hughes then, reluctantly, provided a bottle of his best scotch, and they went back to work.

That night - following the shooting of the more realistic scene - Frank was awakened at 3 o'clock in the morning by a very irate Hughes telling him to come down to the studio immediately. Frank demurred as best he could, but Hughes insisted, and Frank had to get up and go on down to see what he was so upset about. When he arrived they ran the day's rushes. As Gordon's drinking sequence ended, the film, which was not yet cut, kept running and showed a hand appear from the rear, take the bottle from Gordon and return it a few frames later. This was repeated a couple of times - taking swigs of the scotch - and Hughes was mad as hell about it. Frank later confided to me that they'd planned the whole episode just to get *"young high-and-mighty's"* goat. They surely had succeeded!

Roscoe Turner, sharing in the premier's limelight, had first shown up on the coast flying the first airplane that Igor Sikorsky and his Russians had built after coming to this country. It was the S-29A, built in 1924, a huge twin Liberty-engined biplane which Roscoe had been flying around the country promoting various enterprises. I most remember it being called "the flying cigar store" when he was working for the United Cigar Stores. By the time he arrived in California, that promotion had petered out, and Roscoe and the airplane were 'available'.

Roscoe Turner's S-29A "First Flying United Cigar Store" - 1927

306

Roscoe Turner bought the S-29A in 1926; it was the "First Flying United Cigar Store"; then it was leased to Curlee Clothing Co. of St. Louis; and then leased to Hughes. We soon learned that Roscoe was no shrinking violet. He was a darn good pilot in addition to being a superb showman. He joined our Professional Pilots Association and was always a strong and active member.

"Hell's Angels" - The Sikorsky as a German Gotha bomber - 1928

In *"Hell's Angels"*, Hughes needed a Gotha bomber for a scene, and Turner's Sikorsky was the nearest thing available. Hughes chartered it for the movie. In the plane's final scene it was to be shot down and fall spinning with smoke pouring from it. Then, naturally, off camera it was to recover before hitting the ground. Roscoe was not an aerobatic-type of pilot and therefore didn't want to spin the plane. Al Wilson, who would do almost anything for a price, took the assignment. A young mechanic, Phil Jones, went along to operate the smoke-making apparatus, a contraption with about a ton of lampblack and flour in a hopper which was to be expelled as the plane spun downward.

307

During the filming, the "Gotha" went into its spin, the 'smoke' poured out, and then to everyone's surprise a parachute appeared as a man had jumped. The plane continued its relentless spin until it crashed into the ground. Later Wilson stated that he couldn't pull it out, and, after signalling Jones to jump, he had gone over the side. Jones, the poor devil, was killed. Whether or not he ever received Wilson's signal has been an object of speculation ever since. That same night Wilson appeared at a Hollywood night spot sporting a new plaster cast on his broken leg, inviting one and all to sign it as if he were quite the hero. He surely wasn't one in my book - but then he, too, was soon to meet his Maker.

Another time - during the filming of a German airfield scene at Caddo Field - Hughes was way up atop a high tower, and he called out, *"Where's J.B.?"* The word was repeated - *"Where's J.B.? Where's J.B.?"* until finally J.B. Alexander came puffing up all those stairs saying, *"Yes, Mr. Hughes; what do you want?"* *"Oh, nothing, J.B., I just wondered where you were,"* replied Hughes.

A few years earlier, while Alexander was manager of American Aircraft Co. at Clover Field, Howard Hughes was taught to fly there. *"Yesman J.B."* sometimes gave Hughes a bit of backtalk in those days - but he later mended his ways and became one of Hughes' top lieutenants (under Dietrich) until late in the '30's.

But one should never minimize Howard Hughes' capabilities. He became a very fine pilot, an excellent practical aeronautical engineer and was responsible for some very major aviation achievements. I won't dwell too much more on these, for they're all recorded elsewhere - except that there was one thing I was a bit involved with. Hughes was very anxious to break the transcontinental speed record in his *"Special"*, a plane designed by Dick Palmer with the assistance of Max Harlow. In late 1935 he set his first of many records, racing the Special at over 350 mph at Santa Ana, and in 1937 flew it coast-to-coast in under seven and a half hours. When Max worked with Palmer on this plane, he was between jobs - he'd been working at Douglas after his stint with Kinner - and he worked with Hughes only a short time to help perfect the design and the Special's structural analysis. Nonetheless, he told me how astonished he was at Hughes' knowledge of aerodynamics and structures. In 1938, as previously mentioned, Hughes flew around the world in under

308

The Hughes "Special" - "a big engine with a saddle" - 1937

four days with my old 'fired' employee, Lawson Thurlow, as his copilot and navigator. I've just noted with interest that the "Special" has been donated to the Smithsonian. Well, it'll join some other interesting aircraft - including a couple of Waterman models.

This is a good time to comment on the round-the-world craze of the Thirties. It was Wiley Post (whom I'd first met in 1930 when he won the Los Angeles-to-Chicago Air Derby, starting the National Air Races) who was first to electrify the country by flying around the world with Harold Gatty in eight and a half days in 1931 in a Lockheed Vega. *He then did it alone in 1933 in under eight days, a fantastic feat!*

In 1935 I, along with countless millions, mourned the deaths of Wiley and my Santa Monica Canyon 'neighbor', Will Rogers. There's been an awful lot of speculation as to what might have caused their crash in the wastes of Alaska. I lean towards the belief that it was due to disorientation because Wiley had only one eye, though others believe that it was because the pontoons were too large for the plane (they weren't what had been planned) or the wings weren't designed for that fuselage, and/ or the fact that *the plane was out of fuel.*

When Hughes circumnavigated the globe in 1938 his words of praise were for his four crew members *and* the wonder at Wiley's feat. Another flight in this globe-girdling era was attempted by Amelia Earhart in mid-1937, doing it 'the hard way' following the equator. As we'll touch upon later, I was with Amelia before this, her final flight. She was lost over the western Pacific - apparently due to navigational error and the Japanese (See *Amelia Earhart, The Final Story* by Vincent Loomis, 1985).

309

Of course, all of these flights followed the first epic round-the-world flight by the U.S. Army in 1924 flying Douglas planes under the command of (my Berkeley student) Lowell Smith. *(In 1974 I was named a member of the Honorary Committee celebrating the 50th anniversary of this flight, sharing the honors with an historic Who's Who of aviation - but I missed that banquet just as I'd missed the Clover Field takeoff for that flight, being then in the midst of starting the Big Bear Airline.)*

In addition to aircraft manufacturing going through a lot of changes, the airlines were also experiencing a great deal of shuffling in the early 1930's. Boeing received a Post Office contract to take over the airmail from San Francisco to Chicago. Then, they acquired Vern Gorst's Pacific Air Transport running along the West Coast, plus the Eakin's Bach-equipped West Coast Air Transport, and Varney Speed Lines. Sometime later they gathered-in National Air Transport, flying between Chicago and Dallas-Ft. Worth, and thus had the nucleus of America's largest airline. It would be called *United Airlines* following the government's order for Boeing, the manufacturer, to divest itself of Boeing, the airline.

They were just starting to use the new *Boeing 247,* a twin Wasp-powered transport that was a tremendous improvement over the trimotored Fords and Fokkers - *but available only to United Airlines.* Some of the other lines were still flying the last of the *biplane* transports, the Curtiss Condor. During the forced-merger negotiations between TAT and WAE, Pop Hanshue commented about the Condors, *the world's first "sleeper" airliners*, which weren't noted for their climbing ability. He was asked;

> *"And how soon, Mr. Hanshue, will you be able to put Condors on your line from Los Angeles to Kansas City?"*
> *"Oh, not for a long time - a long, long time."*
> *"But, Mr. Hanshue, they'll be out of the factory in six months."*
> *"I wasn't thinking of that. I was thinking of what a hell of a long time it's going to take to tunnel through those goddamn mountains."*

Pickwick Airways had been flying between San Francisco and San Diego, as an extension of their bus service, using Bach transports. They

310

were forced by the Depression and their busline methods to fold, and most of their equipment was grabbed-up by the then-booming Mexican gold mining companies. Bach trimotors had exceptional load carrying capabilities and could operate from short, rugged flightstrips in the desolate mountainous areas where these mines were typically found.

By the summer of 1931 we still hadn't made any deal for the Bach-22, so I decided to tour the country with it enroute to the Cleveland races, taking a paying load of passengers along. My bargain rate of $100-a-head resulted in a full passenger load when I took off early that September. My schedule allowed me to serve as the referee for the Women's Air Derby, making stops coinciding with the ladies' stops.

I've mentioned that the first Women's Derby had been from Clover Field. Will Rogers waved the girls off and Louise Thaden had won that race. This year she won it again, and since I landed at Cleveland a bit ahead, I was on hand to greet the winner. As Louise taxied up to the grandstand, a big crowd surrounded her plane and I hopped on the wing-step and gave her a big congratulatory kiss. I was somewhat taken aback when the photographers said, *"That's great, Mr. Thaden; let's have another one."* Immediately I explained that I wasn't Mr. Thaden - just a good friend - and that her husband Herb was standing nearby, a bit embarrassed, in the crowd.

Louise Thaden was quite a pilot, definitely one of the tops. When the *"99's"*, the premier organization of woman flyers, was founded, she had been the first secretary; Amelia Earhart had been president. Louise had already set altitude and endurance records, and won two Derbys. Later, in 1936, she won the transcontinental Bendix Trophy Race with Blanche Noyes. Also, she wrote the gay little book, *High, Wide, and Frightened.*

Louise's husband, Herb, was TWA's design consultant in the 1930's. He had additional duties as a copilot, though he never was much of one. Herb had joined TWA, hard-up, in the Depression's depths, as I did. In mid-1933 I was flying from San Francisco to Los Angeles with Herb as copilot, and Louise as a passenger. She was working for Beech Aircraft as their West Coast representative. When we were well along on the flight, I told Herb to take over while I went into the cabin and brought Louise back with me to the cockpit. Herb then went back to the cabin while I checked out Louise on the Fokker's controls and idiosyncrasies -

311

for it was a much larger plane than she'd ever flown. She was very shortly doing her usual superlative job of flying.

At that, I then joined Herb in the cabin. Boy, you should have seen the looks of the passenger's faces! What consternation. I immediately calmed them down, telling them who it was flying the plane. Since Louise was almost as well-known as Amelia, there was little further concern as I left her alone, giving her a good crack at piloting a multi-engined job. She was, in addition to being a fine pilot in league with the best of the men, a darn good looker, a real beauty. She was also licensed as a transport pilot, the fourth woman to earn that recognition.

Louise Thaden

But back to the 1931 Races. I again anticipated winning the multi-engine transport race - and it started off looking as if I would. My Bach-22 lept out in front of everyone, but I led only around the first pylon until I was passed by Harvey Firestone of the tire clan. He was racing a souped-up Ford trimotor with the new NACA engine cowlings, streamlined wheel covers and controllable pitch propellers. There wasn't any catching him; he was at least 10-mph faster. I doggedly held onto second place, though, - needing the $1,000 that went with it a lot more than Firestone. Fleetingly I thought that this was his way of getting even with me for my endorsement of Goodrich Tires on my Flex Wing. My second-place finish taught me that *controllable pitch propellers* were here to stay. They had been pioneered by (Seth)Hart-Huestas in Los Angeles, with additional work at McCook Field around 1918. Final development was by Frank Caldwell of Hamilton-Standard, resulting in the *"gearshift of the air"*.

Continuing my tour after the races and hoping to find a customer for the Bach, I soon landed in Washington D.C. Gilbert Budwig was now the Director of Air Regulations of the Aeronautics Branch of the Com-

312

merce Department, and I looked him up along with his old pal, Doc Cooper, whom he'd brought with him to head up the Medical Section. Bud and Doc were running things sort of high, wide and handsome. Along with several cronies, they had a place on Chesapeake Bay where I joined them for a weekend. The weekend wasn't all quiet and peaceful; on Sunday morning one of the Commerce Department's planes swooped low over the 'hideout' and dropped a note telling Bud that his wife, Irma, was back in town. Carol and Irma were the best of friends - and unknown to me, they'd just spent the previous week together in Santa Monica. Hence, Bud was suspicious that I was involved in spying on him for her! Later I finally squared myself with Bud, but the coincidence of that weekend simmered for quite a while.

I then more or less headed home and landed at Ford Airport in Grosse Isle, Michigan, where Upson's "tin blimp" was located. I looked up Vance Breese, who was then test flying for Detroit-Lockheed. He showed me drawings of a very advanced all-metal, low-wing, four-passenger plane. It surely looked interesting and I could understand Vance's hope that Detroit Lockheed would back him.

However, it wouldn't be long until Detroit Aircraft went 'belly up', and shortly after that Vance showed up in California with a Wasp-powered preprototype of this plane, attempting to raise production financing. As I was about the only person around who had recently assembled a crew for building aircraft (the Flex Wing), he reasoned that I'd know how to put together a payroll - a very rare commodity those days. But, I explained to him that my success was only because I'd had a syndicate of fairly wealthy individuals committed before the 'crash'. At the moment I had no prospects for new ventures. He told me that he'd pounded the pavements all over Los Angeles looking for financing, receiving encouragement only from E.L. Cord. Upon hearing this I cautioned him about doing anything with Cord. My own knowledge told me that he'd pick Vance's brains, and then, I'd bet ten-to-one, he'd dump him.

However, with no other options, Vance decided to chance it with Cord. They worked out an arrangement which soon saw him assembling a drafting crew in quarters at the back of the Curtiss-Wright hangars in Glendale. Cord insisted upon a six-passenger, two-pilot airplane, which needed quite a bit more design work. Vance got Cal Tech-trained Ger-

313

ard Vultee, then teaching at the Curtiss-Wright Technical Institute, to moonlight helping him. Everything was moving along nicely, Vance thought, until one day he came down to his office and discovered Vultee at his desk - with instructions from Cord kicking him out. It sounded just like Ford's kicking Graves out! I guess that Vance hadn't read the fine print in his deal with Cord; Detroit-Lockheed's ace test pilot and builder of some great airplanes now found himself on the outside looking in.

The plane's name was changed from Breese to Vultee, and Vultee, with Cord's Airplane Development Corp., further enlarged it into an eight-passenger job. In 1932, it was introduced as the Wright-powered Vultee V-1. During this period Vultee also served briefly as chief engineer for E.M. Smith's Emsco Aircraft Corp. in Downey. After building several V-1 transports at Grand Central Airport in Glendale, Vultee reshuffled his operations, and took over Smith's operation and large property, forming the Vultee Aircraft Division of Cord's Avco. In 1942 it merged with Reuben Fleet's Consolidated to form Consolidated Vultee or *"ConVair"*. Today, Convair is a division of megacorp General Dynamics. Vultee was killed in a crash in 1938.

Soon after returning to Metropolitan I was contacted by the Fairchild Aerial Survey organization about leasing the Bach-22 for a special high-altitude mapping project. This required cutting a 20-inch hole in the plane's floor and beefing-up the structure to support the massive four-lens Fairchild mapping camera and its shock absorbing suspension system. Who should show up as Fairchild's top pilot but one of my Ontario students, Fritz Secor, now a master of map piloting. I checked him out on flying the Bach, and he and his cameraman headed for Winslow, Arizona, where their project was to be based. *Sherman Fairchild's invention of an aerial camera led to the founding of Fairchild Aerial Camera Co. in 1920. In 1926, needing a better airplane to carry the camera, Fairchild founded Fairchild Airplane Manufacturing Corp. He sold 175 aircraft in 1928 and an estimated 1200 by the end of 1929, when he also founded the Aviation Corporation - "Avco".* Apparently, though, the Bach was a better aircraft for high-altitude mapping, hence this job.

Sometime after completing that first assignment, Fairchild contacted me again for a special job mapping part of the San Joaquin Valley west of Bakersfield. The camera was reinstalled and the mapping laid out in detail for me and their cameraman. Fairchild furnished me with a new

314

instrument, a *Paulin* altimeter. It was a combined level flight indicator, altimeter and barometer, *"so sensitive that it will give immediate visual record of variations of 10 ft. in altitude"*. It let the pilot set the precise desired altitude and a needle would constantly indicate whether he was flying too high, right on, or too low. This was a boon to mapping pilots.

We were to map at 16,000 feet, which was about as high as one can fly without oxygen and I didn't have any aboard. I recall that I questioned the cameraman a couple of times to see if we were flying in the right spot, and he assured me that we surely were. Upon completing the flight we returned to Bakersfield, turned the film over to a messenger who rushed it to Fairchild's Los Angeles laboratories, and turned in for the night. In mapping, one never left the work area until you had received the OK that the film was hunky-dorey. A premature departure could simply require another trip.

I was fast asleep when, at about 2 AM, my phone rang itself off the hook and I groggily picked it up. It was Ed Polley, Fairchild's West Coast manager, mad as hell, telling me that we'd mapped an area eight or ten miles east of where we were supposed to. He let me know in no uncertain language that he wasn't paying for it. I was too sleepy to argue, telling him to call back in the morning and I'd do it again exactly as he wanted. At 3 AM the damn phone was ringing again, and Polley said;

"Waldo, exactly at what altitude did you fly?"

"16,000 feet, just as instructed," I replied, "and that Paulin is sure good to fly by."

"Nope, Waldo, you didn't fly at any 16,000 feet. We've done some checking and you picked up a lot more territory - you flew at 19,000 feet," Ed said. And at that news I muttered, "Ed, the problem must be with that new altimeter."

In reconstructing what had happened, we found that the Paulin Altimeter was 3,000 feet off. Whereas we thought we'd been flying at 16,000 feet, we'd actually been at 19,000 feet. This altitude was far too high to be without oxygen, causing a fuzzy mind and the mapping of part of the wrong area. We flew it again using an altimeter that we knew was 'on the money,' with better results.

315

As I've touched on before, Doug and Marion Shearer were our neighbors in Santa Monica Canyon and best of friends. Doug was chief of MGM's Sound Department. He held this "Sound Supervisor" position well into the 1950's. He was doing quite a bit of flying in his Avro Avian, the slick biplane that I'd earlier flown for Lady Heath. Also, he was my partner in the Bach-22 and a fellow member of our Aviation Country Club. One of our club's principal events were fly-in breakfasts at fields all over Southern California. Since we had the largest plane in the club, we always had a full load going to these affairs and often made a bit more than expenses by charging for the flight.

The 1932 Olympics were being held in Los Angeles, and the Junior Chamber of Commerce organized an Air Tour up the coast to publicize it. They chartered our Bach-22, and late that spring I took off on this ballyhooing expedition. Along for the flight were Georgia Coleman and Josephine McKim (Olympic diver and swimmer respectively), the Chamber's manager, my mechanic (Jimmy "Arkie" Frew), and a guest (Leonard Comegys). We headed north to Vancouver, Canada, with many stops in between for the girls' exhibitions. One memorable stretch occurred after leaving Reno. We were headed for Portland, Oregon, over the Siskiyou Mountains, which was very rough and desolate country with patches of snow still visible. The air began getting bumpy, and the ceiling lowered so much that I was sneaking under the clouds following the mountain passes, usually following a road that was sometimes even above us. Looking out, we could see that the cars' lights were on because of the increasing haze, and this meant that there'd be nigh zero visibility by the time we got to the top of the pass. It wasn't the best of flying conditions, but as long as I could see forward I kept going, knowing that I could always turn back if it got too bad. The passengers, especially the girls, were getting a bit skittish. And it surely didn't help matters when they spotted a big boulder beside the road painted with the words *"Prepare To Meet Thy God."*

The remainder of the trip through Oregon and Washington was uneventful, and quite easy because I was flying a route that I'd flown many times for the Eakin's West Coast Air Transport. But on the way home there was an incident that I didn't learn about until arriving back in Santa Monica. We'd landed at Eureka in Northern California for the usual exhibition, and after taking off, found ourselves in murky weather. I was

316

having to fly low, following the ground contours, hedgehopping, so to speak, and apparently we flew over a pasture near Loleta and scared a horse to death. The farmer got the plane's number and raised all sorts of hell about it, claiming that I owed him $160 for the animal. Well, I'd never been much of a horse lover anyway and I retorted, *"Any horse that can't stand the sight or noise of an airplane without having a heart attack isn't worth the Eureka quotation."*

On another occasion, our Aviation Country Club was invited to Jack Dempsey's gambling spa in Ensenada, Mexico, about 70 miles south of San Diego. I carried a full load of paying passengers to this wing-ding, and upon arriving at the very sumptuous and lavish edifice we were personally greeted by Dempsey. Everything was 'on the house' of course, for they fully expected to get back whatever it cost them at least a couple-of-times-over from the tables. However, since I was a teetotaler (except for a rare glass of wine) and a nongambler, I enjoyed a fairly profitable sojourn. The Mexican government soon lowered the boom on this enterprise, and it folded. But, the magnificent buildings stood for many years, with all of the gambling paraphernalia lying helter-skelter in ghostly-quiet rooms. I've seen the place

Jack Dempsey

several times since during the many Newport-Ensenada Yacht Races that I've been in. No one has yet resurrected that memory of yesteryear. The last abortive attempt at gambling in Baja California was in 1958; I guess that it's too near Las Vegas.

Gambling ships were another holdover from the wild and turbulent, gangster-ridden 1920's. During the 1930's one didn't have to go as far as Mexico or Las Vegas to gamble - Vegas was only a wide spot in the road then, anyway. All you had to do was go to San Diego, Santa Monica or Long Beach, climb aboard a water taxi and be whisked-out beyond the

317

three-mile-limit to gambling ships such as the "Tango", "Monte Carlo" and "Rex". Here, wide open gambling was run in a 'speakeasy' atmosphere until crimebuster Earl Warren spelled their end.

But in 1932 we were still on that inexorable road to hard times. The Kinner Aeroplane and Motor Co. hit the skids. Leonard Comegys was the attorney for the receivers and asked that I appraise their remaining assets. Pacific Airmotive's Earl Herring was fortunately appointed trustee. He perceived that there was a viable company underneath the mess - primarily because of all the Kinner engines in use that would be needing parts - and he reorganized the company under Chapter 11 of the Bankruptcy Code. It wasn't long until the revived company got a shot in the arm when the Canadians ordered a quantity of Kinner-powered Fleet trainers (using the 125-hp Kinner B5 engine). Sometime later Ryan would use many, many Kinner 165-hp R5's for their popular World War II trainers. During the war, the company also manufactured cylinders for the adaptation of the Wright Cyclone engine for tank use. Finally, however, Bert Kinner's old company faded from sight. But I'll always remember it for one of its first endeavors - Amelia's KinneR Airster - the plane that I flew in 1926 powered by that historic 1921 three-cylinder Lawrance radial engine.

Late that summer the 1932 National Air races were held. This year the big race to Cleveland was sponsored by E.L. Cord with a whole raft of prizes - from a new Cord car worth around $2,500 (a new Plymouth cost under $600 then) down to a 40th place prize of only $100. I entered the Flex Wing in this race hoping that I'd at least get free gasoline and probably $100 in prize money. Boy, there were surely a lot of broke pilots with that same idea!

During the race I knew that I was no great contender. Another 'slow poke' giving me a somewhat man to man race was James McDonnell in an Menasco-powered Great Lakes plane. Along with Frank Hawks, we were noted in this race as the only pilots who used slide rules attached to our instrument panels to compute drift and perform navigational calculations - a job done automatically today by computers. Mac and I flew a neck and neck race. He ended up beating me by a few points, a place or two. I think that he won $175 while I ended up with my $100.

318

DEPRESSION CLOUDS THE SKIES

Remember February 26, 1911, when Curtiss said;

"Now if we could just take off the wings and drive this thing down the road, we'd really have something!"?

Curtiss tried! In Feb-
*ruary 1917, at the "First
Pan American Aeronautic
Show" in New York, the
Curtiss "Autoplane" - "An
Aerial Limousine" - was
exhibited. Its innovative
concept drew raves, lots of
publicity; but apparently it
never flew.*

That 1911 comment had always stuck in my mind, and here in the summer of 1932 I found myself with a unique opportunity to design and build a roadable airplane for minimal expense. I immediately got to work creating and calculating the best and most logical design which would fufill Curtiss' dream.

My approach was an evolution of the 1909 design-patent of the Englishman, John William Dunne, and of the *"Canard"* concepts of Voisin and Bleriot. Dunne's D-6 of 1911 was the predecessor of the world's swept wing, tailless airplanes. And, his D-8 of 1913 was so stable that Commandant Felix at Deauville, France, casually left the cockpit and walked upon the lower wing - the world's first wing-walker?

*US Army Burgess-Dunne hydroplane
with 9-cylinder Salmson engine - 1914*

*"The Bleriot
Canard, with
the motor and
propeller at the
back of the aviator"
Scientific American,
October 28, 1911*

319

My design criteria for a roadworthy and airworthy vehicle involved, primarily, two areas: wing and tail.

Obviously, the airplane had to be stable, safe and easy to fly, with a low landing speed. These characteristics required a relatively large wing spread, but it was beyond me as to how to incorporate stowable or foldable wings for traveling upon the ground. Therefore, I reasoned that the craft should be able to shed its wings easily, parking them at the flight's terminus in the transition from flying to road use.

The next consideration was fuselage length and tail. An orthodox airplane would be an awkward ground vehicle with its long tail section, so I planned its elimination. Heretofore, the lack of success in building more modern tailless aircraft was principally due to the lack of of airfoils possessing suitable characteristics, namely: zero or negative center of pressure travel; proper thickness; high lift; and low drag. Such airfoils were now available. Additional advantages of a tailless design would be a reduction in overall weight, less head resistance, less cost to manufacture - and a resultant gain in aerodynamic efficiency.

A tailless airplane with its wings shed would thus take the shape of a streamlined coupe. This design would be admirably suited to the efficient use of a pusher propeller which, in turn, would result in ultimate pilot visibility with no forward obstructions. Taking all of these parameters into account convinced me that developing an airplane of this type, with its *ultimate objective* of being a flying automobile, was a logical and reasonable endeavor.

Thinking back to 1909 and 1910, when I'd taught myself how to fly, convinced me that this craft should also have a tricycle landing gear like most of Curtiss' early planes. This arrangement would permit a center of gravity forward of the main supporting wheels, and a *wing attachment angle* approaching zero lift when the airplane was in its static position on the ground. Thus two elements which make the art of flying difficult were eliminated: the inherent tendencies of an airplane with tail-dragger landing gear to ground loop, and to make a second takeoff or bounce when improperly landed. These are both due to the wings of a typical airplane being at their angle of maximum lift at this critical touch-down point. These thus appeared to be naturals for the the short-coupled fuselage of a tailless aircraft, and admirably suited for a modernized tricycle landing gear.

320

Bert Kinner had a low-wing monplane which he had planned to use as a prototype of a folding-wing airplane. Since he had written that project off, I bought its wings from him. I then made a deal with Bob Porter, Kinner's president, to furnish me with one of their 100-hp engines. It was designed for tractor (pulling) use, and therefore this necessitated considerable modification to adapt it for pusher use.

I then proceeded to design and fabricate an airframe that could evolve easily to road use. It was a low-wing monoplane originally incorporating an oleo shock-strut arrangement like the Flex Wing (later abandoned), and a tricycle landing gear. *My objective dictated that this airplane be very easy to fly: nonstalling, nonspinning and almost impossible to nose-over upon landing.*

The completed aircraft incorporated a *modern tricycle landing gear* (steerable nose wheel and shock absorbers on all three wheels), and *elevon control* - both *'firsts'* in American aviation. In getting to the final product I went through the typical problems. My engineering was often 'seat-of-the-pants'; I couldn't afford wind tunnel testing; and many of my results came from the 'cut and fit' school of design. Therefore, there were a few false starts. But I eliminated some development problems by incorporating adjustments that could easily be made during the experimental flight testing period. One precaution was the outfitting of the two seater cabin (side by side seats) with doors that would fall off when an emergency lever was thrown. In case of a crackup, one wanted to get out fast, or if airborne, to bail out easily.

By the time I was ready for the initial flight tests, the runways at Metroplitan were badly deteriorated. Due to the lack of upkeep that the Depression was causing, there were many rough spots and countless gopher holes. By now the plane was largely complete except for side window glazing and such, which mattered little with regard to its airworthiness. It was certainly finished enough to arouse plenty of comment from the "rail birds". These kibitzers were always hanging around the field, and they kept saying, *"Hey, Waldo, what's it you're building?"*. At first I'd go into a lengthy explanation, but after so many *"What's it?"* questions, I simply replied, *"It's a Whatsit!"* and let it go at that. Thus, unknowingly tagging my airplane with the same name that Hooker's men dubbed Matthew Brady's strange black photography wagon during the Civil War.

321

When I had everything assembled and reasonably well checked out, I decided that it was time to give *"Whatsit"* a high speed takeoff run. But, as I was gunning it down Metro's runway, the front wheel dropped into a gopher hole, and the plane flipped over on its back. I had been in this sort of position before, but never while inside an airplane with an enclosed cabin. Feeling trapped and sure that it was going to catch on fire, I hit the panic button, completely forgetting about the emergency door levers. As I was in an upside down position, the fastest way out was ass-end first out the unglazed side window. I soon found out that it was a pretty tricky maneuver. For when my derriere was through the opening - YEEOOW! - all of a sudden I discovered that I'd completely forgotten about the window's crossbrace. This was a piece of tubular steel that cut the open space almost in half. I was crammed into an opening bounded on one side by the brace and on the other side by the jagged remnants of the broken window latch which were digging into my backside. When I felt that pain I recoiled, and was confronted with yet a greater pain as my balls caught on the crossbrace. Literally I was between a rock and a hard place - the most untenable spot that I'd ever been in my life!

But there was no getting around it; I had to get out! I'd twist and turn until the pain jabbing my back became intolerable. Then I'd twist and rotate the other way, trying to pull my testicles past the brace. After repeating this "one pain and then the other" too many times, finally one ball popped over the brace - and after a couple more grunts and pulls, the other one came free. Boy, was I relieved! At that, I quickly wiggled and squirmed the rest of the way and rolled, gasping, away from the plane. I was awfully glad to be alive and, fortunately, no damn eunuch in the process!

There wasn't any fire, but Whatsit was pretty badly battered: the propeller broken, wingtip rudders smashed, and the nose wheel bent cockeyed. We dragged her back to the hangar for repairs, and also decided to increase the wing sweep more than the original 15 degrees - a discovery made on high speed taxi runs before the crash. After calling up Chase Story for another propeller, "Arkie" Frew, Clarence Deyette, Mel Oliver and I got to rebuilding the plane.

Until we'd mastered the aerodynamics of this design, I also thought that a front elevator canard surface like on the old planes might be a good idea. Therefore, while rebuilding, we added a front canard on a

322

forward boom while at the same time sweeping the wings back to 25 degrees. We then put everything back together, and I took her out for another takeoff run. But this time we'd gone too far. She took off much faster than I'd anticipated, and in a split second I'd made a half loop and found myself on my back, 35 feet up in the air.

"If I get out of this with only a broken arm, I'll be lucky," I thought as I cut the switch. Whatsit, still nose high, stalled and slipped back to the ground. The wingtips hit first and crumpled as they took the shock of impact. I came down so cushioned that I didn't even suffer a scratch. But the airplane was a sorry mess, and I was all for just rolling up the project and calling it quits. I was about out of cash, and I couldn't expect my crew to work for no wages. Hell! - I was paying them little enough as it was. But good old Mel Oliver came forward with an offer for him and Arkie to work on it with no wages: just me paying them what and when I could until times got better.

Not affording to turn down an offer like that, we got right to work. After several weeks we had Whatsit, hopefully, flyable again. However, by this time the runways at Metropolitan were in such bad shape that we decided to tow the plane over to United Airport.

At United I used Pacific Airmotive's hangar as my base, and soon I was making high speed taxi runs and lifting her just a few feet off the ground. But I was a bit 'gun shy' about taking her off - possibly because just beyond the south end of the runway was Valhalla Memorial Park, a cemetery with *"The Portal of The Folded Wings"* shrine. It was a burial place for many aviators. Every time you'd take off from United, you'd stare down at all of those tombstones pointing up at you. They seemed like arms reaching to grab you - one's imagination could surely raise hell in such a situation!

Whatsit - "just a few feet off the ground", but this is a later, 1934 photo.

Late one day, while still making high-speed taxi runs, Eddie Anderson, a very good pilot who had been watching, persuaded me to let him give it a try. He only wanted to do a straight lift-off or two, and then give me his opinion on the advisability of a full flight circuit above the field. Saying OK, I carefully explained the unusual flight characteristics of Whatsit. Because of its high thrust line and low-wing configuration, it didn't handle like an ordinary plane. When you gave it the throttle, it had a tendency to nose down; and when you cut it, the reverse happened - the nose came up quickly. This behavior was exactly the opposite of what one would suppose. I told Eddie that if it started to 'gallop', he should give-it-the-gun when he thought he shouldn't, and vice versa, not give-it-the-gun when he thought he should.

Mumbling to himself, Eddie got in Whatsit, taxiing to the end of the runway for his first run. He got off the ground very fast - too fast - and then, upon bringing her down, he started galloping. Confused, he was doing just what I'd cautioned him not to do. On each gallop he'd give-her-the-gun at just the wrong time, until each upward bound was higher than the last. On the final rebound, he landed so hard that Whatsit disintegrated into a pile of wreckage in the middle of the airport. Eddie wasn't hurt much, but that sure looked like the end of Whatsit.

My morale went down another rung, almost to the bottom of the ladder. I now was really broke and knew that I couldn't continue with the project any longer. However, Mel said, *"Hell, Waldo, we've worked on the damn thing so long, why not let me take the pieces home and work on it in my spare time - which I've got a helluva-lot-of now?"* *"Why not!"* I said, and we collected all of the parts and pieces and trucked them over to Mel's. Maybe we'd still fly the darn thing someday.

It was now nearing the end of 1932 and the Depression was becoming worse; *on July 8 the Dow had its lowest close of the century.* We thought we had it bad in 1930 when three-million were unemployed. Now there were twelve-million, *25 percent of the labor force.* But in spite of the greater number of unemployed, the moratorium that had been declared on mortgages in 1930 and 1931 was now lifted, and I found that I had to start the payments again on our Santa Monica Canyon home.

Desperate, I wired Jack Frye, now a TWA vice president in Kansas City, and asked him for a job. I knew that every unemployed pilot in the country had probably hit him up for a job and that TWA hadn't hired anyone for a long, long time, but I thought it was worth the try. Darned if I didn't immediately get a reply from Jack. He stated that he and Paul Richter were going to be in Santa Monica the next day and asked me to meet him at the Douglas factory.

Naturally, the next day I was there, and it was quite a revelation in more ways than one. They were at Douglas to confer about a new transport being built for TWA. It was something far different than anything I'd seen before - a large, twin-engined, all-metal plane designed by Art Raymond and Jack Northrop in response to an inquiry by Frye. Called the *DC-1,* it was the pre-prototype of the famous DC-3, the world's most successful airliner.

But I was there for a job, and that's what I discussed with Jack. He was interested in my trimotor flying experience, informed me that TWA was planning some limited expansion, and hired me initially as a copilot at $190-a-month. This salary would raise to $210-a-month after three months. It was a lot less than what first pilots earned ($400 to $500-a-month) but I wasn't in any position to argue, especially since this was TWA's first opening in almost two years. However, I did get Jack's OK to fly out of Los Angeles instead of Kansas City. At that, I was told to report 'in uniform' to Lou Goss at TWA's Glendale base at Grand Central Air Terminal.

This was a time of almost total stagnation as far as getting promoted was concerned. Before long, it fomented a scheme of harassment of first pilots by some copilots, in the hopes of getting them to quit or get fired. A few copilots were successful, forcing TWA's management to demote two first pilots to copilot status until they were proficient in instrument flying (which was just then coming into wide use). One of these fellows said "To hell with it!" and quit. Since we were both about the same build, I immediately arranged to buy his uniforms. Therefore, the day after being hired, I showed up in a very surprised Lou Goss' office - in the terminal's handsome Mission-styled building - ready to work a week earlier than anyone expected.

The other pilot that had been demoted was Doc Whitney, my old chum from Venice Field days. He was about TWA's oldest pilot and had a very tough time learning instrument flying. However, flying was everything for Doc and he accepted the demotion without a whimper. Since

325

Doc and I were both copilots, I got him to check me out on the duties of the job, returning the favor later.

There weren't any stewardesses or cabin attendants yet on TWA. However, WAE had had *stewards* as part of their crews in *1929*. United had the first *"air hostesses"* in 1930. They were unwelcome additions to the all-male crews, and most suspect to the pilot's wives! The first was Ellen Church and the seven registered nurses she selected as United's nucleus.

But at TWA, we copilots were responsible for taking care of the passengers' well being. This included serving the box lunches (invariably fruit cocktail, fried chicken and rolls); aiding airsick voyagers; and cleaning up their messes. I never did help change any diapers, though! Some aspects of the job surely didn't fit my picture of being an airline pilot, but I either did them or I didn't have a job.

It wasn't too unusual for a flight to be occasionally shy a copilot, as short handed as TWA was then. So, they'd grab some youngster hanging around the field - a mechanic or mail clerk - and thrust him into the copilot's seat, primarily to handle the passenger chores. He'd get a very fast briefing on his duties. Western Air Express made this jury-rigged procedure 'sophisticated' by typing-up instruction forms. One of these quickly drafted Western copilots was a young chap aspiring to become an airline pilot. He had a Monocoupe at the field and was flying it as much as possible in order to build up the required 200-hours time for a transport pilot's license. He was no sooner seated in the right seat than he was handed this form. It was nearing lunch time, and the list said to place napkins on the back of each seat prior to passing out the box lunches. Therefore, aft he went in search of napkins, but all he could find were in a tin box labelled "Sanitary Napkins." Dutifully, he took the required quantity, pinning one to each seatback with the enclosed safety pins. It wasn't long before he learned what he had done and he suffered the first of many years' guffaws. But it didn't slow down his TWA career; he was to become chief pilot for TWA's Eastern Division.

During my own copiloting days I recall a flight to Cincinnati from Kansas City. The ceiling was very low; we were flying under 500 feet in very rough air; and the plane was caroming all over the sky. Most of the passengers were very airsick. There was one little gentleman with a Van Dyck beard in a velvet trimmed overcoat, complaining about everything.

326

in the uniform of a TWA (Transcontinental and Western Air) pilot - note Indian head - 1933

Here was a customer that'd never fly with TWA again, I thought. Just as now, there were comment forms at each seat, and I observed him carefully filling the damn thing out - and I said to myself, *"There's one that management ain't ever going to see!"*. For we had a little trick! After these questionnaires were collected, we puckered up the suspicious ones, read their contents with a pencil flashlight, and tossed the derogatory ones out the window. I'd made a special note to read "Van Dyck's", sure that it would be damning. But darned if he hadn't gone to great lengths praising the crew for the exemplary job we'd done on a difficult flight. That was surely one that management was going to receive!

Another incident that management heard about happened on a flight to the 1933 Indianapolis Race. At Wichita we took on a passenger who, obviously, was feeling no pain. On my final tour of the cabin I noticed that his seat belt wasn't fastened. I leaned over, saying, *"Mister, you'll have to fasten your seat belt."* He then began giving me all sorts of back-talk, to the effect that he was a pilot and he wasn't going to have any punk copilot tell him what to do. After my reasoning failed, I went forward and told Earl Noe, the first pilot, about the problem. I thought we ought to chuck him off because he spelled nothing but trouble. Earl agreed, advised the tower of the problem, requesting assistance if necessary, and taxied back to the terminal. I then went aft and told the passenger that he was being kicked off. Boy! Did he become belligerent. He informed me that he was a big customer of TWA, and that if it were the last thing he ever did he'd see that I was fired.

He was forcibly removed from the plane, cursing all the time, and I'm sure we had some misgivings because customers were scarce in those days. But we went ahead, and later when I wrote my report about the incident I was certain that I'd hear about it. Sure enough, about a week later, Frye called me in 'on the carpet'. He wanted a fuller explanation as to why I'd thrown off Buick's distributor in that area, a very good TWA customer indeed, who had followed up on his threat against me. I explained the story in detail to Jack - and asked that he check it out with Noe. As I left his office I wasn't at all sure that I'd have a job for long. However, he apparently understood our predicament, for I never heard anything more about it. Later in 1933 Noe was killed during an instrument takeoff from Kansas City.

328

But, back to the chores of copiloting. In addition to occasional piloting and cabin attending, you were sometimes ticket taker at smaller stops. And, you often had to climb on top of the plane to assist in gassing it up, cleaning the windshield, and so forth. It reminded me of my first job at Kessler's Machine Shop when I was the 'do anything handy boy', except that now it was around airplanes.

First pilots flew a maximum of 90 hours a month, but there wasn't any limit to how much time a copilot flew, and it wasn't unusual to put in over 125 hours a month - a lot of flying! It was interesting working with the passengers that we had then. They were a more adventurous lot than today, but human nature doesn't change, and we had our share of 'goods' and 'bads'.

My first flight assignment was on the Los Angeles-San Francisco run with stops at Bakersfield, Fresno and Oakland in a Ford trimotor. I flew

with First Pilot Chipino, and I found it very monotonous. But there was the challenge to become proficient in instrument procedures and radio communications.

After a couple of months out of Grand Central, Goss asked me to take the run to Albuquerque, the LA Division's eastern terminus, and then proceed into Kansas City to temporarily help out there for a week or so. Apparently he forgot all about the "week or so". It turned into a four month visit, but I was counting on a raise soon to $210-a-month, and living was good in Kansas City in those early days of 1933. I had a lovely room at the KC Athletic Club for only $25 a month; meals were inexpensive; and I was well prepared with two $50 cashiers' checks that I'd brought along to tide me over 'til payday.

329

Interior - Ford trimotor
1933

But, all over the country banks were closing right and left. Thousands of banks went broke, while countless others were closing their doors under the orders of the governors of twenty-two states. So, I found that I couldn't cash the checks, but that they were nonetheless negotiable. I was able to get by until the new Roosevelt administration passed the Emergency Banking Act on March 9th. This caused the banks to reopen on Monday, after the nationwide banking holiday that President Roosevelt had declared from March 6 to 10. (The next morning, the Kansas City Star headlined the news about the big *earthquake* that had devastated Long Beach on the 10th, killing over 100 people - but a quick telephone call to Carol assured me that she and Janie were fine.)

Now I was officially based in Kansas City. I flew in fair weather and foul, including rain, sleet, snow and hail between Kansas City and Albuquerque and a few times the other way to Columbus, Ohio. Finally, passenger traffic began to grow as TWA was buoyed up for the first time in three long years by a rising stock market and renewed public confidence in the future. They decided to add some new runs, permitting my transfer back to Glendale. In July, I made first pilot; that raise was surely welcome; and I was checked out in the Fords, Fokkers and Consolidated Fleetsters (which I'd first seen in 1930 on a visit to Buffalo). These were eight-passenger single-engine planes that I often flew on the San Francisco run.

As I've mentioned, I had to learn instrument procedures and radio communications - a tough chore for us older, seat-of-the-pants flyers. Both mentally and in actual practice, we had to forget our own body sensations and rely on and properly interpret the instruments. (The Department of Commerce announced SATR, Schedule Air Transport Rating - *"instrument flying"* - in May, 1932) At that time in TWA there were basically two groups of pilots: those of us that had grown up flying during the barnstorming, swashbuckling days; and the younger pilots who had learned their trade from the military and thought of themselves as sharper and better pilots than we were. It was an opinion I found hard to take. At most of the terminus locations, like Albuquerque, we typically shared hotel rooms with other pilots, and during the layovers we'd get into some fine bull sessions on girls, politics, cars - but most of all - flying. The young pilots advocated that pilots should retire at 40, always giving me a sideways glance. I was then 39, and since most of them were

330

in their twenties it was an easy and logical thing for them to say. This age limit has now been advanced so that today an airline pilot is retired at 60 years of age.

Naturally, whenever a man is retired from his love it can cause some grief. It's hard to argue against the ravages of age. As I'm dictating this I feel a bit old myself - having just turned 80. But, I continued flying until I was over 77 years old. Though I surely wouldn't recommend my commanding an airliner anymore, I still find it hard to understand those 'young bucks' in 1933 thinking that at 40 I'd be too old to fly - no sir!

Ford 5-AT Trimotor
1933

John J. Floherty

331

Most of our flights were a combination of passenger and mail, but some were solely mail. They were transcontinental runs using the slick, single-engine Wasp-powered Northrop Alpha - an all-metal plane. We wore both sidearms and parachutes when flying the mail, but it was a very rare occasion when either were used. I never needed them.

Shortly after returning to Grand Central Air Terminal as first pilot, I was flying a run to San Francisco, and drew Doc Whitney, still on probation, as my copilot. Remember, he'd first versed me on a copilot's duties, one of which was the placement of the pilot's and copilot's names in the cockpit rack, in full view of the passengers. The pilot's name was on the left and the copilot's on the right. As we were boarding the plane, I asked Doc to give me his nameplate, prompting him to ask, *"Why do you want it, Waldo?"* *"Oh, I just want it,"* said I - and he handed it to me. When we got to the cockpit's entrance, I placed his in the left slot and mine in the right while motioning him into the left seat. Doc hesitated, thinking there was something funny going on, but he sat there. As we pulled away from the terminal, I told him to take over as I made the last-minute walk through the cabin, checking seat belts and the like before returning to assume the copilot's chores handling the radio.

Doc was on his own - as first pilot - and it was a bit poignant seeing the tears well-up in his eyes. After we were airborne and settled into the flight, he said, *"Waldo, for months now I've been flying copilot for these young kids, half of whom I taught all they know about airline flying, and this is the first time anyone has suggested that I take the plane off."*

"Doc, whenever you ride with me, you'll ride in the left seat," said I. But, that was the only time, for it wasn't long until Doc was relieved from flying and made a station master.

Once, when Clyde and Cotta Forsythe were going east to the Chicago World's Fair, they wanted to fly as far as possible with me as pilot, and I finagled trading runs with Frank Young as far as Albuquerque. My copilot for this flight was Slim Perrette, one of the senior copilots unable to crack the first pilot berth because of the hard times. In 1937, on my recommendation, Slim flew for Studebaker, piloting Arrowbile-2. Around 1939 something went wrong while he was test flying a Northrop trimotor, and he was killed.

That Northrop trimotor was one of the last piston engine trimotor designs, and for many years thereafter this concept, almost antique, was

332

forgotten. Today it's fascinating to see that it's back - this time with jets and the third engine in the tail rather than in the nose!

Other pilots that I flew with at TWA included Dutch Holloway, another of my Berkeley students. Dutch and I flew well together, and tried to team-up as much as possible.

I also flew a lot with Harlan Hall, one of the younger ex-military pilots who had a darn good head for aerodynamic engineering. In 1938, Harlan was assigned by TWA to observe the tests in Seattle of the second prototype of Boeing's first high-altitude, four-engine airliner, the 307 Stratoliner NX 19901. (A similar assignment to mine with the DC-1, see later). In March, 1939, Holland's KLM airline pilots arrived, also to evaluate this plane, and Boeing accorded them every courtesy and latitude in its flying. Unfortunately, Harlan was aboard when their testing of stall characteristics tore off the outer wing, killing him along with nine others in the crash.

Boeing-307 Stratoliner - a July, 1937, illustration.

That summer and fall of 1933 Douglas was in the midst of flight-testing Jack Frye's new dream transport, the DC-1 (X223Y tail number). Since I lived in Santa Monica, Jack, in Kansas City, asked that I observe as many flights as possible, and give him reports on my impressions of

333

the airplane. I was glad to do this and therefore spent a great deal of time around the Douglas factory at Clover Field.

One of their biggest arguments was what engines were to power it, the Pratt & Whitney Hornet or the 710-hp Wright Cyclone. Both of these beauties had evolved from earlier versions, but they were nonetheless still having 'growing pains.' Douglas would often make engine switches overnight in order to compare and evaluate them - and it seemed that almost every time I was riding as observer-pilot, one or the other engine would have some sort of problem, often resulting in a total stoppage. It finally got to the point that both Pratt & Whitney's Marshall and Wright's Ken Boedecker were kiddingly trying to be sure that I was aboard only when the other guy's engine was being tested! Of course, I was not the jinx that they suspected, and my presence was solely due to the timing of my flight assignments.

First of a proud line, the DC-1 "City of Los Angeles" - 1933

These flights were just before controllable pitch propellers came into wide usage. The performance of the DC-1 on one engine with fixed

The DC-1 - over Kansas City - 1933

props was so marginal that we always had to keep an eye cocked for an emergency landing field if the other engine conked out, too. We never had any serious problems, but a couple flights ended with crumpled landing gear and bent props. Eddie Allen worked with Douglas on this test-flying. He was Boeing's top test pilot, and in my view a superb engineering test pilot. He turned the 'wheel' over to me several times, and it was certainly a revelation flying this new plane. It was like none other that I'd ever flown, and a tremendous improvement over the Fords and Fokkers which were then TWA's mainstays.

335

Douglas finally received the new Hamilton-Standard two-speed propellers and decided on the Wright Cyclone engines, though I preferred the Hornets. Then, a decision was made to increase passenger seating from 12 to 14, necessitating lengthening the body and rechristening the modified version - the *DC-2,* May 11, 1934. Thus, there was only one DC-1. Douglas sold it to Howard Hughes for his planned global flight, but he later opted for a Lockheed Lodestar. In what would become typical for Hughes, the DC-1 sat virtually abandoned for quite a spell. Sometime later it was obtained by the Loyalists in the Spanish Civil War, and later crashed while still in Spain, but as an airliner, faithful to its original design intent.

From the DC-2 evolved the historic, world-famous *DC-3,* capable of carrying 21 passengers. It debuted on a Wright anniversary, December 17, 1935. Over 10,000 DC-3's would be built, many still flying today in virtually every corner of our earth. I saw one fly overhead today, and my mind wandered back many years to those first tremulous flights in 1933.

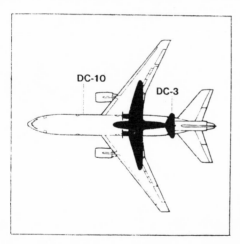

From the DC-3 to today's DC-10 - a comparison in size!

During this period the new Roosevelt administration was 'cleaning house' in Washington. Out went Bill MacCracken's able assistant, Major Clarence M. Young. (Wheeler-dealer-insider MacCracken had resigned in 1929, and Young had been running the Aeronautics job for most of the Hoover years.) Budwig also made his exit at this time.

Eugene L. Vidal moved in with the Democrats to take over the job that I'd hoped for in 1926 - the Director of Aeronautics. He was assisted by John Carroll Cone, late of Arkansas Aircraft Corporation where he'd been sales manager for their popular OX-5-powered Command-Aire plane. Vidal was to be quite a force in aviation in the 1930's and we were

336

to become well acquainted. An ex-army flier known as "one of Washinton's best dressers", he had been one of Transcontinental Air Transport's top people before helping found Philadelphia's Ludington Air Line where I'd first met him. Vidal had married the daughter of the famous Senator Thomas Gore of Oklahoma. They had one son, Eugene Luther Vidal, Jr., "young Gene" who later took his mother's maiden name for which he is now so well known - *Gore Vidal.*

Eugene L. Vidal - 1934

Gene Vidal was a rash and innovative thinker, always coming up with some new and novel idea reminiscent of his earlier airline exploits. He became a favorite of Eleanor Roosevelt, a fact which aided him in no small way in carrying out some of his "constuctive policies".

Shortly after taking office, on November 15, 1933, he put out a memorandum advocating a much broader usage of private airplanes and proposing that this be accomplished by *"a small airplane which will sell for around $700...two-place, low-wing monoplane would require very little attention...landing speed of 20 mph..."* Vidal figured that this "impossible plane" would be a "shot in the arm" to the Depression-beleagured private plane manufacturers - Travel Air, Swallow, Alexander, Laird, Waco, International, Monocoupe, Mohawk, Command-Aire, Stinson, Taylor - oh, there were so many then.

Though I figured that Vidal was naive to think that you could build an airplane for the cost of an automobile, I studied his specifications very carefully. And, I perceived a close parallel to what I'd been working on in Whatsit. Since I was now making good money as a TWA first pilot, I encouraged Mel to accelerate his backyard rebuilding job in the hopes of having Whatsit soon flyable again.

337

But soon after this I learned that TWA was planning to revert to less frequent schedules for the winter months. This was going to put me back as a copilot because I had so little seniority. Not being at all happy with this prospect, and planning to work full time on Whatsit, I asked for an indefinite leave of absence late in 1933. I haven't been back to TWA since.

Chapter 7

1934-1939

Whatsit Becomes the "Air Flivver"
and I Almost Become an Air-Auto Magnate

INTERESTINGLY, Vidal's quest for a "$700 airplane" all but destroyed what little aircraft industry there was still surviving the Depression. The prospect of being able to buy an airplane so cheaply killed the interest in more expensive, conventionally-built aircraft. This ironic result was just the opposite of what he'd hoped for, but in his design criteria I spied a unique opportunity to capitalize upon my Whatsit experience. The revised specifications that were eventually issued were a tough order, but just Whatsit's meat! They called for an airplane with an extreme amount of forward visibility, and the ability to brake immediately upon touchdown without nosing over. The craft had to be able to take off over a 35-foot obstacle after an 800-foot run, and to land within 400-feet after passing over that same obstacle. Additionally, it had to be nonspinning, nonstalling, and with a top speed of at least 110-mph and a landing speed of under 35-mph. And all this had to be done with just a 100-hp engine!

Working hand-in-hand with Mel, we soon had Whatsit ready to attempt flying. In early January 1934 we packed his Model A pickup with camping gear, hitched-on a trailer carrying Whatsit and headed for Rosamond Dry Lake, about 60 miles north of Los Angeles in the Mojave Desert, now part of the huge Edwards Air Force complex.

Rosamond is one of many 'dry lakes' in Southern California, large expanses that are briefly flooded during the rainy season. The heat of the rest of the year bakes them dry, hard and smooth with a surface layer of encrusted salts. This surface is ideal for all sorts of high speed wheeled activities, especially the testing of airplanes. There were no gopher holes, either! *Whatsit was one of the earliest aircraft there.*

We set up camp near the main highway running from Lancaster to Mojave, and later located a cabin adjoining an artesian well. This we found very helpful in trying to make some rough habitation out of this remote and desolate spot.

Whatsit, early configuration, the cabin and us near Rosamond Dry Lake - January, 1934

WHATSIT BECOMES THE "AIR FLIVVER"...

We set-to assembling Whatsit, and shortly had her ready for some initial taxi runs, increasing the speed gradually until she was about to take off. She wasn't as stable fore and aft as I'd like, but I was able to get the nose up and make a few short flights. As I've mentioned, we had built in the ability to make changes, and we soon found the need for the first one. We moved the front canard surface gradually all the way aft until it was almost abutting the plane's nose, rather than a couple of feet forward. Every time that we made a change like this it would alter the center-of-gravity, so I used one of Curtiss' 1910-11 tricks to solve the balance problem. We took an ordinary machinist's bench vice and moved it back and forth along the front boom. When we found that it was positioned properly, we'd simply clamp it tight. There it would stay, no thing of beauty, but doing the job nonetheless. When we determined what we needed to know with the vice, we'd then make permanent corrections within the fuselage using lead weights. We used this vice method again when doing further testing at United Airport, and it sure caused a lot of comment!

My vice-balance trick - not very sophisticated, but it did the job! Note far-forward canard.

341

Carol in Whatsit. Note balance weight clamped on boom, canard position, the soon-eliminated front skid and an original uncut rudder extension - January, 1934

Mel and I tried out a whole variety of arrangements for the wingtip rudders. We went all the way from eliminating them entirely, using spoilers to induce drag (a concept which we found too slow and sloppy), to the other extreme of adding extensions to the normal rudders. Finally, after experimenting with the whole gamut of possibilities, we ended-up with the original rudders with about half of their extensions. These are the same that can be seen today on Whatsit, now in the Smithsonian (though by then we found that we could eliminate the front canard).

After about a week at Rosamond, we thought that we'd learned about all we could with the limited facilities there for making design revisions, and we packed-up and returned to Mel's backyard shop. We then modified the landing gear by moving the main wheels forward, adding shock absorbers and beefing-up the structure. We also installed lead weights in lieu of the vice, and prepared the plane for another series of tests.

We again headed for Rosamond and continued testing, finding that the changes resulted in much-better takeoff and landing performance.

342

Whatsit was starting to fly like a proper airplane, but we were still having one problem. The engine, being a pusher, wasn't getting the cooling it'd been designed for and was overheating. We finally licked this by installing shrouds and baffles at several strategic spots.

Whatsit - NX12272 - final Rosamond configuration - February, 1934

At that, we decided to head for home. Whatsit was now flying so well that I chose to fly rather than use the trailer. After helping Mel load the pickup, I took off, flying over the San Andreas Fault, the San Gabriel Mountains, San Fernando Valley and, finally, the Santa Monica Mountains. There I circled over home, alerting Carol to come and pick me up. This strange bird caused lots of commotion as no one had ever seen anything like it. By the time I landed at Burbank there was quite a crowd waiting. *(In basic principle, Whatsit was virtually identical to today's most advanced aircraft, Beech's Starship-1, designed by John Roncz with canard, swept wing, elevons and engines in the rear.)*

343

News photo: "Waldo D. Waterman...aeronautical veteran...WHATSIT...novel two passenger tailess craft...one answer to America's need for a...flivver plane." February 27, 1934

By now it was early spring of 1934, and a tremendous amount of interest and speculation had been growing around Vidal's dream of a $700 airplane. Even though I never thought that a variation of Whatsit could be built for anywhere near that price, I nonetheless milked the publicity for all its' worth. I was right in the middle of California's news-reel and press business, and had had lots of experience with them. So, I found it easy to make the country very aware of this interesting airplane that "veteran aviator Waldo Waterman has built," and how it might well be just the answer to what the government was looking for. Long ago I'd ruefully discovered that public appeal didn't always lie in what you had to offer - far too often it was what people *thought* you were offering combined with the ability to sell the 'sizzle' to the decision makers!

As such, news of Whatsit's flying was soon known in Washington, and they stayed fully aware of my activities. Vidal hadn't had any luck in finding a manufacturer to build his airplane, and soon political infighting began over the feasibility of the whole idea. Vidal's forces were opposed by those led by his deputy, Cone, who argued that the project was impossible and should be dropped. But Vidal was the boss with his name on the line, and he refused to give in without a fight. It would turn out, much to my chagrin and loss, that I'd be caught in their crossfire.

By this time I'd run out of funds and had to do a bit of promoting with friends for cash. I mainly got it from Doug Shearer and several of his associates at MGM, each chipping-in $100 to $200 apiece as we waited, hoping that something would develop in Washington.

Vidal finally realized that he'd painted himself into a corner: no manufacturer was going to bite. He therefore drafted revised specifications for *"every man's foolproof airplane."* Upon their publication, the industry still insisted that they were just as impossible to meet as the earlier "$700" proposal had been. In spite of their protests, Vidal got $1,000,000 appropriated and announced bidding for 30 airplanes to meet these new specs. However, there was some allowance built into the requirements this time. Nominal variance in landing speed, cruise speed and the like were permitted, but with appropriate penalties.

So, here I was with a flyable airplane already very-close to meeting those 'impossible' specifications. I immediately assembled a few of Max Harlow's top students to work with me in a hangar-office at Clover Field and we drafted a proposal. It included the basic drawings of the airplane, structural calculations and anticipated flight performance figures. Believing that I should have as complete a bid as possible, I arranged an option on E.M. Smith's old factory in Downey for enough time to build the 30 aircraft, and I also optioned 50 Wright-Gypsy engines. These engines were an English design which Curtiss-Wright was building under license. They were a beautiful, 100-hp, four-cylinder, air-cooled engine - but sales had been so poor that after manufacturing only 20 or 30 units, they discontinued production. They still had parts for at least 50 engines, and I made a deal that potentially supplied me with these for only $200 apiece - quite a bargain.

Bid opening was in August 1934 in hot, muggy Washington. About 15 manufacturers submitted bids, including Curtiss-Wright with their Gypsy-powered Coupe, Pitcairn with their 'roadable' Cierva autogiro, and several other innovative craft. Only a few came close to meeting the tough performance specifications. Several manufacturers submitted stripped-down versions of their normal planes, and several more failed to meet the performance bond requirements. When the dust finally settled, my bid was one of the lowest at slightly under $2,500 per unit. Elated I was, but having already been burned once in a Washington bid opening, I thought it best not to count-my-chickens-in-the-coop just yet!

The design that I thought most nearly equalled mine in performance and price was by Hammond Aircraft Corp. of Ann Arbor/Ypsilanti, Michigan at just over $3,000 apiece for their Model Y. This was a two-place, low-wing monoplane with a twin tail boom, tricycle gear and a 95-hp Menasco engine. I knew that the engine alone cost around $900, so it was going to be tough to build a complete airplane for anywhere near $3,000.

At the Commerce Department, I ran into a great deal of negativism about my design. They questioned my calculations and performance claims since there'd been no wind tunnel testing. I'd extrapolated all of my data from my *real* experience with Whatsit, adding anticipated gains from better streamlining and a more powerful engine. It was a result of this skepticism - and the fact that Hammond's design was more conventional - that he was awarded the major contract. I'm sure that Gene Vidal would never have weathered the storm if I'd been awarded it, and then had failed to meet the performance requirements. However, this did little to smooth my feelings - and it was with no great joy that I accepted the 'consolation prize', a proposition to build a *five-foot-wingspan wind-tunnel model* for testing at Langley by the NACA, with the proviso that if the tests were successful I'd then build one aircraft for the sum of $12,500, with the government supplying the engine, propeller and instruments.

With little to foretell just what would happen (for instance, Hammond's contract was cut to 15 units due to problems), I decided that *a part of the loaf was better than none at all* and accepted the government's offer. Working with the Navy's model shop, we soon had the model built and transported to Langley, where I worked with Fred Weick, my old friend from Flex Wing days. He also had submitted a model in the competition, an evolution of his W-1, a tricycle-geared, twin-boom pusher, but didn't pursue it because of his government position. Fred and I worked well together, and soon had the testing completed, with the results confirming virtually all of my claims.

346

Thus, a short while later I headed home with the promise for the single-unit contract. I was not the winner, but at least *second-best overall* and, though unsuspected at the time, I wasn't to have the problems that Dean Hammond would have.

While still in Washington, I had finalized the structural layout and ordered the tubular steel and aluminum skin sheets shipped to Mel's place. Thus, he'd started building the fuselage's framework prior to my return, giving me about a 30-day headstart on the competition - for this was essentially a race to see who could *first* produce a flyable airplane. The winner would surely have a 'leg up' for any follow-up business.

My first task upon returning to Santa Monica was to raise the money to carry-out the contract, even though I was to get progress payments as the work went along. My good friend, Paul Granger, agreed to lend me $5,000 at 6 percent interest, when and if needed. Since I was only making one plane, I chose not to use the Gypsy engine and soon found myself negotiating with my old nemesis, Al Menasco, on behalf of the government for one of his excellent inline, air-cooled, inverted 95-hp models.

Max Harlow, now teaching at Pasadena City College, chose a couple of his best students to help me prepare working drawings in a lean-to office at Clover Field. Then I started scouting around for a facility in which to fabricate the plane. It being 1934, there were an awful lot of choices! One that caught my fancy was an ex-Hudson automobile dealership at 15th and Santa Monica Boulevard. It was located between the Nash and Chrysler agencies, and had 50 feet of street frontage, a showroom, mezzanine balcony, and a service area in the rear. I figured to use the mezzanine for drafting, and the service area for the plane's construction. All-in-all, it looked ideal for my purposes. The rent was low, and I leased it for three months with an option to renew for an additional two months if needed.

In addition to Max's students, I assembled a crew to work with me and Mel. It included my old standby, Clarence Deyette, and Bud Pearson, who'd helped on Whatsit and had been with Bach. Mel, Clarence and Bud were all-around craftsmen, and among them there was hardly a skill that they couldn't do well. Clarence selected the spruce and started assembling the wing spars and ribs, while Mel and Bud worked on the fuselage structure and fittings. Harlow's boys moved ahead with the drawings and calculations with Max checking in every weekend on their

347

progress and making notes and corrections as required. All during this stage I had in the back of my mind the conversion of this design into a flying automobile. Alas, this was a blunder, for many of my ideas slanted to a roadable aircraft had to be scrapped later to fulfill the Vidal requirements.

We weren't very sophisticated when it came to equipment. We had little more than a couple of electric drills, a drill stand, a cutting shear on a bench, a table saw, machinist vice, welding outfit, and the usual assortment of hand tools. We also inherited a long work bench from Hudson's tenancy - which stayed with me for 40 years.

Thus we set to building an airplane - a very unusual one at that. As the work progressed, there was increasing publicity in the papers about what we were doing. It typically referenced a "$700 airplane prototype," which bothered me, but there was little that I could do about it.

My first idea for the landing gear was an arrangement somewhat different from Whatsit's: a single, large wheel in the rear and two smaller, steerable ones up-front about eight-feet apart, supported by a small canard surface. My reasoning was that, at some time in the future, this design would be the easiest for transmitting power to the rear wheel without the necessity of a differential. It would prove to be wrong.

John Geisse was selected by Vidal to oversee this part of the program, and he turned-out to be a rather difficult fellow to work with. Though well-qualified regarding powerplants, he was lacking in knowledge of aircraft structures and his flying ability was barely marginal in my viewpoint. I queried Vidal as to why Geisse had been assigned, and he said, *"If John Geisse can fly and successfully handle the airplane, that alone is sufficient proof of its meeting our goals!"*

We got to see an awful lot of Geisse, and soon he told us that we were way-ahead of most of the other manufacturers building 'consolation' aircraft. He thus began to spend even more time with us, moving us along even faster. We also received our government supplied Menasco engine, propeller and instruments way ahead of schedule, enabling us to keep moving without letup, though the prop wasn't quite what I had planned for.

In a couple of months after my return from Washington, we had the aircraft ready for flight testing, just after the first of 1935, and we decided to use Rosamond Dry Lake again. After tying the plane's wings verti-

348

cally to the fuselage, we hooked it behind my Plymouth and Bud and I towed it to the desert. At this time of year the Santa Ana winds can be very fierce, and as we neared Palmdale our strange caravan was almost swept off the highway. We eventually wrestled ourselves to the lake, wearily pulling in next to the cabin. That was the last time that I would ever try towing an airplane with its wings offering so much area to the wind!

After securing the fuselage and wings so that they wouldn't be blown away, about all that we were able to do that first day was to try and make ourselves comfortable in the cabin. The next day was still howling, so all we could do was partially assemble the airplane. It wasn't until the third day that we were able to complete the assembly and try a few high speed taxi runs. Eventually we got up to around 60-mph, which should have got it airborne - but she wouldn't break loose! Damn, was I discouraged. And try as I might, I couldn't figure out just what the problem was. I found that I could get one of the front wheels off the ground by working the elevons, but the instant I tried getting the other off, the first wheel would drop back to the ground. However, I was finally able to break both wheels free by flipping the controls back and forth, and I immediately found myself flying very well indeed. I eventually perfected that tricky takeoff maneuver so that I could become airborne as I wished. I then did several straightaway flights and a full gamut of flight maneuvers. I knew, however, that I'd have to change the landing gear arrangement back to that of Whatsit - two wheels aft of the center of gravity and a third single, steerable, nosewheel. After spending a couple more days checking flying characteristics I flew her back to Clover Field.

As soon as Geisse learned of our success, he grabbed a flight west and showed up, determined to fly the plane as-is to Washington. I opposed him, sure that it wouldn't do either of us much good in its current state. Finally, I had to have Vidal intervene so as to allow us enough time to make the necessary modifications - though I'd probably have been better off financially if I'd just let Geisse fly her away!

Taking the plane back to our shop, we proceeded to make the revisions, primarily to the landing gear. We ended-up with two wheels aft behind the center of gravity and a third wheel forward as a steerable nosewheel. We also shifted the plane's balance by moving the engine forward about eight inches and the gas tank about fifteen inches. So that

349

everything fit properly, we had to shorten and reweld the tank. This was a tricky task at best, and since Mel was away Bud tackled the job. The welding of aluminum is difficult, more so if it's had any sort of protective paint or coating - but his final result, though no object of beauty, tested out OK. Since it would be hidden, I said, "To hell with it!" and let the unbeautiful thing be installed.

The Waterman "Arrowplane", ready to fly east, Clover Field, July, 1935

When we'd completed this work, the plane was painted black and orange, the Commerce Department's colors, and the government's insignia was affixed on each side of the fuselage. The final touch was applying the plane's number, *NS-13,* which some trickster of Carroll Cone's must have chosen! I then wanted the plane checked-out to the specification's requirements: takeoff and landing performance, and the nonstalling, nonspinning characteristics. The Commerce Department assigned L.U. Hallubeck for that job. I'd known "Hally" for some time as he'd ridden

350

Arrowplane, coming in for a landing - 1935

with me before checking-out Bachs and my Flex Wing. We got along well and the tests went-off without a hitch. Upon their completion Hally signed-off, certifying to Washington that the craft was airworthy. Then Geisse put his name to the completion voucher, thus officially taking delivery of the plane. It now belonged to Uncle Sam (or so I thought).

We tagged this plane *"Arrowplane"*. It was a name that had two origins. Janie suggested it because of the wings' arrowhead shape. And, in the old days when we'd had a helluva time saying *"aeroplane"*, Curtiss had licked the pronouncing problem by saying *"Just say it like an arrow, arrowplane."* Incidentally, the whole thing of what to call an airplane puzzled folks for many, many years. That movie I was in, *"Mantrap"* (1926) came from a best-selling book in which author Sinclair Lewis used these words on just one page; *"airplane"*, *"aeroplane"*, *"air machine"*, and *"hydro-aeroplane"*!

Geisse wanted immediately to fly the plane to Washington and get some badly-needed publicity for the beleagured Vidal forces. Just prior to his departure, I had the noted Commander P.V.H. Weems (author of *Air Navigation,* the book considered the 'bible' of commercial aerial navigation) 'swing' the plane's compass and prepare its correction card. Even though it was late in the day, as soon as Weems finished, John took off, figuring that he'd at least make March Field before dusk. He'd then planned to take off at dawn and fly across America's meanest stretch of desert, crossing the Colorado River at Blythe into Arizona. It would be *hotter than the hinges of hell* at this time.

About three hours after Geisse's departure, the phone rang. It was he, mad-as-hell, chewing me out about the *"damned defective compass that was off by 15 degrees!"* Well, if it had been three or four degrees, I might have reasoned him correct. But 15 degrees could only mean that he wasn't allowing for the normal variation of the area. I told him to stay at March Field and *"take a course in Navigation"* - a comment he didn't think funny. John had done virtually all of his flying in the East where there is little compass variation, and he seemed to be having troubles navigating cross-country in the West. He must have caught on fast though, for he was on his way again in the morning. I began to agree that if John Geisse could fly the Arrowplane to Washington, anybody could - but that was what the whole program was all about!

Before Geisse left, and while we were still modifying the plane, I'd hired Eddie Allenbaugh to help us. Eddie had built a plane or two, and Bud assured me that he knew what he was doing, so I'd given him the job of welding the rear axle on the landing gear. He seemed capable, willing and diligent - the type of innovative employee that I sought. But I over-estimated his welding talents. Geisse, on August 5th, landed at Lordsburg, New Mexico, just ahead of a cloudburst, and taking off the next day didn't see a gully that had eroded across the runway. The landing gear dropped into it, wrenching-off one of the rear wheels and disclosing Eddie's imperfect weld. With the help of the local blacksmith, Geisse soon had it jury-rigged and flyable again, and continued east with no further mishaps, getting loads of favorable publicity at every stop.

Just before the last leg, John stopped long enough to shave, shower, put on a clean linen suit and phone Washington of his coming. Thus, when he arrived over the Capitol 'everyone' was there to greet him: Commerce Secretary Daniel Roper, Vidal, Cone, and loads of lesser lights. John tried a dramatic 'autogiro' landing - coming in steep, almost stalling, with the nose high. I'd designed the plane for this, but only a good pilot could do it right. He smacked-down hard, too damn hard for even the landing gear's long-travel shocks, and with not even a roll it partially collapsed. Later investigation disclosed that the gear failed at the jury-rigged weld. This, combined with Geisse's marginal flying ability, quashed all hope of receiving my final check soon.

Reading the contract's fine print, Vidal's foes seized upon this opportunity to embarrass him and his first *"flivver plane"*. They insisted that the department's engineering section completely retest everything. Not only did this devastate Vidal's hopes, but it really upset my apple cart. I'd come back to Washington on a TWA pass expecting to stay only a few days. I'd checked into the Ambassador Hotel with the thought that I'd soon be headed home with enough money to cover my debts and a bit more. Since, technically, the airplane was still mine - and the 'handwriting on the wall' indicated that they were really going to bear-down, en-

The Washington arrival - Gene Vidal and my Arrowplane - August 12, 1935

forcing even the contract's penalty provisions, I saw nothing but grief ahead. I moved across the street to the Hamilton, a less-expensive hotel.

Nonetheless, with the Arrowplane at Bolling Field, Vidal's people weren't missing any opportunities for promoting it - and their cause. At this time Amelia Earhart was at the peak of her popularity as the *most famous woman aviator in the world*. Being an old friend of both Vidal and myself, she gladly flew the plane with Geisse, and had her photograph taken in it. Also, she commented enthusiastically about it.

*Amelia Earhart
and John Geisse
August 15, 1935*

I headed for Bolling daily, usually in not too good a humor for I didn't know what the engineering guys would throw at me next. They were sure-as-hell reading me the riot act from their book! When we'd partially disassembled the fuselage, they discovered Eddie's unsightly welding job on the gas tank - and, naturally, it displeased them. They insisted upon its replacement, and I called Santa Monica to have the tank's drawings sent posthaste. Upon their arrival, the Commerce Department had Fairchild in Hagerstown make a new tank. When it was completed, I felt a bit ashamed comparing its beauty with our original effort.

As soon as it was installed, I took the plane up for a test. The engine stopped cold, the first time ever for the Arrowplane. After easily gliding in for a dead-stick landing, I figured that the problem was gas starvation. I removed the tank's cap and a great 'whoosh' indicated that a terrific vacuum had built-up. Peering closely, I discovered that Fairchild hadn't quite followed the plans: there was no vent hole!

And, a few days later while talking with Walter Brownell, the department's pilot, we spied gasoline streaming from the Arrowplane. The Fairchild welding job had let loose, proving that beauty ain't everything. We immediately reinstalled the original tank.

As the interminable testing went on and on, I got broker and broker. I started keeping my eye out for old friends, and the first ones I ran into - at the Commerce Department's offices - were the Martin brothers, Eddie and John, of Santa Ana, pioneers of Orange County's airport. I tapped them for a $50 loan. About a week-or-so later, I was again almost bone dry when I ran into Henry King, Fox's "flying director," and he, too, lent me $50.

With funds nipping 'the bitter end,' I moved to the Scott Inn, a boardinghouse about half-a-block from the Hamilton. It catered to lower-scale government employees able to pay little more than the weekly $18 for a room and two daily meals. I was still within an easy walk of the Commerce Department, and from my little cubbyhole room I hunkered-down to continue my battle with that damn engineering section.

Finally, the day came when the Arrowplane had met all requirements but one: the clearing of a 35-foot obstacle with an 800-foot takeoff in still air. Try as I might, I could never quite make it. With a breeze of just a couple-of-miles-per-hour it would have been a snap, but the engineering boys wouldn't give any quarter. I reasoned it best to concede,

355

Me in the Arrowplane - 1935

suffering a penalty assessment for an additional 50-foot takeoff run, and then I *picked up my marbles* and went home. In hindsight, I felt that if I'd insisted upon the propeller first specified instead of the alternate that the government supplied, I could have met the criteria 100 percent. This I demonstrated later, but when you're 2,500 miles from home and down to your last (borrowed) $5, you get a little desperate. After getting aboard the TWA flight home, I began thinking about my next move.

Back in Santa Monica, I used most of the funds from the contract to pay back Paul Granger. I was readying things around the shop for the inevitable move, having no rent money left, when the landlady appeared and tittled, *"When are you moving, Mr. Waterman?"* I was caught a bit off guard - but I noticed a smile on her face. Immediately I reasoned that she wasn't at all sad about losing me as a tenant in spite of the fact that the space had been vacant for over a year before my taking it. She might have something under her cloche that would work to my advan-

356

tage! So, being a good poker player, I remembered my option to renew for an additional two months and said, *"Well, no, I'm not moving out. I'm just shifting things around, getting ready to go into production on some more airplanes."* At that, her face dropped, the smile disappeared and she replied, *"Oh, we were so hoping that you were moving. We have an opportunity to lease the entire building to the Buick people, who want to move into this part of town, and the other two tenants (who were on a month-to-month tenancy) have agreed to move."* Well, I didn't want to take too-much advantage of the situation, but I had no money and nowhere to go.

Santa Monica's Buick dealer had a very handsome building at 5th and Colorado - over 35,000-square feet. But cars weren't selling and they'd been unable to make the mortgage payments, and were now in default. The bank had taken over, but Buick still had over a year's obligation due. So, after some 'horse-trading,' we agreed for me to move into the upstairs of their building while they'd assume the remaining balance on my option-to-renew.

After moving, I found myself in a much-better neighborhood for building airplanes - with twice the area, about 11,000-square feet, windows all around, and a lovely overlook to the ocean only four-blocks away. There was only one hitch - I didn't have any airplanes to build!

I'd already turned Vidal down on one of his suggestions. While still in Washington, Gene had offered me a contract to construct five Arrow-planes if I'd utilize a unique new fuselage fabricating process that had been developed by Early Bird Harry Atwood at Milford, Connecticut. It was an interesting method which appeared to be an evolution of Lockheed's, and Gene had sent me and Geisse up to Milford for a look. I scotched it, though, because Atwood didn't have engineering data substantiating the claims for its structural integrity. I knew that it would therefore suffer from Cone's engineeering group. Later, after Gene resigned from the government, he tied-in with Atwood backing the process (forming Aero Research Co. in 1939), and it became known as the "Vidal Process." But even the promotion of Vincent Bendix couldn't overcome its shortcomings, and it was never utilized to any great extent.

Geisse and I started up to Milford, taking John's teenage son along. We'd checked out a CAA Stinson Reliant, and following our inspection John was preparing to take off when I thought it best to intervene. Tapping him on the shoulder, I hollered, *"John, look at the windsock!"* Well, he did, and was he confused. The wind had changed 180 degrees from when he'd landed the day before, *this being New England!* John was all set to take off with the wind, and that 20-mph tailwind would have cracked us up for sure, just like Charlie Walsh in 1910. At that, John taxied to the other end of the field and made a proper takeoff. But a bit further-on the engine swallowed a valve, and we had to land. After fishing out the valve and corking-off that cylinder's intake, John was all set to take off on the remaining eight cylinders. But I said, *"Hold on, John; you can't fly this plane in this condition because it's technically nonairworthy."*

Darned if John didn't know the law! After detailing to him what might happen if there was an accident while operating the plane in its present condition, he accepted my logic that the plane should be flown with no passengers. John elected to fly the plane back to Washington rather than have me do it (which I'd suggested), and his son and I took the train the rest of the way. Maybe some will think me a bit too cautious, but I've seen far too many tragedies result from just that sort of thing, and I've never been one to stick-my-neck-out needlessly. Maybe that's one of the reasons I'm able to tell you this now!

Though this idea of Vidal's didn't pan-out, there was something else that turned-up from my Washington involvement. At about the same time that the Arrowplane passed its final tests, Harris "Pop" Hanshue was prowling around Washington looking for something to tie-in with (after a stint as president of TWA and Fokker, respectively, and as general manager of Eastern Air Lines). Vidal enthusiastically 'sold' him that the Waterman Arrowplane was the hottest thing around, and Hanshue therefore came to see me, arriving in Santa Monica just before my move to Fifth and Colorado. A *"flying automobile,"* was of as much interest to him as to myself, and I therefore had real encouragement to manufacture the next generation of Whatsit's progeny as I settled into my new quarters.

After discussing the best way to proceed with Max and Leonard Comegys, we decided to take advantage of the Hanshue relationship and tie-in with him. I knew him to be an extremely able, honest and frank individual, remembering how well he'd *cooked my goose* a decade earlier! Late in 1935, we incorporated the *Waterman Arrowplane Corporation* with me as president, Hanshue as vice president, Leonard as secretary

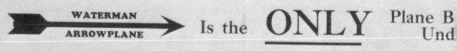

360

SAFETY SPECIFICATIONS

ED by the GOVERNMENT to date
Mar. 1, 1936

SELECT WATERMAN ARROWPLANE

The WATERMAN ARROWPLANE was one of sixteen
tted in the competition. It was one of several designs select-
the Bureau of Air Commerce as meriting a development
ct. In July, 1935, the ARROWPLANE was turned over to
ureau, three months ahead of scheduled delivery date. To
this is the only plane contracted for under the safety specifi-
is to be accepted by the Department of Commerce. The
rman Corporation gets the benefit of the Government de-
ment subsidy without necessity of paying from its own funds.

SAFETY FEATURES OF ARROWPLANE

Safety and performance features incorporated in the
ERMAN ARROWPLANE as dictated by the Department
ommerce included a restriction that visibility of pilot and
nger be unobstructed straight down, upwards to the rear,
forward. The ARROWPLANE has its motor mounted in
of the cabin to satisfy these requirements.

CABIN INTERIOR

The cabin is of all metal construction. Pilot and passenger
de by side. While on the ground the cabin takes the posi-
of a modern low-slung automobile.

UNEQUALED PERFORMANCE

Twenty-six gallons of gasoline is carried, giving a cruis-
range of 350 miles. Short feed lines extend from the tanks
above the engine in the rear of the cabin.
The ARROWPLANE will stop within 87 feet at a ground
d of 35 m. p. h. The front wheel is steerable and directly
ected to the rudder pedals. The plane can be landed safely
a an attitude of five degrees nose down to a complete nose up
ion. This eliminates sixty per cent of the skill necessary to
a normal airplane. Ground looping and abnormal reactions
impossible. Skidded or cross wind landings can be made
out compensating for drift and are entirely normal. A mini-
a amount of skill is therefore required to land the ARROW-
NE.

TAKEOFF TECHNIQUE SIMPLE

With the WATERMAN ARROWPLANE the takeoff is
mplished simply by holding or trimming the stick well back
ing the initial run, and the plane will automatically take off
assume normal climb position. It will clear an obstacle thirty-
feet high at a distance of 800 feet on the takeoff. In landing
ARROWPLANE will come over an obstacle thirty-five feet
a, land, and stop within a distance of 400 feet.

AILERONS AND ELEVATORS

The ailerons are at the extreme rear of the ARROW-
ANE because the wings sweep back. A fore and aft move-
at of the control moves them in the same direction. They there-
e function as both ailerons and elevators. The so-called rud-
s are merely drag elements at each wing tip. They can also
used as air-brakes to shorten the gliding angle.

ARROWBILE FEATURES

1. Non-Spinning
2. Non-Stalling
3. Take-off "Hands-Off"
4. Land in any Attitude Safely
5. Will Fly "Hands-Off"
6. Powered with Automobile Engine
7. Unusual scope of Visibility
8. Long Cruising Range
9. Short Take Off
10. Small Landing Area
11. It Flys, It Drives.

SPECIFICATIONS AND PREDICTED PERFORMANCE OF THE ARROWBILE

Top Speed	120 m.p.h.
Cruising speed	105 m.p.h.
Cruising range	400 miles
Weight empty	1635 pounds
Weight loaded	2200 pounds
Gasoline capacity	26 gallons
Overall length	19 feet
Wing span	38 feet
Climb at sea level	700 feet per minute

DEPARTMENT OF COMMERCE'S WATERMAN ARROWPLANE

361

Associated with Mr. Waterman is Harris M. Hanshue, pioneer in the development of air mail, passenger and air express service in the West. In 1926 Mr. Hanshue organized Western Air Express, and built the small company into the largest individual air system in the country until the merger of Western Air Express-T.A.T.-Maddux in 1930 to form Transcontinental and Western Air, Inc. Under his leadership the pioneer airline expanded from carrying air mail between Los Angeles and Salt Lake City to an air system flying tri-motored airplanes daily from Los Angeles to San Francisco, Portland, Seattle, Catalina Island, Kansas City, Albuquerque, Phoenix, El Paso, Dallas, and from Cheyenne, Wyoming, to Denver, Pueblo, Albuquerque and El Paso. Until becoming interested in the WATERMAN ARROW-PLANE, Mr. Hanshue served as general manager of Eastern Air Lines, large east coast air mail, passenger and express line connecting New York City and Washington, D. C. with the entire south.

Waldo D. Waterman has been an authority on avi in the West for twenty-five years. He was among the fi learn how to fly on the Pacific Coast. From his first days pilot, Mr. Waterman has dreamed of building thousan small, inexpensive airplanes, suitable for the individual o He has devoted practically his entire life to achieve that driv now he has incorporated all of that experience in the WA MAN ARROWBILE.

Just previous to entering the design competition of by the Bureau of Air Commerce, Mr. Waterman was a pil a large airline, flying trans-continental and coast-wise passe and mail planes. In addition to airline experience, he has ma factured and designed many planes, held executive position aircraft manufacturing organizations and airports. In the ea days, his contact with sales and instruction work in aviation further qualified him to analyze the needs of the private ov

WHAT THE PRESS *Said*:

"Tailless Airplane is shown as fool-proof. Eugene L. Vidal cites safety factor as ship refuses to Stall, stops in own length."
—*Associated Press Dispatch*, July 26, 1935.

"As the Waterman tail-less airplane came to a landing at the Washington, D. C., Airport, at the conclusion of a flight from California, it marked the near end of man's long struggle, since the first days of flying, to find a flivver plane that could be manufactured cheaply enough to let every average working man own and fly one."
—*Robert C. Lusch, Popular Aviation Magazine*, November, 1935

FAMILY AIR AUTOS

"The prophets of future practical use of the air as a general traffic highway for private and family airplanes received soul-satisfying evidence on Monday when the new low-price, fool-proof airplane reached Washington from California in the hands of a pilot of the Air Commerce Bureau, which has promoted its development.

"The Bureau sees in this plane the forerunner of a great new mass-production industry comparable relatively to the auto industry.

"The new plane refuses to learn bad habits, such as tailspins—chief dread of private pilots. . .

"The idea of a cheap, safe automobile of the air seems at last out of the dream stage and on the solid basis of practical achievement."
—*New York World-Telegram*, August 14, 1935.

"With the airplane loaded as it was during this trip, the stick could be held hard back, either with full power or without power, without

any possibility of stalling, and this of course removed any wo over stalling or spinning under any conditions. The feature pec to the Waterman airplane is, of course, the lack of the customary
—*John H. Geisse, National Aeronautical Magazine*, September.

"How does it fly?" he (Secretary Roper) asked John H. Geisse "It flies itself," Geisse said. Instead of flying togs, Geisse, was making his first transcontinental flight as a pilot, was weari linen suit and a Panama hat and looked as though he were a busi man on his way to his office."
—*Associated Press Dispatch*, August 12.

"Amelia Earhart, outstanding woman flier and conqueror of oceans, was enthusiastic today over one of the Bureau of Air C merce 'flivver' planes. . .

"She landed to praise the tail-less, bat-like plane. . .

"After John H. Geisse, pilot who flew the strange-looking from the west coast, took the plane aloft, Miss Earhart flew it the dual controls. On landing, she remarked that it handled nice
—*Associated Press Dispatch*, August 15,

"The most important characteristics of the plane are its adaptab to quantity production and the possibility of lower cost even in s production. If this venture proves successful, it is expected th further development will include roadability features, i. e., detach wings and rear-wheel drive."
—*Air Commerce Bulletin*, May 15,

and Max Harlow on the board. Hanshue, with unrivalled Eastern contacts, was to be the main money raiser, and for this was to receive half of the promotional stock, 25 percent of the total issue. I immediately got a couple of Harlow's boys working on new drawings, and we also started preparing a brochure, which wasn't completed until March, 1936.

Before Hanshue became involved in aviation, he'd been a famous bicycle and racing car driver, heading the Apperson Automobile Company's team. Later he was their "Jack Rabbit" dealer in Los Angeles until Apperson folded in 1926, at about the time he tied-in with Chandler and Graves in the Western Air Express venture. Eventually that led to the forced-merger with TAT and the *formation of TWA*. His involvement with Fokker followed, where he became president, but the tragedy of Knute Rockne's death in a TWA Fokker (near Cottonwood Falls in the Flint Hills of Kansas on March 31, 1931) ended the era of wood-framed airplanes, like Fokker, and Hanshue's fortunes dimmed.

I've often speculated about the best potential president of TWA: Hanshue or Graves. Knowing both fellows well, I had almost equal regard for their abilities. Graves probably would have been the best if he hadn't ran afoul of Henry Ford. He was a commendable leader at Bach, and along with Doug Shearer he'd been a trustee of the Waterman Aircraft Syndicate. Both Graves and Hanshue always spoke with a great deal of respect for each other.

Pop took off for New York to raise the funding. But even then we were strapped for money to cover his expenses because the corporation commissioner had required that all funds be escrowed until we'd raised at least $40,000.

With Pop gone, I now devoted all of my time to planning the airplane, and the first major decision was the powerplant. We decided to use a regular automobile engine because it'd cost only about 10 percent as much as an aircraft engine, and also would fit our concept of using as many automotive parts as possible: instruments, brakes, lights, horn and so forth.

It wasn't long before Pop called, needing my help presenting our proposal to some hot prospects in New York. As I packed I planned to make the trip doubly productive by lining-up the auto engine that we'd use, and this would involve us with a car manufacturer.

When I arrived in New York, Pop told me that our first meeting was with Harry Guggenheim, whom he'd known for several years - ever since working with him in 1927 pioneering passenger service on Western Air Express. At that time, Harry Guggenheim had been administrator for his father's *Daniel Guggenheim Foundation for the Promotion of Aeronautics. This was a $2,500,000 fund established in 1926 to help shift the emphasis in aviation away from barnstorming, stunt-flying and airmail to greater areas of public good, such as the development of air safety, instrument flying, and the popularization of both commercial and private flying.* It was certainly a commendable program - one of the many philanthropies of this family whose great fortune came from exploiting the natural resources of western North America and of South America.

Incidentally, it was Hanshue's work with Guggenheim (who had put up the money for Western's purchase of the latest passenger aircraft) that *proved the feasibility of major U.S. passenger airline service,* with such success that the loan was repaid in two years.

Pop and I made our pitch to Guggenheim and he seemed very impressed. In fact, he felt a favorable decision would be made after he'd had his good friend, Charles Lindbergh, check-out our proposal. Guggenheim insisted upon doing everything aviationwise with Lindbergh, whom he'd first met just before Lindbergh's Paris flight. After the flight, he'd given Lindbergh 'safe haven' at his estate on Long Island, protecting him from the hounding press and public, and their friendship blossomed. *One of their many co-involvements was their 1930 assistance to the giant work of Robert Goddard, the man who helped open-up space by inventing the liquid-fueled rocket in 1926.*

Our initial meeting with Guggenheim ended with the setting of the next meeting the following Wednesday, when Lindbergh was to join us for discussion and lunch.

This was late in 1935, and much of the year had seen the grisly and sensational details headlined across the country of the trial of Bruno Hauptmann, kidnapper and murderer of Lindbergh's son. There was a very strange aberration to it all. Lindbergh was feeling threatened and perplexed by the legal-political morass of Hauptmann's trial. It was a very trying period for him - an adultified hero finding it difficult to understand or cope with the public and legal system's reaction to his tragedy.

364

The next Wednesday, Pop and I arrived at Guggenheim's offices for our meeting, but when half-past twelve came and went, we began to get a bit worried over Lindbergh's arrival. We decided to wait before starting lunch and our discussion. Finally though, at 1 PM, we went into the director's room for lunch, still shy of Lindbergh. But shortly after sitting down, in walks Slim, hat-in-hand and holding dark glasses. He apologized for being late, explaining that he'd come incognito on the subway to Wall Street, had gotten lost, and fearing recognition if he asked anyone for directions, ended-up in Brooklyn!

Over a sumptuous lunch, we proceeded to have a very good discussion. Lindbergh was fascinated with our ideas and concepts and wanted to try his hand at flying the Arrowplane, now at the Commerce Department, in order to judge the flying characteristics of our proposed model. After arranging a date for this, I immediately contacted Vidal about borrowing the Arrowplane.

The next day, Thursday, I took the train to Washington; and on Friday flew the Arrowplane up to the Aviation Country Club at Hicksville, Long Island. This was the first of the aviation country clubs, founded in 1929 with an impressive roster of charter members: Charles Lawrance, Chance Vought, Amelia Earhart, Alexander de Seversky, Guggenheim and Lindbergh among others. It was posh, swank and well-guarded. One never got in unless one was a member or a guest.

The Aviation Country Club - Hicksville, Long Island - 1937

On Saturday, Slim and I flew the NS-13 through all of its impressive array of maneuvers. We did short takeoffs, tight-landings, and repeated attempts at spinning and stalling. It wouldn't do the latter two, of course, and this tickled Lindbergh. It was surely good to see him enjoying himself for a change after all-the-hell he'd been going through. And naturally, I was damn-pleased that he was so impressed! Try as I might, though, I couldn't get him to take the plane aloft alone. He demurred, preferring to fly it with me aboard just like Amelia had with Geisse. But he seemed so impressed and pleased that I was sure that we'd have a deal. I was in fine fettle as I returned the plane to Washington the following Monday, feeling certain that Lindbergh's indoctrination in Arrowplane-type flying had been a success.

For the next few days Pop and I killed time. We were in grand comfort, though, staying in the Essex House's penthouse, loaned to Hanshue while its owner was in a warmer clime, it being mid-December. After about three days of staring at each other and muttering, *'No news is good news!',* the phone finally rang. It was Guggenheim, wanting to see Hanshue *alone!* Well, I felt sure that this meant *'bad news,'* and I braced myself for Pop's return. I was correct. Pop told me that both Lindbergh and Guggenheim had been sold on the plane's prospects, but for some reason which they wouldn't disclose they'd be unable to back us! It was a terrific blow.

On Monday morning, December 23, 1935, I picked up the *New York Times* and, stunned, read the headline - *"LINDBERGH FAMILY SAILS FOR ENGLAND TO SEEK A SAFE, SECLUDED RESIDENCE; THREATS ON SON'S LIFE FORCE DECISION."*

I felt like the musician in the King's orchestra which had played so wonderfully that the King exclaimed, *"And I shall fill each of your instruments with gold!"* There I sat with my piccolo.

With the wind knocked-out of our sails, Pop and I decided to head for greener pastures: a fresh start in a new town in a new year. Arriving at the Book-Cadillac Hotel in Detroit, Pop proceeded to call friends and set up appointments. *One of the first was with Charles Kettering (inventor of the self-starter), the man whose technical innovations teamed with Alfred Sloan's administrative abilities to form the cornerstones of General Motors.* We had an interesting luncheon meeting with Kettering, but it

366

got nowhere due to his belief in the airplane solely as a military vehicle. This was very disappointing, for his backing would have been second only to Lindbergh's.

Our next appointment was with Roy Chapin, another of automobiledom's pioneers. He was a founder and the president of the Hudson Motor Car Company and, most recently, Hoover's Secretary of Commerce. He was also one of aviation's earliest boosters, having been one of the very few Americans at Reims in 1909. He'd met Glenn Curtiss then - which led to Curtiss and his wife preceding my visit to the Chapins by a quarter-of-a-century! Roy Chapin had made a name for himself in the development of the automobile industry. One memorable achievement came during the war when he was head of the Highway Transport Committee of the Council for National Defense. He implemented the then-novel idea to move trucks from Detroit to European-bound ports under their *own power* rather than tie-up the railroads for their transport. He thus became the 'father' of the over-the-road truck, and, in effect, of today's massive trucking industry.

Pop and I were picked up at the Book-Cadillac by Chapin's chauffeured limousine. During the ride to Grosse Pointe Farms our legs and feet were kept warm by a huge fur rug (no car heaters then). Upon arriving at their lovely estate, we were met by Chapin, his charming wife, Inez, and their children still at home, including Roy, Jr., today a senior officer in American Motors Corporation. After dinner, Roy regaled us with the story of how, in 1909, he and Howard Coffin, Roscoe Jackson, George Dunham and Fred Bezner, with only blackboard drawings and some floor layouts of their new "Model 20," got the backing of department store magnate J.L. Hudson. Thus began, on a shoe string, one of Detroit's multi-million dollar enterprises. They promoted the car and received many orders even before it had gone into production.

I'm sure that his perilous early days, combined with his love affair with flying, led to his enthusiasm for our ideas. He offered to provide their Essex Light-6 engine to power our *"Arrowbile"*, the name we chose for our auto-plane.

During this time in Detroit, I eventually spent almost five weeks discussing and analyzing possibilities with the engineering departments of General Motors, Ford, Chrysler and Hudson. Each of the engines had

367

to be around 100-hp, and I was classifying them as to weight-per-horse-power, reliability, adaptability to aircraft streamlining and, most importantly, the willingness of the company to provide financial backing in addition to engines and engineering.

My hopes of working with Hudson were soon dampened when studies revealed two major drawbacks with their engine. It had no pressure lubrication to the crankshaft and connecting rods, and had to reach 4,000-rpm to produce the required 100-hp. These shortcomings were fairly typical of auto engines then, regardless of manufacturer. Ford's latest V8 met our criteria, but it didn't fair well into our streamlining plans, and was too heavy. An engine in Chrysler's line, their Plymouth Six, was already Type Certified by the CAA (due to Chrysler's Plyma-coupe entry in Vidal's competition), but only produced 70-hp.

The typical automobile engine of the 1930's was a far-cry from aircraft engines then, let alone of today. I began to think that it was going to be almost impossible to find a suitable one.

Before leaving Detroit, I'd more-or-less rationalized working with Chapin and Hudson, primarily because he'd personally made a $5,000 commitment to our venture, and had promised two engines for our development activities. In addition, one of his sons was very interested in getting into aviation, something which I'm sure swayed both Roy and me.

But we still hadn't yet talked with Studebaker at South Bend, and Pop called Paul G. Hoffman, their new president, and set up an appointment.

Hoffman and Hanshue were old friends from their early days as competitors selling cars on Figuero Street in Los Angeles. Hoffman, when already a millionaire car salesman, became a vice president of Studebaker in 1925, at about the same time that Pop tied-in with Western Air Express. Hoffman had been with Studebaker in its heyday, the 1920's, *the greatest period in American automotive manufacturing*. He had then watched the company's decline due both to the ravages of the Depression and Albert Erskine's dissipation of the corporate coffers. Erskine, president since 1915, embarked on a series of misadventures that included buying ailing Pierce-Arrow and White Motors. That forced Studebaker into bankruptcy and Erskine to suicide. Hoffman and chairman Harold Vance then brought the company painfully back to life, so that when we visited in 1936 was reasonably viable again.

368

Invited to dinner at the Hoffman's, we were greeted by a large and unusual family - five sons, one daughter and two very fine parents who lived a life that appeared formal but warm. The butler supervised the dinner service by uniformed servants, and the children were very well-mannered, although not-in-the-least subdued. Each felt free to speak, joining our conversation, even if briefly. I was very impressed to see this large family so keenly interested in each other's doings. Dorothy Hoffman (nee Brown, from Pasadena), presiding over her brood from one end of the large table, was most charming - one of the loveliest and most gracious women that I've ever known.

After dinner, we retired to the game room where I showed 16mm movies of both Whatsit and Arrowplane in flight. These were very interesting to the kids and, more importantly, to Paul Hoffman. He insisted that we show the film the next day to his engineering staff. We needed little urging; words like these were as balm-to-our-wounds! I've often wondered what might have happened if we'd have gone to South Bend first, and then to Detroit. Psychologically, we may not have been prepared for this opportunity.

The next day Hoffman introduced me to a Mr. Sparrow, designer of recent Studebaker engines, and to Dr. James, their top technical man. After seeing the film, they immediately began studying which of their engines would be most suitable for us. In addition to the support of Hoffman, my pleasure was now doubled when we determined that Studebaker's engines best-met our criteria. Both Sparrow and James believed in inherent lightness, and their latest engines incorporated stressed steel rather than heavy iron below the critical crankshaft area. What's more, they had experimentally upped horsepower into the desired range, from 90 to 105-hp, using multiple carburetors and an aluminum cylinder head. Enginewise, Studebaker appeared to be very far ahead. It seemed that the only thing they were doing wrong was in naming their cars - one model was called the "Dictator," a name becoming unpopular due to Hitler, Mussolini and Stalin.

Although several of Studebaker's engineering innovations were still in the laboratory, they none-the-less demonstrated that their engines could do the job. Our visit ended with Dorothy Hoffman subscribing for $5,000 of stock, and the company for another $5,000, to be exchanged for 50 "Commander" engines at $100-apiece. These engines were to be 'bare', that is, without carburetors or manifolds, but including the starter and generator. It was left-up to us to make any further modifications, just exactly what I'd hoped for. It looked like this budding Studebaker alliance was going to be just what we had been seeking!

Pop and I headed for home, still needing to raise the balance of the $40,000. Remembering the success he'd had in San Francisco raising money for Western Air Express, we first went there. San Francisco was then the financial and business center for the West. Our first contact was Mr. Kingsbury, the president of Standard Oil of California. He liked our proposition and agreed to commit $12,500 if his friend, Herbert Fleishacker of the Anglo-California Bank, would do likewise. Fleishaker needed a bit more convincing than Kingsbury, but finally relented. Then, having collected something over $25,000 in Northern California, we went home to Santa Monica. That money, plus $5,000 apiece from Roy Chapin and Dorothy Hoffman, $500 that I'd gotten from Townsend Ludington and a few other nominal amounts just put us over-the-top.

Therefore, we got the 'green light' from the corporation's commissioner, releasing the escrowed funds and permitting Hanshue to raise more money while we started building airplanes.

Fully expecting to build at least 1,000 Arrowbiles annually, I proceeded to set up an organization that was second-to-none, based upon the premise that a heavy initial investment in tools and equipment would easily pay for itself. Additionally, I was determined to utilize automotive mass-production know-how and methods, and thus *created the first such aircraft assembly line in the United States*.

An insight into our thinking may be seen in our use of *stock* automobile engines. This would have been prohibitively expensive if only a few aircraft were planned, due to all of the engineering and adaptation required. Even costing 10-times-as-much, an aircraft engine would be more economical under those conditions. But in hundreds and thousands, automotive powerplants and other items became reasonable and cost effective. Granted, these were ambitious goals, but we felt confident in reaching them because of the heady publicity we'd already received. Much of it was due to Vidal's program, and also the great coverage we felt certain to get when the first Arrowbiles rolled-off the line. We were sure that this was no *'blue sky'* operation!

The technical problems were monumental. Such a basic item as landing gear required an entirely new design in order to incorporate the road drive. There weren't any wheels, either, to fit our requirements. The method of getting the drive to the road wheels was a tough, tough problem, and even after completing the first couple of Arrowbiles, we were still working on improving it.

We had to determine how to drive the propeller at half-the-speed of an automobile engine, keep the engine as low as possible (for the best center-of-gravity) and still leave at least nine inches ground clearance for the prop tips. Our final design positioned the engine very low, right above the rear axle, with six V-belts controlled by a clutch pulley connecting aluminum-alloy sheaves on both the engine and the propeller shafts, making it relatively easy to change from the flying to the driving mode. The pilot could lower the front end of the propeller shaft, varying the tension for whatever flying condition he desired, up to the point of total slackness for the driving mode which required the disengagement of the propeller.

We incorporated as many standard automotive parts as possible, so long as they met aircraft performance requirements and were not too heavy, thus giving us substantial cost savings. We even included the standard Studebaker radiator and battery. The latter required installing neoprene tubing from the wet cells to the plane's exterior to prevent acid damage when flown upside down. When Studebaker didn't have the parts, we went elsewhere. From Willys-Overland and American Austin, we took brakes, drums, parts of the differential gears, headlights and steering wheel. The reduction between the steering rotation and the front wheel and elevons was done with a planetary gear unit from a Ford Model T. For road use, we incorporated stop lights, sideview mirror and horn. Legally, we were able to classify the Arrowbile as a motorcycle since it had only three wheels and weighed less-than-1,450 pounds. Thus, we could get away with a single headlight and a small license plate, which greatly simplified the streamlining.

Likewise, eight of the 11 instruments were automotive in origin. The only aircraft ones were compass, altimeter and airspeed indicator. Eight automotive instruments cost less-than-half of what the three aircraft types cost! We designed new wheels and tires, a very expensive proposition when one realizes that everything had to pass the rigorous CAA

371

tests, inspections and type certifications. For instance, the wheels had to withstand heavy loads in static tests, and then the entire landing gear had to pass drop tests calculated to rate the units effectiveness for both flying and driving usage. These tests surely caused the CAA engineering staff some headaches! The engine and the drive unit to the propeller were set up on a test stand at Clover Field (where very loud noise could be tolerated) and then run at 90 to 100 percent of maximum horsepower for 150 hours. After being subjected to this grueling punishment, they had to show no abnormal wear upon dismantling.

The drive to the rear wheels (one forward speed, plus reverse) was through floating axles with universal joints splined into a differential of our own manufacture. It had a cast Duralumin case, and the entire unit weighed only 20 pounds.

We'd originally set a goal to raise $250,000 - the amount calculated to permit production of 1,000 Arrowbiles annually. Our enthusiasm about reaching this goal was buoyed by the prospect of every Studebaker dealer nationwide selling them for only $3,000 each *plus* accessories. This figure, we discovered, was far too optimistic! However, as I've already noted, the exhorbitant costs that we incurred seemed small when planning to *sell airplanes in the massive automotive marketplace*.

Mel Oliver, Clarence Deyette, Bud Pearson and Eddie Allenbaugh became the cornerstones of our growing organization. Paul Emmons, a talented ex-Douglas employee enthused with the Arrowbile's concept, became my assistant superintendent, while Max Harlow continued to supervise the engineering, which was done both at Pasadena Junor College and at our plant by two or three of his best ex-students, now full-time employees. At this time, Janie, a freshman at UCLA, prevailed upon me to let her become my full-time secretary. I hated to see her drop out of school, but her help and trustworthiness was something that I certainly needed. Between the two of us we were *"Mugwump"* - Janie was *"Mug"* and I was *"Wump"*.

Janie wasn't the only female boosting our morale. After Amelia's initial flight in the Arrowplane in Washington, she continued to be fascinated with its concept. In 1936 she took a spin with me in the Arrowbile's skeletal framework around a nearby parking lot, happy as a young girl with a new, pretty dress.

372

Taking a spin with Amelia, Santa Monica, 1936

Things were really looking great. Hanshue was back East again, scouting-up the balance of our financing (we'd raised only about 20 percent so far), and I saw nothing but wonderful prospects; like *"Pennies From Heaven"*, what those many Depression-era songs were all about.

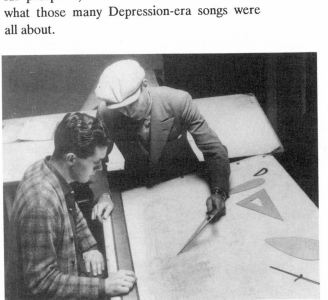

Checking Arrowbile plans - me and Frank Schaffer, 1936

373

Finally, in early 1937, Arrowbile-1, NX262Y, was completed and we decided to test-fly it at Long Beach Municipal Airport rather than haul it out to Rosamond Dry Lake. I then drove it to Long Beach, really tangling-up traffic enroute! Mel followed in his pickup, towing a trailer with the wings, and the next morning we assembled the craft for testing. Long Beach's airport has a long runway ending in a fairly populous area to the southeast (just east of Signal Hill), while all of the land in every other direction was virtually open farmland. That morning the slight breeze was from the south, the direction of the ocean, so that was where I headed for takeoff. I got off the ground with no problem, but as I tried to rise the plane seemed to get more and more sluggish, making me feel pretty uneasy. When I'd reached 200-feet-or-so it seemed like I'd gotten all of the altitude I was going to get. I'd hit the ceiling - but I was able to turn away from the houses, and made a wide sweep as I headed around towards open country. Below me was a new country club and golf course, a development of the Montana Land Company named the *Lakewood Country Club* by landscape architect George Carpenter. (Today *Lakewood* is a sizable city, and also the address of McDonnell Douglas.) Perspiring, I was finally able to line her up for a landing - one which seemed far too fast for the weight and wing area involved.

Touching down heavily and with a pretty hangdog look on my face, I taxied over to where Mel was waiting. Perplexed, we both were trying to figure out the reason for the poor performance when suddenly we spied the trouble. The tape sealing the joint between the fabric and metal along the front spar had peeled away. This formed a vertical ridge about an inch-and-a-half high, literally a spoiler impairing the airfoil and the wing's ability to create lift! It was a miracle that I'd been able to stay aloft at all. After ripping the tape off, I took off again and this time she lept into the air and performed beautifully. *It was a very stable airplane, impossible to spin, stall or perform aerobatically. Yet it possessed all of the maneuverability necessary for landings, takeoffs and turns up-to-vertical-banks. It was a great day - February 21, 1937.*

With two rather than the usual three controls, controlling the plane was a snap. Pushing and pulling of the wheel nosed the craft either up or down. Rotating the wheel caused her to bank *and* turn at any degree without skidding. Also, the tricycle landing gear permitted takeoffs with quite a crosswind - an additional benefit we hadn't counted on.

374

WHATSIT BECOMES THE "AIR FLIVVER"...

Highly elated after several flights, I flew the Arrowbile to Clover Field where I now had a hangar. We were all ready for the next phase - the promotional and newsreel flights. And, it seemed that every newspaper and magazine in the country, plus many worldwide, did a piece on the Arrowbile. We were really getting the sort of press that would make Pop's job easier.

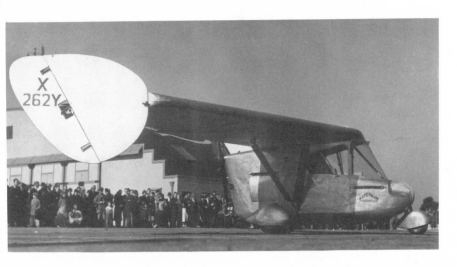

Arrowbile-1 Meets The Press - Clover Field - March, 1937

Me taking her off for the press - Clover Field - March, 1937

Fill 'er up!

Pulled-over by California Highway Patrol Officer Bobby Clark - 1937

Locally, the National Pacific Aircraft and Boat Show was being held at the Pan Pacific Auditorium. This huge exhibit building had been built by brothers Clifford and Phillip Henderson partially from the grandstand salvage of the 1936 National Air Races (which, incidentally, I had been on the contest committee along with Jimmy Doolittle and Amelia Earhart). Cliff was now the top national entrepreneur of aircraft events, and I was closely tied-in to the local ones, being a director of the Los Angeles Aircraft Industry Association.

But this year my participation was primarily because of the Arrowbile. It was our first opportunity to show it off and we did it in a bang-up style. We rigged a huge black-velvet drape between the two halves of the plane so that, looking from one side, it appeared to be flying, while from the other, it looked like it was driving down the highway. We even had an electric hoist to raise and lower the wing. Pretty girls, recruited by Janie, were acting as hostesses, answering questions and showing the film of the Arrowbile both while in flight and on the ground. Ever since my

377

35,000 AMERICANS ARE LEARNING TO BECOME PRIVATE FLIERS

But few of them can yet afford a plane of their own

Today 35,000 Americans are learning how to fly airplanes, more than ever before. This year, almost 2,000 planes will be built for private or nontransport use, an increase of 25% over 1936. In 1936, airplane production showed a 50% increase over 1935. These statistics may foreshadow the long-expected boom in private flying, a boom which began in 1928 and, like so many others, crashed in 1929.

There are 7,000 licensed private pilots in the U. S. today. Last year they flew 30,000,000 miles, half the total flown by commercial airlines. The commuters to the Downtown Skyport (*opposite*) are not typical of them. To the average private flier the expense of flying is still a great strain. Although 140,000 student flying permits have been issued in the past ten years, 125,000 students have dropped flying. Some lost interest, or could not keep in practice. But most of them did not own and could not buy a plane. Cheapest plane produced in any

quantity today costs $1,300. Two-thirds of the planes built for U. S. nonmilitary use last year were in this price class. The planes are safe, easy to fly, can be bought on the installment plan. But $1,300 is a considerable sum and the private flier finds maintenance a burden. A few years ago, the Department of Commerce searched in vain for a safe $700 plane. Among those which passed speed and safety tests, was the tailless *Arrowplane*, built by Waldo D. Waterman of Santa Monica. Mr. Waterman now has a variation named *Arrowbile*, a combination automobile and plane, shown below. *Arrowplane* was never produced commercially and *Arrowbile*, not past all official tests, is still more an interesting experiment than an immediate promise to private fliers. But it does represent one attempt to bring convenience to private flying. Learning to fly is easy. The average adult can manage it in 5 hours. For the things he learns, turn the page.

1 Out of Waldo D. Waterman's garage, his Arrowbile is wheeled. It is more convenient and less expensive to keep the plane in the family garage than in a hangar. Daughter Jane is at the wheel.

2 Down to the airport goes Arrowbile, a wingless, three-wheeled auto, engine driving wheels instead of propeller.

3 At the hangar, the wings are lowered and attached firmly t body. Waterman has seven Arrowbiles under construction of them ordered by Studebaker whose engines power this p

4 The Arrowbile races down the airport runway. Its engine is now linked to propeller which, the plane being a "pusher," is in rear.

5 The Arrowbile takes off. A curious-looking machine, it is made mostly of automobile parts. It has a Studebaker engine and generator, Willys-Overland brakes and differential, Ford steering assembly, battery and radiator.

6 In flight along the coast (*above*), the A: bile has a top speed of 120 m.p.h., can c two passengers 350 miles. Its price is $3.

CONTINUED ON NEXT P

barnstorming days I'd known the value of the carney barker, and we utilized the same sort of spiel, though more decorous, fitting the occasion.

The attendance was tremendous. *"Everyone in aviation" was there: Vincent Bendix, Louise Thaden, Jimmy Doolittle, Ben Howard, on and on. Douglas was showing-off their new DC-3, a "giant" 21-passenger airliner that was the largest craft in the show. But the Arrowbile caused the most comment, and we received the First Prize for the show's best exhibit. We felt that we had the world by the tail!*

At the show we took our first orders at $3,000 each. That was a lot of money in Depression years, but the Arrowbile was still far-cheaper than anything comparable. (The Piper Cub was getting awfully close to Vidal's dream of a "$700 airplane," selling in 1939 for only $995) . And mentioning Piper causes me to comment upon what he and too many others were doing to the aircraft industry, in my opinion. William Piper regarded the making of airplanes as incidental to the making of money. Money was his sole goal, but I guess that's not much different than many segments of American industry today. *(They seem to be ruled by MBA's, accountants and lawyers, with the "bottom line" and the stockprice overwhelming both the product and its quality!)*

Those first orders for the Arrowbile came from Studebaker. Morrow Crumb, their head of publicity, visited the show, saw the crowd's enthusiasm, and after a flight over Los Angeles was completely 'sold.' He recommended that Studebaker buy five Arrowbiles, show them first at the Cleveland Air Races, and then tour them around-the-country, displaying them at the company's many dealers. *It was quite a thrill announcing this sale while the show was still on!*

However, that posed my next problem - getting these five planes completed in time for the races. Fortunately, I'd placed parts orders for ten airplanes and we hurriedly started their final assembly. I still wasn't satisfied with the V-belt road drive, and was working on a small three-speed transmission with an automotive-type clutch which I knew would be better. But these first Studebaker Arrowbiles wouldn't have these because there simply wasn't enough time to incorporate them.

As the Arrowbiles neared completion, we took them to Mines Field (LAX) where they were painted following the Studebaker art department's instructions. Boy, were they psychedelic! But they caught the eye, and we even put grills on to match Studebaker's 1938 line.

Waterman Arrowplane factory (l-r) Arrowbile-1, 6, 5, 4, 3, 2 - July, 1937

Pressed for time, we fudged a bit by taking the original Arrowbile and modified its front end to conform to the Studebaker design, and then rushed the next two so that we'd at least have three planes ready for Cleveland.

I assigned a pilot to each plane who was responsible for flying it for Studebaker upon completion. The first was Slim Perrette - a too-senior copilot who had flown with me at TWA. The second was Jerry Phillips, an ex-barnstormer and well-known movie stunt flyer, and the third was Chuck Sisto, who was recommended by Eugene Scroggie, CAA's flight inspector. We had a helluva time locating him, though. Janie finally dug-him-up, almost literally, for he was digging ditches for the WPA (Works Progress Administration), times being what they were!

Meanwhile, back in Washington, Vidal was having a devil-of-a-time getting any of his *"everyman's airplanes"* flying. Dean Hammond, the

380

Me in Studebaker Arrowbile-2 - August 1937

Taking off, Clover Field - August 1937

(l-r) Harold Vance, me, Paul Hoffman and Morrow Crumb
looking over an ad layout, South Bend, 1937

Dorothy Hoffman christening Arrowbile-3 "Miss South Bend", Clover Field - August 19.

382

program's most successful bidder, was having more than his share of problems in meeting the performance criteria, and at Vidal's insistence had gotten Lloyd Stearman to help him. Lloyd's prime contribution was redesigning the aircraft with a stressed skin, which was far-better but a lot more expensive, too. When they finally reached the flight-testing stage, they discovered that the 95-hp Menasco engine wouldn't budge it at all, and they ended-up with a much more costly 150-hp supercharged Menasco. Even with all that power they still drew quite a few penalty points. However, by this time Vidal was desperate to get anything flying and bent many of the rules, something that hadn't even been thought of for me. But at long last he was able to announce a flyable airplane!

Henry J. Kaiser got involved with the now named Stearman-Hammond Aircraft Corporation, and his backing caused them to move to the San Francisco peninsula, again as Hammond Aircraft Corp. Also, their 30-plane contract had been renegotiated to 12. A few more were sold to private buyers, including one for Rogers Aircraft Corp. in Los Angeles - being carried-on by Emory's mother as a sort of memorial to him. *By this time these (Kaiser-Stearman) Hammond "Y" Model-JH's were selling for around $7,000 apiece, ten-times Vidal's original 1933 quest!*

In Santa Monica, we were racing to complete the three Arrowbiles in time for the Races. Arrowbiles-2 and 3 were soon leapfrogging cross-country, and we were almost finished the remodeling for Arrowbile-1. I had Sisto checked-out flying it, finally turning him loose alone for several practice flights. When everything was completed, he packed his bag, gassed the plane and tookoff early one August morning.

I heaved a sigh of relief as Number-1 faded into the eastern sky, sure that now there'd be three planes at Cleveland. But that afternoon the phone rang 'collect' from Sisto - a problem for sure! He'd made a forced landing at Gila Bend, Arizona, just about the hottest and most desolate spot in the whole country. We had trouble understanding just what had happened - something about the V-belt drive to the propeller not functioning. He'd had to land among a boulder-strewn field, knocking-off the nose wheel, twisting one of the rear wheels and maybe doing some structural damage. Damn! Well, there was little else to do but send Eddie with the trailer to bring Sisto and the plane back to Santa Monica. We still might be lucky and get it fixed-up in time for Cleveland.

383

What a place to land! Note wheel tracks through the rocks

A dejected Chuck Sisto, Gila Bend, Arizona - August, 1937

However, when it arrived back at the factory I saw that we surely wouldn't be able to do that! A fitting in the sheave adjustment had sheared, puzzling-the-hell-out-of-me because it'd been designed for at least 1,500 hours use and had gone only about 50. By questioning Sisto I soon learned about what had happened. He'd been toying with the belt's

384

Alice Faye and me beside Arrowbile-1, "Tail Spin", Hollywood - 1938

tension to see the effect upon airspeed, rpm and vibration, when all-of-a-sudden it broke! Very cooly I explained to him that he wasn't a test-pilot and that that was one damn place to be experimenting! I could have fired him on the spot but for his hangdog look and expressions of wrong-doing. Instead, I put him right to work helping to fix-up the results of his foolishness.

There wasn't any chance now of Arrowbile-1 making it to Cleveland, so I left while Sisto worked at getting it flyable again. Sometime later he flew it in the movie *"Tail Spin"*. Its role always bothered me because the

385

plane didn't have a tail and wouldn't spin, and the backgrounds make you think that the scene was filmed in Central Park - but it was all pure Hollywood! This movie starred Alice Faye, that *"lovely marshmallow sundae of a girl".*

I'd already arranged with both Cliff Henderson and Studebaker for 1938 Studebakers to be driven as 'official cars' at the National Air Races. It turned-out to be a beautiful tie-in with the Arrowbiles, which Slim and Jerry demonstrated daily.

Our performance consisted of flying an Arrowbile in and landing in front of the grandstands. We would then drop-off the wings and drive it around, while the other Arrowbile would take off and perform flight maneuvers. It was quite fascinating, and the crowd gave us a tremendous reception. I'm sure many thought about owning their own Arrowbile to fly on weekends, and then use for commuting during the week (long before freeway gridlock!). And in my daily spiel, we didn't overlook the ease with which the housewife could do her shopping, either!

At the National Air Races, Cleveland, September, 1937

386

Unfortunately, there was a major blight in all of our good happenings. On January 8, 1937, Pop had a stroke while in the East and passed away *(Harris Mathewson Hanshue, 1884-1937, 52 years old)*. I felt a great personal loss, but at that time I had little inkling of how grievous it would be. When Pop died I'd been totally enmeshed in getting Arrowbile-1 completed, and wasn't able to take up any of the financial chores that he'd been working on. I left everything hanging, thinking that we had enough money in the till.

As usual, I was wrong! At about the same time as the Air Races, the country's economy started slipping again, *tumbling into the second 1930's-era depression which would see ten million unemployed by mid-1938.* It wasn't quite as bad as 1932, but bad enough to knock me out of the skies again! As mentioned, our original pricing of around $3,000 per plane was far too low. Events were showing that it should have been nearer twice that amount, and that combined with 'hard times again' started pushing us to the wall. Actually, we never sold any Arrowbiles at $3,000 apiece except to Studebaker, refunding the deposits of all other private buyers. So it wasn't quite as bad as it might seem, but it surely wasn't any roaring success story, either!

But I'm a bit ahead of myself. Following the races, I took to the financing trail trying to pick-up where Pop had let off. I'd already learned that Pop wasn't worth a damn at making a 'selling' presentation. His strength was in knowing the right people and in 'opening doors'. And now I really learned the adage that *"It's not what you know, but WHO you know,"* for I surely wasn't very successful. I only raised about $10,000 more, putting us around $55,000 of our $250,000 goal.

I first tried raising money in Detroit, checking-in with Roy Chapin's executor, for he'd passed away before we'd really been able to get things going. But I couldn't nail anything down, and then went on to South Bend for further meetings with Paul Hoffman and Studebaker. They assured me of their continued involvement, but they were being hit very hard by the economic downturn, were short of cash, and so couldn't advance me any more for the time being. In fact, Hoffman advised me to close down the plant rather than continue our 35-person payroll, for which I had little prospect of paying. It was one of my life's toughest events, having to call Janie and tell her to lay off everyone! I had a crew

387

that had always given far more than they received. With loyalty like that, turning them out into jobless streets was almost more than I could stand.

I did get a commitment from Hoffman to keep enough help to complete the rebuilding of Arrowbile-1, plus an oblique assurance that he'd see that the corporation didn't go through bankruptcy. This in itself meant a great deal to me, for I'd been involved in too many bankruptcies. I had seen them profit only the appraisers, liquidators and court attachees, and I swore I'd never suffer it as a principal.

However, I wasn't giving-up-the-ghost easily! I went back to Detroit for another meeting with Chapin's executor, who then introduced me to Detroit Aircraft Corporation, who, after all of their misstarts, still had a few-hundred-thousand-dollars available. They were governed by a ten man board that had to agree unanimously on any decision. After several meetings with them, I determined that all were for me except for Edgar Evans, who vetoed my every proposition. Later I learned that he had other uses in mind for the funds, which he finally got Detroit's board to back. I was left with nothing but have never blamed Evans, though what he was backing eventually failed! Later he made quite a name for himself manufacturing plastic furniture.

Next I went to Cincinnati for a meeting with Powel Crosley, Jr., millionaire manufacturer of cheap radios and refrigerators, and owner of the Cincinnati Reds. In the early 1920's, shortly after my trying one of Budwig's radios, Crosley offered the public inexpensive sets, selling thousands for only $20 each. He was an aviation enthusiast with several planes, notably Lockheed Vegas. Earlier he'd also produced a cheap airplane, the ill-fated *Crosley Flea*. Therefore I reasoned that he'd be a good possibility to back the Arrowbile - and he was. We had a very good session, until he told me that all of his current efforts were going into a new, cheap automobile! In early May, 1939, Crosley gathered his 200 dealers at Indianapolis and unveiled this new machine. *Dubbed, not surprisingly, the Crosley, it was a "sleek, rakish little convertible," with a two-cylinder air-cooled engine that sold for $325!* Versions of it sold fitfully until 1952, when it disappeared into the American past. My hopes for Crosley died much earlier, though - way back in 1937.

I then swung up to Buffalo for a session with James Rand, chairman of Remington Rand, whom I knew was interested in aviation. He, along with Reub Fleet and others, had backed Ralph O'Neill in the founding of

388

the New York, Rio & Buenos Aires Line (NYRBA). But I guess that its forced-merger with Pan Am caused Rand to lose interest in aviation. I was only briefly able to keep him from toying with a new gadget on his desk, the Remington Electric Shaver.

I met with a few others, Vincent Bendix included, but found that everyone was pulling-in-their-horns, fearful of another 1932. Exhausting possibilities, I dejectedly came home to Santa Monica - to an almost-stilled factory and very meager prospects. I had been able to keep Frank Schaffer on the payroll. He'd been one of Harlow's top students, and he now worked with me completing Arrowbile-1 and a Studebaker-powered Arrowplane, which Hoffman had also authorized.

During this capital-shortage-shutdown-period, Vance Breese showed up one day, and not being at all busy I had plenty of time to listen to the line that he fed me. I was already aware that Vance was test-flying for North American Aviation, and he intimated that their president, James H. "Dutch" Kindelberger, was interested in the Arrowbile. Naturally, this piqued my interest, for I was looking everywhere for financial support in order to keep going. Vance speculated that he might arrange a tie-in between North American and myself since he saw Dutch daily. I'd known Dutch for several years, too, ever since he'd first ridden with me in the Flex Wing.

Well, I fell 'hook, line and sinker,' thinking little of *why* Vance also asked all sorts of questions about the Arrowbile's flying characteristics. Looking back later, I saw more clearly that he primarily asked questions about how I got the Arrowbile off the ground. Being a tailless aircraft, it had virtually no fore and aft moment, and had to be launched by depressing the wingtip elevons to raise the nose. In addition to this short leverage, the other elements of the plane's design had to be carefully positioned in order to make a normal takeoff. Therefore I went into considerable detail, explaining to Vance all of the many problems we'd originally had in solving this baffling phenomenon. Our own solution, finally, was to have the main wheels carry approximately 85 percent of the load, because if the nose wheel was too heavily loaded it required a takeoff speed far too high to gain the right rotational moment.

When Vance left, I had every expectation that I'd soon hear from either him or Dutch. But no such thing happened, and I was quite surprised to read in the papers about a week later that Northrop had de-

389

signed a new aircraft dubbed a *"Flying Wing"* which Vance Breese was putting through flight-tests at *Rosamond Dry Lake!* In 1929 Northrop had built the "Avion", a so-called 'flying wing,' but it had a two-boom tail, and the only excuse that I knew for that claim was that its engine and cockpit were buried within the wing structure. Now it seemed that they'd eliminated the tail and had been unable to break it away from the ground. Vance had been 'picking my brains' to learn how to do it. By moving the landing gear around, like I'd told him, they succeeded.

It has always rankled me a bit that most people believe Northrop was first with an American flying wing. Hell, I'd done it first with Whatsit in 1932 and then with both the Vidal plane and the Arrowbile! It appears that the facts of 'history' are often elusive and capricious. This is particularly true of aviation history, a subject too new to have weathered the strains of hard inquiry and good scholarship.

In the financial crunch, Chuck Sisto was among those that I'd had to lay off, and a short while later I got a call from Jim Webster, manager of Rogers Aircraft Corporation, about Chuck's Arrowbile flying abilities. He'd applied for the job of flying the Hammond "Y" which Rogers had at Union Air Terminal, claiming special talents for piloting this type of plane. Like the Arrowbile, it had two controls, rather than three. I told Webster that Sisto was a fine pilot (hoping that he'd learned his lesson at Gila Bend about going beyond the bounds of caution).

Sisto was hired and spent the next few months flying the Hammond, demonstrating its features to prospective buyers (Rogers was the plane's local agent), giving lessons with its dual controls, and hopping sightseer rides. I took a ride with him, but was pretty unimpressed, and never have considered the "Y" much of a design breakthrough.

Sometime later Sisto was hired by American Airlines as a check pilot, riding with crews to observe their proficiency. One day in a DC-4 over Texas, he was sitting on the floor in back of and between the two pilots, and slyly engaged the gust lock. This is a locking device to preclude wind damage to the aircraft while parked on the ground. His intent was to observe the pilot's reaction upon discovering his control surfaces locked in this totally unexpected situation. He got plenty! The plane went into a steep dive, and the pilot put so much pressure on the controls trying to right the situation that Chuck couldn't disengage the mechanism. The

390

passengers were being thrown helter-skelter, and it wasn't until the plane had fallen about 10,000 feet, with only a couple thousand left before hitting the ground, that Chuck got the pilot to loosen his 'death grip', thus permitting him to release the gust lock. There was a helluva fuss over that incident and the final shake-out was the grounding of Sisto. He would never again be permitted to fly in the United States! Well, that incident kinda backs up the *curiosity killed the cat* proverb. Sisto and his forever-itch to see what would happen 'if' had caught up with him again.

I understand that he then went to the Orient, flew for the Chinese for several years, came home and was, strangely, permitted to take up flying again. I've always liked Chuck, but his damn habits surely cost me dearly, and they didn't help American Airlines much either!

During this time the other two Arrowbile pilots, Perrette and Phillips, had been flying their planes around the country for Studebaker. Perrette, after completing a swing around the Midwest, left Arrowbile-2 in Detroit when he was terminated by Studebaker. Phillips flew Arrowbile-3, *"Miss South Bend"*, through the Northeast; Buffalo, New York, Philadelphia and Pittsburgh, making all of the auto shows helping Studebaker promote their 1938 line. He then flew the plane back to South Bend, where it was stored following his dismissal.

Of course, during all of this period I was as involved as ever in the broader aspects of American aviation.

Shortly after World War I, the Aero Club of America folded, and it became evident a new organization to represent the FAI was needed. As such, Porter Adams of Boston organized the National Aeronautic Association (NAA), initially soliciting aviation's big names to head local chapters. Donald Douglas was the first president of our Los Angeles Chapter, destined to become NAA's largest about the time that I became its president. Adams also persuaded Orville Wright to be the Secretary of the Contest Committee, necessitating his signature upon all sanctioning contracts and competing pilot's licenses. This position was honorary for Orville, and the actual work was done by Bill Enyhart using a rubber stamp for Wright's signature. I chuckle today when someone shows me his license *"signed by Orville Wright"*. Close inspection reveals that it's nothing but a rubber-stamp signature, one which I have on the reissue of my earlier FAI license and which I've never put great treasure to!

Like the FAI, the NAA's power was almighty regarding American air meets, races and other competitions, deriving much of its revenues from the various fees assessed. Initially, most of NAA's staff were aero buffs, but in time Charles Horner, a professional administrator, took charge, assisted by Enyhart. He developed a virtual stranglehold upon the NAA's affairs that wasn't altogether welcome by many of us. I personally clashed with Horner while president of our chapter in 1937, and during the 1937 Air Races I discussed this problem with the race's principal sponsors, Fred Crawford of Thompson Products and Lou Greeve of Cleveland Pneumatic Tool. We agreed that the Horner and Enyhart control should be broken, and I volunteered to solicit proxies against them for the NAA convention in Cleveland in January 1938.

This required a tremendous amount of correspondence and personal contact. Janie assisted me, and both TWA and American gave us passes to get around the country easily. It was late in December, 1937, when we left Los Angeles, bound first for Phoenix, when who should board the plane but Eddie Rickenbacker, Eastern Airline's new president. Warmly greeting Janie and myself, "Rick" joined us in a hand of bridge enroute to El Paso while we talked about old times. It reminded me of the flight that he and Jack Frye had made in the DC-1 in 1934. *They demonstrated its unheard-of capabilities by flying it cross-country in 13-hours-and-two-minutes' flying time.*

I was compiling a list of those who might be acceptable to replace Horner: Rickenbacker, Glenn Martin, Fred Crawford, Jimmy Doolittle and so forth, and was personally contacting each of them. In Washington, I met with Bill Enyhart, a man that I liked personally, but his loyalty to Horner dictated his opposition to our plans. He was amassing quite a few proxies which, he told me, he'd vote in favor of Horner unless I could get Doolittle to accept the nomination. Later I mused that Bill already knew that Jimmy would refuse and that I was playing into a 'stacked deck'. But, nonetheless, I continued my efforts and, even after getting Jimmy's turndown, carried the matter to the floor of the convention where our motion failed and Horner was reelected. In the following year, 1939, we were again unsuccessful in breaking the 'old guard's' hold when Enyhart was elected. But in 1940 we succeeded in getting Fred Crawford to the top post. Unfortunately, World War II was imminent, and the heyday of the National Air Races was over.

During our countrywide swing, we visited with the Hoffman's and I got Paul to provide exhibit space for the Arrowbile in the big Air Industry Show in Chicago in January 1938. After putting Janie on a flight home, I went to Detroit to get Arrowbile-2, planning to fly it to Chicago after delivering a paper on the Arrowbile to the SAE (Society of Automotive Engineers) at the Book-Cadillac Hotel. The paper met with much interest and was later published in their journal, but *the Arrowbile was the real hit of the evening.* I'd demonstrated the plane at the airport, and then had driven it downtown, parking it in front of the hotel. Boy, it surely caused a lot of comment!

After arriving in Chicago, I located Paul Emmons, my employee from Santa Monica days, who had just completed his Masters in Aeronautical Engineering at Purdue University. He was then responsible for Purdue's wind tunnel, and my request for help got him the week off. Paul was a husky football-built fellow, and very knowledgeable about the Arrowbile. As at Pan Pacific, his knowledge and strength were a combination invaluable to me. We didn't have any electric hoists. The airplane was its usual 'hit' - but other than that, there wasn't any monetary gain. I couldn't offset the economic slump that the country was in.

Paul later joined Buffalo's Bell Aircraft, the company that Larry Bell built when Consolidated moved to San Diego. Paul was a chief experimental engineer when Bell was building Airacobras (designed around its deadly nose cannon) in World War II, and was also heavily involved in the design of Bell's XP-59A Airacomet, *America's first jet,* in 1942.

After the Chicago show, I flew Arrowbile-2 to South Bend where it joined Number 3 in storage. Hoffman and I then sat down to discuss the future - which didn't look very bright. 1937 had been a bad year for Studebaker, which meant that it was a bad year for Waldo Waterman, too. Hoffman couldn't justify spending any more money on our venture, and that, combined with the work that Schaffer and I had been doing completing Arrowbile-1 and converting Number 4 to an Arrowplane, caused me to ponder the future with skepticism. The more that I thought over the situation, the more convinced I became that *the idea of a "flying automobile" was of little potential* - elusive and unrealizable. Sure, the concept was fascinating and the public eagerly took to it, but simple practicability foretold an impossible goal.

The public expected 'push button' convertibility, and that was simply unattainable. Like Ford's 1958 "Skyliner" steel top convertible, the Arrowbile worked, but the design compromises were so great that it was doomed. The more I became aware of the engineering problems, the more depressed I became. The dream was so far from reality that its myth began seeping into the marrow of my bones. The Arrowbile would always be a compromise - never the best airplane or a perfect car. My plight was summed-up one day when Victor Flemming said, *"Waldo, that thing is no-damn-good. Did your wife ever come home with a can opener and a cockscrew on the same handle? It'd be a lousy corkscrew and a bum can opener. That's what you have here - and people simply aren't going to buy it!"*

I simmered around the collar when Vic first threw that comment at me, but he was right. Even today I believe that the flying automobile is a dream forever doomed. There have been many attempts, and I'm certain there'll be more, but there's one thing I know: *Arrowbiles 2 and 3 were the best efforts ever. To date, anyway, they are the only ones that ever flew coast-to-coast and performed as they were designed to do!*

Musing on these thoughts, and with Paul Hoffman's assurance that we wouldn't go bankrupt, I headed for home to finish the work on the remaining two planes.

Late that summer, on one of my trips to Studebaker's assembly plant in Vernon, I'd just picked up a check from Hoffman and had gone into the parts department to get a fairly heavy item. A sharp pain hit me in the gut when I picked it up. I recovered a bit, but by the time I got to the car where Carol was waiting, momentary nausea overcame me. We continued on to our dinner date with the Harlow's in Pasadena. But I was feeling so lousy that Carol drove me home right after dinner. Gosh, I felt sick. In the morning I felt even worse, and Carol had the doctor come right over. He diagnosed a ruptured appendix.

They rushed me to the hospital and operated. But chances of recovery were slim as the "wonder drug," penicillin, was unknown then. It looked like I'd suffer the same fate from the same cause as had befallen Glenn Curtiss nine years earlier. But the superlative care from my physician, Dr. Albert Arkush, finally pulled me through. That first operation was followed by four more as the infection spread to other parts of my body. After 13 blood transfusions and a year's hospitalization, they fi-

394

nally said that I was well enough to go home. Gads, I had the scars of cuts and holes all over my torso - but I was alive, alive!

After that terrible bout, I was broke. There were no funds coming in and if it hadn't been for Carol, Jane and my aunts helping out, I'm not sure just how we would have managed.

By the time I was getting ambulatory, Frank Schaffer had completed the Arrowplane and had it ready for test flying. That was something I always did, but not this time - I was still as weak as a newborn lamb. Jerry Phillips was available, however, and he did the flying as I watched from the car. We'd made some improvements in this version, replacing the V-belts with a geared drive unit, but, for some reason or other, it never performed well. I felt somewhat helpless and was sure that if I'd been doing the flying we could have determined the trouble. I did think that a better propeller would have helped, plus the gear drive could be improved. But we finally said, 'To hell with it!', and stored it away in the Colorado Street building.

As I was so damn weak and had negligible prospects for selling any more Arrowbiles, I made the decision to wrap-up the corporation. We returned what inventory we could to suppliers and held an auction that disposed of most of the physical assets and equipment. We kept a couple of Arrowbiles still under construction, plus some specialized parts and fittings only useful to someone making that same type of aircraft, which was no one else!

The original Vidal airplane, NS-13, had been all-but-destroyed when a flood swept Bolling Field. What remained was assigned by the Commerce Department to other projects. The contract under which it was built spelled-out the government's right to the plane's design, but the fact that it lacked type certification meant that it couldn't be put into production. Even though the craft had passed all the tests (except the final drop test of the revised landing gear - which it had passed with the original landing gear) and had never been penalized on this score, the government did not seem to want to proceed. It appeared that their 'eggs' were in the Stearman-Hammond 'basket'.

We did proceed with the Arrowbile's type certification. The Studebaker engine was certified No. 178 in 1937, and the special wheels were issued certification No. 75. The entire airplane had been authorized in June 1938 for the final flight tests and was designated as Model W5A.

We had little thought of any problems in completing these tests successfully. But that was prior to the financial problems causing Studebaker's retrenchment, and of my own physical collapse.

If everything had gone as planned, Studebaker was to move the manufacturing facilities from Santa Monica to South Bend. They'd already set aside factory space, and regardless of the merits of the Arrowbile, this move would have put Studebaker in an admirable position for the tremendous upsurge in aircraft manufacturing caused by the impending war. But, unfortunately, all this never came to pass!

While I was recuperating from my surgeries, the last of the prewar National Air Races was held in Cleveland. It was the first that I'd missed since 1926. I think that there are few who have attended as many as I. I missed being at that 1939 affair very much and was most pleased when Warren Carey, always one of the race's officials, came to my bedside and gave me a full briefing on all that had gone on.

During those interminable months, I had lots of time - far too much, in fact - to think of my past career. So many of my decisions seemed to have been the wrong ones, or at least their results would indicate so. As I lay there, I tried to analyze and reevaluate my outlook, perspective and approach to life, thinking ahead to the day when I'd be up and about again. The more I thought over my failures, the more I came to understand that, too often, I'd set my sights too high, attempting to accomplish things that were simply beyond either my capabilities or my resources. Maybe my goals could have been attained by the teamwork of many; but being such a loner may have precluded my success. I ruminated over the Billy Mitchell - Thomas-Morse affair, the Navy's torpedo plane competition, the air mail fiasco, the irony of the Flex Wing, and finally, the elusive dream of the flying automobile.

I thought of these things while faced with the reality of making a living and paying off all those medical bills. I realized that the post-recovery world for Waldo Waterman would be much different.

396

Chapter 8

1940 - 1944

That Old Song Again - Another War and I'm Teaching For "The Wild, Blue Yonder"

HERE I was, five years after my first involvement with the Vidal competition, with virtually nothing to show for it. However, in the meantime I'd become something of a landlord; since moving into the 5th & Colorado building, I'd been carrying-on a sideline real estate operation. Whenever there was a vacancy in the building, folks seemed to come to me about it as I was the principal tenant. Never one to miss an opportunity, I'd work out a tentative sublease arrangement. Then, I'd hustle over to the owner and lease the space for my normal rate, thus making a few bucks on the difference. In effect, I was performing a building management function, which by 1940 saw me 'leasing' all but the main corner showroom. This handsome space, with high ceilings, tile floors and huge chandeliers, was leased by the State of California for an employment office. They, naturally, insisted upon dealing directly with the building's owner, the Capitol Company, Bank of America's real estate division.

As noted, during my illness the factory had been all but shut down. The only thing going-on was Frank Schaffer's work on Arrowbile-1 and the Arrowplane conversion. Janie had gone to work for a fixed base operator at Clover Field. Her scant income, added to what little I was making from the subleasing operation, wasn't enough to keep ends together. I'd soon have to be making an income myself.

While still hospitalized, Max Harlow had told me about a program just getting started at Pasadena JC, and apparently at many other schools nation-wide: a *Civilian Pilot Training* program (CPT) instituted by the CAA. The students were to get their ground instruction at college, and then their flight instruction at a nearby airfield. After Max told me about this, I mulled over its possibilities and became quite intrigued. When I was getting ambulatory, under the urgings of Dr. Arkush, Max told me that there might be an opening in the program teaching, since the present instructor was not doing a good job. However, I had reservations because I didn't want a repeat of the monotony that I'd found at Berkeley in 1917. Regardless, this was an opportunity to make a living doing something that I knew about, so I set up an appointment with Dr. Sexton, the school department's superintendent.

That day found me still very weak, and upon arriving at the Board of Education I was dismayed to discover that the superintendent's office was upstairs. Gritting my teeth and summoning all of my strength, I negotiated those stairs, holding cane in one hand and grasping the rail with the other. When I reached the top, I was really tuckered-out, but I reasoned that it wouldn't look good entering Sexton's office with a cane, so, after catching my wind, I leaned it against the wall and almost strode into his office. I surely wasn't going to be any cripple looking for a job!

The interview was satisfactory if perfunctory, and upon leaving I had high hopes. So, it was good news a few days later when Max told me that I got the job. I was to teach two groups of ten students, an hour for each group, daily from 10 AM to noon.

The next week, I was apprehensive walking towards my new classroom. Would it be like 1917 all over again? After I entered the room, though, those fears soon disappeared. I discovered a group of starry-eyed kids wanting to learn flying for the joy and excitement of it, not because there was a war going on!

I immediately fused a synergism with these students. Their eagerness to learn coupled with my deeply-felt desire to teach them warmed me. And the fact that there were a couple of girls in the class seemed to

398

heighten this feeling even more. They sure-as-hell weren't going to go off to a shooting war! Those kids seemed to take to flying like a duck takes to water, and these many years later I'm still in touch with several of them. Quite a few of that first group went on to significant aviation achievement.

By the end of that summer of 1940, I was weakening again, and during a three-week vacation I had my seventh operation to clear out some more patches of infection. Laid up during recovery, I was buoyed by the visits of several students as the bond of friendship grew between us.

As we got into the second term, the students found themselves confronted with heavier aircraft and even a bit of aerobatic training. I was successful in expanding the primary student body to 30, plus a group of ten in a more advanced category. The college appreciated this because the government paid them in proportion to how many students were enrolled. Of course, it meant more money for me, too, because I was paid based upon the number of classroom hours I taught. Frankly, in time this program grew into quite a money maker for me, far-more-so than the 'temporary' nature had first indicated.

During this time, the Franklin Aircraft Engine Company (successor to the automobile company) came out with a revolutionary six-cylinder, horizontally-opposed, 120-hp engine. I felt it would be ideal for the Arrowplane in place of the much-heavier Studebaker engine, greatly improving performance. I then made a deal with Hoffman for possession of the Arrowplane, and being better-off financially, I ordered one of these engines.

From then on, I had virtually no contact with Paul Hoffman - but I always treasured his friendship. For many years I followed his extraordinary career as he stepped from private business to become one of our country's greatest public servants. He was administrator of the Marshall Plan in its critical years, 1948-1950, for which modern Europe has so much to thank him; he led the massive Ford Foundation; and later he directed United Nations aids programs from 1959 until his health forced retirement in 1972. When he passed-on in 1974, I knew that the world had lost a great man, and I had lost a true friend. (1891-1974, 83 years old)

As the CPT program continued, it entered its third phase - cross-country flying. Ground school continued both at the college and the field, and there were an ever-increasing number of students. As a result, by the spring of 1941, virtually all of my time was taken-up in this activity. When I reached the time limit of my capabilities, I got the school board to add a couple of my best students as staff. They both taught, and completed their more advanced instruction. Their split-duties earned them split-pay. They got half of what I was paid; I, the other half. This part-time teaching by my staff snowballed, making me substantial proportional earnings .

It wasn't all gravy, though. There was a tremendous amount of paperwork dealing with the Federal government. Thus, I had one of my best girl students, Jerry Britnall, join me full-time as my secretary while still completing her training. As we moved further into 1941, I found that I was enjoying every minute except for the nagging realization that Uncle Sam wasn't doing this solely for altruistic reasons. The rumblings of war were molding our program!

The ever-growing sophistication of the course material brought to bear all of my past training and experience: aircraft design, engineering and manufacturing, plus the stringent demands of instrument flying. I must say that my ability to take my students into the farthest realms of flight instruction resulted in graduates a peg-or-two above the norm. I was even called upon to help neighboring schools groom their students for the rigors of the CAA tests. In later correspondence with the FAA, I discovered that one of those students had been Najeeb Halaby. He was then the FAA's director, and later heavily involved in the aborted American SST project, and president of Pan-Am. During my presidency of the Early Birds in 1964, he was our guest at the annual banquet and particularly liked talking about those times in 1941, plus meeting an idol of his, Matty Laird, the builder of many fine aircraft.

Unfortunately, my bliss was jolted that fall when the Capitol Company advised me that my lease was being terminated. They'd sold the building! This was to be quite a financial blow as I'd lose the subleasing income and my own space, too, though by now I was using it only to store what little was left of the Waterman Arrowplane Company. Racking my brains over this unexpected situation, I remembered that long ago the bank had told me that I'd have first-refusal-rights upon the sale of the property. So, even though I was in no condition to exercise them, I decided to play a little poker.

400

Since I had accumulated some cash during the 'good times' I was experiencing at Pasadena JC, I told the bank that I wanted to buy the building. I then waited with a great deal of apprehension, for their response. A few days later they told me that if I bettered the current offer by $500, I could have it. They even let me to put up only $5,000-down with the balance payable over ten years! *"You've got a deal!"* I exclaimed, and immediately began to raise the money, having about half myself. I went to each of the tenants and told them that I'd discount their rent 10 percent if they'd pay the next twelve months in advance. I raised slightly more than $1,000, and with a personal note borrowed the remaining $1,500. Then, I was the owner - that is, I and the bank!

For once, my timing was perfect. The war was imminent, one of my tenants went broke, and so I had space available when Douglas Aircraft needed it. From then-on I never had any vacancies, and the wartime demand greatly increased the value of the property.

Following December 7, 1941, when we entered the war, all flying of private planes was prohibited within 150 miles of the coast, automatically curtailing the CPT activities. I had to hustle in order to find a spot to carry on, and in scouting around found a likely location. It was at Silver (dry) Lake, three miles or so north of Baker, in the middle of the Mojave Desert. In those days Baker was only a wide spot on the road going to but another wide spot, Las Vegas. There were only a couple of fourth-rate motels there, and a major problem would be the housing and feeding of our students, but I figured that we'd work that out.

The war caused the program to change in several respects. The name became the *CAA War Training Service*, and each student chose courses designated as either Air Force, Army, Navy or Glider. Military-type uniforms appeared, along with a semblance of military training. Although this wasn't altogether to my liking, the financial rewards seemed to soothe this philosophical impediment!

Our staff had grown considerably, with administrative, military and physical education personnel in addition to our regular classroom and flight instructors. There were only four air-conditioned rooms in the motel, one of which I snagged for myself. We erected temporary barracks, and moved one of the classrooms out from Pasadena. (During the Thirties, these temporary classrooms were common sights in the wake of the tremendous damage caused by the 1933 Long Beach earthquake.)

In the meantime, we cajoled Baker's townsfolk into helping bed-down many students. Feeding this large group - 50 or 60 students plus staff - was done by about the only restaurant Baker then boasted.

Pasadena Junior College C.A.A. War Training Service - Baker, California - 1942

The logistics of starting up operations in this forbidding and remote spot were formidable. But after erecting a repair and instruction hangar, the planes were tied down outside, and we were 'open for business' in late January of 1942. However, I'd lost my assistant, Jerry, who'd made instructor and thus became the assistant-coordinator and an instructor at a similar school in Texas. Jane Scott, a graduate of a nearby program, then assumed my office chores - running things in Pasadena and visiting Baker once a month to catch up on things there.

By this time, there were many other schools operating under this CAA program. Ours was the largest within Region Six, which encompassed the 20 units in California, Arizona, Nevada and Utah. Needing better representation in Washington, we organized the National Association of Colleges and Universities in Civilian Pilot Training, Region Six, for which I was elected the regional director. I was now journeying to

Washington several times annually to keep abreast of things, and to put in my two bits worth on impending curriculum and adminstrative changes.

As the war progressed, our program took on more and more trappings of the military. In fact, several of our graduates were already teaching in civilian-operated military flying schools. Shortly after the first of 1943, I decided that I'd had enough of the program, the commuting, and of that damn, hot and dry, Mojave Desert! There were several things that I wanted to work on at my Santa Monica shop, and I therefore tendered my resignation in April. As it turned out (did I already know it was coming?) the entire program was cut back soon thereafter, with the Armed Services assuming virtual total responsibility.

In these days I was reading about Igor Sikorsky's new helicopter. He'd first developed his VS-300 model in 1939, and had it operational by 1941. Ever since 1919 I'd been intrigued with vertical lift, having done considerable work on it over the years. Now I wanted to go further along that line. Also, I had some work which I wanted to do on an automatic transmission I'd dreamed-up during work on the Arrowbile.

I was cogitating on these ideas in Santa Monica one day when the phone rang. It was Bill Stout wondering, *"Just what the hell are you up to these days, Waldo?"*

Just a few days earlier I'd read that Bill was building his own version of a helicopter. So, I replied, *"...just tinkering around on some vertical lift ideas of my own, Bill."* Well, he asked me to catch a plane east right away so we could have a discussion. His operation had just been bought by Consolidated-Vultee (ConVair), and he thought that we could do a thing or two together. Before hanging up I said *"OK!"* for I heard bells ringing. Here was the well-financed opportunity that I'd been waiting for. It would enable me to do research on several ideas that were interesting, me and at the same time work with Bill Stout, an old friend for whom I had tremendous respect.

Mentioning Bill reminds me about the time when I was president of our Southern California Chapter of the NAA. We'd invited him to be our guest speaker, knowing that his talks were always interesting and provocative. He'd just built the first rear-engine production passenger car in Detroit, the revolutionary *"Scarab"*, causing much comment among the auto moguls, little of it favorable, and he was driving one of the nine that he eventually built on a demonstration tour out West (see page 412). It was surely ahead of its time, similar to Volkswagen's Microbus of twenty years later. It sold for around $5,000, a princely sum in those Depression-weary days, and even Bill's famous ballyhooing wasn't drumming up many customers. That was incidental, however, for the evening was a huge success as we savored his humor and testy anecdotes. I've already touched upon Bill's early aircraft developments, including his work with Henry Ford, and there's always more to say about him. He had a fantastic and fascinating ability to turn doodles into practical inventions and mechanical contraptions. *He patented hundreds, and eventually had more technical patents than almost any American save Edison or Land!* It seems strange today that Edison is known to virtually every American, while Bill Stout is lost in our historic wasteland.

Since I am mentioning my chapter presidential days, we had another memorable meeting in early 1937. I arranged for Carl Squier, Lockheed's sales manager, and Harry Wetzel, Douglas's general manager, to be our co-speakers. Wetzel was an old friend, ever since my Jenny-building days. Each had a good sense-of-humor, though being virtually opposite in personalities and philosophies. I therefore anticipated a rousing good time listening to their sparring. At this time, Lockheed's slogan was, *"Look to Lockheed for Leadership,"* a sore challenge to giant Douglas, then the industry's leader with its mighty DC series.

This was the same time that Amelia Earhart was preparing for her globe-girdling flight. She was readying her Lockheed Electra at Union Air Terminal, in spite of the pleas of her good friend, Louise Thaden, about the inherent dangers in her quest. Our meeting was only a few days prior to her takeoff, and I asked that she be our Guest of Honor. Fortunately, the meeting turned-out just as I'd hoped. Squier and Wetzel provided the main course, rare and well-done, and Amelia, the dessert, winning everyone's heart. Little did we suspect that this would be the last time that most of us would ever see her, for her flight west was aborted in Hawaii by a ground loop. It wouldn't be until June when she took off again, this time heading east following the long Equator route, leading to her final flight, disappearing over the southwest Pacific. Words that she'd spoken earlier seem so appropriate now. *"Even though I have lost, the adventure was worthwhile...My life has been very happy, and I don't mind contemplating its end in the midst of it."*

404

But back to 1943 and my meeting with Stout in Dearborn. He went into considerable detail about what his small engineering development organization had been working on. He had merged it into giant ConVair at about the same time Reub Fleet joined Consolidated to Vultee. Reub had occasionally stopped off to see Bill, intrigued (as I was) as to what he was up to. Wanting Stout's genius as part of his organization, Reub bought Stout out in much the same way as Henry Ford had done almost 20 years earlier.

Bill went on ConVair's payroll as director of research, and his son-in-law, Johnny Fisher, was named the group's general manager. *At that time Bill had four projects underway: a low-cost aircraft engine, a helicopter engine, a stainless steel airplane, and a helicopter.* All of these greatly intrigued me. It didn't take much talking for Bill to convince me to join him as their chief engineer. I got a year's contract, plus the proviso that ConVair would buy all of Waterman Arrowplane's remaining assets, including everything at Santa Monica and South Bend, and my Franklin-powered Arrowplane, which I'd now completed.

Arrowbile-1, converted to a non-roadable Arrowplane - with horizontally opposed 6-cylinder, 120-hp Franklin engine

405

This would leave me owning virtually nothing from that era. Also, when we attempted to locate what was at South Bend, we made a sad discovery. Arrowbiles 2 and 3 had been destroyed, apparently when the Army took over Studebaker's proving grounds where they were stored.

Stout's low-cost aircraft engine was to be used for powering the *"Skycar"*, the airplane that they were developiong. This project was being managed by Julius Dusevoir, a superb machinist but a prima-donna of the first order who, we discovered, couldn't back up claims for certain of his ideas. This engine was touted as a marvel that'd *"weigh 100 pounds, develop 100 hp, sell for $100 and in one hour, a man with one wrench could disassemble it and then put it back together in another hour!"*

Victor Raviolli was in charge of the second project, a 130-hp helicop-ter engine being developed for the Air Force. He was a brilliant chap possessing one disconcerting trait - a heavy suspicion of my 'old fash-ioned' engineering know-how! I had to enlist my old friend, Cornelius van Ranst, to assist me in communicating with him. Later, Ravi would be credited with designing Ford's overhead-valve V-8 engine, and went on to become chief engineer at American Motors.

The third project, the "Skycar II", (a name Stout had first used in 1931), sounded like a flying automobile, but it wasn't. It was a somewhat conventional high-wing monoplane with a twin-boom tail similar to the Hammond "Y", but was built of stainless steel. By this time, though, they realized the impracticability of stainless steel, and were changing it to Duralumin.

The fourth project, the helicopter, fascinated me the most. The mockups revealed a very advanced design, one in which I was itching to have a hand. Additionally, there were several less-important items under discussion and development, all which would fully challenge my interests.

Stout's organization was located on Telegraph Road in Dearborn, where were the drafting and design rooms plus the administrative offices; the mockups and experimental work were carried out in a shop a couple of miles away which Bill had used ever since his parting with Ford. Also, they were leasing a second shop, fully equipped with the latest machines and equipment, permitting us full-latitude in creating almost anything that we could dream up.

After leasing our place in Santa Monica Canyon, Carol and I drove to Michigan, checking into the Dearborn Inn. We soon found that this wasn't to our liking, and we were spending almost every weekend at the Stout's lovely place on Green Lake. Shortly, the van Ransts helped us locate an apartment near where they lived, but its thin walls soon caused us to look elsewhere. Carol finally found more suitable quarters in Franklin Village, but by now it was getting into winter, and our habit of sleeping with the windows open didn't set too well with the landlord! Franklin Village, though, was about midway between Dearborn and Green Lake, and we stayed there until our departure the following year.

At the labs, due to my broad background and title of chief engineer, I got involved in all the projects. But, because of my aeronautical background, Raviolli reasoned that I didn't know enough to advise him on engine design. Therefore, I had to resort to a backhand method of getting my comments to him since he'd threatened to quit if I continued 'interfering.' Ravi worshipped van Ranst, so we retained Van as our consultant and thus decoyed around Ravi by having Van tell him whatever I was concerned about!

There was one problem, however, that neither Ravi, Van or I could lick. The engine had air-cooled cylinders, similar to Wright J4B's, of cast aluminum with integral cooling fins and a cast iron sleeve shrunk into the cylinder's bore. The engine's design required that a heavy shear load be transmitted through these castings. This resulted in fractures which eventually caused this design to be scrapped. It wasn't any fault of Ravi's, though, - it was simply that the state-of-the-art in casting alloys and cylinder design then was behind our aspirations.

At this time, van Ranst was with Ford, where he'd redesigned a 12-cylinder water-cooled aircraft engine into a very successful eight-cylinder tank engine - the war's major American tank engine. It was made at Ford's massive River Rouge plant, where Van was technical manager, and he invited me for a plant tour. Fully expecting to trudge through a messy factory, I was surprised to be met by Van with a Lincoln Continental convertible, top down, in which we toured in grand style.

In addition to the four principal projects at the Stout labs, I discovered that they had a couple of roadable airplane concepts being worked on. And I suspect that these may have been much of the reason for my involvement. By this time, however, I'd already cooled on this idea and tried ducking any further commitment, though not with total success.

The one project still fascinating me was the helicopter, and one aspect of its development particularly intrigued me. In the early 1920's I'd first become interested in the plastic forming of compound curves for aircraft structures. This was a long, long time before the fiberglass and plastic resins that are so common today - I was thinking more along the lines of what the Loughead brothers had developed in Santa Barbara using thin wood veneer and adhesive layups. Now, in 1943, knowledge had advanced considerably and the plastics age was brimming with myriad potentials. Thus, I set up a small laboratory at Dearborn, equipping it with an array of apparatus and assigning an employee that appeared knowledgeable in plastics to work with me. One of the projects we worked on was the fabrication of the tail boom used on both the helicopter and the Skycar, using an internal mold covered with fiberglass and polyester resin. We also experimented with the use of thermoplastics for nose sections, fairings, wheel pants and large fuselage midsection panels. However, due to the short-comings of my assistant plus my own limited time, we never made much headway. It was somewhat of a hobby and sideline as far as I was concerned. Also, the state-of-the-art in plastic composites was still quite primitive, and as nothing compared with today's *"advanced composites"* of boron and graphite - something that Ryan Aeronautical did breakthrough work on in the late 1960's.

During this time, Julius Dusevoir, working on the "$100 engine," developed a patented way to join two butt-ended shafts with a coupling that had its containment milled into it. Supposedly, it could be used for attaching wheels to axles, axles to axles, etc, and he'd designed the crankshafts for both the helicopter engine and the "$100 engine" incorporating this joint. It enabled the crankshaft to be assembled in pieces using standard ball or roller bearings (instead of babbitt) and appeared to have tremendous potentials. As testament to our faith in it, we even used the Dusevoir Joint for attaching the helicopter rotor to its vertical power shaft. We got astounding results testing these joints, and ordered a machine for producing them on a production basis, setting it up in Plant 2. But after we'd made several joints on the machine, we made a disturbing discovery. Upon testing, they didn't measure-up in any way to the handmade ones. This puzzled me, and I started to ask questions. A study of the prototype joints revealed that they'd been very carefully *hand-lapped* to tolerances impossible to obtain with a machine. Well, at that the en-

408

tire Dusevoir joint program evaporated into thin air, soon followed by the engine project for much of the same reason: we found that we couldn't make many of its parts on a machine with any reasonable economy.

Most of my time, however, was spent on the helicopter project. It was in the mockup stage when I arrived, and I immediately got involved with everything in its structural design, except the main rotor and gear boxes, which Timken-Detroit Axle were doing. I designed most of the main structure, plus the tail rotor and its adjustable mechanism. But we realized that we'd need an expert from the autogiro industry to design the main rotor assembly. Therefore we hired Burke Wilford as consultant. He was one of the vertical-lift experimenters in Philadelphia. From then on, he came over bi-weekly and worked on the design of the main rotor, its hub and drive mechanism.

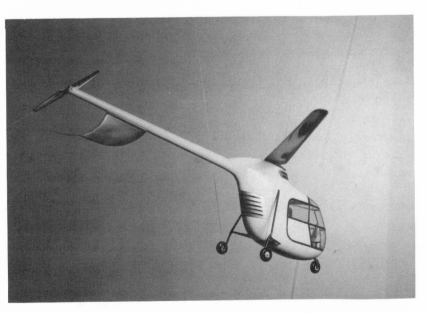

ConVair Stout-Waterman Helicopter Model - 1943-44

I was also involved in the design of two types of main rotor blades. One was a foamed material covered with wing fabric; the other plymetal, very thin Duralumin backed with spruce veneer to prevent oil-can-

409

ning and wrinkles. Both of these were built around a long, tapered chrome-molybdenum core.

We chose a couple of Franklin's latest engines to power the helicopter. These were variations of their six-cylinder, 150-hp models designed for vertical rather than horizontal use. I went up to Syracuse to observe and approve their final tests. One was then installed in the helicopter and we took it to ConVair's Stinson factory in Wayne, Michigan, for testing. Stinson was managed by Ed Shelton, whom I'd known before as Menasco's general manager, but I'd never seen eye-to-eye with. However, now that we were both working for ConVair, I'd best keep our relationship at least 'workable,' even though he was a production man with little use for research and development.

With the helicopter tethered, we began the testing, but the rotor vibration was so great that it almost shook everything to pieces. Wilford's design wasn't worth a damn, and it was 'back to the drawing board!'

At this time there were only three successful American helicopter designs - Sikorsky, Bell and Frank Piasecki in Philadelphia. *(Cierva's Autogiro Company of America had the basic patents in this field.)* We would have been in very select company if we'd had a good rotor design.

Both Stout and the powers-that-be at ConVair, San Diego, still felt that the flying automobile had promise, and in spite of my resistance they insisted upon working on it. We now had Arrowbile-1 at Dearborn, minus its wings, and Bill was certain that it could be successfully driven down the road trailing its folded wings. Try as I might, I couldn't dissuade him, so one day we rigged-up a set of dummy wings and sent him off for home. Well, the road to Green Lake is a heavily-travelled truck route, and it wasn't long until I received a call from him, wildly exclaiming that he'd almost been blown off the highway and *"I'll be damned if I'll drive the damn thing again!"* Reminded me a bit of Rosamond!

Another concept which we worked on was a variation of the Arrowplane, using the flying wing idea but incorporating flaps. It was very tough to use flaps in a tailless aircraft due to the pitching moments set up by differing flap positions, but after a lot of experimenting and relocation of the design-modified flaps, I was successful in making it work. The result evoked interest in San Diego, and they soon sent one of their best test-pilots to fly this *"Waterman flying wing with flaps."* Apparently it had a considerable effect upon aircraft that ConVair was presently designing

410

- delta wing planes with elevon controls. Later, this sort of design appeared on their Sea Dart, followed by the F-102 and F-106.

After I'd settled-in at Dearborn I contacted Eddie Allenbaugh. I knew he had an inventive bent and I suggested that he join us. He came east, hankering to carry out some of the flying automobile ideas that I knew he'd been secretly working on when he was with me. But everything came to a screeching-halt when he refused to sign the patent waiver required of all ConVair employees. I understood his reluctance to part with something that he thought he'd created, but I could also understand the corporation's claims, because they were providing the funds and the facilities. I was sorry to lose Eddie's potential contributions.

In early 1944 I received a letter from a reporter in Philadelphia, enclosing a greatly-embellished account of a wonderful aircraft invention that'd supposedly solve all of our problems. Called the *"Spratt Wing,"* it could be built cheaply, was automatically stable and would do virtually all the things we'd been seeking for the private plane owner - or so the claims went. It consisted of a very lightweight, flying boat-type hull suspended from the wing by a flexible joint atop a pylon. This enabled the craft's wing to tip fore and aft or up and down sideways - the sole and entire control concept! There were no tail fins, elevators or ailerons - simply a tipping wing attached to control levers. It was powered by a 65-hp Continental engine connected by a long shaft to a pusher prop. After reading this, I mused some wild thoughts and replied (tongue in cheek), *"If your Mr. Spratt can do all of these things, we certainly want to get together with him. We're looking for good ideas, and he surely sounds like he has the world by the tail on a downhill pull."* Much to my surprise, Spratt was on the phone about a week later, wanting to come over and show off his invention with photos and movies. We set up an appointment.

At about this same time, ConVair's engineering vice president, Mac Laddon, swung through Dearborn and didn't like what he saw, summarily firing Stout's son-in-law, John Fisher, and putting Ed Shelton in his stead. At that I said to Bill, *"There goes Stout Research!"*. The climate of fruitful research and development we had would be far different from the penny-pinching production environment which I was sure that Shelton would institute. The close relationship that Bill and John and I'd had, transcending a normal eight-to-five day, was destroyed. There'd be no more after-hours and weekends spent jawboning over questions and

411

Bill Stout and his Scarab, and me and my Arrowbile, Santa Monica, 1937

problems. But maybe that was what San Diego wanted, knowing how close we three were. They surely succeeded, completely knocking the wind out of our sails!

The development activities under Shelton now slanted away from aircraft and onto a Greyhound bus chassis project. It was to utilize aircraft-type welded steel construction, and be powered with the Franklin air-cooled engine, all of which was interesting, but really not down my alley.

Complicating matters, Spratt arrived, and his demonstration seemed to prove all of his claims! Bill got excited, insisted that I hire him and, though unenthusiastic, I consented. However, from then on, I dragged-my-heels implementing his ideas, which earned me the displeasure of both Stout and San Diego. Finally, I was pressured into bringing Spratt's original machine to Dearborn to develop into a flyable craft that we could fly over Green Lake, near Stout's home.

412

When this machine arrived, I looked it over carefully and soon perceived his secret. He had the structure so whittled down that it at best measured up to only half of Stout's axiom, *"The goal is to simplicate and add more lightness."* There was so damn little structure remaining that it would be able to fly only in smooth air in a non-maneuvering condition! It was so light that one of the critical parts had a load factor of only one-and-a-half, so low that any sudden movement would cause its failure.

So this climate of innovative retrenchment, combined with the advent of the Spratt Wing, put me into a more and more untenable position. The more I knew of the Spratt concept, the more it seemed best to try it out first on a Stinson test-bed vehicle. But as project after project was lopped-off in favor of the Greyhound and Spratt projects, I was overruled again and again. Management would brook no interim steps in getting Spratt's idea flying!

It was obvious to me that Spratt's concept depended upon air that was absolutely still and stable so as not to upset his craft, which depended so much upon its extremely low center-of-gravity. I was certain that any turbulence or violent maneuver would make it uncontrollable. But the more I protested, the more suspect I became. I'd already been overridden by San Diego about pursuing the roadable airplane, and I am sure my continuing contrariness on this made me a burr under Mac Laddon's saddle. Therefore, in spite of my opinions the decision was made to develop a totally new Spratt aircraft, and, upon its completion several months later, Skycar IV was taken to San Diego for testing and demonstration. Hah! Its performance was so marginal that the whole project was soon cancelled, to the tune of hundreds-of-thousands-of-dollars washed down the drain.

Spratt's theory was very interesting, and had appeal to others. Vincent Bendix had dropped a bundle in it before Spratt approached us. And, after spending that time with us and ConVair, San Diego, Spratt went on to Boeing, Seattle. At none of these places was he able to make the theory work successfully, and I understand that he is now back in Philadelphia. His idea is similar to one that has become popular in hang gliding - the Rogallo glider (Francis M. Rogallo, Wing Patent, 1951). At least one aircraft manufacturer, Ryan, used this concept in their interesting line of "Flex Wing" craft.

413

When Mac Laddon put Ed Shelton in charge, it pretty much spelled 'curtains' to the projects that interested me. Laddon especially saw little future in the helicopter. And since we were unable to get a good main rotor design, he axed it. He thought that we were wasting our money tinkering with plastic airplanes and components, and shelved that, too. The helicopter engine problems, and the truth of Dusevoir's "miracle joint" only made matters worse. Then, about when my contract was up for renewal, ConVair announced that the Stout and Stinson facilities in Michigan were to be moved to their Avco plant in Nashville. Well, that clinched it for Carol and I. We'd had enough of the Midwest's climate and ConVair's corporate logic, and I told Bill that I'd be returning to Santa Monica. That news seemed to dishearten him very much, and he soon also decided not to move to Nashville, in effect giving the coup-de-grace to Stout Research.

For me, the final disappointment came when we completed the new cantilever wing for the Arrowplane. After attaching it to the fuselage, the craft was sent to Stinson's plant for final touch-up and upholstering. I was looking forward to its flight tests, convinced that the performance would be far superior. But with all of the shuffle of moving to Nashville, coinciding with my resignation, I never did see it fly or hear of its performance. Sometime later, hoping to acquire it, I contacted ConVair and could only learn that it'd been shipped to Nashville and then, seemingly, vanished. I would surely like to know what became of it.

The helicopter project disappeared into thin air, too. When everything was being wrapped up, it was given to a ConVair engineer that, I understand, lived in Florida, and I heard nothing more of it.

I would guess that 'ole-rough-and-tough' Mac Laddon was now licking his chops. He'd sure-as-hell put the finishing touches to Stout Research, something which he'd never wanted in the first place. It's interesting, though, that after all of Laddon's derogatory comments and actions regarding helicopters and plastics, he later became a director of Palo Alto's Hiller Helicopter, and put his son into the fiberglass fishing rod business in San Diego. Then, to top that off, in 1955 we became *next-door neighbors* on Point Loma!

Although wartime, I had plenty of gas coupons due to my association with Stout Research, and Carol and I drove tandem for home. We planned to stop enroute in Ogden, Utah, where Dr. Arkush was stationed, for some remedial surgery. When we got on the highway headed west, it was surprising to see so few cars. We would often go for an hour and see only one or two. The country was deep into the war effort, and from the sight of things, totally committed to it.

Dr. Arkush was now a Navy Captain, and he placed me in a civilian hospital and operated on my hernia while Carol stayed at their home. When I was up and about again, I surely wasn't fit for driving, so we arranged for a young couple to drive my car on to Santa Monica while Carol drove me leisurely to San Francisco, where we stayed with our old friends, Skip and Virginia Warner, for a couple of weeks. Then it was down California's spectacular coastal Route 1, hugging the Pacific, to home.

Thus ended my only extended time away from California. It had been a rich, full, and interesting experience, even if it was not very profitable. But more than anything else, we were richer from our intimate relationship with the Stouts. Our friendship with Bill and Alma would continue for many years.

Chapter 9

1944 - 1953

Fisherman, Land Developer, House Builder - and Having a Ball

BACK in California after the ConVair debacle, I gradually started a new lifestyle, and more-or-less retired. As we'll see, a financial windfall helped my transition to a less hectic, more satisfying and relaxing pace. I was never too far from flying or aeronautics, though, and these years were punctuated by many aviation activities.

During our time in Michigan, Douglas Aircraft had taken over all of my building, except for the state's employment offices. Since I wanted to continue several research projects, I leased a place in nearby Ocean Park and set up *Waterman Research Engineering Co.* to work on a vertical lift concept I had in mind. It differed considerably from typical helicopters. I also continued my work on the automatic transmission that I'd started for the Arrowbile.

I didn't have much of an organization: just myself, an older model maker that'd come west following Stout's dismantling, a draftsmen moonlighting from Douglas, and my cousin, Homer Wood. Homer, a graduate of Cal Tech, had been chief engineer at Menasco and was the one who'd told me what to expect from Shelton. He was now with Garrett, helping to develop their revolutionary small jet engine. Later he'd establish his own consulting organization.

The work I'd done with Studebaker and around Detroit convinced me that the automatic transmission was the coming thing for automobiles. I thought that there'd be quite a market for a unit smaller and less-costly than those already used by GM and Chrysler.

I proceeded to build a workable, full-scale prototype, but it vibrated too damn much, and after spending quite a bit of time and about $3,000 on it, we finally had to call it quits.

It was about this time that the Waterman Ranch reentered my life. At first it was a bit of a headache, but eventually it gave me the first real measure of financial security that I'd ever had.

My grandfather had developed a rich silver mine in the 1880's, and had homesteaded a section of land (one mile square) across the Mojave River from where he built the stamping mill and miners' housing, a settlement originally called *Waterman Station*. The property lay dormant following the collapse of the silver market, until around 1908 when my adventurous Aunt Abby Lou Waterman tried to make it into a model farm, raising alfalfa in the fertile river bottom.

Remember, following my crackup in 1910, I had been sent there to convalesce from my broken ankles. In later years, still deeply attached to the property in spite of what I'd suffered through, I would often stop-by when passing through *Barstow,* now Waterman Station's name. Eventually Aunt Abby died, and the place became rundown. Her sister, Anna, was very upset about the shape it was in, and darned if one day she didn't deed it to me!

Following the tremendous wartime migration to California, the post-war years saw an unprecedented real estate boom take place around Los Angeles. Fortunately, the Waterman Ranch adjoined Barstow, now one of the larger desert communities, had a ready source of water in the Mojave River bottom, and thus appeared 'choice' for development. Thus, I began subdividing it and offering parcels for sale.

Though sales were slowed due to the California Real Estate Commission's stiff requirements, they still kept up at a steady pace until, after several years, I'd sold off the entire 640 acres - and in the process made myself quite a comfortable nestegg.

417

Therefore, during 1945-46, I was involved in both the research facility in Ocean Park and the ranch in Barstow. The ranch was a long, hot drive away, but I soon solved that problem when the government began selling-off surplus planes from the war. The one that I was interested in was the Vultee BT-13, often called the "Vultee Vibrator", a basic trainer built in great quantities (over 11,000) for the Army Air Corps. They were being offered for only $900 each, and I went to Chino to pick one up. Upon arriving, I learned that the price was to be halved within the week. Since I already had my $900 certified check, I simply placed an order for two, and in a few days returned to take their delivery. It seemed like 1922 all over again!

I then successively flew each plane to Metroplitan/Van Nuys Airport, staked each down, and began cannibalizing one in order to re-work the other for full compliance with CAA regulations. Soon I had a proper vehicle for making those Barstow trips!

In 1945 our home was feeling a bit cramped, and I began construction of a new one on a lovely lot on Amalfi Drive, still in Santa Monica Canyon. It was our 'dream house', incorporating everything we wanted and adding up to over 5,000-square feet! With lots of glass, concrete, an acoustically-designed room for Carol's piano, and many other unusual features, it was considered 'way out' - very functional and modern - and caused much pro and con discussion, which didn't bother me a whit.

And, loving the ocean almost as much as flying, I bought a 25-foot cabin cruiser. Soon, though, I replaced it with a larger, 32-foot craft built in San Pedro. This boat was capable of trips in a radius of around 150 miles, and I therefore got quite involved in deep sea fishing. But soon I bought actor Jon Hall's beautiful 38-foot boat, named it *Caronell* after our grandaughters, and did a lot of Catalina Island crusing.

Some of my trips would take a week or two, and one of my most compatible 'crew members' was Max Harlow, who loved to go out during vacations from his teaching at Pasadena City College. Dick Short also often accompanied me. He was the son of Mac Short, Lloyd Stearman's chief engineer and later became president of Lockheed's Vega Aircraft.

Other activities kept me from spending all my time on the water, however. Our new home had a large workshop, of course, and I moved all of the remaining Arrowbile parts there. I wanted to construct one more example for the Smithsonian's collection. I'd already restored the

418

(l-r) Carol, me, grandaughters Carol and Nell, and Jane and son-in-law, Adrian Blackwell

Whatsit, which the Smithsonian had likewise wanted; they had it first shipped to storage in Chicago, and then to permanent space in Washington where it is now. In addition to working on the Arrowbile, I also had an automobile project in the works. (I'd acquired a chassis from a burned-out Studebaker Champion: power train, wheels, axles and frame.) I proceeded to build a streamlined body using aircraft drop tanks, huge plexiglass windows, and ended-up with a very futuristic vehicle that I termed the "Bug Car", sort of a copy of Bill Stout's Scarab.

I also developed an automatic transmission based upon a modern stick-shift syncromesh transmission fitted with an automatic gear changer. It was an interim design, between the old style manuals and the new Hydra-Matic and other automatics being jointly developed by Borg-Warner, Ford and Studebaker.

I reasoned that there might be a market for my design, and bought a 1947 Studebaker Commander coupe in which to install and demonstrate it. I then headed east that summer on a trip designed to get me to the

419

*Me in Whatsit, enroute to
the Smithsonian - 1946*

Cleveland Air Races, before heading for Studebaker, Bendix, and then Detroit.

As usual, the Hoffmans warmly greeted me, even though Studebaker was already committed to the Borg-Warner program, along with Ford. I then went to Ford, and was greeted by my old associate, Victor Raviolli, who was working on Ford's new overhead-valve engine. I also touched base with General Motors and Hudson (now American Motors), but not Chrysler, for they already had their "Fluid Drive". Finally, I had no option left but Kaiser-Frazer, Detroit's newest manufacturer.

I had a devil-of-a-time finding out just who to see there, so imagine my surprise when I finally walked into the 'right man's office' and came face-to-face with Dean Hammond, my old Vidal airplane competitor. Trying to sell those airplanes for $7,000 apiece had blown their Stear-

420

man-Hammond (Kaiser) project higher than a kite, but apparently Dean had gotten Henry J's confidence, and had been functioning with Kaiser in various trouble-shooting capacities. I chuckled and said, *"What in the hell do you think you're doing, Dean, sitting here as chief engineer of an automobile company?"* He laughed and said, *"Waldo, I was just wondering the same damn thing!"*

Well, he knew that he couldn't kid me about his knowing anything about automotive design - but he said, *"Here I am!"* - and I proceeded to outline my proposal. Dean said that he'd see that it was properly evaluated by their engineering group - but that he, *"...sure as hell, was not about to make any decision, yea or nay, about it."* The net result, though, was finally zero, and before heading home I decided to spend the weekend at Green Lake with Bill and Alma Stout.

My hybrid-transmission had come to naught, but it did give me a chance to renew some old aquaintances. This was my last visit to Green Lake. Soon, the Stout's were moving to Phoenix to join their daughter, since son-in-law John Fisher had rejoined his brother in a construction company there.

I continued working on Arrowbile-7. It was eventually to go to the Smithsonian in 1957. It was somewhat different from the 1937 version, and I therefore dubbed it the *"Aerobile"*. It had wing number N54P.

Initially I'd designed it around the six-cylinder Franklin air-cooled engine, but due to the wide range of engine demands, road use (utilizing 20 percent of the power) and flying (80 to 100 percent), a liquid cooling system was much more desirable. As luck would have it, at about this time the Tucker automobile (another of Detroit's postwar hopefuls) was announced, powered by a six-cylinder *water-cooled* Franklin. Fifty of these engines were produced before Tucker went bankrupt, and I thus was able to make a deal for one of them. This engine was one reason I changed the name to Aerobile, for the Arrowbiles had all been Studebaker-powered. Also, it used an angular geared shaft with a clutched automotive transmission in the road drive, encased far better than the original belt and sheave drive units had been.

I made other changes, too. With the higher 166-hp engine and less weight, I was able to make the plane a three-place job, moving the pilot forward a bit and leaving room for two passengers where the original seats had been. I also greatly simplified and eased the wing attachment

421

and detachment. The wing was now one-piece, and after releasing the lock bolts and dropping the main struts (plus the wingtip *parking* struts), you could simply raise it from the body with a built-in electric jack and drive away. This method of attaching-detaching had been my intent all along, but the pressures of getting the first planes ready for the 1937 Air Races forced me to put it off. Now I had plenty of time! Also, the control system connection was perfected to eliminate manipulation when changing from ground to air or vice versa.

Aerobile-7, Gillespie Field, El Cajon, California - 1957

*Franklin-Tucker powered Aerobile-7 -
the culmination of my flying automobile
development - 1957*

423

On several of my fishing jaunts I'd become reaquianted with San Diego, which was growing by leaps and bounds. As a boy I'd said that I didn't think that San Diego was the place for me to stay and build an aircraft manufacturing enterprise. I had felt that it was a little 'one horse town' and would never amount to much in aviation. Boy, was I wrong!

Four of the biggest firms in aviation either grew up in San Diego or moved there. Consolidated moved from Buffalo in 1935; Ryan Aeronautical started with young Claude Ryan in the Twenties; Solar Aircraft, founded by the Prudden brothers, now makes gas turbines as a division of International Harvester; and Rohr in Chula Vista now specializes in aircraft components and mass transit equipment. And, there's been lots of cross-pollination along the way. Fred Rohr started by working for Ryan Airlines while they were building Lindbergh's plane; and later, one of the Prudden brothers was with Claude Ryan as his principal assistant - at about the same time George Prudden built the trimotor that we used to scare-the-hell-out-of Loop Murphy.

I guess that in the early days I was thought of as a crazy, harem-scarem kid that didn't know any better than to fool around with flying machines. Therefore, I never considered my hometown as the place to start doing the things I had in mind because my ideas were far too advanced for their conservative thinking. Hmmmmm.

So, when we decided to sell the 345 S. Amalfi Drive house, San Diego was to be our new home location, and I started prowling along the Point Loma waterfront looking for our next nesting spot. To make a long story short, we eventually purchased a 94-foot sailing yacht named *Zahma,* and moored her in the northeasterly part of the yacht club harbor.

She was a beautiful, classic ketch (designed by Benjamin Bowdoin Crowninshield, and built around 1915 by George Lawley & Sons in Massachusetts) - a long way from new, but basically in good condition. This was a big step in more ways than one: moving from a 5,000-square foot house into a 94-foot sailboat, *and* returning to the town of my youth.

Meanwhile, I had negotiated a lease with the Port District for a location on San Diego harbor's new Shelter Island, which included rights for my own pier and a site for a research laboratory. As soon as the harbor department completed the road, I commenced work on a 24 by 40-foot building and 200 feet of pier and floating dockage. At the same time, we undertook an updating and refurbishing of Zahma.

424

Zahma, my 94-foot Crowninshield ketch, moored off of the San Diego Yacht Club

When these were completed, we moored her just off of the south end of the *San Diego Yacht Club,* which I had now joined as a Flag Member. After working out some problems with utilities, we soon had telephone service and ample electricity aboard to set up housekeeping with all of life's modern conveniences, TV included.

But we had a devil-of-a-time storing all of the things that were impossible to get into Zahma. Much of it I put into the Colorado Street building, and when my Shelter Island building was completed, much was moved there, including the unassembled parts and pieces for Aerobile-7.

We took Zahma out-and-about off San Diego many times, and occasionally we'd take her on cruises as far as Catalina Island. These were quite an undertaking for such a large boat, especially since I preferred to use sail rather than power whenever possible. Thus, we'd take along guests that were not only good companions but, also, good sailors. Setting sails on a 94-foot ketch is no easy task!

After living aboard Zahma for three years or so, the novelty started wearing thin. The chores of keeping a boat of her size shipshape were colossal, and I was no J.P. Morgan! Therefore, we started looking around Point Loma for a place to live. We'd earlier exhausted the water-front possibilities - and now figured that we'd rather have a place higher up which took in a better view.

Some years earlier the Marston (department store) family had ac-quired what is probably the most spectacular private property in San Di-ego - *ten acres as far out and as high up on Point Loma as possible.* How-ever, its steep contours turned out to be too difficult for them to handle, and Walter Trepte bought the property. (If you recall, back in 1911-12, I'd borrowed the Cameron engine from Trepte's that Charles Walsh had hocked there, using it to power my tractor biplane.) Walter Trepte had taken over the family business, and had built-up the largest construction company in the area, building many military installations during the war, plus countless other projects. I'd known Walter since high school days, though we never went to the same grade school. Anyway, he'd acquired this property and proceeded to carve it into parcels of approximately an acre each, allocating the choicest to members of his family. But they were all choice, and several other wealthy families became neighbors in this private preserve, with its precipitous road going from the bottom to the top of the hill, where the view was truly fantastic. *It looked out over all of San Diego Bay, North Island, Coronado, downtown San Diego and, into the distance, the mountains of Mexico. (See opposite page 1.)*

Our good friends, Donald and Thelma Burnham, had a home in "Trepteville" - and thus introduced us to this site. One evening at the Burnham's we learned that their neighboring property, Walter Trepte Jr.'s bachelor pad, was on the market because he'd now married and was living in a more suburban area. We immediately looked it over. It needed a lot of remodeling, but it surely had all of the potentials that we were looking for. We purchased this home on the uppermost of the acres, and though its view was partially blocked by the other homes, it was nonetheless spectacular in almost every respect. We then planned the changes that we wanted to make in the house, and the remodeling went on while Carol and I continued living on Zahma.

426

Soon our new home at 354 San Gorgonio Street (today a gated and private "Kellogg Way") was ready to move into, and we undertook the selling of Zahma - no easy chore, but finally accomplished, though the story of her final days is another book in itself!

Earlier, I'd been negotiating with Jacques Cousteau, who had wanted to buy my Shelter Island site and pier as a base for his various endeavors - which we are all so familiar with now. However, the Port District was giving me such a rough time that it was delaying the deal. They wouldn't let me charge Cousteau any more than the actual cost of the improvements that I'd made on the site, and this soured me on their methods of administering both the harbor *and* trying to mind my business, too. Though I didn't pretend to have any commercial goodwill to sell, values had gone up so dramatically in the few years since I'd set up my facility that I simply could not accept their presumption. In fact, things dragged on to the extent that Cousteau was proffered and accepted a location in Monaco - now an international showplace - and a group under the name of Submarine Operations aquired my site. Doug Fane, Jon Lindbergh (Lindbergh's son) and Lamar Boren, set up a marine diving service there that achieved world renown. So San Diego missed the opportunity to have Cousteau - from my perspective because of their ridiculous rules and regulations. Sub Ops later turned over the site to a hotel development, the Half Moon Inn, and in the meantime I moved to a leased portion of a building adjoining the San Diego Yacht Club for my own research and development work, which continued until 1974.

Chapter 10

1954 - 1972

Building and Racing Sailboats, Building and Flying the Planes of Yore

SO here I was with all of my activities on the premises of the San Diego Yacht Club, living in a home on a beautiful property with a fantastic view - with nothing to do except enjoy myself.

Since joining the yacht club in 1951, I'd been an active member, not only in the *predicted-log races* with Caronell - but also as chairman one year of the Security Committee, another year of the Slips and Docks Committee, and more recently, of the Challenge Committee - the heart of this racing-oriented yacht club (one of the three or four oldest in the country, founded while my grandfather was California's governor). This committee handled the negotiations for all of the biggest races: the Lipton Cup and the San Francisco Challenge Race, among others. It was very interesting work which I got a lot of fun out of, while, at the same time, performing a service for the club. In fact, as I'm dictating this, we're about to enter the 1974 Challenge Race, and although I'm no longer a member of the committee I plan to be part of our rooting section in San Francisco - in large part because this race is one in which I

428

was responsible for our club's participation and have been identified with ever since.

Another important race which I had quite a hand in for several years was the San Diego to Acapulco Race - a major ocean-racing event covering 1,400 miles down to that exotic Mexican resort. The first year that this race was run was in 1953 - and there weren't many contestants. The race had originally been the brainchild of one of the clubs in the Los Angeles area - but their lack of success prompted them to move its sponsorship to San Diego. Since I had one of the most powerful two-way radios on Zahma, I was initially involved in order to communicate with John Scripps on the Novia - a participant in each race until her sinking. Since I became thoroughly familiar with that first race, I then advocated that our club assume its sponsorship the following year, 1954.

The club did this, asking me to act as the co-ordinator of the activities. That race was to start in the ocean, outside of the harbor and just south of the tip of Point Loma. However, we had a bit of trouble. Zahma was the committee and starting boat, loaded-up with race officials and many sightseers - but we couldn't see a damn thing because of a solid pea soup fog. We ended-up milling about, getting lost and having a couple of near collisions with the yachts trying to get ready for the start. Finally we got everybody together and worked our way back into the mouth of the harbor, between Point Loma and Zuinga Jetty, where the fog wasn't so thick, and we managed to get the race off to a somewhat murky and sloppy start.

At this juncture, we decided that running a race of this scope should be an every-other-year event, and decided to hold the next one in 1956. For that race, another boat was used for the Race Committee, and the start was moved further into the harbor, in the main channel between Shelter Island and North Island. This time our problems were tide and wind, or the lack thereof. The current was running out of the harbor at a lively clip, but there was but a whisper of a breeze. This resulted in several boats making it across the starting line too soon, and then not being able to make it back for a second start without the use of their engines - a forbidden thing. The Race Committee hastily put their heads together and formulated a new rule, permitting those boats to restart using power to get into position but taking a two-hour penalty.

Prior to and in preparation for this race, Carol and I drove over to the Stouts in Phoenix, and with them, plus Wilma and John Fisher in a second car, we took off into the 'uncharted depths' of Mexico, planning to drive all the way to Acapulco. The Stouts and Fishers went as far as Ciudad Obregon, below Guaymas, before bidding us farewell - or better said, *Vaya Con Dios,* for that was what we needed on those roads! That was the last I saw of Bill - he passed away just a short while later (March 16, 1880 - March 20, 1956).

This trip was my first and last of driving in Mexico. The route we were following, along the Gulf of California and the Pacific until turning inland toward Guadalajara, was then a most primitive affair. Both on that stretch and later, into Acapulco, there were many places where we had to ford streams and rivers where no bridges existed. One time we used the railroad bridge, bumping across the ties - Boy!, that'll surely jar your fillings loose - and a couple of times the job was accomplished by floating the car across on a ferry rigged from two canoes. We really felt like Halliburton or Johnson - but we finally made it, and I then arranged with the Acapulco Yacht Club for the race's finish.

Back to the start of the race, which was a bit fouled up as noted. Immediately after the start, being the race chairman, I was taken aboard the Coast Guard cutter *Perseus* to accompany the yachts to Acapulco. There the Mexicans were the best of hosts, but they were soon sadly to learn about some of our not-too-commendable Yankee tricks, resulting in an erosion of camaraderie over the years.

Ever since the evolution of modern plastic technology, I had been keenly interested in it - possibly doing the most along this line while with Bill Stout in Dearborn. In 1957, it was announced that a company in Sausalito, on San Francisco Bay, was bringing out a 41-foot sloop, designed by the great Phillip Rhodes, and made with the new 'miracle' material - fiberglass-reinforced plastic. They were offering this boat at a price far-cheaper than a comparable wooden-hulled vessel, apparently convinced that its construction costs would be considerably less than wood. Well, having observed so many sailing races, and being intrigued with plastics, I couldn't resist this bargain. I immediately headed for Sausalito.

I worked out a deal with Coleman, the boat builders, to represent them in San Diego and thus acquire my first *Bounty-class boat* for a 20

430

percent discount, the same that I'd receive for any additional sales I made. This *Bounty-41* was delivered in September 1957, and I planned to enter it in the 1958 Acapulco Race. Stephen Newmark, a prominent yacht broker in the Los Angeles area, was named their distributor there. He had won the 1956 race in his *Eventide,* a 38-foot ketch. Being the two Bounty representatives in Southern California, we decided to combine our talents in one boat for the 1958 race. I was delivered Bounty No. 5 long before Newmark, so we proceeded to transfer much of the special gear from the Eventide to my boat. Kenny Watts, then possibly the best sailmaker on the coast (San Diego's Lowell North was just beginning), was to supply the sails for Newmark's Bounty, and we thus planned to use his sails on my boat and include Watts as our sailing master. We put together a top-notch crew and figured that we had a terrific chance to win this race.

There were only two or three boats that were real competition. The one I most feared was *Carousel,* an Owens cutter skippered by San Diego's master yachtsman, Ash Bown. Each boat was rated upon a handicap basis, and Carousel and my boat, *Lady Bountiful,* were almost equally rated, with mine having to give him 36 minutes-or-so for the race - a pittance, I thought. Another boat was a 10-meter (a boat of around 65 to 70 feet in length, of a class one notch below the America's Cup 12 meters) named *Windward* - very fast with a very high rating. Other than Carousel, though, only *Minstrel,* a 36-foot Lapworth, dogged us neck-and-neck the entire race. Windward was out front, out of sight, and we knew that the only way we'd beat her was by the capriciousness of the winds.

The night before we were to finish, Windward had already finished, and we calculated that to beat her, we must finish by 10:30 the next morning. As dusk descended, Carousel was just ahead of us and Minstrel to our stern - and we'd have to bear down hard to win. We elected to move in near shore and sail along the breaker line - a somewhat risky venture that would gain us what little offshore breeze existed. When the glimmer of dawn started to break, we saw the promontories lying northwest of Acapulco and knew that the finish line was very close. However, we couldn't see hide-nor-hair of either Carousel or Minstrel, and were in quite a quandry as to where they might be - ahead or behind. Regardless, we kept moving toward the finish - but as the sun came up, the wind

431

went down, until we were about two miles from the line and it was *dead calm*. There is possibly no more heart-rending situation for a yachtsman - there we sat doing '360's' while we watched Carousel's mast behind us, slowly gaining in size! The offshore winds were coming up before the wind that was closer in - and before the breeze reached us, it had made Carousel fully visible. We figured that Minstrel wouldn't be far behind her. The 36 minutes that we had to allow Carousel now started to feel like the seconds-of-doom ticking away.

I'm reminded now of the time I was trying to locate some gear for my boat in Ensenada - and the local fishermen were helping me. They were greatly surprised to learn that I couldn't use my motor during the race - and thought me a bit teched or stupid not to. Well, this was surely one of the moments that the thought passed through my mind - but like Bobby Jones, it was but a flicker, because in both golf and sailing, honor and sportsmanship rate very high.

Finally, the winds that were moving Carousel reached us - and we started to gain momentum again. We then moved across the line - but seven-minutes-too-late to beat Windward. Then there was nothing to do but bite our nails until Ash Bown crossed the line - and by this time the wind had picked up considerably, and he came barreling-in, finishing in a time to not only beat us, but Windward, too. Then, as if it were dregs in the cup, along came Minstrel and beat our time by three minutes - *all this after a race of 1,400 miles!*

Out of the 37 boats entered, we then ended-up fourth overall and third in our class - not bad, but a lot less than we'd counted on. It was a disappointment, and I was quite down and out about it - not in a bit of a good humor for all of the parties and festivities that marked the completion of this race, lasting for several days until all of the boats finally arrived. In the years since, hundreds of boats have competed in this race - and I at least have the satisfaction of knowing that only a handful have ever beat Lady Bountiful's time in 1958.

We stayed over in Acapulco about ten days after the race because I had a hot prospect interested in buying Lady Bountiful - but the deal blew up and Frank Martin flew down to crew on the long trip 'uphill' back to homeport. As is usual, when you have a corinthian crew, they aren't expected to share in the nitty-gritty, humdrum chore of sailing the return leg - and you, as the owner, are stuck with that. When Frank arrived, he and I and a young Mexican who claimed sailing knowledge powered-out of Acapulco early one morning, soon setting the main sail for a trip planned to include several stops. I intended to stay with the boat until we got to Puerto Vallarta, about 400 miles up the coast, and then if everything was going OK, leave the boat to be sailed the rest of the way by the young bucks.

As I mentioned, the trip north was uphill in the sailing sense, for most of the prevailing winds were northwesterly, and it was nigh impossible to get much headway from them. Therefore, the mainsail was up primarily to steady the boat while the engine and the propeller drove us along. Not planned as motor sailers, these boats had little fuel storage, and we had the gas stacked around the cockpit on the deck (a common practice) in eight 50-liter drums (approximately 15 gallons). One night I was at the helm when we were about two days out, somewhere off of Punta Lizardo, and Frank was getting his 40-winks, when the Mexican youth went below to prepare coffee. Our stove was an alcohol one which had to be preheated and properly processed in order to start, and he'd assured me that he knew how to do it. After quite a spell I spotted something really flaming-up below - and I hollered to Frank to find out what was going on. Frank popped out of his bunk and rushed down to find that the drip pan under the stove, brimming with alcohol, was aflame - having ignited when the boy struck a match to light the burner. Frank grabbed the blazing pan and brought it topside to heave overboard - which he almost didn't do. It just missed the stern by an inch-or-two. If his aim had been off a bit more, this story probably would have ended - for on the stern we'd placed two leaking gasoline drums on some padding. By this time the padding was fully saturated - but we'd placed the drums there in full knowledge that it was as far as possible from any fire source. Well, we surely lucked-out that time!

We stopped a couple of times enroute - once at a very beautiful cove near Zihuatanejo (a just-discovered paradise) and also at Manzanillo, about two-thirds of the way to Puerto Vallarta. Just before arriving at Vallarta we ducked into another picturesque tropical cove, where we spied Windward and a couple of other boats idly moored. By the time we arrived at Puerto Vallarta, our fuel was running low. They had no shore facilities, but there was always a crew with canoes to ferry visitors ashore. We tied our empty drums together and floated them to the beach. Then they were refilled and again floated (gasoline being lighter than water) out to the boat and lashed down, a common procedure in these primitive, out of the way spots.

After staying there for a couple of days, we awoke on the morning of our departure to find ourselves about ten miles out to sea, almost to the mouth of Bahia de Benderas. Apparently we hadn't gotten our anchor well-hooked or had used too little scope. It was now hanging straight-down, far from the bottom. We were lucky - for all we had to do to correct that goof was to start the engine, winch the anchor back up and motor sheepishly back to port. It was another lesson almost learned the hard way.

Later that afternoon I caught my flight to Tijuana, just across the border from San Diego, and the next morning Frank and the Mexican youth headed for Cabo San Lucas, the tip of the Baja California peninsula, where they were to refuel before heading for Ensenada, the final Mexican port where they were to clear customs. I figured that this trip would take them at least four days. Boy, was I surprised when they arrived in San Diego three days after leaving Puerto Vallarta. They'd made a fast stop at the cape, and then had skipped Ensenada, knowing that the Mexicans cared little whether they made the customs stop - an attitude not shared by the U.S. authorities where we cleared customs at San Diego, and where an awful lot of Mexican booze gets dumped into the drains every year. I was very glad to see the Lady back safe-and-sound, and then paid off the Mexican lad, and gave him his plane ticket home with a 'Well done.'

We now sat down to rerace the race, somewhat like Monday morning quarterbacking, for a discussion of what changes we should do in order to make the boat more competitive. In San Diego then, it hardly mattered what one did to his boat - Ash Bown seemed to win, regardless. However, looking back on what I've learned since, I certainly wouldn't have started that race with the sail combination that we had, for it precluded our capitalizing on the wide variety of wind conditions that we encountered. We did conclude, though, that the Bounty-class ably demonstrated the virtues of fiberglass construction, and that it was *surely the coming thing in yacht building.* Lady Bountiful was the first sizable yacht using this new construction in Southern Californian waters - it was the harbinger of the many thousands of boats plying these waters today.

434

It wasn't all good with the boat, though. Whereas Rhodes was probably one of the finest designers in the country, what Coleman, the boat's builder, had done with his design was not the best. They altered it enough to end-up with an out-of-balance boat and had to add 500 pounds of cast iron ballast in the forepeak, above, rather than below, the waterline. This resulted in a heavier boat to move through the water, and a slightly longer waterline which penalized the boat's handicap. We also thought that its design was slanted too much toward cruising rather than racing. We thought that it'd be better with the cockpit moved forward enough to allow a two-berth aftercabin, which would also improve the live-aboard habitation. The sum total of these thoughts dictated that I obtain a Bounty hull and then finish the boat to my own specifications.

Hence, I went up to Sausalito and worked out a deal with Fred Coleman for a bare hull with the clear-cut understanding that I would never refer to it as a "Bounty" since Coleman feared that my endeavors would reflect badly. I had no fears on this score - wanting only to possess a fiberglass-laminated Rhodes-designed hull which would then be "Waterman" from there on. The hull was completed in mid-1957, and trucked to San Diego where I had it put in the water beside Lady Bountiful. We had to fill it half-full of water in order to keep it from capsizing as there was no ballast installed yet. In the meantime, I'd been working on the design of the boat - and our final effort was something which racing sailors would appreciate but not anything that would get raves from the ladies. It was a rather austere, no-nonsense, cambered flush-deck design. Passengers like to look out of the windows of a typically stepped-deck boat; there were none in mine. This boat was designed to have the lowest handicap possible as a racing machine - a boat designed with the same parameters as when I designed the Gosling for Cecil deMille, but hopefully with better results.

There was a whole complex of things that I made decision after decision on - one was the use of lead rather than the iron ballast which Bounty had used. Lead was more expensive - but it was heavier and would thus allow its placement to be the lowest possible within the hull's built-in ballast pocket, and so give a better center-of-gravity in relation to the entire displacement. Also, I eliminated installing the forepeak ballast that Lady Bountiful had. Frank and I worked on the boat for many

435

months - quite a job installing the interior bulkheads, floors, lockers, head (toilet), galley, ice box - on and on - including the engine mounting, mast and rigging, sail track, cockpit and helm.

An article in the paper said, *"Waldo Waterman...is attacking the problem of beating Ash Bown...with a slide rule in one hand and the ocean handicap rule book in the other."* Well, if innovation would do it, I was surely going to give it a helluva try.

One of the more interesting things I did - which evoked a lot of comment pro and con - was my method of steering the boat. I installed a vertical helm which looked a lot like an airplane control stick, placing it well forward in the cockpit; putting the helmsman away from the crew's activities where he could better judge them, the sails and the boat's relative position during a race. The position of the 'whip staff' helm was both in the center of action but completely out of the way of the various operations that the crew had to undertake - such as the almost continual winching and tailing of the sheets, primarily the jib, during a race. Incidentally, this type of helm was very common on old sailing ships - just proving the adage that there's nothing new under the sun. Regardless of the chuckles and comments on this arrangement, I have yet to take a racing skipper sailing with me that was not impressed with it when I turned the helm over to him. It's quite revolutionary, and I sometimes wonder why more boats don't use it.

As the boat was nearing completion, more and more folks wanted to know what its name was to be - and finally it was tagged in much the same manner as Whatsit. I told them that it was to be a similar boat to Lady Bountiful - but stripped of all unnecessary encumbrances. After awhile I conjured the name *Lady Godiva* - and the name stuck. However, many thought that my description envisioned a boat lacking in amenities below. Quite the contrary, for upon her completion, Lady Godiva had everything Lady Bountiful had, plus a bit more; it just wasn't as visible.

The first tests with the finished boat were quite encouraging. We immediately had her measured for handicapping and entered her first race. I don't recall just where we placed in that race, but we were among the top finishers and Lady Godiva was a top contender in San Diego yachting for several years. I originally had a vision of entering her in the 1960 Acapulco Race. But one reason or another kept me from doing it - primarily because the Mexicans were becoming less cordial and were exploiting the Yankees. I probably can't blame them, for we 'gringos' were not always the model of good guests.

However, I did enter eleven *Newport-to-Ensenada* Races in a row. This annual race is possibly the largest yacht race anywhere - attracting well-over 500 entries in a whole spectrum of classes. *It's always started in the ocean off Newport Beach on the Friday of Mexico's Cinco de Mayo holiday - their "Fourth of July" - and finishes at Ensenada, about 60 miles south of the border.* The mobs that converge upon Ensenada, both yachtsmen and landlubbers, are something to behold - but not altogether something to be proud of. The carousing and hi-jinks suffer an awful lot of retelling, and suffice it to say that trying to get a beer in Hussong's is an experience you'll long remember. Some skippers often have to motor home shorthanded - like the time one of Dick Wheeler's *Karama* (a classic 10-meter yacht) crew pushed a Mexican cop into the pool at the Capri Motel. Boy, there was hell to pay for that!

Regardless, as a yachting competition, it's a first-class race - run very seriously. I'm proud to state that I won my class five out of those eleven races, and three other times I was in the top three class finishers. One year I came within two boats of winning overall - a reasonable feat out of half-a-thousand boats. That particular race was won by my eternal nemesis, Ash Bown.

I only beat Ash once - and won $10 to-boot. Ash, being the perpetual winner that he was, always liked to put a bet on a race - which we had done in this case. As we neared the finish, we were quite far apart laterally but about the same distance from the finish, he on one side of the channel and I on the other. We were working like beavers on both boats trying to squeeze every last ounce out of the wind, when Ash had to cross the channel on a converging course. In front of him was some shoal water, and the tide was such that I questioned whether he'd clear the bottom. As he came through this area, he was about 100 yards from me and slightly ahead - and he hit bottom, stopping dead in the water. His crew had the spinnaker pole over the side in a flash, wresting Carousel free - but the delay was enough to allow me to scrape by the finish line about a half-minute ahead of him. I won the $10, but learned a lesson - never, never bet on a race with Ash Bown! And speaking of Ash reminds me of

437

My Lady Godiva - the Rhodes-41/Waterman-1 - Newport-Ensenada Race - 1966

another pretty good sailor, but a totally different type of individual - Dennis Conner:

> *Dennis crewed for me several times on Lady Godiva. He grew-up around the San Diego Yacht Club and could be very difficult. He was damn good at sailing a boat, but knew it and didn't hesitate to emphasize it. Ash Bown was the only skipper he sailed with that he would knuckle under to. I think he owes Ash for most of his techniques. During my tenure as Chairman of the Challenge Committee, Dennis was always wanting to get on that committee, but I always turned him down - telling him that was the work for the older hands and that we needed him out there winning the races rather than trying to do so before the race as we tried to do in the Committee. Using his out-and-out gall he promoted himself as a crew mem-*

438

ber on three of the four America's Cup Challengers. It paid off by his finally becoming Co-Skipper of the America's Cup winner Courageous. Jerry Driscoll, skipper of runner-up Intrepid, would not give him any crew spot - if he had, he might have kept Dennis off Courageous, thereby winning the spot for Intrepid. The last time Dennis crewed for me, he came to me afterward and told me that if I expected him aboard again it would only be as skipper. That ended him on Lady Godiva.

Interestingly, in my first Ensenada race I was up among the leaders at the finish (though we wouldn't know the exact standing until all of the boats were in) and Fred Coleman came bounding aboard saying, *"Waldo, we certainly showed them up this time with the Bounty, didn't we?"* I retorted, *"What do you mean 'we,' and what do you mean, 'Bounty'?"* I then reminded him that he'd insisted and I'd agreed that this boat would never be called a Bounty - advising him not to refer to it in any such way in his advertising. Well, that took the wind out of his sails a bit, and was the last I heard on that score. Many others inadvertently referred to Lady Godiva as a Bounty - and if I were there, I corrected them and referred to her as simply a Rhodes-41 hull - *for she was the Waterman-1.*

In capsule form, this gives you a bit of the picture of my sailing activities - which I carried on until around 1970 when age and decrepitude ended my high seas adventures.

During this period, I was always, naturally, tinkering with airplanes. Frank Martin assisted me in completing Aerobile-7, and in August 1957, I took it to Gillespie Field, just east of San Diego, for flight-testing. When I was satisfied that everything was hunky-dory, I told the Smithsonian that it was ready to go, and in the late spring of 1959 they had a Maryland National Guard Fairchild C119 cargo plane pick it up while on a training flight. We rolled the automobile portion through the Fairchild's big cargo doors, and placed the wing in a special cradle for the flight to the Smithsonian's Silver Hill facility, where it was assembled and checked over. Every time it headed over for permanent display in the Smithsonian's main museum, it seemed that some politician would sidetrack it in favor of displaying some other aircraft from his home district. This happened so many times that I finally suggested that they put it on display at Silver Hill, where it now resides.

You may ask, what happened to the other Arrowbiles? Number 6 (really a rebuild of No. 4) had been used in Dearborn for a mockup of the folding wing and had demonstrated the inadvisability of Bill Stout's idea of a folding-wing flying automobile. Afterwards we'd installed a fully cantilevered wing which I felt would greatly increase the plane's speed and overall performance. The plane went to ConVair, and was still there when I resigned. But I have been unable to find hide-nor-hair of it since.

Arrowbile-5, designated NR18934, the last one completed, ended-up at Studebaker's proving grounds when the Army took over during the war. I presume that it met the same fate as did Nos. 2 and 3 (NR18932 and NR18933). Number 1, originally NX262Y, was the one Chuck Sisto landed in the boulder patch and was later rebuilt. It appeared in the Alice Faye movie before being shipped to Dearborn, where it was cannibalized until there was no airplane as such left.

Lets go back to Point Loma and see what other things were going on with me during this period. Just as I was closing the escrow on 354 San Gorgonio, I learned that Mac Laddon, my old nemesis from ConVair days, had purchased the senior Trepte's home - now that Mrs. Trepte had passed away - which was right across the driveway from our new home. This bothered me a bit, for he and I had never seen eye-to-eye, and I credited him with blowing-up the Stout Research activities. However, I decided it best to keep an amicable and neighborly appearance, though I presume that we both said a thing or two about the other when our backs were turned - but that's life.

There were other pioneers living on Point Loma with whom I was great friends - Reuben Fleet, Fred Rohr and, most particularly, Claude Ryan - a fellow yacht club member with whom I spent many, many enjoyable hours. Claude was especially intrigued with the airplane reproductions that I was soon to get involved with, often accompanying me when I went to test-fly these planes (page 445). Of course, between the two of us, we could regale each other and our friends with more yarns and embellished anecdotes than any other two old aviators around.

After the Aerobile departed, I began to get the itch to have another plane. A few years previously I had attended an auction where a six-cylinder Franklin was on the block. As I walked in, I waved casually to the auctioneer, Milton Wershow, whom I'd known since the early Arrowplane days. Much to my surprise, he immediately said, *"Sold to Waldo Waterman for $35!"* I had no idea as to what he'd knocked-down, but I knew full well that it would be something that he knew was both a bargain and useful to me. Lo-and-behold, it was this Franklin engine, which had originally cost the Navy around $2,500 and now for me, $35!

I then started thinking about building a modernized version of a 1911 Curtiss pusher powered with this engine, provided I could find a suitable set of biplane wings. Thanks to Mort Larson, I found a set at the Cal-Fritzen Propeller Company of Torrance. They were from a Vought VE-7, the Navy's first American-built single-engine fighter; originally built in 1920, and so successful that it remained in service through the Twenties. I immediately bought them, and also ordered a wooden pusher propeller.

I then built a mockup with the help of Stephen Ballas, who had previously helped me build a Popular Mechanics/Fly glider for the Smithsonian. We had a lot of fun, and the work progressed speedily during that spring of 1965, and we finished the assembly in Mort's hangar at Palomar Airport. I did two or three test flights, and when I was satisfied that everything was properly tuned, I announced to the press that there would be a public showing and demonstration of this plane on July 1st, the anniversary of my first flight in 1909. I named the plane the *Early Bird* because I wanted to impress upon the public that it had been *The Early Birds of Aviation who had laid the foundation upon which the Space Age had been built.* It served the cause very well. The plane received a terrific amount of press and publicity, and even made Janes' *All's The World's Aircraft* in 1966.

The Early Bird was soon a popular attraction at air shows. The first of any prominence was the All American Air Carnival in November 1965 at Palm Springs. The event was highly-publicized, and had attracted participants from all over the country: racers, aerobatics, parachute jumpers - all sorts of aviation hi-jinks.

There were a couple of other old planes there. One was a copy of the 1909 Bleriot that had first flown the English Channel, originally built by Canada's Calgary Institute and powered by a 65-hp Continental engine. The other was a more authentic copy than mine - a Louisiana-built replica of a 1911 Curtiss pusher, powered with an 85-hp Continental engine. Both of these were owned by Frank Tallman of Tallmantz Aviation

441

My Early Bird - Franklin-powered, 1911 Curtiss-copy - 1965

based at Orange County Airport. These fellows had cornered most of the Hollywood flying by this time - and just a bit earlier, Paul Mantz (Maentz, originally) had been killed while filming the final scene for *"The Flight of the Phoenix."* Tallman was a superb pilot, also, but due to a nonaviation accident he'd lost his left leg and didn't fly either of these exposed-position airplanes.

The carnival included the International Aero Classic, a race scheduled between the Bleriot and the Curtiss. I suggested that we make it a three plane affair (with the full realization that it wasn't a fair contest because of my plane's much-faster speed). I assured the other two pilots that I'd stay well-clear of them, making wide turns and sometimes double turns around the pylons in order to make for a more spectacular show. We took off, and I jumped way ahead immediately. I circled the pylon directly in front of the stands completely before going around it a second time, giving the other planes a chance to catch up with me. For five laps I was continuously doing something that would drop me back and then bring me up ahead again. On the last lap, the chap piloting the Curtiss decided that he was going to pull a fast one. He cut the last pylon entirely and made a beeline straight for the finish, which normally would have put him ahead of me. However, I had a few tricks up my sleeve too, and I flew that last lap a bit higher than usual so that I could size up the entire situation. When I saw what he was doing, I dove down, using up all of my altitude as I built-up enough speed to finish a few yards ahead of him. Boy, did the crowd roar their approval - and the press really ate-it-up, too. From this race I was tagged, *"Waldo The Great - King of the Pylons,"* though I'd first earned some notoriety along this line at the 1929 National Air Races, 36 years earlier!

There was another item of interest at Palm Springs. Arthur Godfrey was there, ballyhooing the just-introduced Lear Jet, selling for around $500,000 apiece. We worked out a gag wherein Godfrey would act as the Lear Jet salesman and I would amble up, looking it over - and he realizes that I'm a potential customer. He then launches into a sales pitch, and we banter back and forth awhile until, finally, I ask if my plane would serve as a down payment on the jet. Godfrey says he can see no reason why not - and wants to see my airplane. When he does, he decides that it isn't quite an acceptable down payment for a half-million-dollar airplane, and our 'deal' is off. This skit was repeated on television and later on several other programs.

443

Afterward I flew the Early Bird far and wide to air shows and fly-ins all over Southern California. And, on December 17, 1967, I made a formal presentation of it to the San Diego Aerospace Museum.

By now I had achieved quite the *aviation elder statesman* image. Ironically, I was possibly getting more publicity than at any time before because of my building and flying of unusual and vintage aircraft. *I was considered the senior commercially-licensed aviator in the country,* and in spite of my years, I was having the-time-of-my-life - typically flying in excess of 100 hours annually.

In 1968 I was installed in San Diego's *International Aerospace Hall of Fame* along with John Glenn, Richard Byrd, Theodore von Karman, and Manfred von Richthofen; I joined the Wrights, Curtiss, and Bleriot plus my old friends Reuben Fleet, Claude Ryan and Fred Rohr. This, I guess, was one of the compensations for growing old. Of course, this sort of philosophy ties in well with my long-spoken adage that it's the mistakes that we make that teach us something - that it's through our failures that we progress and, hopefully, finally succeed.

During the course of my work on the Early Bird, I became associated with the Experimental Aircraft Association - a group numbering many thousands who are either rebuilding antique aircraft, building their own airplanes, or engaging in related activities. Just as for me in 1910, one of their biggest problems was finding a light but powerful engine. Many EAA'ers were using the Volkswagen engine. However, it was only powerful enough for small single-seaters. I was intrigued with the engine in the Chevrolet Corvair - a six-cylinder, air-cooled engine that could develop 140-hp and weighed but 220 pounds, somewhat Franklin-like; I planned to develop and adapt it for aviation.

In place of the V-belts that I had used in the Arrowbile for engine speed reduction, I turned to a new type of cogged belt which mated with cogged drums on both shafts, resulting in an ideal combination of a belt's flexibility *and* a gear's precision.

The engine was built-up from a 1968 Corvair short-block and required considerable modification. I had to perfect a straddle-bearing system to protect the crankshaft, devise a dual ignition system, and make numerous minor mechanical changes. And of course, there was an air-

444

Corvair-powered Chevy Bird, Claude Ryan with camera, Palomar Airport, September, 1968

Henry Artof

445

plane to build around the engine. The wing, tail and control surfaces were scavenged from a wounded Cessna 140. The design was a high-wing monoplane, all-metal construction and similar to the Early Bird.

Upon its completion, I tagged this plane the *Chevy Bird* and took it to Palomar Airport for the required 50 hours of flying. This engine proved to be very sound and capably ran its 50 hours with no difficulty. When I had completed these FAA requirements and the plane was permitted unrestricted flight, I found that the Chevy Bird and I were in great demand for air shows throughout Southern California.

After flying around 150 hours in this plane, I wrote a series of six articles for the Experimental Aircraft Association's magazine, *Sport Aviation,* detailing the process of converting the Corvair engine for flight purposes. In 1969 I attended the annual get-together of this group - the EAA Fly-in - and was honored by being awarded the top prize for the best *literary effort* of the year.

When I returned to San Diego, I'd been determined to have my own seaplane to fly around the harbor. It was an old dream, and now the Chevy Bird became the *Chevy Duck.* My first problem was locating suitable pontoons. Eventually I used an Edo for the main center pontoon, and two small, scow-types built from quarter-inch plywood, fiberglassed and attached to the landing gear legs on the Chevy Bird. They acted as both pontoons and sponsons, giving sufficient lateral stability to prevent capsizing, though they looked sort of odd. But I was more concerned about having a seaplane to flit about in rather than making any contributions to the art!

After some test hops, I did my first major flight on December 30th, 1969 for the benefit of the TV and press. They had cameras set-up on Shelter Island, and also a fast boat with which to follow and photograph me. I was at an altitude of around 400 feet and flying nicely when, for the first time ever, the engine stopped cold. I immediately had to swing into the wind for a dead-stick landing. It was the first landing, other than straightaway, that I'd attempted in the Chevy Duck, but I came in with no undue problems, much to the delight of the photographers. One fellow from the Union got a classic shot of me at the moment of engine failure, a great contrast between the Chevy Duck and a huge aircraft carrier in the background.

446

George Smith

My Chevy Duck, between Shelter Island and North Island - December 30, 1969

Joe Holly

447

Joe

Me in Chevy Duck, starting dead-stick landing, San Diego Bay, December 30, 1969

Upon landing I had to be towed back to the club - a bit sheepish - and began investigating the cause of the engine failure. I found that my shoulder straps, which were flapping loose because I was wearing a Mae West, had gotten caught in the cog belt drive, entangling themselves around the ignition wiring and completely yanking it out. This accounted for the stoppage!

Another of my airplane projects in these years was a replica of the Wright Kitty Hawk Flyer - the Wrights' first powered aircraft. I built this for Donald Gilmore, formerly chairman of the Upjohn Pharmaceutical Company, for his museum near Kalamazoo, Michigan. Through the Smithsonian, I was able to secure a complete 40-plus page set of the drawings, which had been prepared by the National Cash Register Company's staff while the original flyer was undergoing restoration in Dayton.

Bruce Gustafson

Gilmore Wright Flyer - 1966

449

Before leaving the Gilmore Wright Flyer, I think it would be interesting to comment on the Flyer's engine - of which I also received drawings. The engine was a four-cylinder, 4-inch bore and 4-inch stroke, having an aluminum cylinder block with cast iron cylinder sleeves. It had an overhead camshaft, fuel injection, magneto make-and-break ignition and pressure liquid cooling. Its design was not unlike the superb Miller-Offenhausers of a later era - or of 'engineering breakthroughs' being offered the automotive public today. *(It's said that the last piece of automotive innovation was made in 1934 with the introduction of Reo's "self-shifter" automatic transmission - everything else was tried and proven long before.)* It is rather astounding to me, though, that this original Wright engine developed only 12-hp while turning at 1,200 rpm, whereas the Offenhausers of approximately the same size put out 600-hp at 9,000 rpm. (We made only a mock-up of this engine for the Gilmore Flyer.)

In my building of this Flyer, I reread much of the Wright's history and reacquainted myself with their achievements all over again. They were very forward thinkers and innovators. However, once they'd developed something that did the job reasonably well, they were very reluctant about changing or improving it, and they refused to build an airplane without incorporating it in its structure.

They took out many patents to protect their position and preclude others from infringement, and defended their patent rights *to the letter -* attempting to make anyone building an airplane pay them a fee of 20 percent of the cost of manufacture, and then collecting an additional tax on almost all flying of the plane, such as $100-a-day for each time it was flown in an exhibition. The Wright's conduct so beleagured Louis Paulhan on his national air tour following his 1910 triumphs at Dominguez that he finally threw up his hands in disgust and fled home to France (to sell Curtiss aeroplanes!).

The results of this behavior led to very slow technical advancement for Wright machines. They were still using skids while Curtiss, myself and others had long been using wheels. Every Wright airplane up 'til around 1915 used wing warping instead of ailerons, chain-driven propellers spinning in opposite directions, and many other features that even then were outdated and old fashioned.

450

As I've mentioned, Glenn Curtiss was the Wrights' main competitor and a source of great irritation to them. Curtiss was a fantastic innovator and a seat-of-the-pants engineer, though lacking formal training (remember the sewer pipe determination of the center-of-gravity), but he had the intelligence, aggressive drive and common sense to solve his problems one way or the other. He built all of his planes on a modular basis - the wing panels were a five-and-a-half-foot span (except for the center section which was an even six feet), and he always used a four-and-a-half-foot chord. He could then take a pile of parts and within a few hours produce a biplane, monoplane, seaplane or a triplane with from five to seven bays - tractor or pusher. Even his first flying boats utilized this same modular scheme. The result was that, within a week's time, he could try out a half-dozen ideas that would have taken the Wrights much, much longer and, thus made him appear far more versatile in producing new and workable ideas.

This impression was further heightened by the Wrights' being very prone to secretiveness whereas Curtiss would give his advice openly to anyone that he considered worthy of his assistance, even to those making virtual copies of his designs.

Of course, this was at odds with the Wrights' almost paranoid insistence upon the rights of their patents. Only a few companies took out Wright manufacturing licenses - most notable being The Burgess Company in Marblehead, Massachusetts, plus several foreign concerns. (Later Burgess became a subsidiary of Curtiss, specializing in seaplanes while at the same time building Wrights under license.)

The relentless pressures of progress doomed this rigid Wright patent adherance, and the coup de grace was rendered by the Great War which forced both the Wright and Curtiss patents into a common patent pool. However, all was not black and white in this picture of the Wrights and Curtiss, there were *shades of gray* as to the wisdom and propriety of both their actions several times during their careers. But, though I will admit to some prejudice on Curtiss's part, I in no way want to detract from the Wrights' achievement.

I'm relating these comments to show the vast differences that existed between the Wrights and Curtiss. I shudder to think of them ever during

451

their *active* careers allowing the merger of their names as it came about in the *Curtiss-Wright Corporation* in 1929, though I understand that Curtiss then did smile about it. I, of course, knew Glenn Curtiss very well, but I never knew either of the Wrights. The Wrights and Curtiss lives are fascinating stories about which every American knows a smattering - typically far more about the Wrights than about Curtiss. I well-recommend further study of their careers by anyone interested in the *American Dream* and the quality of man's inventiveness. Without the *equally substantial* contributions of *both* the Wrights and Curtiss, we would surely not have reached the wonderful heights that we have. As Harry Bruno (that era's foremost aviation observer) said, Curtiss is *"the one American whose name as a pioneer ranks with that of the Wright brothers."*

During a later trip East to supervise the installation of the Gilmore Wright Flyer, I swung by the Smithsonian. While there, I learned that National Educational Television (NET) wanted a flyable reproduction of the Kitty Hawk Flyer for a documentary, and in due course I offered to build them an 80 percent-size flying reproduction.

I'd started construction and had it about 30 percent complete when NET advised me that they were placing their order elsewhere. It seems that they'd picked my brains and then awarded the contract to Jack Lambie, a teacher in Fullerton, CA, who used his students to work on the project. He was an authority on several types of gliders, but wasn't as knowledgeable as I on the Wright Flyer.

But this didn't stop me, and with Erik Larson helping, it wasn't long until we had the Flyer complete enough to move out to Palomar Airport for final assembly and flight testing. On its first flight it proved very difficult to handle - understandable, since it was a true reproduction and 20 percent undersize. We were using a 40-hp 450-cc Honda motorcycle engine which developed considerably more power than the original engine had, and the airplane showed real promise. However, after three flights and three crackups, we decided that we'd better take a new approach, and were aided by a fortunate turn of events.

I learned that there was to be a huge transportation display by the Department of Transportation at Dulles Airport in the late spring of 1972, "Transpo '72." I thought that having a reproduction of Cal Rodgers' Wright *Vin Fiz* at this show would be very interesting.

452

My flyable Wright Kitty Hawk Flyer - 1971

The Flyer, configured as Rodgers' Vin Fiz - and my last solo - 1972

So we redid the Flyer as the 1911 Vin Fiz, changing the tail structure and eliminating the very troublesome biplane elevators in front.

We were almost ready to ship the Vin Fiz to Washington when I received bad news. My last FAA medical examination had unacceptable results due to new, more stringent hearing requirements, and I found myself *officially grounded for the first time in my life.*

I, of course, resisted this edict, using the pretext that I was to fly in an FAA-sponsored event at Dulles, but to no avail. I did sneak a few more flights in the Vin Fiz, though, the last on *May 15, 1972, my final solo.* I then turned it over to the San Diego Aerospace Museum.

To finish this last chapter on my active career in aviation, I'd like to end where I began, with the Chanute-type of glider which I first flew in 1909. I'd already built two replicas of my original glider, one for the Smithsonian and one for San Diego. I was now intrigued at what might happen by modernizing this design with a cleaner wraparound of the fabric, more rounded corners, increased wing area and a swept-up tail. I hoped this last feature would cure failed flights by eliminating the tail hitting the ground just prior to takeoff.

In the fall of 1972, Stephen Ballas and I had completed the glider and took it to some hills near Otay, south of San Diego. My old wobbly legs weren't adequate to fly a hang glider any more, and I was certainly glad to have Steve step 'into the breach'. We made a series of flights, with several glides the full-length of the available hill - something over 600 feet. This was quite a contrast to my glide of 125 feet in 1909. After several more flights, we felt that this glider had fulfilled its mission, and it was then put in the San Diego Aerospace Museum alongside my 1909 model. That glider has aroused considerable interest in the burgeoning cult of hang gliders - being referred to as a *Classic* in contrast to the kite-like Rogallo models. Universal Studios used a glider built from my design for a sequence in a television series on NBC in 1974.

454

Me and my 1972 version of my 1909 glider

Stephen Ballas flying the glider - over 600 feet, at Otay - 1972

455

It seems like I'm becoming quite the elder statesman of hang gliding, too. It's a lot of fun to see this fascinating sport have such a resurgence after a span of half-a-century.

That about wraps up the saga of my life in flight, though by no means does it spell 'finis'. I'm sure that I will be actively following what goes on for many years yet - and in my manner, putting my two bits in from time to time.

Doug Fronious in a 1972-1909 glider - Torrey Pines, San Diego - 1974

456

Chapter 11

1974

Some Final Recollections and Reflections

OVER the years, and particularly in the early Twenties, we used to have many bull sessions about flying. Many of these were in social affairs including our wives and girlfriends. The pilots talked, and the women listened. As I look back on it, it is understandable why some of the girls were so horrified at the idea of flight. They heard all of the things that could go wrong in flying, but didn't have much concept as to the cause or rare frequency of these problems. It left them with a mental picture that created a lot of home opposition and lost loves.

Fire was the main thing that would drive you to the ground faster than anything else, and several aircraft were more vulnerable to it than others. We were skittish about certain Boeing seaplanes, the Standard J-1's, and the all-metal German Junkers. Most fires in these craft could be traced to fuel line ruptures, and once a fuel line broke, gasoline under pressure squirted out and really created an inferno. When the Federal government took over aircraft regulation after the 1926 Air Commerce Act, one of their first directives outlawed pressure-type fuel systems, and

457

thereafter this type of fire greatly diminished. The De Havilands (Americans typically dropped the second "L") that the Post Office and the Army were flying were especially dangerous in the event of fire and were thus tagged with the ominous *"flying coffin"* nickname. Also, the pilot sat well forward, immediately in back of the plane's Liberty engine and just in front of the huge gas tank between the two cockpits. The pilots ruefully referred to themselves as the *fried meat in the sandwich,* for in a crash the gas tank would hurtle forward, crushing them into the engine. This arrangement was improved by moving the pilot to the rear cockpit and the mail compartment forward.

Parachutes ("aerial life preserver") were something few of us used due to their expense and because the low landing speed of the planes then made it more prudent to ride the plane down rather than bail out if an engine failed. Also, few of us knew how to clear the aircraft or how to land in a parachute without injury, particularly in windy conditions or on rough terrain. *About the only thing that would drive us over the side with a parachute was a good hot fire beginning to singe our tail feathers!*

During the war years, 1914-1918, there was a lot of development work on parachutes, much of it at North Island, which finally culminated in the modern pack-type of chute at McCook Field in 1919. The first users were the pilots flying the Air Mail and, after Bane's order, the Army test pilots at McCook Field. As I mentioned, Harold Harris was the first to use one in earnest when an experimental Loening monoplane became uncontrollable, although some say the first emergency jump was made by Air Mail pilot C. C. Eversole on February 18, 1921.

But the cause of most of the bailing-out by test pilots was due more to higher speeds than to fire. At over 150-mph it was found that the wind buffeting got so severe that the control surfaces began shaking violently. This induced so much flutter that sometimes the stick thrashed so hard that the pilot couldn't hang onto it - so he'd lose control and be forced to go 'over the side' while his plane tore itself to pieces. It wasn't long, though, until this problem was solved by proper static balancing of the control system.

There was a lot of talk about having transport passengers wear parachutes. But there were serious problems with that - like if everyone tried to bail out at once, or if some refused to go. Another idea was to bring the whole airplane down, passengers and all, with one big chute. The

458

September 1921 issue of *Popular Science* pictured this concept on its cover (see next page). There was a lot of experimenting along this line by Roscoe Turner, and he found that the many diverse surfaces of the airplane could cause the chute to windmill, hopelessly fouling the shrouds and causing an even greater disaster. Two or more chutes were tried, but the costs, bulk and complexities ruled that out, also.

We had endless discussions on how to land a disabled airplane. We came to the conclusion that all engines failed sometime, and that it was wise to fly a route which always provided some sort of landing spot below you. This wasn't possible all of the time, but leaning in that direction surely saved a lot of lives and broken-up airplanes. Remember, I laid out the route for the Big Bear Airline that way - and that forced landing over Box S Springs proved its wisdom.

The airplanes that we flew typically had landing speeds of only around 35-mph, and in a crash landing there were ways of avoiding or lessening injury in spite of the frailties of the aircraft. At Ontario, I trained my students on where it was best to land in case of an engine failure. As the entire countryside was planted in some form of agriculture, there was quite a choice: alfalfa or hay fields; and groves, orchards and vineyards (some of California's first wineries were in this area). I found that a forced landing in an orange grove really broke an airplane up because the trees were short, tough and stubby. The problem with walnut trees was that they were quite tall, and you could get a nasty fall after you'd landed in one. However, peach trees were ideal - just the right height, and pliable enough so that the impact was cushioned and usually wouldn't totally break up the airplane. In fact, one time I landed a Jenny in a peach tree and all it took to fly away again was a new propeller. A grape vineyard was just about the worst place to be forced down. It was an absolute certainty that you'd dig the nose in and turn the plane over on its back while you were still going at a fairly good clip, far worse than what happened when Elon Brown rolled Brand's Mono Eagle into the Los Angeles Country Club's rose garden.

We had many discussions about flying over cities. We concluded that the best thing to do in a forced landing was to head for an archway or a large doorway - and go right on through, wiping the wings off in the process. This would absorb the shock while letting the body of the aircraft - with the pilot safely within - come to rest inside of the building.

459

100 Useful Things to Make at Home

Popular
Science

Founded MONTHLY *1872*

I know of at least two such cases where the airplane was virtually destroyed but the pilot's life was saved. The bad thing, though, was the danger this placed upon whomever might be in the building! In a forested area, if you could line up two good, substantial trees, around ten feet apart and fly between them, then a walkaway-crash-landing was very much in order. Of course, these emergency procedures dictated that you flew the airplane at just above its stall speed - as slowly as possible. These same guidelines were followed by the best Hollywood stunt pilots when they crashed into houses, barns and the like, *all in their day's work.*

Certain techniques involved in a water forced landing also made it possible to escape without injuries as long as you still had control of the airplane. However, the plane's sinking still left considerable danger. When Carol and I were flying the Flex Wing from Buffalo to New York, following the Mohawk and Hudson river valleys, there were few places for a forced landing except the river. Unthinkingly, I briefed Carol on what to do in case we were forced to *ditch* (though we didn't call it that) in the river. Quite awhile later I found out that she had taken my cautionary words as a terrifying possibility. That - coupled with the other incidents on that trip - (the hairy takeoff from Chicago, the blind landing at Wauwatosa, almost being shot down on the Aberdeen Proving Grounds, the near-miss with Jimmy Doolittle, and the weaving through the oil derricks in Oklahoma) all spelled-out what was to be her (almost) last flying experience. *She'd had enough!*

In those early years there were several types of airplane controls. My Waterman Tractor of 1911 had what could be considered a normal *stick* (from Santos-Dumont) and rudder bar control. That is, fore and aft motion of the stick controlled the elevators, lateral motion of the stick controlled the ailerons and the rudder bar controlled the rudder. However, my rudder function required a push on the right side in order to turn left, and vice versa, just the opposite of what developed later. Of course, a kid's coaster was controlled by pushing on the right to go left and this, therefore, seemed perfectly natural to me. In later years it became apparent that the rudder control did more than just turn the airplane around the vertical axis, and that pushing forward and down on the rudder pedals should cause the plane to bank or go down *on the side that was pushed.* As a result, all of the controls from about 1915-on that used the rudder bar or foot control were rigged in this manner.

461

The Wright control system typically consisted of three vertical levers. Two duplicate levers (one on each side) were for the *elevator*. The pilot in the left seat was called *"a left hand pilot"* because he maneuvered the lever with his left hand, while the pilot that sat in the right seat would do so with his right hand. A third lever in the center controlled the wing warp and the rudder. When it was pulled to the rear, it raised the left wing and depressed the right wing; when pushed forward, the reverse was true (see photo, page 85).

At the top of the central control lever was a hinged hand lever (the *split-handle* lever) connected to the *rudder*. This was rigged so that when the warp control lever was moved fore or aft, the split-handle lever's *lateral* movement controlled the rudder movement to overcome the added drag of the wing warping on the down side, theoretically producing a banked condition without any yaw or turning effect. These were unnatural operations requiring that a student pilot spend many hours sitting in the at-rest Wright, working the controls and observing their reaction. The Wright control system was obsoleted by the Bell-Curtiss AEA aileron combination, patented Dec. 5, 1911, (evolved from Santos-Dumont's *14 bis*), which by 1915 was in common usage.

But in these early years any pilot who had learned to fly with one system was greatly handicapped on another. Witness the tragedy that befell Silas Christofferson. My own problem in flying right after World War I was that I'd mainly flown the Curtiss shoulder-yoke and steering wheel system, the Wright lever system (a small amount) and the Waterman tractor reversed-control system. I found it quite difficult to make the transition from these systems into what soon became quite standard - *the stick control in my Jenny.*

The early Jennys had a wheel in place of a laterally-moving stick. This had been introduced by Deperdussin in France and was known as the *"Dep"* control, mispronounced *"Death"* by some. It was used in my Boeings and is still used today by all large aircraft and a few small ones. If one placed the hand that he normally used for the stick on the top-center of the wheel, the motions were identical for transition. But if a person learned on a Dep control using two hands, transition was more difficult. Another problem developed from positioning of the throttle. If the student learned on a plane with a right-hand throttle, he obviously used

462

his left hand on the stick - or vice versa. A pilot with limited experience naturally didn't like to make basic changes like this; therefore when confronted with this problem he flew with the hand he preferred on the stick and crossed the other hand over to operate the throttle. When the pilot became proficient, this made no difference.

In the early postwar days, flying the *"Aerial Mail"* for the Post Office was a pioneering and risky profession. One of their pilots was a chum of mine from middle school days, John Ordway (Jack) Webster. During the war he became an Army pilot, and then a Post Office pilot flying between Cleveland and Chicago. His last flight ended in a crash landing at Cleveland, and though he escaped being crushed, he was severely burned, surviving only because of a fast rescue by his buddies. He returned to San Diego and passed away many years later of natural causes.

Webster was one of the 'lucky' ones. Far too many pilots lost their lives as a result of the Post Office's arbitrary management. An Aerial Mail pilot's life expectancy was only *four years,* and *singed* letters were prized by philatelists! It's almost always been the case - even from the very early days - that the pilot has the final word on whether or not a flight should start, particularly in case of hazardous flying conditions. However, the Post Office gave their division managers the right to decide whether a flight would go or not. In one case, the manager at Bellefonte, Pennsylvania ordered the pilots to fly, regardless of the weather conditions. He, of course, ran into a great deal of opposition which he dealt with by threatening to discharge any pilot who refused to take off. Many crackups and not a few deaths resulted, and this caused the pilots to band together to fight these irrational edicts. Sometimes they would simply fly to the next emergency field and declare the flight off. At times they would select a newly-plowed field to land in, causing at least a turn-over, a broken propeller, a mangled rudder, and often more damage. These not so subtle maneuvers began to be understood by the Post Office's management. They realized that there was little they could do to combat them and finally retracted the rule that *"The mail must go though",* allowing the pilots the final word.

This episode wasn't too different from my own experience with Mrs. Eakin when we were starting West Coast Air Transport. But, fortunately, it hadn't taken any lives to convince her otherwise - only money.

463

Much of what I've recounted here came from Gilbert Budwig. As noted, Bud was one of the original handful of Post Office pilots. He shared the honors with such notables as Ira Biffle, the man that taught Lindbergh how to fly; Jack Knight (a Frank Clarke look-a-like), the pilot whose epic flight in 1921 ensured the completion of the first transcontinental Aerial Mail flight; and Mike Brown, the mentor of all the younger pilots.

When it came to notifying next-of-kin, the Post Office could be quite thoughtless. On at least two occasions, when a pilot was killed, his body was simply placed in a pine coffin and shipped to his wife or his parents, freight-collect, with no additional explanation. And, in at least one case, the arrival of this macabre package was the first news that a pilot's wife was a widow. The Post Office obviously was not accustomed to losing its carriers, and didn't have any procedures to cope with this situation as their bureaucracy slowly ground-away, snuffing-out the lives of some fine young men. (89 crashes killed 19 airmail pilots in 1920 and 1921.)

Some other aspects of early airline flying may be interesting. Practically all airlines used either the Fokker F10's or the Ford-Stout "Tin Goose" trimotors. The Ford had a capacity for twelve passengers, the Fokker, ten; and there were few provisions for their comfort. For meals, box lunches and thermosed hot coffee would be passed out, with the pilot and copilot often having to pay for their own. Passenger lunches were usually stored in the aft compartment, which was also used as the toilet room and sometimes as a luggage compartment. The toilet consisted simply of a seat with an opening downward, like a privy, and anything resulting from its use simply dropped from the airplane. Because of the slipstream, all of it didn't hit the ground; often a layer built-up on the rear tail surfaces. Naturally, the toilet room door was (supposed to be) locked when over towns.

When Spatz's *Question Mark* Fokker landed, it was moved into Metropolitan's main hangar so that we could handle the crowds and also give the crew an opportunity for a news conference. As general manager of the field, I ordered that no one but the plane's crew or those with press passes could get close to the aircraft. Clyde and Cotta Forsythe were there and, naturally, very interested in this flight, so I gave them passes. Cotta was a very lovely and beautifully-groomed lady - she always had a perfumed and embroidered hankie in her purse. She very-much wanted a souvenir of this historic event, but of course there wasn't anything we could detach from the airplane to give her. As she was wandering around, she spied a substance encrusted upon the tail surfaces just above her head. Thinking it was engine oil, she took her hankie and rubbed a bit off on it. I noticed what she was doing and I told her what it *really was*. At that, I was immediately given the hankie for disposal in the hangar's trash can!

Beyond the experiences of flying, I would be remiss unless I mentioned some of the men who helped make aviation what it is today, most of whom have been my friends over these many years.

Grover Loening, a somewhat starchy fellow, was one of the most outstanding. He was the first American to receive a degree in aeronautics (Columbia, 1910) and had started out as a young man in the Wright's tent at Governors Island, N.Y., in much the same manner as I had in Glenn Curtiss' tent at Dominguez. As such, our perspectives have been somewhat at odds over the years, mine being Western and his Eastern; but I have admired his achievements. In 1913, he joined the Wright Aeronautical Corporation briefly, and later, while with the Army Aero-

The Loening Amphibian, "A Patented and Proprietary Article" - 400-hp Liberty - 1926

465

nautical Corps at North Island in 1915, was responsible for breaking them away from building pusher airplanes with the ancient chain-driven propellers, wing warping and the like. With his brother, Albert, Grover then formed Loening Aeronautical Engineering Corporation. They manufactured seaplanes, amphibians, and a high-wing monoplane, the Loening M-8. It was similar to my Gosling and Ryan's B-1, but a bit larger and tailored to the military market with a more powerful 300-hp Hispano-Suiza engine. After an impressive decade-or-two of innovative contributions, Grover retired and became a director of Grumman Aircraft Engineering Corporation. He joined us at our Early Bird's reunion in Boston in 1974 (page 91). Though he never was much of a pilot, he qualified easily for membership because, when he was designing and building airplanes, he always insisted upon flying with the test-pilots in order to know firsthand what changes and modifications should be made.

Another rather flamboyant chap was Chance Vought, whose name is still around as part of the Ling-Temco-Vought (LTV) group. Chance was quite a flashy dresser and a social luminary. He built several credible airplanes in Connecticut, and then formed the Chance Vought Corporation. Vought and Grumman were the Navy's favorites for many years. You'll recall the Vought VE-7 wings I used for the Early Bird. In 1928, Vought teamed-up with Bill Boeing and Fred Rentschler, forming United Aircraft & Transport, the predecessor of United Airlines. Chance died many years ago, but his career is still remembered.

During the early years, Russia had a very impressive position in aviation, one that they have not ever relinquished. Following their 1917 revolution, two fine men came to this country - Alexander de Seversky (1894-1974) and Igor Sikorsky (1889-1972).

In Russia in 1913, Sikorsky had co-designed the Le Grand, a huge aeroplane which was the world's first with four engines. Sikorsky arrived with a group of White Russians (as differentiated from Red, or Communist), many of them former noblemen. He set up shop in an old hangar at Roosevelt Field, on Long Island, and first built a twin-engine transport, the S-29-A (Roscoe Turner's *"Flying Cigar Store"*). After 1928, Sikorsky flying boat models S-38 and S-39 became very familiar, particularly when shown in lectures and the movies being flown to the remote corners of the world by Martin & Osa Johnson.

466

Sikorsky S-38 over a smoggy lower-Manhattan, ca. 1929

The first time I met Igor was in the mid-Twenties. I had a devil-of-a-time understanding his then-limited English, and hardly any of his crew spoke it well, either. Sikorsky continued developing his flying boats, which Pan American used in the mid-Thirties to span the oceans. And in 1939 he built and flew the forerunner of today's helicopters, the Vought-Sikorsky VS-300.

Alexander de Seversky had also served in Russia during The Great War - as a fighter pilot completing an incredible 56 missions after the first one in which he lost a leg. Arriving in this country, he joined the staff of Billy Mitchell, and that's when I first met him. Seversky showed a great flair for engineering and design; but he also was a superb pilot, a top-notch executive, and a strenuous worker right up to his death. Both his book, *"Victory Through Air Power,"* and his remarkable aircraft (most notably the Republic P-47D Thunderbolt) caused him to be hailed by President Franklin Roosevelt as one who helped give the United States control of the air in World War II.

Seversky and I used to share the same table at the annual banquets of the *Society of Experimental Test Pilots,* as we were both honorary fellows of that hallowed organization. He was a most fascinating man.

467

The *"Lockheed"* brothers were a very interesting trio. They made several major contributions to both aviation and other facets of American life. There was Allan and Malcolm Loughead and their half-brother, Victor. Victor, spelling his name Lougheed, was the first one that I knew anything about. He was a bit of a renegade, and wrote the book, *"Vehicles of The Air; a Popular Exposition of Modern Aeronautics with Working Drawings,"* a treatise on aviation for 1909. I cherished my copy for the large fund of information it contained. There was one sad thing about it though. Victor threw-his-lot-in with the claims of John Montgomery, whose theories were contrary to the best-known and accepted aerodynamic and design theories of the day. Victor, I believe, wrote the book in order to capitalize upon Montgomery's claims, as he had a financial agreement with him. He backed Montgomery's family in a lawsuit against the Wright brothers and the government, claiming that every airplane built during World War I was an infringement of the Montgomery patent. After a lengthy and sometimes acrimonious trial, the whole thing was thrown out of court as unsubstantiated.

During the 1920's, brother Malcolm spun off from aviation to invent and promote the automobile hydraulic brake, first used by Chrysler. He was the first to adopt the handle *"Lockheed"*, and the term *"Lockheed brakes"* soon became almost generic. His success provided the funds that helped Allan launch his venture with Fred Keeler, forming *Lockheed Aircraft Company,* predecessor of today's giant. I've already touched upon much of Lockheed's early development, and of Gilbert Budwig's early involvement. My good friend Max Harlow was also a factor in Allan Lockheed's development of the Alcor Duo-4 and 6.

There are *so many* other names who contributed in some way in bringing aviation to its present state. Many I've not touched upon; some possibly because their philosophy was somewhat alien to mine by being in aviation primarily for the money and not for the challenge of aviation. My own limited success in aviation - through luck or the lack of it - has been more personal than public, more aerodynamic than financial.

When I was very young, I had determined to make aviation my life's career. I realize now that what achievement I accomplished could have been done by many others if they'd had the same chance, determination and background that I'd had. I had many, many opportunities in avia-

468

tion, most of which I recognized and pursued. The results, though, have been limited and fraught with failure and heartbreak.

The first big disappointment that I had was the inability of Kenneth Kendall and I to complete our aeroplane, in order to take it to the 1910 Dominguez Air Meet. I always felt that if we'd have gotten it there, even with the very poor performance that we eventually achieved, that we would have received a considerable amount of recognition and possibly some of the prize monies available to the California amateurs.

My real ambition in that era was to become an exhibition aviator, as that seemed to be where the glamour and money existed. Fortunately, I was overruled by what I now suspect was a conspiracy between my mother and Glenn Curtiss to sidetrack me into an engineering education. Although disappointing at the time, this was a fine thing as far as my future was concerned. Otherwise, I probably would have soon ended my flying career by reason of the statistical average lifespan of the exhibition flyers then. Even those that did not die in a spectacular crash seemed to fade into oblivion. On the other hand, many of those that chose to follow engineering and manufacturing found their names emblazoned upon the annals of aviation history.

The construction of the flying boat, which I started at Berkeley, was another case in frustration. If we'd been able to complete it, we could have demonstrated a breakthrough in flying boat hull design. I can point with some pride to the photographs of our partially-completed work which, when compared with others of this time, indicate how advanced the design was. Naturally, it was a major disappointment to have this project curtailed - particularly at the time of youthful college exuberance.

And when the Great War came along, I was turned-down at North Island as a cadet-pilot on account of my badly broken-up feet. This dashed what dreams I had of becoming a Hun-downing ace. However, I later took pride and consolation from my many Army Aviation School students that went on to memorable exploits of their own, while always warmly remembering me.

Another disappointment was U.S. Aircraft Corporation. Just when we finished our first contract and were negotiating for a follow-up, one which could have been profitable, the war ended and no new contracts were issued. By this time, at only 26-years-old, I was running things. I considered this a tremendous opportunity lost.

After moving to Venice and establishing Waterman Aircraft Manufacturing Co., I proceeded to make the next of my mistakes by taking Billy Mitchell's advice literally, bidding on only the 50 and 100-plane quantities for the Thomas-Morse MB3A contract. Boeing (which at that time wasn't much bigger than I was) bid on the whole 200. They thus had a lower-per-plane figure than my bid and won the entire contract. I should have been less greedy and stuck by my original intent of pursuing the Navy torpedo plane contract, for which three contracts were to be let. I am sure that I would have received one of those. I find it quite interesting, though somewhat melancholy, to compare my drawings with those of the three successful bidders and to see that my concept had several points of advance over each of them.

As you recall, times were very tough in the early Twenties and the loss of these contracts necessitated the shutdown my operations. The citrus frost-prevention and Heat Mill episode followed, which carved out a couple of years of my life. I got no great financial reward save the satisfaction that I contributed something that's now practiced worldwide.

In looking over my Ontario and Big Bear operation, I can see where I made many mistakes. Yet some concepts that I had could have been highly successful if they had been carried to their conclusion.

All through my activities, I always had my sights set too high, and invariably went after a project underfinanced. Boy! I surely had my foot in the door in deals and projects that proved very successful to others, such as Douglas and Boeing!

Sometimes I was simply too-far-ahead - witness the Vidal competition and the Arrowbile. Even with the advances that have been made in the last quarter-century, that concept still seems to be intriguing, but really not possible to achieve. That was my problem in several other concepts: aviation was not yet ready for them, or they ended-up being solved in some other way, like the Flex Wing. And, in 1946, in a discussion on the future types of aircraft, I said that *the plane of the future might be called the 'flying body' - because I think that fuselages are going to get larger and larger.* Today's 'wide-bodies,' like the Boeing 747, certainly seem to prove-out that prediction.

In spite of all of these ups and downs, I can't help but feel a certain amount of satisfaction in what I've come to and have attained. I am sitting here in the spot that I picked 55 or 60 years ago as the place where I

470

wished to retire. I've had my yachts, my seaplane, my own pier and a freedom of life that is enjoyed by few people. My wonderful wife, Carol, has been with me through all of these years - through the thick-and-thin of it - and she has been a constant rock on which to lean in those times of travail and weariness. Our daughter, Jane, and her family, Adrian, our grandaughters, Carol and Nell, have all been a source of love and loyalty, for which I am very thankful. All in all, it's been a wonderful experience.

And thus we come to what appears to be the end of my tale. At this writing (1975), both Carol and I are still hale and hearty, though a bit weary and bent with the years. My hope is that you have found the reading of my life and times as much fun as I have had in both living it and of telling you about it. Good bye.

"Time, like an ever-rolling stream,
bears all its sons away;
They fly forgotten,
    as a dream
dies at the opening day."

Isaac Watts, 1719

The End

Me, at the San Diego
Yacht Club, 1971.
Photo by Jack Carpenter

471

PROFILE

Waldo Dean Waterman
June 16, 1894 - December 8, 1976

1908-12	San Diego High School.
1909-10	Waterman-Kendall Aviation Partnership, *17.*
1910-12	Glenn H. Curtiss, Los Angeles & San Diego, helper & pupil, *21.*
1912-16	University of California, Berkeley, *92.*
1917 30 June	Married Carol E. Coulter; one daughter, Jane, *108.*
1917	Head, Dept. of Flight Theory, Military Aeronautics, University of California, Berkeley, *108.*
1918-19	General Manager, U.S. Aircraft Corp., Redwood City, *115.*
1920-22	Waterman Aircraft Co., Venice, CA, *117.*
1923-24	Barnstorming aviator, *160.*
1925-27	General Manager, Ontario Aircraft Corp., *(Ontario-Big Bear Airline)* Ontario, CA, *173.*
1928-29	Chief Engineer & test pilot, Bach Aircraft Co, *217.*
1929-30	General Manager, Los Angeles *Metropolitan Airport* (Van Nuys), *239.*
1930-31	Waterman Aircraft Syndicate *(Flex Wing), 285.*
1932-33	Pilot, TWA, *325.*
1934-39	Waterman Research Engineering Co. *(Whatsit), 321.*
1935-1938	Waterman Arrowplane Corp. *(Arrowbile), 358.*
1939-43	Coordinator, Civilian Pilot Training, Pasadena City College, *398.*
1943-44	Chief Engineer, Stout Research Division, ConVair, *405.*
1945-74	Waterman Research Engineering Co., *(Aerobile), 416.*

1909	Aero Club of San Diego.
1920	Aero Club of Southern California.
1920-30	Professional Pilots Association, president, 1924.
1929-76	*Early Birds of Aviation,* Life Member, president, 1939.

472

1937	National Aeronautic Association, Los Angeles Chapter, president.
1965-	Experimental Aircraft Association.
1965-	OX-5 Club, *"Mr. OX-5"* 1964; Hall of Fame 1971.
1966	Honorary Fellow, *Society of Experimental Test Pilots.*
1968	International Aerospace Hall of Fame, San Diego.

| 1929 | Altitude record (20,820 feet), carrying 1,000 Kg. load, *273.* |
| 1929 | First Place, Air Transport Race, National Air Races, *279.* |

1909 1 July	First solo flight, Chanute-type glider, San Diego, *13.*
1911 28 June	First solo flight, Curtiss biplane, North Island, *59.*
1972 15 May	Last solo flight, Waterman-Wright *"1911 Vin Fiz", 454.*

Smithsonian Institution:

    1909 *Popular Mechanics Glider,* replica.
    1932 Waterman *"Whatsit",* original.
    1937 Waterman *"Aerobile",* flying auto No. 7.

Inventor and holder of several patents in the aviation field. Credited with designing and building the world's first *"Flying Auto";* the first plane with shock-absorbing wings; the first American tailless flying wing monoplane; the first modern tricycle landing gear, etc. Author, *"Nomenclature for Aeronautics,"* 1917, plus many other articles and papers, i.e., Society of Automotive Engineers, 1938.

CHRONOLOGY

1804-53	George Cayley, English - father of "Aerial Navigation".
1842-48	William Henson & John Stringfellow, English - powered monoplane model.
1856	J.M. LeBris, French - albatross-shaped, man-carrying glider.
1857	Felix du Temple, French, powered airplane patent.
1867	Wilbur Wright born, died 1912.
1871	Orville Wright born, died 1948.
1871	Alphonse Penaud, French, rubber-band-powered model airplane.
1876	A.N. Otto - practical four-stroke gasoline engine.
1878	Glenn H. Curtiss born, died 1930.
1880	William B. Stout born, died 1956.
1884	H.F. Phillips - airfoil sections published.
1893	Lawrence Hargrave, Australian - "box kite" design.
1894	*Waldo Waterman* born, died 1976.
1894	Octave Chanute - *Progress in Flying Machines.*
1891-96	Otto Lilienthal, German - first man to fly and control gliders..."*to fly is everything*"
1896 May 6	Langley's *"Aerodrome"* - first American unmanned powered flight (photos by Alexander Graham Bell), *8.*
1899	Wright brothers built large kites.
1901	Charles Manly - 52-hp five-cylinder radial engine (from Stephen Balzer rotary), for Langley's Aerodrome (2.4 lbs. per hp, lightest ratio until 400-hp Liberty).
1901 Aug 14	Gustave Whitehead (1874-1927) - powered flight of Lilienthal-like Model 21, Connecticut.
1900-02	Wright brothers built man-carrying, Chanute-like gliders.
1903	Leon Levavasseur's *Antoinette* - ultra-light engine, *17.*
1903 Dec 17	*Wrights fly in manned powered flight.*
1904	Esnault-Pelterie - use of *ailerons, 13.*
1905 Jun-Oct	Wright 20-hp powered *"Flyer No. 3"* - first *practical* airplane.
1906 Feb 27	Samuel Pierpont Langley dies, age 72.
Sep 13	Alberto Santos-Dumont, Brazilian, thought he was first to fly (in Hargrave-like craft, in Paris), *7.*

474

1907-08	*Waldo Waterman's first large kites, 6.*
1907 Oct 1	*Aerial Experiment Association* formed by Mabel and Alexander Graham Bell, Curtiss (*Director of Experiments*), Selfridge, McCurdy & Baldwin.
Nov	First time European stayed in air a full minute in an airplane.
Nov 30	First American airplane company - Curtiss Motor Vehicle Company.

| 1908 | *THE YEAR THAT THE LIGHT OF THE DAWN OF AVIATION BLAZED FORTH.* |

Mar 12	F.W. "Casey" Baldwin flew the AEA *"Red Wing"*.
May l4	Wrights were flying again...having not flown since 1905.
May 19	Lt. Selfridge flew the AEA *"White Wing"* (killed Sept. 17, 1908, while a passenger with Orville Wright, *9*).
May 21	Glenn Curtiss first flew the AEA *"White Wing"*.
July 4	Curtiss, in AEA *"June Bug,"* was first to fly kilometer in the U.S., winning the *Scientific American's* prize, *8*.
Aug 8	Wilbur Wright first flew in Europe.

1909

July 1	*Waldo's first successful glider flights, 13.*
July 25	Louis Bleriot was first to fly the English Channel.
Aug 22-29	World's first Aviation Meet, Reims, France - Lefebvre, Paulhan, Farman, Latham, Bleriot, and Glenn Curtiss, the lone American, won the coveted *Gordon Bennett Trophy*.
Nov 22	The Wright Company incorporated.

By year's end, three aviators had died.

1910

| Jan 10-20 | *First American International Aviation Meet,* Dominguez Field, Los Angeles - the French: Paulhan, Maisson, Miscarol and the American group: Curtiss, Clifford Harmon, Hamilton, and Willard; with Cortlandt Field Bishop as chief judge. *Waldo meets Curtiss, 18.* |

1910

April First flight, Waterman-Kendall airplane - *Waldo* broke both ankles in crackup, *31*.

 Lincoln Beachey joined Curtiss. Orville Wright said that Beachey was *"the greatest aviator of all."*

Sept 2 Blanche Scott, *first American woman pilot* - taught by Curtiss at Hammondsport.

Nov 14 Eugene Ely flew *off of* USS Birmingham in a Curtiss.

Dec 26-31 Second Dominguez Meet.

At year's end, 32 flyers had died.

— —

1911 In early 1911, there were only about 150 airplanes and 26 pilots in the US; by year's end there were over 300 "private aviators", plus 16 that had been killed.

Jan 17 Curtiss Camp (new experimental grounds) established on *North Island* (San Diego) - Curtiss and Lt. Ellyson, USN; Lts. Kelly, Beck & Walker, US Army; Robinson, Witmer, & mechanics, Merrill and Cooper, *35*.

Jan 18 First ship *landing and takeoff;* Ely in a Curtiss and USS Pennsylvania, San Francisco. (Ely killed Oct. 9, 1911)

Jan 26 Curtiss flew *first practical seaplane* (at North Island), *40*.

Jan 28-29 Curtiss had first Air Show in San Diego (Lt. Ellyson's "first flight"), *35*.

Feb 17 Curtiss "flew" to, and was *hoisted on and off,* USS Pennsylvania, San Diego, *46*.

Feb 26 Curtiss flew *"Triad"* at North Island, *first amphibian, 48*.

May 8 Navy ordered two Curtiss planes, *"birthday"* of Naval Aviation.

June 28 *Waldo first flew in Curtiss "Lizzie" at North Island, 59.*

Dec 10 Calbraith Rodgers in *"Vin Fiz"* completed first transcontinental flight at Long Beach, CA (where he crashed and died four months later).

From Sept 17, 1909, to March 8, 1911, approximately 1,000 learned to fly, many of whom were to die in this precarious infancy-of-flight period.

476

1912

Jan 20-28 Third Air Meet at Dominguez Field, Los Angeles
Feb 29   *Waldo's* tractor-biplane demolished, *83.*
March 1   *Waldo,* as passenger, crashed with Herbster at North Island, demolishing *one-third* of USN aircraft, *75.*

At the end of 1912, the U.S. Army had 12 aeroplanes and six licensed pilots; the Navy had three Curtiss and two Wright aeroplanes.

_____

1913

Nov 25   Beachey did first American loop in a Curtiss over polo field at Coronado/San Diego (killed at San Francisco Pan Pacific Exposition, Mar 14, 1915, *102).*

_____

Early *Navy* pilots: 1 Theodore Ellyson, 2 John Rodgers, 3 J.H. Towers, 4 Victor Herbster...52 1/4 Forrest E. Wysong.

Early *Army* pilots: 1 Frederic Humphreys, 2 Frank Lahm, 3 Benjamin Foulois, John Walker, Paul Beck, G.E.M. Kelly.

US *Marine* Corps: Alfred Cunningham (Aug 1912).

Civilians, licensed by Aero Club of America under authority of Federation Aeronautique Internationale, FAI: 1 Curtiss, 2 Lahm, 3 Paulhan, 4 Orville Wright, 5 Wilbur Wright...56 Glenn Martin.

Jack Carpenter (G.J.,Jr.) was born in Southern California, seven miles from where America's first air meet was held. He grew-up as a sky-struck kid, trudging out to Long Beach's airport when 9 years old (where he flew with Earl Daugherty in 1928, though remembering nothing of it). He first met Claude Ryan as a 12-year-old when taken to San Diego by Ryan's father, his Sunday school teacher. Also, he didn't wash his hands for days after shaking Wrong-Way Corrigan's hand in 1938!

Jack spent many days of his youth in San Diego, where an uncle's Point Loma home overlooked the bay and North Island, and he also later lived on Point Loma. He was with Ryan Aeronautical for a couple years, when he co-managed the program to build the *first* advanced composite supersonic flight surface. Membership in the San Diego Yacht Club introduced him to Waldo in 1967, and to many luncheons with both he and Claude Ryan. Once, after taking an Air Force Colonel to the member's lunch, he exclaimed *"I've just had lunch with history!"*.

An amateur historian since a private interview with Alexander Kerensky while a freshman at Illinois College, Jack has had a life-long interest in understanding *"how things really were"*.

This book began in 1974, shortly after Jack moved to Massachusetts. Initially there was the exchange between he and Waldo of over 40-hours of tapes. Their transcription, and many, many cross-country editing communications with Waldo followed. Eventually, after several more years of on-again, off-again work, he reached the conclusion, this book.

Jack entered the Navy as a pilot candidate in World War II, but when commissioned in 1946 had never begun flight instruction. He has degrees from Notre Dame and Stanford universities, and lives with his family in Andover, Massachusetts, where he is active in real estate development.

478

ACKNOWLEGEMENTS

Those that helped: in an endeavor with the scope of this tale, there were those individuals whose contributions, assistance and comments are invaluable. My thanks, therefore, to the many that have helped, and especially to (alphabetically, just like the FAI in 1909!): Bert Buckborough, Owen Clarke, Jay Connolly (cover design), Chuck Haberlein, Bob Hilton, Ken Naylor, Susan Pfluke, Sandy Roca (co-editor), Joan Rolfe, Jack Searles, Bob Tardugno, and Scott Young (our "desktop publisher").

PHOTOGRAPH CREDITS

When, in 1974, Waldo and I started this project, we planned to use his own large photographic collection - but the 1978 San Diego Aerospace Museum fire scorched that! Therefore, out thanks to the sources listed below. Also, in a few cases we have reproduced several photographs and illustrations of poor quality where no better examples are extant

Our particular thanks to Paul Matt (though too late, now), to Charles Haberlein of the Naval Historical Center, and to Phil Edwards of the Smithsonian Air and Space Museum Library. Also, to the San Diego Historical Society, the San Diego Public Library, and the Union-Tribune Publishing Co. Chere Negaard of the Northrop Aviation History Library was most helpful, as was Kevin Harkins and Howard Rozelle. Also, thanks to First American Title Insurance Co., the California Historical Society, the Schlesinger Library of Radcliffe College, and the Glenn H. Curtiss Museum.

California Historical Society/Ticor-LA: 21

California State Library: 2

Curtiss Museum, Hammondsport: 72

Downie and Associates: 375 (top), 405, 442 (top), 445 (top)

479

First American Title Insurance Co.: 26 (composite)

International News Photos: 344

International News Reel: 289 (top)

Matt, Paul R.: 82, 83 (2), 96, 133, 146, 149, 174, 273-274, 340, 341 (Ray Russell), 342-343, 350 (Ray Russel), 380, 381 (lower), 386, 422 (2)

National Air and Space Museum, Smithsonian Institution: 39 (lower), 76 (lower), 77 (top), 109, 280, 373 (lower), 376 (lower), 382 (2)

Northrop Aviation History Library: 268-269

Schlesinger Library, Radcliffe College: 147

TWA: 251

Union Tribune Publishing Co.: 447 (2), 448

US Naval Historical Center, collections of T.G. Ellyson and J.L. Callan: 25 (Willard), 36 (2), 37-38, 39 (top), 41, 42 (2), 43 (3), 44 (2), 45 (2), 47 (bottom), 48, 50, 51 (middle and bottom), 52 (bottom), 53 (2), 61, 63, 64 (3), 65 (3), 66, 68 (2), 69 (3), 70 (3), 76 (top), 77 (bottom), 79, 80 (bottom), 81 (2), 84 (2), 85-87, 97-98

BIBLIOGRAPHY

ABOVE AND BEYOND - ENCYCLO-PEDIA OF AVIATION & SPACE SCIENCES, Vol. 1. Chicago, 1968.*

Adams, Jean; Kimball, Margaret; Coll. w/ Eaton, Jeanette. HEROINES OF THE SKY. Garden City, NY: Doubleday Doran & Company, 1942.*

Allen, C.B.; Lyman, Lauren D. THE WONDER BOOK OF THE AIR. Chicago-Philadelphia-Toronto: The John C. Winston Company, 1941.*

Allen, Richard. REVOLUTION IN THE SKY. Brattleboro, VT: The Steven Greene Press, 1964.

Angelucci, Enzo. AIRPLANES FROM THE DAWN OF FLIGHT. New York: McGraw-Hill Book Company, 1971.

AVIATION IN THE UNITED STATES. Washington, D.C.: Naval History Division, 1965.*

Balchen, Bernt. COME NORTH WITH ME - AN AUTOBIOGRAPHY. New York: E.P. Dutton & Co., Inc., 1958.*

Baxter, John. STUNT. Garden City, NY: Doubleday & Company, Inc., 1974.

Beamish, Richard J. THE BOY'S STORY OF LINDBERGH THE LONE EAGLE. Philadelphia-Chicago-Toronto: The John C. Winston Company, 1928.*

Bower, Chaz. THE AGE OF THE BI-PLANE. Englewood Cliffs, NJ: Prentice-Hall, Inc., 1981.*

Bowers, Peter. FORGOTTEN FIGHT-ERS, U.S. ARMY. New York: ARCO, 1971.

Briddon, Arnold E.; Champie, Ellmore A.; Marraine, Peter A. FAA HISTORI-CAL FACT BOOK - A CHRONOL-OGY 1926 - 1979. Washington, D.C.: Department Of Transportation Federal Aviation Administration, 1974.*

Brownlow, Kevin. THE PARADE'S GONE BY. New York: Alfred A. Knopf, Inc., 1969.

Bruno, Harry. WINGS OVER AMER-ICA, THE STORY OF AMERICAN AVIATION. Garden City, NY: Halcyon House, 1944.*

Buchanan, Lamont. THE FLYING YEARS. New York: G.P. Putnam's Sons, 1953.

Burke, John. WINGED LEGEND. New York: G.P. Putnam's Sons, 1970.

Byrd, Richard E. DISCOVERY - THE STORY OF THE SECOND BYRD ANTARCTIC EXPEDITION. New York: G.P. Putnam's Sons, 1925.*

Byrd, Richard E. LITTLE AMERICA. New York-London: G.P. Putnam's Sons, 1930.*

Byrd, Richard E. SKYWARD. New York: Blue Ribbon Books, 1936.*

Caidin, Martin. GOLDEN WINGS - A PICTORIAL HISTORY OF THE UNITED STATES NAVY AND MARINE CORPS IN THE AIR. New York: Random House, 1960.*

Cameron, Robert. ABOVE LOS ANGE-LES. San Francisco, California: Cameron & Company, 1981.*

Canby, Courtlandt. A HISTORY OF FLIGHT. New York: Hawthorn Books Inc. Publishers, 1963.*

Carlisle, Norman; Cleveland, Reginald; Wood, Jonathan. THE MODERN WONDER BOOK OF THE AIR. Philadelphia-Toronto: The John C. Winston Company, 1945.*

Chant, Christopher. FANTASTIC AIR-CRAFT. London: Roydon Publishing Company, New York: W.H. Smith Publishers, Inc. (Gallery Books), 1984.*

Chaplin, Charles. CHARLES CHAPLIN. New York: Simon & Schuster, 1964.*

Chatfield, Charles Hugh & Taylor, Charles Fayette. THE AIRPLANE AND ITS ENGINE. New York: McGraw-Hill Book Company, Inc., 1928.*

CHRONOLOGY OF SIGNIFICANT AEROSPACE EVENTS. (25th Anniversary) United States Air Force, 1972.*

Collins, Francis A. THE BOYS' BOOK OF MODEL AEROPLANES. New York: The Century Company, 1910.*

Conot, Robert. A STREAK OF LUCK, THE LIFE AND LEGEND OF THOMAS ALVA EDISON. New York: Seaview Books, 1979.*

Corn, Joseph J. THE WINGED GOS-PEL. New York: Oxford University Press, 1983.*

Corrigan, Douglas. THAT'S MY STORY. New York: E.P. Dutton & Company, 1938. Signed.*

Cresswell, Mary Ann & Berger, Carl (compilers). UNITED STATES AIR FORCE HISTORY. Washington, DC: Office of Air Force History, 1971.*

Curtiss, Glenn H. CURTISS SOUVENIR BOOK AND DAILY PROGRAM. New York: White & Wood Co., 1911.*

Curtiss, Glenn H.; Post, Augustus. THE CURTISS AVIATION BOOK. New York: Frederick A. Stokes Company, 1912. (Post's personal copy, signed)*

Davies, R.E.G. THE WORLD'S AIR-LINES. London: Oxford University Press, 1964.

Davis, Burke. THE BILLY MITCHELL AFFAIR. New York: Random House, 1967.*

Davis, Warren Jefferson. THE WORLD'S WINGS. New York-London: Simmons-Boardman Publishing Company, 1927.*

481

Devon, Francis. MR. PIPER AND HIS CUBS. Ames: Iowa State University Press, 1973.

Dickey III, Philip S. THE LIBERTY ENGINE 1918-1942. Washington, D.C.: Smithsonian Institution Press, National Air And Space Museum, 1968.* From Hunsaker estate.

Dwiggins, Don. THE AIR DEVILS. Philadelphia: J.B. Lippincott Company, 1966.

Dwiggins, Don. THE BARNSTORM-ERS. New York: Grosset & Dunlop, 1968.

Dwiggins, Don. ON SILENT WINGS - ADVENTURES IN MOTORLESS FLIGHT. New York: Grosset & Dunlop, Inc., 1970.*

Dwiggins, Don. THEY FLEW THE BENDIX RACE. Philadelphia-New York: J.B. Lippincott Company, 1965.*

Earhart, Amelia. LAST FLIGHT. New York: Harcourt, Brace & Company, 1937.*

Earhart, Amelia. TWENTY HOURS AND FORTY MINUTES. New York: G.P. Putnam's Sons, 1928.*

Floherty, John J. 'BOARD THE AIR-LINER. New York, Garden City: The Junior Literary Guild & Doubleday, Doran & Company, Incorporated, 1934.*

Fokker, Anthony H.G. & Gould, Bruce. FLYING DUTCHMAN. New York: Henry Holt & Company, 1931.

FORTUNE. New York: Time, Inc., May 1934.

Fraser, Chelsea. FAMOUS AMERICAN FLYERS. New York: Thomas Y. Crowell Company, 1941.

French, Joseph Lewis (Ed); Intro. by Eddie Rickenbacker. ACES OF THE AIR. Springfield, MA: McLoughlin Brothers, Inc., 1930.*

Funderburk, Thomas R. THE FIGHT-ERS, THE MEN AND MACHINES OF THE FIRST AIR WAR. New York: Grosset & Dunlap, 1965.*

Furnas, J.C. GREAT TIMES 1914-1929. New York: G.P. Putnam's Sons, 1974.

Gann, Ernest K. BLAZE OF NOON. New York: Henry Holt & Company, 1946.*

Gann, Ernest K. A HOSTAGE TO FOR-TUNE. New York: Alfred A. Knopf, 1978.*

Gibbons, Floyd. THE RED KNIGHT OF GERMANY: The Story Of Baron Von Richthofen. New York, Garden City: Garden City Publishing Co., Inc., 1927.*

Gilbert, James. THE GREAT PLANES. Ridge Press, 1970.

Gill, Brendan. LINDBERGH ALONE. New York-London: Harcourt Brace Jovanovich, 1977.*

Glines, C.V. FROM THE WRIGHT BROTHERS TO THE ASTRO-NAUTS. New York: McGraw-Hill Book Company, 1968.*

Golding, Harry (Ed) THE WONDER BOOK OF AIRCRAFT. London-Melbourne: Ward, Lock & Company, Ltd., ca. 1930.*

Greenwood, James. THE PARACHUTE. New York: E.P. Dutton & Company, 1964.

Greif, Martin. THE AIRPORT BOOK - FROM LANDING FIELD TO MOD-ERN TERMINAL. New York: Mayflower Books, Inc., 1979.*

Grooch, William Stephen. SKYWAY TO ASIA. New York-Toronto: Longmans, Green & Company, 1936.*

Harris, Sherwood. THE FIRST TO FLY. New York: Simon & Schuster, 1970.*

Hatfield, D.D. DOMINGUEZ AIR MEET. Inglewood, California: Northrop University Press, 1976.*

Hatfield, D.D. LOS ANGELES AERO-NAUTICS. Inglewood, California: D.D. Hatfield, 1973. Signed.*

Hatfield, D.D. PIONEERS OF AVIA-TION. Inglewood, California: Northrop University Press, 1976.*

Hatfield, D.D. AEROPLANE (OR FLYING MACHINE) SCRAP BOOK, NUMBER 1. Inglewood, California: Northrop University Press, 1976.*

Hatfield, D.D. AEROPLANE (OR FLYING MACHINE) SCRAP BOOK, NUMBER 2. Inglewood, California: Northrop University Press, 1971.*

Hatfield, D.D. AEROPLANE (OR FLYING MACHINE) SCRAP BOOK, NUMBER 3. Inglewood, California: Northrop University Press, 1975.*

Hawks, Frank (Capt.) ONCE TO EV-ERY PILOT. New York: Stackpole Sons, 1936. Signed.*

Heindell, Howard J. THE FLIGHT ACROSS THE ATLANTIC. New York: Curtiss Aeroplane & Motor Corporation (issued by Dept. of Education), 1919.*

Heinmuller, John P.V. MAN'S FIGHT TO FLY. New York-London, Funk & Wagnalls Company, 1944.*

Higgins, C.A. TO CALIFORNIA AND BACK. Chicago: Atchison, Topeka & Santa Fe Railroad, 1893.

HISTORY OF FLIGHT. American Heritage Publishing Co., Inc., 1962.*

Holland, Rupert Sargent. HISTORIC AIRSHIPS. New York: Grosset & Dunlap, 1928.*

Holmes, Donald B. AIR MAIL - AN IL-LUSTRATED HISTORY, 1793-1981. New York: Clarkson N. Potter, Inc., Publishers, Dist. Crown Publishers, 1981.*

482

Howard, Frank; Gunston, Bill. THE CONQUEST OF THE AIR. New York: Random House, 1972.*

Howard, Fred. WILBUR AND ORVILLE - A BIOGRAPHY OF THE WRIGHT BROTHERS. New York: Alfred A. Knopf, Inc., 1987.*

Jablonski, Edward. ATLANTIC FEVER. New York: The Macmillan Company, 1972.*

Jablonski, Edward. FLYING FORTRESS. Garden City, New York: Doubleday & Company, Inc., 1965.*

Jablonski, Edward. LADYBIRDS: WOMEN IN AVIATION. New York: Hawthorn Books, Inc., 1968.*

Jablonski, Edward. MAN WITH WINGS. Garden City, NY: Doubleday & Company, Inc., 1980.*

Jablonski, Edward. SEA WINGS. Garden City, NY: Doubleday & Company, Inc., 1972.

Jane's. ALL THE WORLD'S AIRSHIPS - 1909. ALL THE WORLD'S AIRCRAFT - 1913. ALL THE WORLD'S AIRCRAFT - 1919. New York: ARCO, 1969.

Jensen, Paul. THE FIRESIDE BOOK OF FLYING STORIES. New York: Simon And Schuster, 1951.*

Jordanoff, Assen. FLYING AND HOW TO DO IT! New York: Grosset & Dunlap, 1932.*

Jordanoff, Assen. MEN AND WINGS. Curtiss-Wright Corporation, Airplane Division, 1941.*

Jordanoff, Assen. YOUR WINGS. New York-London, Funk & Wagnalls Company, 1937.*

Juptner, Joseph P. U.S. CIVIL AIRCRAFT (Vol. 1, 1962 & Vol. 2). Los Angeles: Aero Publishers, 1964.

Keats, John. HOWARD HUGHES. New York: Random House, 1966.*

Keller, Michael David. FIFTY YEARS OF FLIGHT RESEARCH: A CHRONOLOGY OF THE LANGLEY RESEARCH CENTER, 1917-1966. Washington, DC: National Aeronautics and Space Administration, 1966.*

Ketchum, Richard. WILL ROGERS, HIS LIFE & TIMES. New York: American Heritage, 1973.

Kinert, Reed. AMERICAN RACING PLANES AND HISTORIC AIR RACES. New York-Chicago-Toronto: Wilcox & Follett Company, 1952.*

Koehl, Hermann; Fitzmaurice, James C.; von Huenefeld, Guenther. THE THREE MUSKETEERS OF THE AIR. New York-London: G.P. Putnam's Sons, 1928.*

Langley, Samuel Pierpont. THE "FLYING MACHINE." (McClure's Magazine) New York: S.S. McClure Company, 1897.*

Law, Bernard A. (Major) FIGHTING PLANES OF THE WORLD. New York: Random House, 1940.*

Lawrence, Joanne T. AVCO CORPORATION: THE FIRST FIFTY YEARS. Connecticut, Greenwich: Avco Corporation, 1979.

Lawson, Ted. W. (Capt.) THIRTY SECONDS OVER TOKYO. New York: Random House, 1943.*

Leadabrand, Russ; Lowenkopf, Shelly; Patterson, Bryce. YESTERDAY'S CALIFORNIA. Miami, FL: E.A. Seemann Publishing, Inc., 1975.*

Leigh, Howard. PLANES OF THE GREAT WAR 1914-1918. London: John Hamilton Ltd., 1934.*

Lewellen, John; Shapiro, Irwin. THE STORY OF FLIGHT FROM THE ANCIENT WINGED GODS TO THE AGE OF SPACE. New York: Golden Press, 1960.*

Lewis, Sinclair. MANTRAP. New York: Harcourt, Brace and Company, 1926.*

Lieberg, Owen S. THE FIRST AIR RACE--THE INTERNATIONAL COMPETITION AT REIMS, 1909. Garden City, NY: Doubleday & Company, Inc., 1974.*

Lindbergh, Anne Morrow. HOUR OF GOLD, HOUR OF LEAD. New York: Harcourt, Brace Jovanovich, 1973.*

Lindbergh, Anne Morrow. LISTEN! THE WIND. New York: Harcourt, Brace and Company, 1938.*

Lindbergh, Charles A. OF FLIGHT AND LIFE. New York: Charles Scribner's Sons, 1948.*

Lindbergh, Charles A. THE SPIRIT OF ST. LOUIS. New York: Charles Scribner's Sons, 1953.*

Lindbergh, Charles A. THE WARTIME JOURNALS OF CHARLES A. LINDBERGH. New York: Harcourt Brace Jovanovich, Inc., 1970.*

Lindbergh, Charles A. WE. New York-London: G.P. Putnam's Sons, The Knickerbocker Press, 1927.*

Loomis, Vincent; Ethell, Jeffrey. AMELIA EARHART, THE FINAL STORY. New York: Random House, 1985.*

Lorentz, Gunnar; Hommerberg, Sigge. BERNT BALCHEN. W. Nygaard, Oslo: Forlagt Av H. Aschehoug & Co., 1946. Signed by Balchen.*

Lundborg, Einar. THE ARCTIC RESCUE. New York: The Viking Press, 1928.*

Mason & Windrow. KNOW AVIATION. Garden City, NY: Doubleday & Company, 1973.*

McMahon, John R. THE WRIGHT BROTHERS, FATHERS OF FLIGHT. Boston: Little, Brown & Company, 1930.*

Miller, Francis Trevelyan. THE WORLD IN THE AIR, VOL. I. New York-London: G.P. Putnam's Sons, 1930.*

Miller, Francis Trevelyan. THE WORLD IN THE AIR, VOL. II. New York-London: G.P. Putnam's Sons, 1930. Blank "salesmans' copy".*

Mittelholzer, Walter, et al. BY AIRPLANE TOWARDS THE NORTH POLE. Boston-New York: Houghton Mifflin Company, 1925.*

Mohler, Stanley & Johnson, Bobby. WILEY POST. Washington, DC: Smithsonian, 1971.

Mondey, David, F.R.Hist.S., Editor. THE COMPLETE ILLUSTRATED ENCYCLOPEDIA OF THE WORLD'S AIRCRAFT. New York: A & W Publishers, 1978.*

Montague, Richard. OCEANS, POLES AND AIRMEN. New York: Random House, 1971.*

Mosley, Leonard. LINDBERGH/A BIOGRAPHY. Garden City, NY: Doubleday & Company, Inc., 1976.*

Munson, Kenneth. AIRLINERS FROM 1919 TO THE PRESENT DAY. New York: Exeter Books, 1983.*

Munson, Kenneth. PIONEER AIRCRAFT - 1903-1914. New York: Macmillan & Company, 1969.

Nadeau, Remi. LOS ANGELES FROM MISSION TO MODERN CITY. New York-London-Toronto: Longmans, Green And Co., 1960.*

O'Brien, P.J. WILL ROGERS/AMBASSADOR OF GOOD WILL/PRINCE OF WIT AND WISDOM. Chicago-Philadelphia-Toronto: The John C. Winston Company, 1935.*

O'Dwyer, William J.; Randolph, Stella. HISTORY BY CONTRACT... MOTORIZED AVIATION...GUSTAVE WHITEHEAD. West Germany: Fritz Majer & Sohn, Publisher, 1978.*

O'Neill, Ralph A. & Hood, Joseph F. A DREAM OF EAGLES. Boston: Houghton Mifflin Company, 1973.*

Oppel, Frank. EARLY FLIGHT - FROM BALLOONS TO BIPLANES. Secaucus, NJ: Castle, 1987.*

Pearson, Lee M. WRIGHT B-1 ENGINE HISTORY. Washington: Bureau of Naval Weapons, 1963.*

Phelan, James. HOWARD HUGHES: THE HIDDEN YEARS. New York: Random House, 1976.*

Putnam, George P. SOARING WINGS. New York: Harcourt, Brace and Company, 1939.*

Rae, John. AMERICAN AUTOMOBILE MANUFACTURERS. Philadelphia: Chilton, 1959.*

Redding, Robert & Yenne, Bill. BOEING - PLANEMAKER TO THE WORLD. Greenwich, CT: Bison Books (Crescent Books, Div. Crown Publ. Co.), 1983.*

Rickenbacker, Edward V. FIGHTING THE FLYING CIRCUS. Garden City, NY: Doubleday & Company, 1965. Signed.*

Rickenbacker, Edward V. RICKENBACKER. New Jersey: Prentice-Hall, 1967. Signed.*

Rolfe & Dawydoff. AIRPLANES OF THE WORLD. New York: Simon & Schuster, 1969.*

Ronnie, Art. LOCKLEAR; THE MAN WHO WALKED ON WINGS. New Jersey: A.S. Barnes & Company, 1973.

Roseberry, C.R. THE CHALLENGING SKIES. Garden City, NY: Doubleday & Company, Inc., 1966.

Roseberry, C.R. GLENN CURTISS: PIONEER OF FLIGHT. Garden City, NY: Doubleday & Company, Inc., 1972. Signed.*

Rosenbaum, Robert A. (Ed). BEST BOOK OF TRUE AVIATION STORIES. Garden City, NY: Doubleday & Company, Inc., 1967.*

Ross, Walter. THE LAST HERO: CHARLES A. LINDBERGH. New York: Harper & Row, 1968.

Rubenstein, Murray and Goldman, Richard M. TO JOIN WITH THE EAGLES. Garden City, NY: Doubleday & Company, Inc., 1974.*

Saunders, John Monk. WINGS. New York: Grosset & Dunlap, 1927.*

Seamans, Robert C. Jr. "ACTION AND REACTION", Minta Martin Lecture, Massachusetts Institute Of Technology, 1969. Signed.*

Shamburger & Christy. COMMAND THE HORIZON. New York: A.S. Barnes & Company, 1968.

Shrader, Welman A. FIFTY YEARS OF FLIGHT: A CHRONICLE OF THE AVIATION INDUSTRY IN AMERICA, 1903-1953. Cleveland: Eaton Manufacturing Company, 1953.*

Solberg, Carl. CONQUEST OF THE SKIES. Boston-Toronto: Little, Brown And Company, 1979.*

Stout, William B. SO AWAY I WENT! Indianapolis: Bobbs-Merrill Company, Inc., 1951.

Swanborough & Bowers. U.S. NAVY AIRCRAFT SINCE 1911. New York: Funk & Wagnalls, 1968.

Tallman, Frank. FLYING THE OLD PLANES. Garden City, NY: Doubleday & Company, Inc., 1973.

Taylor, John W.R. A HISTORY OF AERIAL WARFARE. London: Hamlyn Books, 1974.

484

BIBLIOGRAPHY, continued

Terzian, Kathryn & James. GLENN CURTISS, PIONEER PILOT. New York: Grosset & Dunlap, 1966.*

THE WPA GUIDE TO CALIFORNIA - THE FEDERAL WRITER'S PROJECT OF THE WORKS PROGRESS ADMINISTRATION FOR THE STATE OF CALIFORNIA. New York: Pantheon Books, 1984.*

TIMETABLE OF TECHNOLOGY, THE. (Editors-Authors, various) New York: Hearst Books, 1982.*

Toland, John. SHIPS IN THE SKY - THE STORY OF THE GREAT DIRIGIBLES. New York: Henry Holt & Company, 1957.*

Turnbull, Archibald D. and Lord, Clifford L. HISTORY OF UNITED STATES NAVAL AVIATION. New Haven, CT: Yale University Press, London, Geoffrey Cumberlege, Oxford University Press, 1949.*

UNITED STATES AIR FORCE HISTORY. Washington, DC: Office of Air Force History, 1971.*

UNITED STATES NAVAL AVIATION - 1910-1970. Washington, DC: Department of the Navy, 1970.*

UNITED STATES NAVY - FIRST TO FLY THE ATLANTIC. The Flight Across The Atlantic. New York City: Curtiss Aeroplane And Motor Corporation, 1919.*

Van Deventer, C.N. AN INTRODUCTION TO GENERAL AERONAUTICS. American Technical Society, 1974.*

Villard, Henry Serrano. CONTACT-- THE STORY OF THE EARLY BIRDS. New York: Thomas Y. Crowell Company, Inc., 1968.*

Weiss, David Ansel. THE SAGA OF THE TIN GOOSE. New York: Crown Publishers, Inc., 1971.

Whelan, Russell. THE FLYING TIGERS. New York: The Viking Press, 1942.*

*Personal collection of Jack Carpenter.

INDEX

487

489